CLASS IN THE
COMPOSITION CLASSROOM

CLASS IN THE COMPOSITION CLASSROOM

Pedagogy and the Working Class

GENESEA M. CARTER
WILLIAM H. THELIN

UTAH STATE UNIVERSITY PRESS
Logan

© 2017 University Press of Colorado

Published by Utah State University Press
An imprint of University Press of Colorado
5589 Arapahoe Avenue, Suite 206C
Boulder, Colorado 80303

 The University Press of Colorado is a proud member of
The Association of American University Presses.

The University Press of Colorado is a cooperative publishing enterprise supported, in part, by Adams State University, Colorado State University, Fort Lewis College, Metropolitan State University of Denver, Regis University, University of Colorado, University of Northern Colorado, Utah State University, and Western State Colorado University.

ISBN: 978-1-60732-617-5 (paperback)
ISBN: 978-1-60732-618-2 (ebook)

Library of Congress Cataloging-in-Publication Data

Names: Carter, Genesea M. (Genesea Mackenzie), 1979– editor. | Thelin, William H., editor.
Title: Class in the composition classroom : pedagogy and the working class / [edited by] William H. Thelin, Genesea M. Carter.
Description: Logan : Utah State University Press, 2017. | Includes bibliographical references and index.
Identifiers: LCCN 2016049359| ISBN 9781607326175 (pbk.) | ISBN 9781607326182 (ebook)
Subjects: LCSH: Working class–Education (Higher) | College students' writings. | Classroom environment. | English language–Composition and exercises–Study and teaching.
Classification: LCC LC5015 .C55 2017 | DDC 808/.0420711–dc23
LC record available at https://lccn.loc.gov/2016049359

Cover illustrations, clockwise from top left: © Sean Locke Photography, © Straight 8 Photography, © Luis Molinero, © Pop Paul-Catalin. All illustrations from Shutterstock.com.

CONTENTS

CLASS IN THE
COMPOSITION CLASSROOM

INTRODUCTION

William H. Thelin and Genesea M. Carter

Travis, eighteen, had just started his first year at the University of Wisconsin–Stout. An undeclared major at Wisconsin's only polytechnic, he came to UW–Stout hoping to major in something practical. He chose Stout because it is a few hours' drive from home, the people were friendly during his campus visit, the college town was small, and his application was accepted. Travis, like many of the students at UW–Stout, is from a small rural farming community and does not know what he wants to do yet. He is pretty sure he wants to stay in Wisconsin and maybe become a manager of a local Menard's, a regional home-improvement box store, or own a construction company back in his hometown.

Travis grew up on a family farm. In high school he worked twenty to thirty hours a week helping his parents with the farm. During the summers, he also got a job at the local 3M factory. His parents, Bob and Jackie, both graduated from high school and spent a few years at the technical college although they never attended a four-year university. Their expectations were always for Travis to get a bachelor's degree and find a job that would pay him more than the hourly wages at 3M, the best-paying job within a few hours' drive. But they did not want Travis to move too far away; they wanted to keep the family together.

Like many working-class students, reading and writing are not all that interesting to Travis. He has little experience in reading for pleasure, and his parents never took him to the library as a kid. In fact, he stopped reading for fun altogether in the third grade and, instead, started hunting, playing hockey, and fishing. Writing is something he associates with homework and English papers. He thinks of himself as an okay reader or writer, but he would rather be doing something else.

Travis does enjoy his English 101 class at UW–Stout, however. The professor is engaging and interesting, and Travis especially enjoys the fact that he does not have to write any literary essays in this course. The most difficult part of the course for him, however, is how time consuming writing is. He is expected to write rough drafts, participate in peer reviews and conferences, and then revise his drafts before submitting them. And

DOI: 10.7330/9781607326182.c000

Travis is not completely convinced that the time and effort is really worth it. He is not going to become a writer, after all. Besides, none of his family members are writers, and they all have jobs. Travis approaches English 101 like many students do: he puts in the effort to try to get the grade he wants, but he is not convinced English 101 can benefit him much. Thinking about the applicability of English 101 beyond the grade is not something Travis has done—or knows how to do—yet.

Teaching students with Travis's background and mindset requires that writing instructors develop an awareness of and appreciation for the diverse factors that shape the students who enter their classrooms. For instructors like us who teach working-class students—whether at institutions that draw a heavy percentage of working-class students or at institutions where working-class students are blended into classrooms with middle- and upper-class students—there is a need for "developing both awareness of working-class culture and an effective working-class pedagogy," writes Sherry Lee Linkon.[1] Awareness of working-class students' needs coupled with an effective pedagogy, Linkon suggests, "better[s] our chances of engaging and inspiring them."[2]

Although Travis's story represents one type of working-class student, there are many working-class students who do not resemble Travis. Some working-class students come from households with parents who have bachelor degrees; some working-class students live in urban and suburban areas; some working-class students are resistant writers; and some working-class students love writing and their English classes. The variance in the descriptor *working-class student* makes the term particularly difficult to define, as many other working-class scholars have illustrated.

WORKING-CLASS STUDENT DEFINITION

We cannot speak of a "working class" in American life or among student populations without understanding the underlying class system. Yet, *class* is a contested term. Definitions range from those based purely on the type of job a person holds (blue collar versus white collar) to those that see a systemic relationship between classes determined by who controls the means of production. Theorists clash about whether the lived experience of a given group of people is more important in understanding class than what Max Weber called the "life chances" of those same people,[3] or the "cultural capital" they might wield, as Alvin Gouldner first suggested.[4] Much is made of the existence of a middle class, which, if a distinct class and not just a form of worker, clouds some tenets of traditional Marxist theory.

Furthermore, *class* can be used casually, as when a person says that a breach of etiquette showed "no class" on the part of the perpetrator. *High class* is associated with elegance and dignity, if not necessarily wealth. *Low class* refers to coarse or inappropriate behavior. Such common usage confuses the issue of class and what it means to be working class. We will not pretend here that we have arrived at a definitive answer to the question of definition. Contributors to this book also disagree with each other. But we can review important understandings that influence our conception of the working class, moving from the systemic forms of class to the characteristics of students we might see in our classrooms.

Michael Parenti divides classes into two categories or columns, A and B. He describes those in column A as living mostly "off other people's labor."[5] They might have a salaried position, but that is not their main source of income. He further states that in this class,

> there are several hundred thousand adults . . . who do not work, not because they are retired or infirm or unemployed or institutionalized or raising children. They do not work because they do not have to. They have what we call "private" or "independent" incomes; that is, they get enough money to live—usually quite well—from the money they possess. Their money does not come from their own labor but the labor of others.[6]

Column B, he explains, contains the other 98 percent of humanity "who live principally off wages, salaries, bonuses, fees, commissions, and pensions."[7] They might have some savings or investments, but that income is not enough to live on. While this group as a class does not share a culture or an identity—they are not consciously aware of being in this class—the labor of its members creates the incomes for both column A and column B.

Parenti feels this relationship is exploitive, not symbiotic. He documents that the ruling class (column A) maintains its hold over this working class (column B) through a

> supporting network of doctrines, values, myths, and institutions that are not normally thought of as political . . . these supportive institutions help create the ideology that transforms a ruling-class interest into a "general interest," justifying existing class relations as natural and optimal social arrangements.[8]

Parenti acknowledges many differences among those he categorizes into column B, but it is clear he believes minimum-wage workers and bookkeepers have more in common than they know.

We acknowledge that this relationship between owners and workers creates the class system, and its impact on society, as Parenti explains it, is not one we question. We see much value, in fact, in showing students from differing backgrounds how much more they have in common with each other than with the column-A people, who prosper from all our work. However, we believe that within this large category, stark differences exist that differentiate a working class from a middle class. We temper this common understanding of class, though, with the work of Michael Zweig. We feel it builds on Parenti through Zweig's understanding that class is related to access to power.

Zweig sees class as a system in which people are both connected to each other and made different from one another in the production of goods and services. Class extends itself into the "political and cultural dynamics of a society."[9] In attempting to distance his definition from others, he states,

> Class is not a box we "fit" into, or not, depending on our own personal attributes. Classes are not isolated and self-contained. What class we are in depends upon the role we play, as it relates to what others do, in the complicated process in which goods and services are made. These roles carry with them different degrees of income and status, but their most fundamental feature is the different degrees of power each has.[10]

Autonomy, then—the level of our ability to control aspects of our lives, especially those involved with work—is a large determinant of our class standing.

Zweig is concerned with common misperceptions of class. He does not feel a person's job determines his or her class, using as an example the difference between a truck driver who owns his own rig and is, thus, a "small entrepreneur" within the middle class, and the truck driver in the working class who works for a freighting company. He further explains:

> Images of the working class too closely identified with goods-producing blue collar workers miss the point. Only 21 percent of people [in the working class] are in goods-producing industries (mining, construction, and manufacturing). Over 70 percent of all private sector nonsupervisory employees hold white collar jobs in wholesale and retail trade, finance, insurance, and real estate, and a wide variety of business, personal, and health-related service industries.[11]

While he does not spend much time exploring the adjunct-labor system of academia, he does suggest that part-time college instructors, too, are part of the working class.

Zweig ultimately asserts that most people should not be considered middle class. He believes, as the title of his book states, that when seen through his definition, the majority of our country's population is working class—62 percent according to his calculations.[12] This division of class views the middle class as a small managerial and professional group that is caught in between—and that has its access to power determined by—the "two great social forces of modern society, the working class and the capitalist class."[13]

Class can also be associated with education, which is our focus with this collection. While understanding many dimensions of class that he later explains, Alfredo Lubrano conducted his research with the assertion that the "dividing line between working class and middle class" is education.[14] He knows other factors play into it, but he sees a person's level of education as crucial. If true, this view validates Lynn Bloom's assertion that the university is a "middle-class enterprise" that should work at changing working-class students into students with the values of the middle class and the aspiration to join it. While we find her claims a bit problematic for the very reasons Irvin Peckham asserts in *Going North Thinking West*, working-class students are perceived by what they lack in comparison to their middle- and upper-class counterparts. Carolyn R. Boiarsky, with Julie Hagemann and Judith Burdan, developed seven characteristics of working-class students that are informed by the "sociological, cultural, and psychological sites" they arrive from:

- They have grown up in families who earn less than the medium income earned by professional families.
- Their parents work in blue-/pink-collar or nonprofessional service jobs.
- They are first-generation college students.
- They exist in an authoritarian environment with little control over decisions related to their own lives. (Decisions related to work are made by management and decisions about their lifestyles are made by parents.)
- They live in a world governed by rules and procedures.
- They work at jobs rather than in careers, perceiving the job not as an end in and of itself but rather as a means to pay for their life outside work.
- They are often paid by the hour, with time becoming a measure of their worth.[15]

Although many variables complicate Boiarsky, Hagemann, and Burden's characteristics, these features provide an overview of the influencing factors that shape working-class students. These factors lead to behaviors instructors see when they encounter working-class students in the writing classroom. One of these concerns is linguistic in nature. Basil Bernstein first posited the notion of "restricted" and "elaborate" codes regarding verbal expression. Bernstein associated working-class students with restricted codes that did not translate well into the expectations of school.[16] Restricted codes rely on implied understandings among members with shared cultural backgrounds. Elaborate codes make no such assumptions and are, thus, more explicit. Middle- and upper-class students express themselves through elaborate codes.[17] Some of these features were verified by Annette Lareau's research on families from different class backgrounds.[18] So in terms of classroom behavior—what an instructor observes—differences attributable to class are seen, as working-class students are less explicit.

Research, from Bowles and Gintis to Anyon, also reminds us that working-class students have been educated in directive, mechanical ways while students from wealthier school districts have been allowed more creativity and are expected to engage materials in more critical ways. Bowles and Gintis suggest that schooling is meant to reproduce class divisions in our society, as working-class students learn to obey orders to succeed in the types of K–12 schools they are placed in.[19] Thus, working-class students enter our classrooms believing education is done to them, to use Ira Shor's words, not something they actively do.[20]

We also know exposure to reading marks the working-class student as different from those more privileged. Working-class homes often do not have as much reading material in them as middle-class or wealthier homes have. Working-class students do not see their parents reading as much. It has also been documented that working-class neighborhoods contain fewer libraries for children to visit. As a result, working-class students in college have not done much extended reading on their own and see reading as work. While they might have been read to as children—fairy tales or other such standard fare—reading is rarely an enjoyable activity to them as they get older. Furthermore, they might lack some traditional cultural references—the type E. D. Hirsch discussed thirty years ago—and are likely to have a more limited vocabulary.

Working-class students' purpose for education is an additional consideration for instructors. Linkon explains that the majority of working-class students do not intend to "becom[e] academics" even if they share a "cultural background" with other academics from a working-class background. For most working-class students, Linkon writes, academia is a means to an end, a better job.[21] Working-class students are extremely hard workers who want opportunities for socioeconomic mobility. Yet, they might also resist or sabotage both teaching and learning, as Shor has theorized, due to their estrangement from the academic project.

Society in general has much to learn about class. Education, especially composition studies, must respond to features of teaching that subtly or blatantly alienate working-class students and set up further obstacles for them to overcome in order to succeed. Along the way, we also must see what working-class students can add to our understanding of teaching and to higher education in general.

We feel that composition studies' current scholarship regarding social class has not focused enough on the application of class understandings to first-year writing instruction. Some volumes have focused on the backgrounds of working-class academics. Some scholars have discussed the teaching of class theory to students. A few articles and books have outlined pedagogical practices that work toward emancipatory goals. *Class in the Composition Classroom* stands alongside such scholarship but contributes to the field in different ways. Given the variations in working-class populations and institutions of higher education across the nation, we do not offer chapters that merely give advice on what to do, as easy importation of a pedagogy from one group to another violates our pedagogical beliefs. Rather, this volume adopts an honest examination of what teachers are teaching to working-class student populations, as well as why certain theories should be implemented (or disregarded) given the particulars of any specific population.

We gave our contributors a draft of this introduction as a way to offer a lens through which they could discuss working-class students in their chapters. We desired that the contributors understand the underlying conceptions of class we find articulated in Parenti and Zweig, but we felt the issue in front of us was pedagogical, so we wanted them to concentrate on the particular features we outline from Boiarsky, Hagemann, and Burden and the others cited above. As we suggested earlier, though, attempts to define class feel confining, and some of our contributors resisted our interpretation (see especially the chapter by Marie-Roper and Edwards). Ultimately, though, our contributors fleshed out the experiences of working-class students in ways that illustrate the pedagogical issues on which we wanted to focus. We divided this book to allow for variations in our understanding of "working class" while highlighting real students in real situations concerning the teaching and learning of writing. The sum of the collection adds to the existing knowledge in important ways. We feel a working-class pedagogy must emerge in composition studies. We must respond to John Alberti's seminal article on second-tier institutions of higher learning. Tony Scott's research into the influence of adjunct labor, largely located in working-class institutions, must be accounted for. The collection in front of you, then, gives concrete evidence for what a working-class ethos can produce in terms of practice and scholarship. We can make a difference. Our contributors demonstrate this.

PART 1: THE WORKING-CLASS STUDENT:
REGION, EDUCATION, AND CULTURE

The first section examines a range of students' identities from home literacies to gender and sexual identities to access issues. This section highlights the diversity of students with working-class backgrounds or experiences while dovetailing pedagogy with students' voices. These stories illustrate previously unexplored definitions of working class while also celebrating and appreciating the wealth of knowledge working-class students bring with them into the classroom.

Aubrey Schiavone and Anna V. Knutson's chapter, "Pedagogy at the Crossroads: Intersections of Instructor and Student Identities across Institutional Contexts," explores the intersections of their identities and students' identities. With experience teaching working-class students at the University of New Mexico and Salisbury University in Maryland, respectively, before moving to the University of Michigan, where the population of working-class students was significantly less concentrated, Schiavone and Knutson affirm the importance of instructors' reflecting on the effects of their own pedagogies, as those pedagogies have been developed teaching different student populations.

"No Homo!: Toward an Intersection of Sexuality and Masculinity for Working-Class Men" by Robert Mundy and Harry Denny examines the experiences of working-class men at St. John's University and Pace University who must negotiate gender and sexual politics on the college campus. Through interviews with male students within the composition classroom, Mundy and Denny's research uncovered a theme they are calling "No Homo!" that illustrates the fragility of masculine identity. Mundy and Denny's research illustrates how the writing classroom affects and influences male students' perceptions of and beliefs about masculinity.

Aaron Barlow and Patrick Corbett, in "Implications of Redefining 'Working Class' in the Urban Composition Classroom," address the shifting definition of working class from socioeconomic to sociocultural. They explore the implications of this shift in a first-year composition classroom at New York City College of Technology (City Tech). The authors examine what it means to be working class in twenty-first-century Brooklyn, as well as how writing instructors are working to serve the working-class student population at City Tech, where traditional conceptions of working class cannot be applied to their student population.

Cassandra Dulin analyzes the California State University (CSU) system's Early Start program in "California Dreams: Working-Class Writers in the California State University System," exploring how this CSU programs affects working-class students at CSU Bakersfield and CSU

Stanislaus. Through on-site interviews with current writing program administrators and individual and statewide programmatic data analysis, Dulin shows how one of the largest university systems in the country is impacting working-class students.

Jacqueline Preston's "The Writing Space as Dialectical Space: Disrupting the Pedagogical Imperative to Prepare the 'Underprepared'" applies Kenneth Burke's work on identities to challenge the idea of the "underprepared" working-class student. Preston suggests FYW students are not as marginalized or underserved as many would like to believe; instead, they are individuals actively, purposefully, and meaningfully engaged in an ongoing and complex discursive process as they learn to engage and respond to the world around them.

Edie-Marie Roper and Mike Edwards investigate in "Changing Definitions of Work and Class in the Information Economy" how the use of digital tools, especially those associated with white-collar rather than blue-collar work, are affected by composition students' and instructors' self-awareness of class or lack thereof. The authors have direct experience with working-class living, one as a participant in the federal government's TRIO program for first-generation, low-income college students and the other as an enlisted United States Army soldier who benefitted from the GI Bill. They use interviews with Washington State University composition instructors and students to advocate for a new perspective to replace the older industrial-economy model of class that accounts for the economic value of digital work within the writing classroom.

PART 2: PEDAGOGY IN THE COMPOSITION CLASSROOM

This section provides readers—instructors, teaching assistants, program directors, scholars, and others invested or interested in composition pedagogy and practice—with stories that illuminate the ways in which writing instructors develop classroom curriculum, practice, and strategies to support the working-class students in their classrooms, colleges, and universities. Our collaborators do not advocate for an easy importation of curriculum from one institution to another, but their essays provide insight into how pedagogical practices can be used to bolster students' identities, experiences, and needs.

In "Telling Our Story: 'College Writing' for Trade Unionists," Rebecca Fraser illustrates the importance of integrating fiction and nonfiction readings and writing assignments into course materials to help trade students write (and share) their own stories. Using her experiences teaching college writing at SUNY Empire State College,

Fraser suggests that trade-related readings inspire working-class students to recognize the job-specific intelligence they have while also celebrating their work lives. She suggests that trade union students need curriculum that encourages reflection upon and celebration of their identities, as it can move them beyond the stigmas they have about themselves.

In her chapter "Emotional Labor as Imposters: Working-Class Literacy Narratives and Academic Identities," Nancy Mack explores pedagogical approaches to the memoir and literacy-narrative assignments. Mack suggests that these assignments encourage students to explore the challenges they face as their identities develop and change while also encouraging students to critique the emotional labor they invest within issues of literacy.

Liberty Kohn, in "We're all Middle Class? Students' Interpretation of Childhood Ethnographies to Reflect on Class Difference and Identity," considers an argument and analysis essay he assigns in his Winona State University composition course in which students grapple with Annette Lareau's ethnographic readings about working-class and middle-class children. His classroom research illustrates that students do not self-identify in easily patterned ways, further illustrating the difficulties in defining working-class culture.

Holly Middleton explores her "writing-as-advocacy" pedagogy and curriculum in "Pedagogies of Interdependence: Revising the Alienation Narrative for Cultural Match." As an instructor at New Mexico Highlands University, an open-access, Hispanic-serving intuition in northern New Mexico, Middleton asked her students to adopt the role of advocate, in which they were asked to read, write, and act on another's behalf, bridging the "compassion gap" often existing between middle-class and working-class people. Trading advocacy roles, as well as applying theories to the classroom that teach students interdependence and independence, allows students to celebrate and respond to each other's communities while also encouraging their agency as writers and citizens.

In "Never and Forever Just Keep Coming Back Again: Class, Access, and Student Writing Performance," Missy Nieveen Phegley explores the intersection of technology, access, and students' writing proficiency scores. Analyzing five years of data collected from Southeast Missouri State University (SMSU) students' writing-proficiency scores at the end of Composition 1 and Composition 2, Phegley highlights the challenges working-class students face when writing with technology—particularly because many students do not have computers or the Internet at home.

PART 3: WHAT OUR STUDENTS SAY

Students' voices are a vital part of pedagogical inquiry. Without including them in our work, we cannot adequately refine our pedagogical practices, develop new curriculum, and impact programmatic policy. Therefore, in this section our contributors share their classroom and programmatic research as a means toward publicly sharing their students' voices. In addition, these essays offer thoughtful research questions writing instructors may want to adapt and explore within their own classrooms.

In "Social Economies of Literacy in Rural Oregon: Accounting for Diverse Sponsorship Histories of Working-Class Students in and out of School," Cori Brewster shares data collected from interviews conducted with rural, working-class students attending twelve Oregon two- and four-year colleges. Brewster's data illustrate that working-class students' literacy sponsorship opportunities vary drastically, and this reality means educators must adopt a more nuanced understanding of students' lives—where they have come from, where they envision going after college. The diversity of students' sponsorship also brings to bear broad implications for curriculum, assessment, pedagogy, and policy.

Brett Griffiths and Christie Toth explore the importance of understanding the relationships among poverty, class, and literacy learning for students in the two-year college setting in "Rethinking 'Class': Poverty, Pedagogy, and Two-Year College Writing Programs." Their article presents two case studies from radically different two-year college communities—one on the outskirts of Detroit and the other controlled by the Navajo Nation—to examine how poverty shapes the teaching practices within the composition classrooms at these two campuses.

According to James E. Romesburg in "Retrograde Movements and the Educational Encounter: Working-Class Adults in First-Year Composition," writing instructors who teach "mixed-generation" composition classes—nontraditional and traditional student populations—must challenge the ideological clichés that emerge from our youth-focused educational system. Romesburg shares his findings from quantitative and qualitative data gathered from three hundred first-year composition students and a range of their instructors at the Columbus University, a university that encompasses a large working-class and nontraditional student population. Ultimately, Romesburg calls for composition instructors to develop pedagogies, practices, and policies that decrease the friction between traditional and nontraditional students while increasing their collaboration and communication.

Genesea M. Carter, in "'Being Part of Something Gave Me Purpose': How Community Membership Impacts First-Year Students' Sense of

Self," explores how her English 101 Discourse Community Identity Profile can support working-class students' transition to higher education by encouraging them to explore ways in which their discourse communities cultivate their identities. Using data collected from her English 101 section at the University of Wisconsin–Stout, a regional university and Wisconsin's polytechnic, Carter analyzes her students' profiles and accompanying reflections to highlight which communities her first-year, working-class students value and why they value them.

"Literacy Development as Social Practice in the Lives of Four Working-Class Women," by Gail G. Verdi and Miriam Eisenstein Ebsworth, is an interview study of four working-class women who grew up and lived in the New York metropolitan area. Verdi and Ebsworth's questions unpack the family literacy practices the women experienced growing up to discover how literacy practices in childhood can affect the success (or failure) of some working-class students.

We look at this collection of essays as a start of a broader conversation about the importance of valuing the class component of marginalized student populations. Much care must be incorporated into pedagogies and curricula so as to respond to our students' identities and our students' needs. The teaching of writing is difficult even among affluent populations. Our contributors have delved into the recesses of working-class pedagogies. Their struggles should inspire us all. We have no easy answers. But with this collection, we begin to form a concrete examination of the myriad factors influencing what we do as instructors of writing—and how our students perceive our efforts.

Notes

1.   Linkon, *Teaching Working Class*, 6.
2.   Ibid., 6.
3.   Weber, *Economy and Society*, 302.
4.   Gouldner, *Future of Intellectuals*, 61.
5.   Parenti, *Land of Idols*, 55.
6.   Ibid., 55.
7.   Ibid., 57.
8.   Ibid., 85–86.
9.   Zweig, *Working Class Majority*, 11.
10.   Ibid., 11.
11.   Ibid., 31.
12.   Ibid., 30.
13.   Ibid., 20.
14.   Lubrano, *Limbo: Blue-Collar Roots*, 3.
15.   Boiarsky, ed., *Academic Literacy*, 12–13.
16.   Bernstein, *Class, Codes and Control*, 146–47.

17.   Trudgill, *Sociolinguistics*, 132–35.
18.   Lareau, *Unequal Childhoods*.
19.   Bowles and Gintis, *Schooling in Capitalist America*.
20.   Shor, *Empowering Education*.
21.   Linkon, *Teaching Working Class*, 2.

PART 1

*The Working-Class Student's Region,
Education, and Culture*

1

PEDAGOGY AT THE CROSSROADS
Instructor Identity, Social Class Consciousness, and Reflective Teaching Practice

Aubrey Schiavone and Anna V. Knutson

While composition instructors are frequently encouraged to recognize the intersectional identities of their students, including social class identity, we assert in this chapter that it is equally critical to recognize the identities of composition *instructors*. Too often we assume instructors of college composition classes are universally middle- and upper-class individuals who must be attentive to the needs of their working-class students. While this, in many cases, may be true, we would like to make two related assertions: (1) socioeconomic diversity exists in the ranks of composition instructors, and by overlooking that, we miss a major puzzle piece central to our understanding of class in the composition classroom; and (2) regardless of socioeconomic status, instructors must be reflective about how their own social class background might influence their relationships with their students. In other words, we challenge all composition instructors to consider rigorously the role socioeconomic status plays in how they empathize (or, conversely, don't empathize) with their students.

As two teacher-scholars of writing who identify with working-class identity in varying ways, we believe reflections on the role of social class in our own teaching practice may provide a useful example for other composition instructors. We both recently transitioned from teaching at universities with high concentrations of working-class students, with whom we largely identified, to teaching at a more privileged institution with a low concentration of working-class students. In light of our assertion that composition instructors should reflect rigorously on the role of their own social class identity in their relationships with their students, we believe our transition into a more privileged institution

DOI: 10.7330/9781607326182.c001

provides a unique exigence for reflecting on how we interact with various student populations.

In this chapter, we explore the intersections of our identities and students' identities across specific classroom and institutional contexts in order to advocate for teaching practices that are at once reflective and contextually sensitive. We discuss the demographic profiles of three institutions, analyzing the contexts in which we have taught and presenting parallel trajectories of instructors who began teaching writing in universities particularly hospitable to working-class students before moving to Midwest University (MU), where the campus climate tends not to recognize or welcome working-class students. We then use student texts composed at these different institutions to reflect on the results of transferring our respective pedagogical approaches from one institution to the other. Ultimately, we advocate for pedagogies responsive to student demographics and for self-reflective teaching practices that view class-based tension as a potentially generative site of teaching and learning. We argue that these two goals—reflective teaching practice and contextually sensitive pedagogy—are linked: reflective teaching practice allows instructors to consider their own identities as well as how these identities may be enacted within the local conditions of particular institutions. As we argue for broader adoption of reflective teaching practices, we also demonstrate this practice throughout our chapter, reflecting on our own teaching and learning narratives.

THEORETICAL FRAMEWORK

As teacher-scholars of writing, we recognize there is much work to be done in helping working-class students make connections between their experiences in higher education and their experiences in their home communities. We are particularly interested in helping students reflect on and value both these spheres of experience even though they are at times disparate and even conflicting. More specifically, we seek to learn from our students how they use the strengths they bring with them to their college environments even as those environments might overlook or discount working-class students' strengths. In essence, we view students as experts on their own identities, home communities, and attendant literacy practices, and we organize our pedagogical approaches so as to access and encourage that student expertise. Through narrative and reflective writing assignments, we hope to make space for students to reflect on and express their home literacies and to view those literacies as strengths that can aid them in their college experiences.

Working-Class Students

Existing literature recognizes working-class students' experiences as distinct from those of their upper- and middle-class peers. For example, literacy learning can be especially fraught for working-class students who may perceive that they cannot successfully draw from their home literacies in new educational environments. Since perceptions of dissimilarities between domains of learning may prevent students from transferring knowledge across learning environments,[1] these students may resist drawing on literacies from their home discourses in the context of college writing. We use narrative and reflective writing to position our composition classrooms as spaces in which all students, including working-class students, can feel safe to reflect on their shifting identities and literacies. These narrative and reflective assignments offer us opportunities as teachers to read and listen empathetically and to learn from our students' expertise about their own social class experiences rather than making assumptions based in our own limited perceptions of students' social class identities. Furthermore, these types of assignments provide instructors with opportunities to critically reflect on their own positionality in the classroom, particularly as it pertains to their own social class identities.

Narrative Writing

Since working-class students in first-year composition courses are often making sense of their own shifting identities, as well as the influence of higher education on those identities, narrative writing may offer a means of supporting these students' identity development. The potential for narrative writing to combine expressivist and cultural studies approaches to teaching writing may be particularly relevant to working-class students.[2] For example, Nancy Mack's multigenre folklore writing assignment, David Seitz's work memoir project, and Donna LeCourt's literacy autobiographies all combine narrative and reflective elements to better support working-class students.[3] These kinds of narrative assignments allow working-class students to make sense of the identity marker of *working class* itself.[4] In addition, working-class people often use narrative to articulate their own experiences with work, the very experiences that label them working class.[5] As writing teachers, we value narrative writing for its potential to help working-class students make sense of these experiences; additionally, we value the ways in which narrative writing can allow teachers to encounter students' own meaning-making processes concerning social class rather than imposing our perceptions or understandings of social class differences in the classroom.

Important to note is that narrative is often perceived by working-class people as a way to articulate differences in individual experiences, values, and identity without necessarily challenging collective or group values.[6] This potential for narrative to allow difference within sameness might be especially powerful for working-class students moving between home and academic literacies because, as Seitz articulates, these students "require conviction, rather than critical uncertainty, to face the odds against them."[7] Because narrative and reflective writing pedagogies invite students to bring fraught moments of identity (re)construction into the writing classroom, they may offer working-class students opportunities to develop and express such conviction. Where teacher practice is concerned, narrative and reflective assignments create opportunities for teachers, regardless of their social class identities, to perform empathy,[8] "listen respectfully,"[9] and better understand their students. With these benefits in mind, we have developed assignments that encourage students to write their own narratives that may help them reflect on their developing identities.

Reflection

Our discussion of reflection in this chapter is twofold: we are interested in reflective assignments in the composition classroom as well as teachers' uses of reflection to improve their pedagogical practices. As previous scholarship has suggested, reflection might be a powerful site of identity formation for students as well as teachers. Because reflection may allow learners to reflect on their experiences while engaging with an audience, and because it entails setting goals and evaluating whether these goals are met, reflection provides insight into both learning and teaching.[10] In addition, by providing space for individuals to explore their identities as members of multiple communities, reflection can allow both teachers and students to engage with socioeconomic difference at the individual, classroom, and institutional levels.

However, along with the benefits it may offer teachers and students, reflection may also pose risks. When educational institutions require students to reflect on their own abilities, we must be conscious of how students' social and educational experiences might influence these assessments.[11] Namely, students may under- or overestimate their abilities in ways that reproduce inequities, which may present a particularly high risk for marginalized students such as working-class students. In addition, reflection may become standardized through programmatic requirements, thus defanging it of its honesty and possibly its capacity for identity formation.[12] Even with these risks, there is great potential for reward in terms of creating a space where students and teachers can explore the relationship between their identities and institutional spaces in which they operate. In the case of working-class college students, reflection, if designed and scaffolded purposefully, can create a space for students to reflect on the connections and conflicts between their incoming literacies and those valued in their new institutional contexts. Furthermore, for teachers, reflection may offer a window into students' identities, learning experiences, and the intersections of these, thus providing opportunities for instructors to (1) better understand students from a wide variety of backgrounds and (2) explore the ways in which they relate to students from a wide variety of backgrounds.[13] As a result, reflection might be a particularly fruitful pedagogical practice for instructors seeking to understand the role of social class in their classrooms.

CONTEXTS OF RESEARCH

In this section, we use Carnegie classifications, student demographic data, and institutional mission statements to contextualize our three sites of research: Midwest University (MU) (where we both currently teach), East Coast University (EU) (where Aubrey began her teaching career), and the University of the Southwest (SU) (where Anna began her teaching career). These demographic snapshots offer a sense of the overall campus culture at each institution, and we emphasize that both EU and SU seem to have campus cultures that support working-class students more so than MU's does. Although there are several initiatives currently being developed at MU intended to support first-generation college students and transfer students, many of whom are working class, the climate of the institution tends to privilege the experiences, needs, and values of middle- and upper-class students. These varying campus climates presented important implications for us as we sought to teach varied populations of students at different institutions. Campus climate also provided us with opportunities to think carefully about the implications of social class differences in our classrooms, and we reflect on these opportunities in the analyses that follow.

Midwest University

MU is classified as a large, four-year, primarily residential, public research university with very high research activity and lower rates of transfer-in. MU is also classified as "more selective," whereas SU and

EU are both classified as "selective."[14] Working-class students' experiences of isolation or exclusion from campus culture tend to be intensified or heightened at more selective, elite institutions, where populations of working-class students tend to be less concentrated and often less vocal.[15] In addition, individual students might identify themselves as working class, or be identified by institutions as such, according to complex and varied factors including education, income, financial-aid eligibility, work, lifestyle, and familial differences. For example, at MU in 2013, only 13 percent of the total first-year student population identified their parents as having "no college" or "some college" as opposed to the 87 percent of the total first-year student population that identified one or both their parents as having a bachelor's degree.[16] These low percentages stand in marked contrast to nationwide 2012 CIRP data in which approximately 40 percent of first-year students at public universities report that their parents have some or no college.[17] In addition, data for MU students' family income reveals working-class student populations to be in the minority at that institution. For example, in 2012, 63.1 percent of first-year students' parents earned $100,000 or more per year and 22.7 percent of first-year students' parents earned $250,000 or more per year; these percentages for parents' income are far above national averages, confirming that the MU student population is overwhelmingly upper-middle and upper class.[18] In the sections that follow, we reflect on how the presence of this kind of wealth and privilege on campus influenced our awareness of social class dynamics in our classrooms.

Along with these student demographics, MU's mission statement also offers some indication of the campus culture of that institution, which might in some cases be alienating to working-class college students. This mission informs much of the campus culture students perceive through their interactions with administrators, faculty, staff, and peers at the university. The mission states that the university's goal is "to serve the people of [this state] and the world through preeminence in creating, communicating, preserving and applying knowledge, art and academic values, and in developing leaders and citizens who will challenge the present and enrich the future."[19] While references to serving "the world" and the "preeminence" of the university might seem far reaching, at MU this mission is a perceivable part of the daily culture of the university.

In addition, MU's mission names its primary activities as "research and creativity, education, and service." Unfortunately, these primary activities offer little indication of the everyday experiences of working-class students on campus. Even when working-class students are interested in activities the university explicitly values, such as research and creativity, they are also interested, out of necessity, in activities the university does not value outright, such as succeeding academically, surviving financially, finding spaces of social support on campus, developing professionally, and preparing to give back to their communities of origin. MU also identifies as a strength its "tradition of balance between academic decentralization with strong central support for governance, infrastructure, and services." However, this decentralization can manifest as the isolation of resources in particular departments or offices, and working-class students often lack access to resources or expertise in how to navigate this division of services. This is not to say all working-class students feel isolated at all times at the university; instead, the university's mission offers an indication of the overall campus climate working-class students regularly encounter and may respond to in a variety of ways. Similarly, this mission statement offers some indication of teacher positionality and the climate in which teachers at this university pursue their various teaching goals. As writing instructors deeply invested in supporting working-class students, the campus climate implied by the university's mission statement gave us pause as we wondered how best to acknowledge social class dynamics, including our own and students' social class identities, in our classrooms.

East Coast University

EU is classified as a medium, four-year, primarily residential, public master's-granting university with lower rates of transfer-in. Interestingly, in 2013, only 13 percent of EU's student population was identified as first generation, a comparable percentage of students to that at MU.[20] Both institutions' populations of first-generation college students fall significantly under that of the national average at public four-year colleges and universities. In 2011, EU identified 8.1 percent of its total undergraduate population as "low income" by federal government standards, by which "low income" is calculated at about $33,525 per year for a family of four.[21] In 2011 at MU, 10.8 percent of students' parents earned less than $40,000 a year, and only 8.1 percent of students' parents earned less than $30,000 a year.[22] So, where low-income students are concerned, EU and MU are again comparable, and again, both institutions' populations of "low-income" students are much lower than national averages.[23]

However, EU's mission statement does offer some indication of campus culture and its concern for working-class students. EU states its mission as "offering excellent, affordable education in undergraduate liberal arts, sciences, business, nursing, education and social work and applied

MA and doctoral programs."[24] EU's mission also explicitly names concerns for "gainful employment, and life-long learning," acknowledging a population of working-class students who often value such qualities in their pursuit of higher education. Its concern for applied graduate programs as well as preprofessional undergraduate programs, including education and nursing, also suggests that the university has in mind working-class students who often value professionalization in addition to academics.[25] Overall, this mission statement offers some indication that EU recognizes and values the complex contexts influencing working-class students' college experiences. This institutional recognition of working-class students' presence on campus tangibly influences approaches to teaching and learning at that institution. For instance, while teaching writing at this institution, Aubrey often felt comfortable and supported in disclosing her own working-class background to students in her classes when such disclosure was relevant and appropriate. In other words, the institution's readiness to acknowledge social class distinctions means teachers can confidently do so in their classroom practice as well.

Southwest University

SU is classified as a large, four-year, primarily nonresidential, public research university with very high research activity and higher rates of transfer-in. In 2008, SU had the highest concentration, 35.8 percent, of Pell Grant-eligible students of all flagship universities in the US.[26] In contrast, in the same year, Midwest University was one of the ten flagship institutions at which Pell Grant eligibility fell below 15 percent. SU is also a Hispanic-serving institution (HSI) and a so-called majority-minority institution—as of 2009, white students constituted about 43 percent of the student population, while 37 percent were Hispanic and 7 percent were American Indian (in contrast, for example, to 0.21 percent American Indian students at Midwest University).[27] Although SU does not report family income or parental level of education in its public institutional data, the socioeconomic diversity of its student population is supported by a state scholarship, which guarantees tuition at local postsecondary institutions to residents of the state who graduate from high school in-state. Although K–12 educational resources and socioeconomic factors, of course, still affect students' eligibility for the scholarship, the scholarship serves to increase access to higher education for local students, resulting in a campus more representative of the demographics of the surrounding region in terms of socioeconomic, racial/ethnic, and linguistic diversity than most flagship institutions.

Working-class students are also supported at SU through two TRIO programs—Student Support Services, which provides support to students who are low income, first generation, and/or disabled; and the Ronald E. McNair Postbaccalaureate Achievement Program, which seeks to prepare students from historically excluded populations for graduate school.

SU's mission statement reflects its commitment to serving the school's surrounding communities as well as its emphasis on professional education, which might be of particular interest to working-class students.[28] The statement refers to the state's local communities twice: once in reference to the mission of preparing students to "contribute to the state and national economies" and in the goal to "actively support social, cultural, and economic development in our communities to enhance the quality of life for all [residents of this state]." This aspect of SU's mission statement reveals the university's commitment to its surrounding communities, which are socioeconomically diverse, and the students who come from these communities. The brief mission statement refers to its healthcare programs twice, in terms of its commitment to "growing excellence in teaching, research, patient care, and community service" and in its goal to "deliver health care of the highest quality to all who depend on us to keep them healthy or restore them to wellness." This commitment to professional programs may be of interest to working-class students who are pursuing higher education in order to have access to new professional opportunities.[29] Overall, SU's campus climate supports socioeconomic diversity through its stated values and support structures for working-class students.

These distinct institutional settings and attendant campus climates presented interesting challenges for each of us as we transitioned from our respective MA programs to doctoral work and teaching writing at MU. In the following section, we describe our experiences with teaching narrative and reflective writing at these institutions—detailing how campus climate influenced our experiences with teaching particular populations of student writers.

PEDAGOGICAL DATA

Keeping in mind the institutional contexts outlined above, we analyze narrative and reflective assignments from our own curricula as a means of demonstrating how instructors adapt to different student populations. Through analyses of students' responses to assignments, we also hope to demonstrate reflective teaching practice and its usefulness for making sense of social class divisions in varying university contexts.

Narrativizing Class: Aubrey's Data

When I began my teaching career at EU, the first assignment sequence in a department-wide composition curriculum was a narrative-argument sequence titled the Social Significance Argument. This assignment combined narrative and argumentative writing as it prompted students to identify a social issue and make some argument about that social issue using a combination of personal experience and source material as evidence. The overarching goals of this assignment were to support students in discovering that public arguments usually stem from issues of personal importance. The assignment sequence also offered students practice in critical reading and thinking, research, and source integration. As an instructor, I found this assignment allowed me to get to know my students and their interests early on in the semester. I also found this assignment aligned with my own developing goals for teaching writing; namely, this assignment allowed students to practice academic writing skills but with topics they were personally invested in and with which they had some prior experience or expertise. Part of the assignment sequence consisted of reading narrative arguments by authors including Richard Rodriguez, Adrienne Rich, and Susan Bordo. In reading and teaching these published narrative arguments, I often identified myself to students as working class and a first-generation college student. In this particular institutional setting, students' contributions to class, comments in conferences, and descriptions in their own narratives often expressed markers of social class I perceived as indicating students' working-class statuses as well. Not surprisingly, I often found it easy to relate to students who described experiences similar to my own, students who talked and wrote about places and people familiar to me: their working mothers and fathers; their extended families who lived with them in their homes on and off over the years; the varied and numerous workplaces they populated as working teenagers; their high-school teachers who inspired them to pursue college; and their aspirations to pursue careers that allow them to serve their home communities. Often, these students were working class. I learned from these students and their stories readily and often and felt welcome and confident in sharing my stories with them. In this institutional setting, my perception of campus and classroom climate allowed me to identify easily with my students and the narratives they composed for the course.

Interestingly, social class was not usually the explicit focus of students' essays in the writing courses I taught at EU. Instead, social class divisions were often a kind of subtext or undercurrent in the narrative arguments students composed. For example, Katie's narrative described her high-school experiences participating in an extracurricular club focused on volunteerism and community service. Katie described these experiences as evidence for her argument that "schools should offer more community service based clubs . . . and encourage students to get involved in many different types of community service activities." Katie's argument did not address social class directly or explicitly, but her narrative of her experiences revealed social class to be an undercurrent in those experiences and in her argument. In one example, Katie described volunteering at a Christmas toy drive in her local community: "While walking past all the families, I noticed that there were so many types of families there including people of different ethnicities and what looked to be different classes." In describing the families she was serving, Katie was careful not to assign particular social class identities; instead, she offered her perception and assumptions that the families she was serving belonged to "what looked to be different classes." Moreover, Katie hinted at individuals' intersectional identities as she noted the different ethnicities and social classes she encountered. When I encountered Katie's narrative, this willingness to acknowledge multiple identity categories for individual people and her hesitation to assume and assign social class identities to particular groups of people resonated with my own trepidation about being labeled by others according to my social class status. Katie's recollections in her narrative also resonated with my own investment in inviting people to self-identify rather than assigning identity labels to individuals I encounter. Katie went on to reflect on her experiences with community service: "I have come to realize that I am destined to help others and want to encourage others to become more involved as well. Others need to recognize how fortunate they are for what they have and realize that they should give back to their community." In this reflective moment, Katie did important work, recognizing privilege and encouraging others to do similarly. Katie's explicit focus on community service in her essay meant social class issues bubbled up and surfaced where appropriate; as a reader of Katie's narrative, I was able to confront those social class issues readily. Katie's treatment of social class allowed me, the instructor, to feel comfortable and reassured in my decision to identify openly as working class.

In transitioning to MU and carrying a similar reading and writing assignment sequence to FYC classrooms at that institution, I found that the content of students' narrative arguments was markedly different from students' work at my previous institution. At MU, students' narratives often revealed them to be middle and upper class. When I began assigning narrative arguments at MU, I experienced new challenges in students' uptake of that assignment. Interestingly, these students were often explicit about social class and social class differences in their narratives, and this explicit attention to social class divisions created some tensions for me as I read students' narratives.

For example, Lizzy's narrative, titled "More than Money," combined her own high-school experiences with data about the effects of poverty on high-school drop-out rates to argue for the broader adoption of "early intervention programs that encourage students to stay involved in school and help them along that process." While this is an important argument, and one relevant to my own interests as a teacher and researcher, I did experience moments of tension as I encountered Lizzy's narrative. In her narrative, Lizzy positioned herself as much more privileged than most of the students in her high school. Lizzy described this population: "In the public high school I attended, many students did not come from such a privileged background, but rather lived in poverty and abusive households, and an alarmingly large amount of these students dropped out of school." While my own identity most likely places me on a spectrum somewhere between Lizzy and her high-school classmates she described as living "in poverty," Lizzy's focus on privilege, poverty, and social class certainly created tensions for me as I encountered her narrative. The conflation of poverty, education, and violence as Lizzy described her peers especially worried me. Encountering Lizzy's narrative prompted me to reflect on my own high-school experiences as well as my own social class identity, wondering how I had been perceived by others and by my students. Even as Lizzy stated her own privilege, demonstrated empathy for her peers at certain moments in her narrative, and argued for early intervention to better support those peers, I experienced concern and confusion as I wondered how to communicate to the Lizzy that while this empathy might be well intentioned, there is a degree of indignity in choosing to speak for another person or for a population of people whose experiences might be more nuanced than we can perceive as outsiders. I asked myself how I could encourage her to nod toward these nuanced realities instead of painting her peers' experiences in broad strokes, and I wondered how my own positionality as a working-class teacher was coloring my perception of Lizzy's argument.

Lizzy went on to describe in more detail her own position in her high school: "I stuck out like a sore thumb in my first experiences of high school. I carried my books everywhere and avoided confrontations in the cafeteria instead of encouraging them." As Lizzy described her own privilege and her own feelings of difference from her high-school peers, she readily recognized and deciphered differences and attributed those differences to social class. In the FYC classroom, my realization of students' awareness of social class difference heightened my own self-consciousness as a working-class person tasked with instructing privileged students to write for academic contexts. While my working-class identity is one I have often worn with pride throughout my life, in this moment of transition to a university with a student population and campus climate that exuded privilege, I felt silenced. I wondered how to balance empathy for students' narratives with my authority as an instructor in a classroom where I felt constantly the competing interests of being a graduate student, an instructor, and a person who identifies as working class.

Similar to Lizzy's, Sasha's narrative argument, titled "It All Comes Down to Money," engaged with issues of socioeconomic status and schooling, in this case the influence of financial-aid systems on students' experiences applying to and attending college. While describing her college acceptance experience, Sasha asked, "How can we as a society tell students over and over again that education is the only way to succeed in our society when we are preventing capable students from going to college by keeping a failing financial aid system in place?" As evidence for this argument, Sasha described her own joy and exhilaration at being accepted to her first-choice university followed by panic when she received a financial-aid award that was decidedly smaller than she had expected. From these experiences, Sasha argued that "the current financial aid system is failing hundreds and hundreds of students who rely on the system to go to college." Similar to my reaction to Lizzy's narrative, when I encountered Sasha's narrative, I found much that resonated with me, but I also experienced moments of tension between my identity and Sasha's. As she reflected on her experiences, Sasha recognized that many other people experience similar challenges to attending college. Sasha explained that, even though her financial-aid package was not as helpful in covering college costs as she had hoped, she had help: "Luckily, my dad is currently able to cover the tuition fees, but if my mom had to pay for college by herself, I definitely would not be attending the school that I am." Sasha's narrative, like Lizzy's, shows her acute awareness of socioeconomic differences and their influence on experiences of schooling.

While Sasha's narrative is one that resonated with my own experiences and anxieties around attending college, her narrative also worked to bring those anxieties into my experiences navigating my role as a writing instructor. Perhaps Sasha's and my social class identities are not that different from one another, or perhaps they are; our particular social class identities were not necessarily the source of the tensions I experienced. Instead, the tensions I experienced in encountering this student narrative had to do with my role as a teacher of writing, one who in this particular context was feeling silenced and was choosing to keep her own social class identity private. In concluding her essay, Sasha stated, "I do admit I am a lucky case. Many individuals who do not receive financial aid simply cannot attend college. It isn't their grades or their standardized test scores or even their extracurricular activities. It all comes down to numbers. Numbers of students applying to college and increasing zeros on tuition costs. Money." This complex network of educational and financial structures is one I felt personally close to and wary of. Sasha's desire to analyze these systems necessitated that I, her instructor, reflect on and reconsider my own identity and my own positionality within these structures.

These complex, nuanced, and abstract interactions between students' identities and my own occurred simultaneously with more concrete aspects of teaching writing. I sought to instruct students in crafting academic arguments, signaling audience awareness, and integrating sources. I also sought to position myself among this student population that felt distant and unfamiliar to me. Through reflective teaching, I constructed ways to pursue these goals in tandem in my new and different teaching contexts.

Reflecting on Transitions: Anna's Data

In this section, I will discuss my transition from teaching at SU, an institution with considerable socioeconomic diversity, to MU, an institution with lower numbers of working-class students. My own experiences as an undergraduate at another highly selective research university were shaped by several markers of class identity, including my need and desire to stay close to my community, my need and desire to work during and after college, my status as a community college transfer student, and my status as a first-generation college student. As a result, when I noted aspects of students' experiences that, in my reading, marked or indexed working-class identity, I felt a sense of solidarity and affinity with the socioeconomically diverse students at SU. However, my transition to teaching at MU was marked by tension between my identity and the identities I felt were enacted by many of my students. In this section, I explore my own reflections on and reactions to some of the markers of social class identity I noted across both student populations. Ultimately, I attempted to use my perception of the differences between my students and me as a productive tension that would help me cultivate a reflective teaching practice.

When I began teaching FYC at SU, I designed a reflective question-naire asking students about their experiences with education, language, and literacy. Although the questions have been substantially revised over time, the three-pronged goal of the assignment was (1) to lay the groundwork for building an interpersonal connection with students, (2) to prompt students to tell me about their experiences, and (3) to ask students to engage in low-stakes reflective writing with the goal of easing them into the frequent reflective assignments embedded in my curriculum. Through my analysis of students' responses to the questionnaire, I consider how my reactions to aspects of students' identities served as an opportunity for reflecting on tensions between instructor and student identity in service of improved pedagogical practice.

When assigning the questionnaire at SU, I reviewed the handout with the class, explaining key terms to students. When I came to the question about level of parental education, I explained what the term *first generation* meant, and I identified myself as such, thus disclosing this aspect of my identity to the whole class. However, when assigning the questionnaire at MU, I did not identify myself as first generation due to my perceptions of the institutional climate. However, I did complicate this decision later in the semester by offering students a writing sample in which I identified as first generation as a prop for a peer-review mod-eling exercise. This was my subtle way of embedding my disclosure in another activity as a means of reconciling my identity with a campus cli-mate I perceived as unwelcoming to first-generation college students.

Students' responses to the questionnaires helped me get a sense of who was in the class and what sort of support they might need. At SU, I found students' experiences seemed to share many similarities with mine; however, at MU, I found my experiences didn't square as neatly with those of this student population. Although this tension initially caused me some discomfort, I ultimately used it as an opportunity to reflect on the cultural divides between some of my students and me and to consider how I might strategically position myself in my classroom to inspire students to reflect on their own privilege and the inequality embedded in US higher education.

In the SU questionnaire, I asked, "Where are you from originally? If it is not [local state], then what brought you here?" In keeping with the demographics of the student population, the majority of student respon-dents came from in-state, and many of these students had been born and raised there. Although local students didn't always explain their rea-sons for staying, I identified with them based on their decision to attend a university in their hometown: I had chosen my own college based on geographical location since attending my four-year institution allowed me to stay in the same city as my family, my job, and my community while paying in-state tuition. Some students provided this information in a matter-of-fact manner, and others offered this information with more pride and enthusiasm. Others offered a range of emotions: for example, one student responded to this question by saying, "Unfortunately, I have been born and raised right here in [City], [State]." The conflicted tone of this statement resonated with me, as my own decision to attend a college in my hometown had been primarily one of necessity. Students largely took this opportunity to claim allegiance to the region, or to reflect on their stance toward it; no local students in the nine sampled here discussed the reputation of Southwest University as a factor drawing them to the institution.

However, in response to a similar question on the questionnaire at MU, the majority of students explained their decision to move in terms of the prestige of the institution. Although the phrasing of the question stayed the same after I moved to MU, the geographical unit changed— that is to say, instead of naming the state in which the university was located, I named the city. While SU is located in a large city, MU is located in a smaller city, arguably a college town. Although it is of course understandable that students who move to a city to attend college would explain their decision in these terms, I found it striking that when asked why they had moved to a particular city, students took this question as an opportunity to talk, indeed, about the reputation of the university. This move seemed to resonate with the language of exceptionalism that informs the institutional culture at MU. Many students drew on general aspects of the reputation of the institution, multiple students suggested they had wanted to attend MU for some time, and several students made explicit references to the accomplishments of the university's athletics program. Finally, multiple students offered legacy narratives in terms of generations (i.e., how many generations of their family had attended MU) or individuals (i.e., an aunt or a sibling, for example, attended MU first and drew the student's attention to the university). The emphasis on the reputation of the institution, and the tendency of students to refer to specific mechanisms by which they became invested in the reputation of the institution (i.e., sports, family legacy), seem to echo the sentiments expressed in the mission statement: this is a prestigious school where leaders (and legacies) are developed.

Although the questionnaire did not ask students directly about their class identifications, it did ask about the education level of their parents, which may be one potential marker of class. While reading students' responses to the question "Do you consider yourself to be a first-generation college student (i.e., parents did not complete college)? If so, how has the college experience been so far?," I found myself identifying with the many SU students who stated in the questionnaire that they were first generation: "Yes, I am a first-generation college student. So far my first semester was jam-packed with one too many encounters with my good friend, trial and error." In addition, I noted there were many students who appeared to be unclear about their first-generation status: there were many "Yes and no" or "Sort of" responses to the first-generation question, often from students who had parents with some college and no degree. These complex narratives of identifying as first generation resonated with my own experience understanding my familial educational background and beginning to find language to describe it.

In contrast, at MU, in keeping with the demographics of the institution, only one out of ten students identified as first generation ("I am a first-generation college student. So far the experience has been a good one, but a lot is being thrown at me at once and it can get slightly overwhelming"). My reactions to the rest of the responses to this question were varied since students tended to offer brief, incomplete responses in contrast to full sentences for every other question (perhaps indicating discomfort with the question) or in-depth explanations about how many members of their family had graduated from college. Although it is understandable that this question might make students from more privileged backgrounds feel uncomfortable or obligated to overexplain their backgrounds, this overexplaining still served as a moment of tension for me. One outlier was a student who responded by saying, "No, my Dad was the first-generation college student in my family." This response indicated some awareness of previous generations having not attended college, and it interestingly seems to suggest that every family has a first generation to attend college, projecting a future in which everyone eventually obtains access to college education. This same student demonstrated a high level of social awareness in response to a question about which communities he belonged to: "I consider myself to be a part of my family community, and my friend community. Both of these communities largely consist of upper-class, Caucasian individuals." This student's awareness of the role of race and class in his own life seemed to align with his statement about his family's educational background.

Finally, there were interesting contrasts between the institutions in terms of how students discussed their decisions to pursue their majors. In response to the questions "What is your intended area of study? Why does it interest you?," many SU students stated that they had decided to pursue a college education in order to have access to a specific profession. For example, one student said, "I am studying political science and Latin American studies. I would love to have a job in international relations, such as an ambassador. I am in love with Latin American culture and language (I take Mayan, Spanish, and Portuguese classes)." In addition, multiple students framed their professional interests as a means of giving back to the community. For example, one student stated, "I want to major in psychology and minor in both Spanish and Art. Eventually I would like to become an art therapist and do a lot of volunteer work with underprivileged kids and families." Similarly, another student said, "I am majoring in Biochemistry. Ideally, I'd like to go to Medical school so one day I will literally be saving lives, but I am not sure how realistic this goal is. However, I will never know unless I try, right?" Yet another student stated she intended to major in pharmacy because "pharmacists are pretty much the last people to speak with people about their medications such as making sure that they do not share medications and dispose properly of the ones that they do not use . . . I want to protect everyone though educating them about [addiction] and then keep them from the horrible situations drug abusers face." These three students evoked the themes discussed earlier from SU's mission statement: the goal of preparing students for the workforce so they can give back to local communities, particularly through healthcare professions.

While the majority of SU students focused on the professional outcomes of their choice of major, two students expressed their interest in their major in terms of both their professional and intellectual goals. One student framed his biology major (with minors in chemistry and psychology) not only in terms of his career goals but also his interest in research: "Those areas interest me because I want to go to Pre-med and become a neurologist . . . I want to discover how to cure a person that has anorexia or bulimia." Similarly, another student stated, "My intended major is psychology because I think it is incredibly fascinating to understand why people are the way they [are]. I feel like it is a question that can never be completely answered and that's what I love about it! I want to be a forensic psychologist so I'm really eager to see what all I can learn." The only student in this sample who didn't mention a specific profession still managed to discuss her career path in her explanation for choosing her major: "My intended area of study is currently American Studies. I'm drawn to this degree program because it allows me to explore and expand my intellectual horizons. Since I don't quite know what I want to go for career-wise, this is perfect for me. I get to take interesting and challenging classes and enjoy my coursework."

All of the SU students who consented to participate in this study framed their choice of major in terms of their professional goals, which resonates with SU's stated goals of professional development.

Interestingly, at MU, the tenor of students' responses to this question changed dramatically. Instead of explaining their choice of major in terms of professional opportunities conferred by that particular degree, MU students tended to frame their interest in their major in terms of intellectual "interest" or "fascination" rather than professionalization. It is, of course, understandable that students, when asked why their major interests them, will discuss their majors in terms of interest; however, it was intriguing to me that students at SU overwhelmingly framed their educational choices in terms of their career aspirations, while MU students tended to frame their choice of major in terms of interest or inquiry. Although I, of course, understand the logic behind pursuing an academic subject due to interest or fascination, I certainly identified more with the students at SU who framed their academic interests in terms of professional aspirations.

In light of my reflections on my experiences teaching across institutions, I suggest that teachers should understand that their own identities will inevitably influence the ways in which they perceive the identities of their students and that they should, as a result, be deeply reflective about the ways in which they navigate their particular institutional culture. Even though the transition was not necessarily seamless, I ultimately found satisfaction in teaching at MU. I hope that by continuing to develop my reflective stance toward teaching, I will be able to adapt to teaching within any other institutional cultures I encounter in my career.

CONCLUSION

In this chapter, we have sought to reflect on the ways our identities might influence our relationships with our student and the ways these relationships might affect our teaching practices. We have used the tension created by moving from campus climates that felt relatively hospitable to working-class identities to an institution that tends to privilege middle- and upper-class values as an exigency for reflective teaching practice. By reflecting on student narratives and her experiences encountering them, Aubrey realized that transitioning between different institutions necessitated that she reconsider her own definitions of good teaching. When she encountered a population of students with whom she easily identified, she thought that easy identification was good teaching—that being a good teacher meant finding points of synthesis and resonance with your students. When she encountered a population of students with whom she did not easily identify, she began to recognize points of difference or tension between herself and her students as potentially productive teaching and learning moments. After reflecting on her reactions to the ways in which students at SU and MU talked about various factors that influenced their educational choices, Anna began to recognize that her perceived distance from students at MU could serve as a point of productive tension. She could draw on that tension to help students reflect on their origins, to learn from students about the complexity of class identification, and to help her serve as a mentor to the few first-generation students in her classes, who were likely working class as well. Both Aubrey's and Anna's analyses demonstrate that while it is certainly important to consider students' complex, intersectional identities in the classroom, teachers should also reflect on their own positionality in relation to their students and to their institutional climate.

Based on our analysis of our teaching practices and student responses to them, we recommend instructors from all backgrounds (1) learn more about students in their local context through institutional mission statements, demographic data, and thoughtfully designed questionnaires; (2) reflect on the ways instructor identities may converge with and diverge from student identities; and (3) consider how these factors may affect (implicitly or explicitly) dynamics in their classrooms. Well-scaffolded reflective and narrative assignments are two specific pedagogical practices that can support each of these goals. We highlight the importance of instructors *from all backgrounds* engaging in this process. Indeed, reflecting on intersections between instructor and student identity might be particularly critical for instructors coming from middle- and upper-class backgrounds.[30] Because privilege is so often invisible to those who have it, it might be especially important that instructors from more privileged backgrounds be aware of and sensitive to the presence of working-class students in their classrooms.[31] In this way, reflecting on the effects of their own pedagogies on various student populations is an essential skill all teachers of writing must develop, and institutional transitions are critical opportunities for such self-reflection.

Notes

1.   Bergmann and Zepernick, "Disciplinarity and Transfer"; Driscoll and Wells, "Beyond Knowledge and Skills"; Jarratt et al., "Pedagogical Memory"; Nowacek, *Agents of Integration*; Reiff and Bawarshi, "Tracing Discursive Resources"; Rounsaville, Goldberg, and Bawarshi, "From Incomes to Outcomes".

2. Burnham, "Expressive Pedagogy"; Fulkerson, "Composition at the Turn"; McComiskey, *Teaching Composition.*

3. Mack, "Ethical Representation"; Seitz, "Making Work Visible"; LeCourt, "Performing Working-Class Identity."

4. Lindquist, "Class Affects, Classroom Affectations"; Seitz, "Making Work Visible."

5. Lindquist, "Class Affects, Classroom Affectations"; Seitz, "Making Work Visible"; Tingle, "Opinion: The Vexation of Class."

6. Lindquist, *Place to Stand.*

7. Seitz, "Making Work Visible," 210.

8. Lindquist, "Class Affects, Classroom Affectations."

9. Mack, "Ethical Representations," 61.

10. Yancey, *Reflection in the Writing Classroom.*

11. Ketai, "Race, Remediation, and Readiness"; O'Neill, Moore, and Huot, *Guide to College Writing Assessment*; Schendel and O'Neill, "Exploring the Theories."

12. Scott, "Creating the Subject of Portfolios."

13. Yancey, *Reflection in the Writing Classroom.*

14. *Carnegie Classification of Institutions of Higher Education.*

15. Stephens, "Cultural Mismatch"; Guerra, "Coming Out as Poor at an Elite University."

16. *University of Michigan Student Profile Comparison*; University of Michigan Office of Budget and Planning, *The Michigan Almanac*; University of Michigan Student Life Research, "What Proportion of UM Students?"

17. Pryor et al., *American Freshman.*

18. *University of Michigan Student Profile Comparison*; Pryor, *American Freshman*, 29–33.

19. University of Michigan, Mission and Integrity, "Mission Statement."

20. Carrie A. Tingle, Office of University Analysis, Reporting, and Assessment at Salisbury University, e-mail message to author, February 2, 2015.

21. US Department of Health and Human Services, "2014 Poverty Guidelines"; US Department of Education, Office of Postsecondary Education, "Federal TRIO Programs: Current-Year Low-Income Levels." The US Department of Education defines "low income" as those families whose "taxable income for the preceding year did not exceed 150 percent of the poverty level amount." In 2011 the US Department of Health and Human Services set the poverty level amount at $22,350 per year for a family of four.

22. *University of Michigan Student Profile Comparison*; University of Michigan Office of Budget and Planning, *Michigan Almanac.*

23. Pryor et al., *American Freshman*, 29–33.

24. Salisbury University, "Salisbury University Mission Statement 2014."

25. Terenzini et al., "First-Generation College Students".

26. "Pell Grants."

27. de Leon, *2009–2010 Diversity Report Card*; University of Michigan, Office of the Registrar, *University of Michigan Total Enrollment Overview.*

28. University of New Mexico, "UNM's Mission."

29. Terenzini et al., "First-Generation College Students," 16.

30. Hartsock, "Feminist Standpoint," 285.

31. McIntosh, *White Privilege and Male Privilege.*

2

NO HOMO!
Toward an Intersection of Sexuality and Masculinity for Working-Class Men

Robert Mundy and Harry Denny

We have struggled with the adjectives students, particularly men, assign us in classroom settings. If our identities as white, male, working-class academics seem transparent and privileged, our gender and sexuality work counterintuitively. In public spaces, particularly when with students, Rob is a "guys' guy" and Harry is the "ambiguously gay" guy. We both have come to embrace our identities, particularly our masculinities and how their performativity enables men who share our background a certain degree of comfort with us, especially for those men who have historically felt out of place in writing classrooms. During classes and conferences, our masculinity provides access to men who traditionally doubt the academic benefits writing offers—as they often suggest writing is not what "real men" do. Whether reflecting on Rob as the "dude," complicating the identity politics his male students face, or on Harry's waxing and waning status as "one of the boys," we are continually struck by how first-generation/working-class college men, like ourselves, struggle for intimacy and connection in writing classes.

As educators, we are aware of the potential role our own "confessional narratives," to borrow a term from bell hooks, might play in inspiring students to participate in a deeper, albeit problematic, inquiry into the forces that shaped and continue to shape their experiences as both expressive and socially conscious writers.[1] Like Irvin Peckham, we share a suspicion of the scrubbing of first-generation/working-class students of their legitimate resistance to academic- or middle-class-coded ways of thinking and expressing themselves (ourselves) through prose.[2] Donna LeCourt notes that working-class students are given a Faustian bargain in most college writing classes (and throughout all of higher

DOI: 10.7330/9781607326182.c002

education)—being asked to surrender authentic self, affect, and ties to home/neighborhood in exchange for marginal assurance of material gain or entry into the middle class and its dubious security in postmillennial America.[3] Of course any rhetorics of self, authenticity, and communication, whether for/of working- or middle-class people, are discursive inventions that lack any "real" referent. On that front, what our study offers here is neither new nor striking, but we wish to further complicate the existing conversations by pointing to the doubly confounding experience for working-class men in writing classes; the pressure to surrender their primary discourse for the power of academic/disciplinary/class-coded ones is confounded by the intersectional role of gender and sexuality in constructing/deconstructing who they are or are becoming. These men simultaneously embody the privilege of men in a patriarchal society and the marginality of working-class identity in academia and society generally; further, they struggle with signifying their masculinities in ways that conform to and confound the sensibilities of a more bourgeois notion of performativity in which cool reason and affect rule supreme.

This qualitative study, in which we promised to release neither the names of the interviewees nor the institutions, interviews with men who identify as first-generation college students, extends from our own experiences, asking men who share our background to speak into their own experiences and the identity politics they negotiate among the often-different worlds of home, college, and the wider public. As the men of the study reflected, the writing classroom is often an area requiring vigilance and hyperawareness of how masculinity signifies and not a "safe contact zone."[4] We first discuss the method and theory that drove this study, focusing on how we selected, interviewed, and coded our participants' responses, and then present our participants' powerful responses to the proximity of sexuality to the expression of/reflection on gender in their writing classes.

COMING TO TALK WITH MEN: THOUGHTS ON METHOD

This study was developed to explore how sociocultural and socioeconomic markers intersect with gender identity and was conducted through semistructured interviews that were subsequently coded using grounded theory methodology.[5] Participants were identified through conversations in composition classrooms and courses that required enhanced writing, such as English and First-Year Experience, at the participating comprehensive institutions—a private, urban university and a suburban, public college. Although the nine participants all identified as working-class male students, their identities—raced, ethnic, and sexual—varied, along with their origins, encompassing provincial to urban lives. During the interviews, participants discussed their backgrounds, families, and education/work experiences as a means to develop a narrative regarding the role writing has played in previous identity creation and to what extent writing has acted as a means to embrace and/or isolate any sense of self from present academic and/or social expectations. Our work focused on the following aims: determine how sociocultural variables affect first-generation college males' sense of self; consider how their writing speaks to this self-awareness of or affinity with conventional notions of gender; understand the extent to which writing relates to the exploration of their gendered identities.

A standard set of questions was used throughout the interviews (appendix 2.A) and garnered codes that reaffirmed common markers of masculinity but also revealed a number of powerful themes. We named an especially powerful theme No Homo!, which reflects the concern the men of the study had about the manner in which their gender and sexuality signify in self-presentation, whether in the interview, the classroom, or through their writing. In the larger context of the research, the participants discussed several aspects of male identity and performance—construction, maintenance, and subversion; however, "No Homo!," as a unit in and of itself, focuses primarily on exclusionary aspects of masculinity and gender policing. Throughout the interviews, the participants riffed on this very trope, the notion that masculinity exists under the watchful eye of the male gaze—an act of surveillance for men, and by men, and given the gendered understanding of writing, the participants inevitably took up or balked at the challenges presented by the act of writing.

The practice of policing masculinity by Othering men who display what is thought to be homosexual sentiment is widespread in pop-culture taglines. From rap singer Kanye West to the NBA's Roy Hibbert, "No Homo!" is a playful speech act that alludes to an unwavering fear of misinterpretation of homosocial activity, as audiences might read even sentiment as code for homosexual identity. The utterance reflects what Eve Sedgwick[6] describes as "male homosexual panic" or what Judith Butler[7] has cited as a heterosexual anxiety that extends from the fear that the heterosexual ideal is nearly impossible to attain, let alone replicate. Crass as "No Homo!" may be, the expression indexes the fragile nature of masculinity, wards off the misinterpretation of acts and words as homosexual, and works to police and reinforce hegemonic masculinity. The phrase serves as a spoken means of signaling self-awareness of a homoerotic subtext and simultaneously distancing oneself from it, firmly reestablishing identification with a perceived heterosexual norm. For men, even the slightest gaffe—"Don't get me wrong"—can cast their (compulsory) heterosexuality in doubt.

Such policing of words and thoughts is the everyday practice of the language of their lives. Throughout the study, the participants alluded to this phenomenon, almost apologizing for moments in which they breached their unwritten "No Homo!" pact with other men. To talk about their lives as working-class men and their emotions signals an uncertainty that is tantamount to crossing the discursive boundary into homosexuality, which is evidently consonant with sensitivity, reflection, and doubt. Throughout the interviews, the participants were attuned to the "boy code" and the "mask of masculinity"[8]—a kind of swaggering posture boys embrace to hide their fears, suppress dependency and vulnerability, and present a stoic, impervious front."[9]

CRYBABIES TO SISSIES, SISSIES TO FAGS: CHANNELING THEORIES OF SEXUALITY AND MASCULINITY

Throughout the study, "No Homo!" was intimated, even called out directly at times. The working-class men could feel it in the air, a moment in which a line was crossed, a time to ensure that their masculinity was still fully intact in light of their previous thoughts. Although the spoken utterance has become mainstream, its sentiment—the hyperawareness and sensitivity working-class men, in particular, have about masculine performativity—is timeless and ubiquitous. In this policing of masculinity, men are left with two feasible responses: take up masculine, heterosexual rhetoric or duck and cover. In avoiding the feminine and/or homosexual (each read as provisionally middle/upper class in men), both identity markers that shape working-class masculine performance, men rarely challenge heterosexuality, just as masculinity often goes without ever being problematized. Consequently, hegemonic masculinity and heterosexuality retain a sense of what is thought to be natural/normal. As Butler notes, however, the binary opposites of heterosexuality and homosexuality are far more intimately connected than is often perceived.[10] For "natural" to exist (heterosexuality), a counterpoint identity marker must be mobilized. The oppositional is expressed through discursive representations, while the norm gains meaning through inference.[11]

In "doing gender," the physical act of interpretation Candace West and Don H. Zimmerman suggest, a standard is formulated by which a certain gender performance is assigned authority.[12] In this design, gender is regulated according to a preexisting norm and overseen by those who have been afforded authority according to their performative proximity to said position. However, as the work of Michel Foucault[13] and later Butler[14] determines, authority extends beyond the simple act of regulation. Instead, gender capital is accrued and maintained through the discursive act of naming and thus creating the Other as a means to bolster the norm. The Other is brought into existence through discourse, the confession, as Foucault notes, which distinguishes clear parameters for what is culturally acceptable.[15] Seemingly undetected, the norm is made natural through the inclusion and immediate marginalization of the Other. In the case of working-class men, men already Othered by economic forces, they are inscribed as another Other through the discursive protocols of gender and sexuality.

C. J. Pascoe's ethnographic work in *Dude, You're a Fag* speaks directly to "fag discourse" and the spectacle it creates.[16] The fag epithet acts to out any male who is not conforming with the prerequisites of masculinity. Its homophobic nature teaches men that to act other than masculine—according to an extremely limited notion of gender—is tantamount to being homosexual, and if a man continues this behavior, he himself will become a fag as well. Through this vitriolic language, masculine norms are created and maintained. We argue that this masculine norm is further class coded, that men with greater economic (as well as social and cultural) privilege have more latitude in how they perform their gender, particularly in mixed arenas like colleges and universities. As noted throughout the larger research project, gender identity[17] is learned through experience, across all social interactions.[18] When acting according to the norm, working-class men are rewarded with membership in a filial community. However, when performance does not meet expectation, males are subjected to disciplinary measures, as evidenced in fag and "No Homo!" rhetoric. Pepper Schwartz notes that when one behaves outside the constructed norm, "psychic or physical violence follows in order to preserve normative heterosexual role playing along narrowly constructed and strongly idealized stereotypes."[19]

According to Pascoe, in practice, "the lack of masculinity is the problem, not the sexual practice or orientation."[20] This attitude suggests that men see the homosexual as having the least amount of masculine capital possible, and in calling a heterosexual male a *fag*, that individual is reminded of what is at stake when they do not capitulate to the norm. In essence, the "No Homo!" response is a byproduct of fag discourse. It conditions men to understand heterosexuality and masculinity as being interchangeable, one and the same, and the former, heterosexuality, can and should police the latter, masculinity. Pascoe continues: "A boy could get called a fag for exhibiting any sort of behavior defined as unmasculine (although not necessarily behaviors aligned with femininity): being stupid or incompetent, dancing, caring too much about clothing, being too emotional, or expressing interest (sexually or platonic) in other guys."[21] When masculine rhetoric is understood in this context, outside strictly sexual terms, we see how much effort is put into policing masculine ideals and to what extent the homosexual is used to clarify what is permissible. When stating "No Homo!," men act to get in front of a *fag* label, fully aware that what they have said or done would be cause for correction. To some degree, "No Homo!" is the opposite side of the same coin; it preemptively serves to discipline the self before others have the opportunity to do so. Through homophobic rhetoric and its ability to police bodies, hegemonic masculinity is reproduced. According to Pierre Bourdieu, this language is the verbal representation of symbolic violence, the real, physical implications men may face when they perform what may be perceived as anything other than the masculine ideal.[22] The act of qualifying one's words, regardless of how innocuous they may be, brings to light masculinity's complicated connection to sexuality; to be perceived as gay is a threat to what "real men" signify as and perform.

In the case of this study, talk about writing and masculine identity led many participants to introduce sexuality into the conversation. As fag discourse and the "No Homo!!" response suggests, one's sexuality is always in play and on display. If writing and the humanities are understood to be feminized, as mentioned earlier, then it should be of no surprise that any talk of writing would elicit similar commentary. Anne Watson, Michael Kehler, and Wayne Martino's work makes this very connection between hegemonic masculinity and male schooling, noting that masculine norms complicate the educational experience.[23] Wayne Martino, through his work with male students, further supports this logic. According to one of his subjects, "English is more suited to girls because it's not the way guys think. . . . Therefore, I don't particularly like this subject. I hope you aren't offended by this, but most guys who like English are faggots."[24]

For several straight working-class men in the study, uneasiness with the conventions of masculinity and its intersections with sexuality became evident when talk about writing and personal identity fell closer to the margins of permissibility. Although these men did not approach the conversations we had with the same sense of sexualizing or gendering certain subjects, as previously noted, what transpired during the interviews both supported and challenged the very notion that aspects of men's lives are off limits, particularly when speaking with other men.

The interviews allowed the participants to speak into the paradox of working-class masculinity in classrooms: they're pressured to engage in what they see as a coded activity of reflection and expression, insight they have been conditioned to understand as inherently suspicious of and challenging to their very identity. Further, to put those thoughts into discourse (in papers, journals, etc.) or to talk about them in the semipublic space of classrooms and conferences is to be forced to utter those thoughts and to perform their identity in ways fully incongruent with the bourgeois sensibility of the "politically correct" arena of middle-class education. At minimum, they come to signify as uncouth asses; at worst, they are racist, sexist, homophobic, and nationalist bigots. To our participants, sexuality was never far from their thoughts. The repeated move to the topic, however, suggests that their understanding of masculinity is swept up in feelings about sexuality and class. We were not surprised, considering the power the male gaze holds over men. In an intimate setting such as an interview, the participants addressed how they understood themselves as men, working-class men, first-generation men in college. They did so publicly, with a male interviewer taking notes as they spoke. For the participants, this experience was just another physical representation of the male gaze.

The men in this study taught us how powerfully the language and physical performance of masculinity are policed, especially for the working class. They conceived of masculinity on a spectrum of privilege, with heterosexual masculinity positioned at one end (valued as dominant, privileged) and the homosexual analog positioned at the opposite extreme (as marginal, Other). Predictably, the men we interviewed positioned themselves, in practice, somewhere between both extremes. Those men who did not fulfill the athletic ideal, which was how hegemonic masculinity was most clearly presented in the interviews, were on high alert—reserved, guarded, and, at times, apologetic for their identities, suggesting that being a man is an all-or-nothing project and fraught with the prospect of being relegated to the disfavored extreme of homosexuality.

Sexuality was the marker by which masculinity was understood and subsequently policed during the interviews. Although other topics—for instance, class—certainly created issues for these men, these topics did not, at least at this juncture in their lives, interrupt their collective sense of masculine self. To be perceived as gay was a misstep that required immediate justification and resolution; disloyalty to working-class identity, however expressed, was just not comparable in scale or intensity. Just as Pascoe's research attests, the participants understood talk of masculinity as an articulation of the male gaze.[25] The complicated power of hegemonic masculinity was realized as Participant 2, a college athlete and team captain, turned talk of classroom experience into a forum for discussing sexuality. In the moments just prior to describing a scenario, he distanced himself from the direction he was taking with his responses to our questions. Catching himself as he talked about a time in which he used writing as a way to resolve an issue he was having in his relationship, he moved forward to make clear that he was only willing to go so far, and his immediate move toward sexuality signaled a topic that would not be negotiated. Although gender and sexuality are completely different aspects of one's identity, he understood sexuality as a component part of his gendered self: to be straight is to be masculine; to be gay is to betray masculinity. He continued his interview with a standard male narrative, reflecting on aspects of his life and identity that afforded him authority: "To be a male and an athlete is macho, kind of, you know what I am saying? It's cool to be a male athlete—you know. It's almost like we are supposed to be athletes. As kids, everybody plays a sport." Indeed, athletics are common components of male socialization. However, the participant's position as a college athlete was lost on him. He never realized that although a good percentage of men participate in sports, only a small number excel. The most interesting or, at least, most telling aspect of his thoughts relates to his conceptualization of the ideal man. In his estimation, men are to be athletes, and by extension, he was simply the one who best filled the role that was created with him in mind. If masculinity is a contest, he just happened to be the one who was winning.

Participant 2 was warm, courteous, interesting, and forthcoming with his comments. He is not the image to rally against, either. Throughout his interview, he appeared as though he was attempting to speak on behalf of men as a whole, to play the role he was assigned as a gifted athlete by acting as the de facto male authority. This assumed position, however, did not always play to his advantage: "In class it's kind of stereotypical. Like, you know, 'Oh, he's an athlete. He plays baseball. He plays a sport. He can't get in-depth in writing and stuff.'" Participant 2's interview reveals a man who is privileged and at the same time hampered by his position, possibly benefiting from an authority he himself never directly requested. As a male, he realized his individual identity was limited by the larger strictures placed on men by the prevailing social order. He saw his individuality lost to a collective sense of gender: "It's a group. It's 'How do you guys feel?' That's how it has always been. Ever since high school. Not ' How do you [as an individual] feel about this?' It has always been about the group." To some extent, his thoughts suggest he is primed to contest standard notions of masculinity. However, as he continued his interview, it was clear this negotiation was only possible when it provided him with greater opportunity. He could not see the forest for the trees, taking issue with masculinity only when it impeded his growth.

Repeatedly throughout his interview, Participant 2 discussed moments in his classes in which it felt better to remain silent. In these academic settings, he was not the voice of authority. The moment in which he contested basic gender prerequisites seemed like an eternity ago as his attention quickly shifted to moments in which he acted to regain his authoritative standing.

> That is another topic I do not like to talk about. Homosexuality. I would say that, abortion, and religion. If I have to tell you, let's write it on paper. Let's make sure it stays between, you know, me and you. In one class we were speaking about an athlete, the gay athlete, Jason Williams [*sic*]. We were talking about him. [Name of another baseball player in the class] and I kind of had the same view on it, you know. And the whole . . . it was literally me and [baseball player's name] against the wall, and the whole class was coming at us. Questions were flying at us. We had a different view than other people. Because people were saying, "Oh, it's no big deal. It's not a big deal." We were saying, "How do you know? You are not on a team. You don't shower with guys." You know what I mean? It was back and forth between us two and the whole class.

His comments draw attention to how power gets played out in social spaces. The manner in which he approached the topic of homosexuality, and by extension the class, was with a privileged voice. He was no longer championing male individuality; rather, he was the embodiment of fag rhetoric and "No Homo!" discourse.

As we spoke, he relived moments in which masculine norms were challenged on his baseball team by a gay man. According to his thoughts, homosexuality was something he was not entirely opposed to, provided it did not disrupt the social order within the locales he most identified with: "If you want to be gay, that's fine. That's totally okay. That's all right with me. Am I against it? You know, uh, in some cases yes, and in some cases no." Homosexuality was acceptable, in his estimation, if it existed on the margins; it had no place, however, in sports or the home, spaces he viewed synonymously as heterosexual. According to his line of thinking, homosexuality disrupts the heteronormative family: "Every child should experience a mom and a dad. No child should have to deal with that." His logic saw the team, the locker room, and home as one and the same. These were spaces that were not to be blemished by homosexuality. Although he was "okay" with it, as he noted, sexuality seemingly fell under his jurisdiction. Homosexuality was acceptable, by his own admission, but not everywhere. Not where he stood. Not on his watch.

As he continued recounting the event, his frustration with his classmates and the larger class became apparent. His ire, initially directed at those classmates who approached the conversation without knowing the rules of "guyland," [26] quickly turned to another man in the conversation: "The other guy in the class was on the side of 'what's the big deal?' And even though he is a male, he isn't an athlete. The subculture of the athlete makes a huge, huge, huge difference. Huge difference." Participant 2 had moved forward in an attempt to show this young man the way. He had explained that being gay wasn't so much the issue; the stigma of being feminine was most troubling. But he and his teammate were outnumbered, their authority greatly diminished by a space that didn't play to or fear their reaction. As the talk of homosexuality and the locker room came to a crescendo in the class, according to Participant 2's reflection on the event, his teammate felt obligated to make clear his sexual preference, a response Participant 2 felt was necessary in the moment: "I have a girlfriend! I like girls! I don't like guys!" In a similar final shot, Participant 2 made his stand: "You people don't know what it's like to shower with someone that is gay. You know, 'cause I do. I had a gay teammate, and I had to step in the showers. You guys don't know how it is." With their positions on sexuality being challenged and the sanctity of the boys club of the locker room in doubt, Participant 2 and his teammate acted on behalf of the heterosexual gestalt. To be gay was not for real men, an attitude and identity they sought to embody. The liberal class was missing the truth behind their words, in their estimation. In a culture that has become accepting of homosexuality, masculinity, "true" male behavior, would only be pushed so far.

For the men of the study who identified as heterosexual, gender was determined on a spectrum, an identity that dare not drift toward the polarized, homosexual Other. However, for the only openly gay man who spoke with us, masculinity and sexuality worked far more congruently; his sexuality, although subjugated, did not alter how he understood himself as a man. He just happened to be a gay man, but a man nevertheless. Participant 7, the son of an immigrant mother and stepfather, understood masculinity as a far more fluid identity than did the straight men of the study. Although his instincts told him his gendered identity was not solely tied to his sexuality, his experiences made him quite aware of the expectations that come with being a working-class male.

Early in our discussion, Participant 7 reflected on his writing, an act, as per his thoughts, done in private in an attempt to put words to emotions so as to articulate, in some sense, how he understood himself as a man: "I would write, and I would just write down everything that I would feel. And you know, I would write stuff . . . I would write about stuff that I wasn't comfortable talking to other people about. Umh, you know, like, about my parents or about myself because I was discovering myself when I was in middle and high school. These were things I wasn't able to talk to anyone about because I didn't know how to approach it." At the opening of our dialogue, Participant 7 was feeling out Rob to see whether he was a safe confidant. Participant 7 was prepared to give an honest account of his experiences with writing; however, he was unsure, as his repetitive use of "stuff" as a euphemism for homosexuality attests, of how Rob would respond. In time, however, as Participant 7 grew more comfortable, he began to open up about his sexuality. In doing so, he addressed the manner in which he was outed and subsequently required to remain silent.

> A topic I like to talk about are gender roles and sexual orientation. So, gender roles, I have written about that in my journals. I've written about how, you know, my stepfather had a stubborn, strong mindset about men and very old-fashioned ideas about what men do. Yeah, then I talked about sexual orientation. When I was in middle school, I had met a, uh, guy who, umh, he, he basically opened my doors, and was starting to see that I was having . . . I liked guys. He was like, "This is not what God intended you to be, so you can't do this." Just something like that.

As a working-class man, his outlets were limited. His home, a space occupied and surveilled by his stepfather, and his larger culture, a working-class school and community, were dominated by a pervasive sense of "traditional" masculinity. At seemingly every turn, Participant 7 was silenced and marginalized, as his performance signaled a breaking with gender normativity—the steadfast notions of organized religion and economy that undergird much of the working class's understanding of masculine identity.

Prior to looking further into Participant 7's experiences as a gay man—the times in which he hid from being the fag, the moments he and others uttered the apology of "No Homo!"—how he conceptualized writing in comparison to Participant 2 is rather telling. What is interesting is that both men saw writing as a private act. However, what they concealed in their journals was in reality quite different, not so much regarding intent, as they were both hiding to some extent, but rather regarding what they were hiding from. Participant 2 saw writing as surreptitious, an act that mirrored the masculine identity he seemingly supported. Policing men to watch over their movements and words is largely done in silence. Likewise, calling someone a *fag*, whether outing an individual as homosexual or suggesting their actions are feminine in nature, is done in select locations, spaces in which the dominant male position holds its greatest amount of power. The male gaze operates to shame men in front of other men. Writing passively rather than engaging publicly was done to avoid being challenged. As for Participant 7, his writing was responsive to the sheer number of spaces in which male rhetoric holds sway. He wrote in silence as a means to search for his identity, as the public spaces he moved through were all possible locales in which he could be shamed for his sexuality. As he reflected on those days alone, he penned a narrative about transition, one that is aware of the repressive nature of masculinity, but one that finds strength in the act of self-discovery.

If Participant 2's strength was in his ability to silence oppositional voices in public spaces, Participant 7's courageousness was evident in his desire to make his private thoughts public, although he was quite aware of what was at stake. In some sense, this act works to reappropriate spaces, filling voids purposely left silent with subversive language as a means to garner greater public standing. Throughout his interview, he spoke of moments in his life in which he was shamed for his sexuality. In doing so, he provided a first-hand account of the homophobic language of masculinity. However, unlike many of the narratives that take on this topic, his culminated with a call for greater dialogue.

As he shared his stories, the conversation was more cathartic than painful. This interview, as a conduit for his stories, gave a perspective on working-class masculine identity, particularly the experience of a man of color. Although he occasionally strayed from topic to topic, the majority of our time together was spent discussing his family. The apologies he was asked to make were cultural, as he was a first-generation American. How his family understood masculinity was dated, overtly patriarchal, and his outlets were minimal.

> My mom was silent. She was also a traditional person herself. She just believed in staying home and not going to school or work. She has never worked. . . . I take that back. She has never worked a legal job. She was just a maid. She was just a maid for other houses. She is not going to get a social-security check. She is not going to get a pension when she is sixty-five . . . so, umh, she wasn't someone I could say, "Oh, I'm discovering myself." Then my mom would be like . . . she would agree with my stepfather who would say, "Oh, you have to follow religion. You have to do this, and you have to . . . this is the way of God. And this is all this stuff." I was pretty much by myself.

In moving from one country to another, the finer points of the lived experience are easily lost in the daily attempts to fulfill basic needs. His mother's time was spent working, as he noted, dead-end jobs. Much of her identity was predicated on her husband's thoughts and wishes. His siblings, although supportive—his sister was presently providing him with a place to stay—were taxed by their meager beginnings. His brother's and sister's apparent lack of empathy might have been a front for their own struggle for security and stability.

> I didn't have anyone to talk to. You know, you have all of these guys, having the same mindset as him [his father], and then my mother really never had a voice, so I could never really talk to her about anything. My sister and my brother had their own lives, so they never really, you know, got in touch with me about a lot of stuff. And, you know, they never really gave me the access to talk to them about what I felt or what I agreed or disagreed with.
>
> I wish I could tell her [his sister] more. I don't know how she would react because . . . I feel like there are certain things as to what you can say. You know, I feel you need to build it up first and not go straight to it. I wish I could say, "Oh, I dated this guy." I've dated a lot of guys. They know about it. But she is not completely comfortable talking about it. I am not completely comfortable talking about it.

Participant 7's isolation was most apparent during this exchange. Although his sister was progressive, as he noted, she was still not prepared to engage him in a discussion of his sexuality. Talk of this nature fell outside what was permissible in their homes. They both to some extent were conditioned to treat difference with silence.

Lost in the working-class immigrant experience were their voices. The voice that did, however, resonate was that of his stepfather. As Participant 7 noted repeatedly, his stepfather was the authority from which he sought cover: "He wanted me to be somebody that I naturally wasn't. Somebody that I never wanted to be. . . . He says I am too weak and, you know, too passive. 'You are too slow,' and, you know, 'you're not tough,' you know, this and that."

Although he was aware of Participant 7's sexuality, "suspicious" as Participant 7 noted, his stepfather forged ahead with a rather classed sense of vitriol. In Participant 7's home, he repeatedly heard of all he lacked as a man, all he should apologize for. According to his stepfather, he was deficient in the qualities that define a man: being outspoken, stoic, physically and emotionally strong. Participant 7's mannerisms, comments, and general demeanor, although authentic in nature, signaled him as Other. According to his stepfather, he should in some sense work to correct these character flaws and apologize for his actions, as he was performing antithetically to the male norm. For Participant 7, simply attaching "No Homo!" as an afterthought would do little to correct either his identity or its performativity. "No Homo!" would signify that his gender was inextricably tethered to his sexuality, so attaching "No Homo!" would only work to foreclose his sense of self.

In his Brooklyn neighborhood, Participant 7 heard similar sentiments and watched men perform in line with his father's thinking. He first realized he was gay because he was told so by a classmate. In some sense, he was outed; however, the manner in which Participant 7 reflected on this moment was not regretful, as one might suspect. His sexuality, now spoken aloud, was stronger, as he attested. He no longer had to hide because there was no secret to conceal. Speaking about his experiences and himself, he seemed to be living each moment again, except this time with a greater sense of confidence, no longer quietly and submissively penning "No Homo!" in his journals but making his sexuality known when given the opportunity. He concluded the interview with the following: "Some men are afraid to talk about it, so they may not be able to put it on paper. Maybe they won't even . . . some people don't talk about it for the rest of their lives. Some men just live in the closet their whole life and not express themselves. It's a shame that men do that. Because, you know, there is no definition of what a man should be." This passage was a fitting end to his interview, as it brought our conversation full circle. During the interview, he spoke about the silence that comes with being the gay son of immigrant, working-class parents. Speaking of his stepfather and the men of his neighborhood, Participant 7 noted just how embedded sexuality and gender are in his culture and community. These aspects of identity are rooted in the rhetoric of his home and the streets he walked. Class notions of masculinity take shape in the schoolyard and classroom. His journals, as he noted, were filled with a powerful voice, one that only had strength on the page. In public, to speak candidly would result in some sexual epithet. However, at this stage in his life, he was done with apologizing for his sexuality and his performance of masculinity. If "No Homo!" is to silence, he was prepared to do the opposite.

Although the previous narratives are powerful, they are not indicative of the common male experience. Both participants introduced so far had powerful voices that stood in opposition to one another. For the majority of men, gendered identities are not always hegemonic (Participant 2) or marginalized (Participant 7) but rather in the middle—a space of negotiation. These men are gender's greatest performers. They strain and contort to avoid the male gaze. They present themselves as confident and powerful, even as they are insecure. However, Participant 1's public presentation of masculinity was far different than his more private performance of it. Throughout the interview, he was uncomfortable with how he signified as a man. Unlike Participant 2, overtly heterosexual, and Participant 7, openly gay, Participant 1 was neither. He claimed no position on sexuality nor did he divulge his own. Rather, he spoke of what he assumed he should be, and in doing so, the power masculinity holds over men became apparent, seeing as he was in all actuality policing himself, censoring in the moment the words he uttered. And when this internal monitor failed him, letting a word slip or a gesture slide, he was quick to qualify the thought or action as not being homosexual, as he feared it was being read.

When Participant 1 initially spoke of athletics or his past girlfriend, he seemed to be posturing. As he grew more comfortable, he slowly changed his affect and became quite self-conscious. He began this shift with a commentary on the locker room, a public space that functions under scrutiny similar to that of a classroom, a place in which he was once comfortable but now felt the gaze of his peers: "Umh, when I was on the basketball teams . . . you know . . . the basketball teams I was on were very masculine . . . hypermasculine . . . athletic stereotypes . . . . They were for the most part . . . they were . . . you know, you had the guy's guys . . . you know . . . sex in the locker room . . . talk about sex in the locker room." His time in the locker room, although originally defined as space in which he felt great comfort, was soon described in quite different terms. In reality, it was a space that caused him great anxiety. When he reflected on these moments, he was reminded of the sexually charged language of the space: "It wasn't an environment I was totally comfortable in, umh, I didn't really talk to many of my teammates from back then." Gone was the bravado of the former athlete identity he initially presented. In its place was a far more honest man, one who was realizing that his former presentation of masculinity was quite possibly coerced, even fictitious. He continued to discuss how he attempted to avoid detection as an outsider.

> At least when you are being quiet and you are, I guess, I guess shy and people don't deal with you, you can at least say that this isn't who I really am . . . they are not . . . they just don't like this face on me, and I am fine with that. But, you know, if they react the same way to who you really are, that is a bit, I think, scarier. So, I think you are just better off putting on an act that way.

In a setting that called for, as he noted, a hyper sense of masculinity, he knew he could not live up to the standard. He also knew that to draw attention to himself and his "masculine deficiency" would bring him additional unwanted attention. As he noted, sports, although still an area of interest, became something he wrote about rather than a participatory experience. Similar to Participant 2 and Participant 7, Participant 1 sought to write as a means of escape. However, if Participant 2 did so to avoid challenge and Participant 7 to find a voice, Participant 1 receded to the private act of writing for cover, quite possibly creating a private space for negotiation.

As we concluded, Rob asked if Participant 1 had any questions for him. His response changed the entire interview: "To be blunt, when I was talking . . . I was thinking, 'Is he thinking that I am gay?'" When Rob asked what would have possibly given him that impression, he responded:

> First of all, I am kind of self-conscious about my voice being high pitched. Another bit is, you know, the use of the word *friend*. I think the way I was using it a bit can be blurred. Umh, you know the whole issue of identity, I guess, you know. A lot of when we talked about identity now or when you hear identity in the media is about . . . you know . . . sexual identity. Some things are in the back of your mind sometimes. Nah, the other thing was. I think, when you talk about not fitting in with other guys, that's usually one of the telltale signs.

His voice, his relationships, and/or his inability to fit in with the guys individually or collectively could have signaled him as Other. Truth is, it could have been anything. Somewhere in the midst of our discussion, the conversation for Participant 1 became less about his experiences and more about not challenging his sexuality. His interests in writing and/or his inability to fit in with peers signaled, to him, a possible misstep in terms of how he was presenting himself. Throughout the interview, he noted the distinction that existed in his life between his working-class community and the middle-class schools he attended. The academic identity he hoped to fulfill was problematic, as he noted, when he was in his neighborhood or in the locker room. He understood that he had to vary his performance; however, he had trouble doing so, something he noted. Participant 1 wondered how his sexuality was being perceived, and he never seemed to move beyond concern for how it was being read. In both cases, this moment and the locker room scenario, male response was driven by perception. Masculinity becomes a performative response to the surveillance or perceived surveillance of men by men.

Masculinity for these young men is something to be guarded at all times, for all constituencies, in every context. The performance of masculinity hinges on an image of empowerment and overt heterosexuality, all the more critical and uncomfortable in spaces of writing where critical thinking fosters doubt when believing and shoring up is often the instinctual response. For the men in our study, the prospect of becoming critical, even "objectively" challenging a core belief that has interpolated their subject positions, is confounding, as Peckham duly notes.[27] For working-class men, those who are often already lacking social, cultural, and economic capital, to be anything less, to be less masculine or to be gay, would only further marginalize their identities and underscore their alterity, albeit always already fictive. Three of the participants in the study explicitly addressed sexuality, unprompted by any of the common questions posed. Although some held authority and others worked from marginalized positions, what was constant was the notion of surveillance. As men, regardless of their proximity to the hegemonic norm, they were all quite aware of their public presentation of masculinity. For the first two participants, their identities were seemingly fixed. The athlete, at least for the time being, would continue to hold the most authority in the majority of public spaces. As a straight, white athlete, he was the embodiment of the norm. Participant 7's early life had been spent not covering but crafting a public persona. Participant 7 did not fear a *fag* label because he was comfortable with being a gay man. That was not the case for Participant 1. For him, a man who wanted to be perceived as masculine, sexuality was far more problematic. That said, ironically, sexuality was not the issue, per se, as it was never noted. Being gay for Participant 1 was never about the physical act of sex with another man; it was tied up in characteristics often identified as feminine—his voice, for example. Sexuality is ambiguous (like everything else). In the matrix of what determines masculine ideals, homosexuality is perceived as the position farthest away from hegemonic masculinity. Could one be both masculine and homosexual? Could one be feminine and heterosexual? For Participant 7, the former was just fine. For others, as was the case for Participant 1, the isolation and anxiety of signifying as both feminine and heterosexual was cause enough for him to monitor each and every one of his words, to say "No Homo!"

TEACHING FROM "NO HOMO!": IMPLICATIONS FOR THE EVERYDAY

In the highly performative, scripted state of masculinity, our research indicates that sexuality, perceived or otherwise, determines male status. Ironically, the men who participated in this study also found the very act of being interviewed, doing so in a public setting, to enact a parallel "checking" of one's gender and sexuality. The interviews invited men to get in touch with privately held notions of gender and sexuality, and that very self-reflection, metacognition, signified a sort of transgressive play on how one does (perhaps ought to do) public articulation of gender and sexuality. Although the writing classroom can be a pedagogical arena that facilitates a class-coded discovery and expression of authentic, felt selves and identities, perhaps spaces to become more critical of social conventions, they just as often indoctrinate the uninitiated into the middle-class/academic performance of rhetoric. Young working-class men, at least the ones we interviewed, find those spaces fraught with risk where they feel as if they cannot express and speak freely without risking or causing damage to their public face, a collection of self and presumed public identities that at once confer them status but also make them threatening representative of a status quo the academy offers up for unless challenged. Of course, these men are participants in many conversations happening within writing classrooms and across their learning and teaching environments. The discursive landscape for male students is a pedagogical terrain where a subtext of gender politics is palatable and inscribes a social protocol that many men do not feel they can challenge and still succeed academically. The material consequences are too great. For the majority of men, those who perform similarly to Participant 1, their only response to the gaze upon them—what they know to be real and present—is to, again, utter "No Homo!," removing themselves from the pedagogical inquiry of the space.

For both Rob and Harry, as teachers, as men, as first-generation academics, the insight our participants share resonates with our own experiences of needing to be hypervigilant about our sexualities and masculinities in the classroom. Just as our male participants feared the transgressive moment of being too gay, "No Homo!" occasions represent never-ending speech acts that license and police away the performative risk at the intersection of masculinity and sexuality. In Rob's classrooms, his affect makes possible a sort of bond with men that's without risk for many of the men he encounters, yet being "one of the guys" simultaneously refuses him the cred and capital of the conventional male faculty member, who often embodies the elite patriarchal masculinity of academe. Harry, for his part, though self-identified as a working-class male, is always already relegated out of the discursive domain of "one of the boys." The more legible his sexuality, the more likely the recoil, as Participant 2, the athlete, explained in his description of the intrusive, menacing, unwelcome gay man in the locker room. This figure, whose sexuality represents a contagion of sorts, both shores up and challenges dominant sexuality. The push-pull Harry represents dovetails with the very logic of the academy with which our participants had a complex and unresolved relationship. Rob, to the contrary, represents the potential reconciliation—if he can negotiate a presence, perhaps his path is one to follow, emulate. Whatever the trigger—being interviewed, writing about personal experiences, getting in touch with one's emotions through sharing in public—masculinity is thoroughly performative, a scripted endeavor inside and beyond the classroom, and when men are not perceived as masculine, they are to ask for forgiveness, to be "No Homo."

APPENDIX 2.A

Interview Questions

1. What do you hear when you hear *writing?*

2. What comes to mind when you think of a writer?

3. Which of these qualities apply to how you would describe yourself or how others would describe you?

4. Where or how do you think about these aspects of who you are? For example, do you talk with friends and/or family members?

5. Do you use writing as a means to explore or better understand yourself? If so, what classes and/or experiences have been most helpful?

Notes

1. Peckham, *Going North Thinking West.*
2. hooks, *Teaching to Transgress.*
3. LeCourt, "Performing Working-Class Identity in Composition."
4. Pratt, "Arts of the Contact Zone."
5. This study was approved by the St. John's University Institutional Review Board. Protocol #0213–091.
6. Sedgwick, *Epistemology of the Closet.*
7. Butler, *Gender Trouble.*
8. Pollack, "Real Boys," quoted in Foster, Kimmel, and Skelton, "'What about the Boys?,'" 13.
9. Foster, Kimmel, and Skelton, "'What about the Boys?,'" 13.
10. Butler, *Gender Trouble.*
11. Messner, *Politics of Masculinity.*
12. West and Zimmerman, "Doing Gender."
13. Foucault, *History of Sexuality.*
14. Butler, *Gender Trouble.*
15. Foucault, *History of Sexuality.*
16. Pascoe, *Dude, You're a Fag.*
17. Butler, *Gender Trouble.*
18. Connell, *Masculinities.*
19. Schwartz, "Social Construction of Heterosexuality."

20. Pascoe, *Dude, You're a* Fag, 55.
21. Ibid., 309
22. Bourdieu, *Language and Symbolic Power.*
23. Watson, Kehler, and Martino, "Problem with Boys'."
24. Wayne Martino, quoted in Watson, Kehler, and Martino, "Problem with Boys,'" 357.
25. Pascoe, *Dude, You're a Fag.*
26. Kimmel, *Guyland: The Perilous World.*
27. Peckham, *Going North Thinking West.*

3
IMPLICATIONS OF REDEFINING "WORKING CLASS" IN THE URBAN COMPOSITION CLASSROOM

Aaron Barlow and Patrick Corbett

In this chapter, we explore the disconnect between New York City College of Technology (City Tech) students' working-class subjectivities and the traditional implementation of first-year composition (FYC) pedagogy. We articulate the relationship between institutional realities, pedagogical tradition, and students' needs and how these intersections of institutionality and students' lives do not connect our students' working-class subjectivities to the educational project of FYC. We raise three questions we believe must be explored as part of the process of creating tangible changes to how teachers and scholars of FYC approach urban working-class students.

- How do we identify urban working-class students as working class in a positive, and productive, way?
- What aspects of composition pedagogy in its contemporary application devalue working-class students' subjectivities?
- How should we position ourselves within the diversity of working-class students' values and perceptions about literacy, language, and education to *serve* a contemporary working-class population?

A cultural disconnect exists between instruction for working-class students and the working-class subjectivities they bring into the classroom. Even as FYC has developed into one of the few courses (if not the only one) all students take, its present usefulness in our students' lives is limited. Writing teachers have invested decades in finding ways of bridging the gap between the methods of higher education and student learning potentials. Still, urban opportunity-granting institutions struggle to connect to students in the classroom and advance them toward an enduring and useful education. Here at City Tech, one of the most entrenched barriers preventing FYC from fully serving our urban working-class students is the social reality of class at our institution. FYC instruction is

DOI: 10.7330/9781607326182.c003

complicated by a hidden, but acute, divide between how class (particularly the working class) is addressed institutionally and as part of pedagogy, and the realities faced by our students.

We must understand our urban working-class students beyond rigid socioeconomic and sociocultural definitions that reify the working class as an economic and social marker of identity. Historically, being marked as working class corresponded to perception of such students as having unfavorable learning habits and deep resistance to institutional authority, which is remedied through pedagogical intervention. We must break away from this attitude and move to a more nuanced reflection of problems and contexts that simple models cannot address. At City Tech, our working-class students individually represent complex subjectivities formed out of *radically diverse* backgrounds. What we see through our existing models limits our understanding of the subjectivities our students' bring to their educations and the usefulness of these subjectivities to student learning.

At City Tech, our urban working-class students have experienced traditional pedagogy (and how it structures power and authority) their entire educational lives. They are inured to it. If we do not reach out with a more nuanced understanding of what role class plays in our interactions with students, we do little more than continue the social reality in which our students are marked as "working class" through extant institutional and pedagogical discourses. If we seek no new insight into how our teaching practices affect our students' subjectivities, we continue to build barriers around the very ideology of class we expect students to overcome.[1] If learning involves negation and shifts in subjectivity, we must respect our students' subjectivities as authentic, even valuable to our own work, and the locus of both being and belonging in our students' lives—not as problems to solve through pedagogy. To connect with urban working-class students, all faculty must recognize the extent of difference, of course, but must also continually reassess their own subject positions within the class structures of institutional power and legitimacy and must triangulate these with our students' realities.

URBAN WORKING-CLASS STUDENT DIVERSITY

Founded in 1946 as the New York State Institute of Applied Arts and Sciences of the City University of New York (CUNY), the mission of City Tech was to develop a "technically proficient workforce" out of returning World War II veterans. The core of City Tech's educational philosophy has been to offer students a learning experience connecting technical training with liberal arts. City Tech has developed sixty-six associate and baccalaureate degrees that serve a student population of staggering multicultural, multiethnic, and linguistic diversity.[2] As CUNY's technical college, City Tech provides working-class students the opportunity to emerge as skilled professionals holding both the technical skills necessary to perform in STEM-related fields and the broad range of perspectives provided through general education and the liberal arts.

City Tech students cannot be represented by traditional working-class definitions. Diversity at City Tech is a living force that inflects every aspect of our institutional character and operations. Even though students' families earn median annual incomes of less than $30,000 (in expensive New York City), the construction of our students' subjectivities has as much to do with their complex cultural backgrounds as it does with family income or the fact that many of them work as they pursue their educations.[3] City Tech students arrive from 138 countries and most live in homes where English is not the primary language (62 percent).[4] Many do not identify with traditional markers of ethnicity because the complexity of their backgrounds defies simple categorization (e.g., students may self-identify as Indo-Caribbean, or Arab-Brazilian). Their extended families often reside on two or more continents, come from multiple ethnic backgrounds, speak many languages, and have substantial differences in educational attainment.

While most City Tech students are not economically privileged, their significant cross-cultural competencies are valued by faculty in the classroom. Our colleagues throughout the college deeply respect our students' ethnic, religious, and linguistic differences (one could not teach here otherwise). However, when these differences are stretched to include our students' working-class backgrounds, the conversation often moves from respect to frustration. The mismatch in expectations between student and teacher is rooted in unexamined assumptions about class and its contribution to subjectivity. Working-class students' subjectivities contribute to their own expectations about what they will be learning, how, and to what end, just as our subjectivities as faculty contribute to *our* own expectations. Though City Tech students are labeled working class by economic and cultural definition, their representation of what this label means is different from how they are *defined* in the classroom.

This disconnect between class, subjectivity, and learning has serious pedagogical implications in writing instruction. Beyond the pedagogies of identity, the subjectivities formed by diverse groups of urban working-class students are distinct from those of their instructors, regardless of the teacher's own background. When faculty make assumptions about the nature and value of the subjectivities of their students (or overlook them entirely), we are creating barriers, depreciating the complex subjectivities working-class students bring through their cultural environments. We compound the problem by developing classroom instruction that shows working-class students that their subjectivities are not recognized or valued because these subjectivities do not correlate with the identities or intellectual goals valued in FYC.

INSTITUTIONAL CONDITIONS OF WORKING-CLASS EDUCATION

As a course sequence traditionally rooted in the study and expression of identity, FYC is deeply imbricated in issues of class, but our pedagogy often fails in examining the relationship among subjectivities, particularly working-class subjectivity within the context of conflicts between instructors and institutions. Teachers of writing, through education, professional development, and the folkways of experience have understood what constitutes effective teaching in their field since the 1970s. Yet, our ability to realize long-term, systemic, and effective change has been slow.

Even though we understand what makes pedagogy effective, and know how to guide our students to praxis when they come to us ready and willing to learn in a way we recognize, we are faced with institutional conditions born out of the increasingly manifest poverty of public funding, of systemic mandates that serve a surveillance bureaucracy more than students, and a staggeringly diverse student population that lacks familiarity with traditional higher education teaching methods and ideological imperatives. Within this cluster of material, ideological, and cultural conditions, implementing the best pedagogical advances of our field is an ongoing challenge.

Like its peer institutions, City Tech has difficulty graduating the students it serves. City Tech loses about a third of its entering students by the second year, almost half by the end of two years. Close to one-quarter of its students have earned associate or baccalaureate degrees after five years.[5] Part of the problem is that support for students outside elite US institutions is dwindling precipitously. There are institutional, cultural, and political reasons for this loss, but one tendency is to blame the ideology and work ethic of faculty. This devaluation of the subjectivities of faculty, of relegating their professional vocation to delivering and assessing content under an increasing paucity of resources, creates an environment in which subjectivity is categorically devalued in the learning process.[6] New emphases on delocalized assessment, continuous "quality" improvement, and rote technological solutions to pedagogical issues play significant roles in the material and instructional conditions of the classroom and the extent to which subjectivity can be valued. Yet even "techniques such as reducing class sizes, applying different pedagogical methodologies, offering psychological and societal interventions, and . . . utilizing technology ultimately will offer smaller potential for improvement in student learning" than do teacher contributions because it is that nexus of interpersonal interaction and subjectivity formation that guides the learning process.[7]

Two policy directions affect the extent to which individual subjectivities can be explored, particularly in the classrooms that serve working-class students. The first, "teacher proofing," is "the practice of limiting the autonomy of individual teachers [in order] to produce a more uniform and controlled experience" through increased curricular control and pacing, high-stakes testing, standardized course content, and rote instruction.[8] Teacher proofing sees the teacher not as people who have their own individual subjectivities but as assembly-line workers. The assumption is that variability in teacher skill and student populations can be lessened through breaking tasks down into simpler components with increased oversight and decreased autonomy. At CUNY, we have our own teacher-proofing initiative, Pathways, which is an attempt to regularize general education over the first two years of college across the entire system. Teacher proofing is always top down (Pathways was imposed by CUNY's central administration), with its goals imposed on teachers and students by forces far from the classroom.

The second direction starts from the dynamic of teacher-and-student interactions and depends on goals developed by students in conjunction with their teachers. Instead of teacher proofing, this emphasis on personal relationships gives both teacher and student an opportunity to continually hone skills and knowledge in a fashion appropriate to the individual. It is not based on assessment or external oversight and goal setting but on growth from the individual student's starting point. This direction, one most writing teachers are familiar with, owes a great deal to the progressive ideals of John Dewey and his work's influence on twentieth-century United States education.[9] This direction begins by recognizing the subjectivity of the teacher as valuable in the learning dynamic. Ideally, it would also afford the same value to the subjectivities of individual students, but this does not happen automatically. Though basic to the disciplinary framework of FYC, valuing the subjectivities of students is an approach frequently hamstrung by institutional limitations. It is effective only when student and teacher cocreate a meeting point from each other's cultural subjectivities.

Given institutional constructs inimical to appropriate instruction (e.g., large class sizes, limiting physical spaces, and inflexible curricular structures), moving urban working-class students through FYC in a way that values individual subjectivity as a crucial aspect of learning can be challenging. Students and policymakers blame writing teachers for lack of success, and all too often, in hallway and water-cooler talks (and occasionally in print), writing teachers blame students or, at least, their working-class subjectivities. Though improvement does not rest on the faculty alone, our most immediate contribution to urban working-class student success will come from understanding students' needs and quandaries, both cultural and institutional, and from acting with these in mind. While we can make little immediate change in institutional contexts, we *can* reexamine, as Ira Shor suggests, our relationships with working-class students—the "already-existing conflicts" present in the classroom, in the institution, and within socially unjust economic systems. Equally important, we can focus on the students themselves, their own conflicted relationships with socioeconomic and cultural realities, and what they struggle with as they further their education.[10]

CRITIQUING THE "WORKING-CLASS IDENTITY"

Though City Tech students fit many working-class demographics, they do not fit traditional assumptions about the working class—a problem manifest in FYC, where the politics of identity is typically made overt as a matter of ethical pedagogy. One of the dangers of trying to define a class or group other than our own is that we end up looking at the other group *only* in terms of our own. Conversely, when we try to define our own class, we have very little to compare it to, usually having no substantial knowledge of other groups. As a result, when we compare teacher and student identities, our benchmarks are often clichés and assumptions based in our own subjectivities.

Much traditional scholarship of working-class identity fails to consider how the powerful working-class subjectivities our students bring into the FYC classroom are *hidden subjectivities* without easy correlatives in the scholarship of identity. Further, working-class subjectivity is at odds with the identities students at colleges like City Tech believe they come to college to acquire. At the same time, like faculty everywhere, few of the teachers come from working-class backgrounds. Writing teachers too often operate on outdated visions of what it means to be working class. They carry forward old assumptions, including

- that the liberal arts and humanities will enlighten working-class students about themselves and the world;
- that the value of composition pedagogy can be exported to other (frequently vocational) departments and programs without a mutual exchange of disciplinary perspective;
- that class and ethnicity can function separately as relevant concepts affecting learning outcomes; and
- that individual courses like FYC can, by their very essence, promote working-class students' progress toward relevant educational goals.

THE SOCIAL REALITY OF BEING WORKING CLASS IN THE FYC CLASSROOM

However we fight to improve education, we must not pretend to be out to free our students from slavish adherence to a "system" that we, by virtue of our positions, remain slaves to. Like Thoreau's "statesmen and legislators" in "On the Duty of Civil Disobedience," many of us stand "completely within the institution." We are governed by what Luc Boltanski defines as social reality, not reality "as it is actually experienced by individual actors in the diversity of everyday situations" but "reality as a whole, resting on a framework of formats, rules, procedures, knowledge and tests that purport to be generally applicable, a reality sustained by institutions that determine its shape."[11] But insomuch as social reality contributes to ours and students' subjectivities, we have become comfortable within ours and uncomfortable with our students'. In doing so, we prepare our working-class students to accept, among other things, institutional limitations on the value of the education they seek. If we do not begin examining and questioning our own class-based assumptions and engage the experiential realities of each of our working-class students, we risk throwing a tunic of emancipatory rigmarole over the already substantial vestments of tradition. We end up appearing just as many of our working-class students already imagine us: guardian priests of an insider tradition of which they cannot, or will not, partake. They wouldn't be far from wrong.

To make matters worse, we continually develop a prescription for scholarship and even learning based on conventions and artifices known only to insiders. Our insistence on teaching particular citation formats, for example, is an alien practice to those not trained to it. Worse, it is a set of conventions that has little extrinsic necessity outside academic life. Our working-class students see citation as institutional make-work, but the real role it plays is one of ensuring conformity to a discourse that has much more to do with institutional tradition and faculty values than it does with a useful organizational practice for students.

[Citation] is the means by which the "real" is instituted. To cite the other on their behalf is hence to make credible the simulacra produced in a particular place. . . . To cite is thus to give reality to the simulacrum produced by power, by making people believe that others believe in it, but without providing any believable object.[12]

With our instruction in citation, we promote conformity to a pattern of "knowledge" based on old assumptions about language, influence and heredity—not about an experiential reality our students will need to carry forward in their education and their lives.

We don't often question such assumptions of our own, though we constantly ask students to question theirs. This unequal ground raises our cultural attributes above theirs, creating a standoff. Few students are going to jettison their cultural baggage on the say-so of a teacher. More widely, fallout includes criticism of universities for "political correctness," a reaction to the arrogance of intellectuals in believing their views of the world are more accurate and appropriate—and better—than those of others. Though we on the faculty may pride ourselves on being cultural warriors, we are all defenders of a cultural status quo, adhering to rule-bound organizations and educational processes. We carry within us cultural norms we are rarely willing to recognize. There is no fundamental or essential necessity to the formalisms of citation in our FYC students' lives, and for most there never will be.

Of course, teaching writing involves cultural norms and expectations as much as development of abstract competencies. Nothing about FYC can be simply skill based; everything about it is affected by traditional means of dividing people into class categories through language. When we say our students can't write, we are not telling the full story: our students may well be able to communicate on paper, and effectively. What they can't do is write within the conventions we consider standard.

REACHING OUT TO WORKING-CLASS STUDENTS

Because FYC pedagogy occurs within narrow curricular structures of general education and writing faculty's own education and professional development, harmful assumptions about the role of writing and communication are easily propagated and amplified, both within the degree paths of our students and in writing pedagogies. Even the liberatory pedagogies typically associated with class-based politics may fail City Tech students and those like them, preventing them from expanding their subjectivities and from producing desired educational outcomes. As Shor writes, "Exercising various kinds of agency in an unequal setting where they lack formal authority, students also resist/engage/manipulate the teacher."[13] An us/them battle line can quickly form. Students have "become resilient experts in the skill most taught by mass education—spitting out and spitting back the official syllabus force-fed to them year after year."[14] The teacher cannot change this by demand, and depending on how we are theorizing our working-class students, we might never reach or engage them at all.

The ideological models about working-class students found within composition scholarship help us theorize composition as a middle-class enterprise but do not value the working-class subjectivities of FYC students. Following Henry Giroux, Beth Virtanen claims that working-class internalization of the ideology of the dominant culture often reinforces working-class positions[15] and categorizes working-class students as

- Those Most Likely to Succeed;
- Reluctant Scholars;
- Unlikely Candidates;
- Those Who Choose to Not-Learn.

Virtanen's model captures the resistance of working-class students but categorizes it as a condition with a continuum of success depending on how resistant working-class students are. Those Most Likely to Succeed are the students who willingly divest themselves of their working-class identities. They see themselves as "better" within the meritocracy of pursuing the American Dream. Their limitation is that they still perceive a distance between the working class they are leaving behind and the middle class to which they aspire.[16]

Virtanen's students categorized as Those Who Choose to Not-Learn are the most resistant students, ones who challenge authority, who recognize (often unconsciously) the vast inequality in educational systems. They do not want to join the traditional middle class. These students "take from education what they see will enhance their lives, and they strongly reject the notion that higher education requires leaving their home communities. Attaining a higher education is an experience in finding out what is insightful in one reality and merging it with their prior sense of how things are."[17] Unfortunately, these working-class students are the ones we overlook as difficult, those with perspectives least valued in our classroom because they defy the ideological project and identity politics of FYC disciplinary thinking.

In articulating FYC as a "middle-class enterprise," Lynn Bloom writes that FYC addresses aspects of social class that are "enabling students to think and write in ways that will make them good citizens of the academic (and larger) community, and viable candidates for good jobs upon graduation."[18] Of course, "Composition is taught by middle-class teachers in middle-class institutions to students who are middle class either in actuality or in aspiration—economic if not cultural."[19] Composition cannot be removed from questions of class. City Tech students cross ethnic, class, and social lines, each one creating a new pattern of cultural interactions and learning possibilities. As a result, City Tech's working-class students cannot be modeled or reached as members of a single politicized class; they resist class-based identities and the very politics of class. So, instead of relying on what we've learned about the working class, especially in relation to the middle class, we must approach them as individuals immersed in a myriad of identities that share certain subjective experiences, with unique configurations in each particular classroom.

COMPOSITION PEDAGOGY BEYOND TRADITIONAL
NOTIONS OF THE WORKING CLASS

Many working-class students at City Tech believe their educational failure is endemic—that even being at the college is itself a failure of not obtaining admission to a more prestigious institution. Coupled with the barrier created by our assumptions as faculty, this belief guarantees that the walls between student and teacher and student and institution almost always remain intact and that student success rates remain low. Unfortunately, teachers, given short semesters and heavy teaching loads, haven't time to explore individual student backgrounds; they start instead with generalized assumptions about the cultural backgrounds of even individual students, and they often end there. These assumptions must be challenged, and a new flexible and individual-centered means of approaching FYC classrooms in colleges such as City Tech must be established even in the face of a rigid social reality.

It's worth repeating that the concerns we express are not new. Scholars of education and writing have explored them intensely for decades. For a variety of reasons, the changes called for in scholarship have not appeared in the classrooms that serve working-class students, so this is where we must now focus. Prevalent older and ineffective assumptions persevere, including the "banking model" of education Paolo Freire and two generations of scholars after him have critiqued. Nearly fifty years after James Moffett wrote that "a child is not an empty vessel when he enters school; he comes replete with a set of abstractions about the world and himself," classroom teaching still fails to account for working-class students' subjectivities.[20] As Shor claimed in the nineties, "Students are creative, intelligent beings, not plants or blank slates or pegboards for teacherly hammering."[21] As a discipline, we accept these commonplaces wholeheartedly, but they have little impact on the educational lives of urban working-class students, perhaps because we cannot describe the content of the vessel, the subjectivity of the student, any more than we can describe the vessel itself.

As teachers, we spend a lot of time attempting to create and illuminate goals for education. We are trained to talk about "outcomes" and craft careful statements describing what they look like and why they are necessary. Yet this work has little impact on the individual learning of working-class students. That's because, in part, we spend very little time at the other end, with "incomes." Perhaps instructors are satisfied that the standards for entering students place them all at the same basic level, but such uniformity is unlikely. Anyone who has taught FYC at a college like City Tech knows classrooms are likely to contain both fluid and confident writers and those close to being functionally illiterate. To make matters more complicated, working-class students are coming from various cultural and economic backgrounds. *Writing* can mean quite different things to different students—and the goals represented by attendance at college can be as widely divergent.

THE INERTIA IN FYC INSTRUCTION

Lack of teacher understanding of working-class cultures has acculturated the affected students to certain forms of performativity as students in a writing classroom. For many City Tech students, there is an additional range of cultural reticences creating resistance to the kinds of writing assignments found in FYC classrooms, especially if they concern family and background. Our students may find family a private matter and wish to keep it so. A student may have grown up behind a Chinese restaurant, a family of five or more living in two or three rooms—possibly even in an undocumented situation—and may not want to describe home life or even relate stories of parental life back in Guangzhou, where the living situation may have been even worse.

Many young immigrants and children of immigrants are more interested in looking forward, not back, and others do not wish to share their private lives with faculty. City Tech students often work at jobs in which they serve people much like their instructors or their families—or people who appear to be of that class, one distinct from their own. They are in college because they don't want to stay in such jobs—and they do not expect their teachers have had any experience in similar situations; they don't believe their teachers could understand anything they say about their work. Having been trained in "proper" behavior in service roles, they know those they serve have very little interest in them. They can even feel patronized when interest is expressed.

This situation is further complicated by questions of ethnicity and race. Race, in particular, has an impact on almost every facet of instruction and programming in schools like City Tech, especially because our working-class students are also students of color, even though many would not identify as either. bell hooks writes that

> throughout the history of the civil rights struggle to end racial discrimination, exploitation, and oppression, freedom has often been determined by the degree to which people of color have access to the same privileges as white peers. Embedded in this notion of freedom is the assumption that access is all that is needed to create the conditions of equality. The thinking was: Let black children go to the same schools as white peers and they will have all that is needed to be equal and free.[22]

There is no way teachers, on their own, can overcome the failure of this belief. There are factors that simple race avoidance can never address or overcome, one example being shame.

> Many black students with excellent academic skill and talent are performing poorly in academic settings because they are shame-based and in settings where shaming is a common practice. In many cases simply the experience of being "judged" activates deep-seated feelings of shame. Messing up, performing poorly eases the anxiety. If the fear is that they will be found wanting, then as soon as they can inappropriately act out so that they are indeed wanted, they can feel better. There are serious taboos against acknowledging shame. Individual black students and colleagues have broken down emotionally as we talk in my office about negative experiences in predominately white academic settings. They voice shame about feeling shame.[23]

The combination of race, class, and institutional hierarchy makes it unlikely that any of these barriers can be overcome—even when one of them has been reduced through identity, a black teacher working with black students, for example.

THE SOLUTION IN THE PROCESS

At their best, FYC teachers take to heart the advice of the members of the Society of Friends at Balby in 1656, who wrote, "These things we do not lay upon you as a rule or form to walk by, but that all . . . may be guided: and so in the light walking and abiding, these may be fulfilled in the Spirit, not from the letter, for the letter killeth, but the Spirit giveth life." Each semester, effective FYC instructors go through a process of learning along with their students; class structures and syllabi must be reevaluated and rebuilt in light of individual experience. No formula fits every situation.

One suggestion that has proven useful at City Tech is to keep syllabi lean so they don't drive the courses. An outline of course regulations and a short schedule is all that is necessary for FYC. It can also be useful to allow the students to suggest alteration of certain requirements and dates as set out on the syllabus, moving a weekly deadline from Friday to Saturday for e-mail submissions, for example, after students explain that the work schedules for many of them make the weekday deadline difficult. Minor actions can have a major impact, for they give students an understanding that they can—and should—be actively involved in their courses far beyond simply responding to assignments.

Standardized "outcomes" and course goals exclude too many students from success. We can see this in the way, institutionally, we treat nonnative speakers of English or even those whose dialects are nonstandard. Though there have been attempts to recognize differences in dialect as acceptable parts of higher education, these attempts have failed. The reason is simple: US power structures use dialect as a sorting mechanism. Students, though they may be proficient in communication within their native languages and dialects, are considered deficient when they enter US higher education without being able to handle the narrow forms and conventions of US written communication. Their skills are swept aside; they are placed in remedial environments, as though they have failed when, in fact, they are simply differently abled.

One of the first things an FYC instructor can do is sidestep the cultural arrogance most of us carry. We can do this in two ways: first, we must challenge our own generalizations, our imagined outlines of our students and their possibilities. Second, we can create a strict agenda for the teacher and a corresponding freedom for the student, the opposite of what we normally attempt. This approach should cede some classroom control to the students, keeping teacher interference to needed support. The position of the teacher, as their role becomes more regimented and, indeed, restricted, moves from the center of the course experience to the side. From this new place, the teacher keeps priorities in proportion: "The basic problems of understanding what someone else says to us, or of putting thoughts into words, can and should be separated from mere decoding of letters and mere transcribing of speech, which involve only perceptual and motor skills, not thought and emotion."[24] We teachers might always keep in mind that "when students can connect what they are learning to accurate and relevant prior knowledge, they learn and retain more. In essence, new knowledge 'sticks' better when it has prior knowledge to stick to."[25] To teach, we must know what the students know.

The universes of discourse each student operates within are often quite different from the standardized one created by the contemporary mania for easy assessment. Standardization reflects the assumptions, the social reality, of a particular and well-educated elite. Standardized exams in writing are chosen by faculty and reflect *their* cultural biases and understandings, carrying the expectation that those of the students will be no different. Students often fail from lack of familiarity, not lack of skill. For this reason, it becomes useful to allow students to develop writing topics through a process of exploration. This is an old composition strategy, of course, but it is often abandoned in situations in which students seem particularly passive, as they can seem at City Tech.

The question for the FYC instructor is, how do I design student-enacted exercises that utilize a student's own cultural strengths within a milieu alien to that student's culture? The answer cannot be universal; it will never fit within the pattern of standardization increasingly imposed on US education. The answer requires a great deal of institutional confidence in individual instructors and their judgment, something few higher education administrations, in our assessment-happy environment, are willing to develop.

One of the first steps toward creating an environment in which the student feels unfettered by the constraints of the instructor's belief is deemphasizing the necessary hierarchy of the classroom itself. Active student learning should not be imagined to center on passive reception of teacher lectures. Freire explains why, writing that "leaders who deny praxis to the oppressed thereby invalidate their own praxis. By imposing their word on others, they falsify that word and establish a contradiction between their methods and their objectives."[26] The purpose of large-group activity should be coordination of other activities and motivation of students toward those activities—or provision of a singularity (such as watching a film, theater presentation, or lecture) that will be useful to subsequent and more individualized activities. In any case, such large-group activities should never dominate the course but should be seen as tools enhancing individual writing projects.

Instead of relying on prepared prompts and exercises, writing topics should be developed through student interest and knowledge. Teacher, what do you want? should be a question kept well in abeyance, with students working within their own prior conversational universes to develop topics. What do you talk about with your friends? What does your family discuss? What comes up at work? What do you think about and dream about during any free time? These and other questions, when carefully formulated to keep the student from feeling cornered or pushed, can lead to the generation of personalized topics that can, without intrusive manipulation, become the basis for genuine and effective writing. In their prior coursework, students have only been taught to select topics that will meet with teacher approval. They will continue to do so unless the teacher deliberately moves from a controlling centrality. Taking a lesson from South African black activist Steve Biko, we teachers must understand the necessity for space where students can develop decision-making skills. They cannot do this under our direct supervision, but we teachers are often too nervous (or are too much under institutional constraint) to give students this necessary freedom.

Just as whole-class instruction is too teacher centric, technologically mediated individualized instruction also confines students through visions developed outside their personal experience. Both are useful, but each removes communication from the one-to-one interaction so should not be the center of the FYC experience. Lou Kelly, author of *From Dialogue to Discourse: An Open Approach to Competence and Creativity*, argues that writing works best when it starts with discussion, then moves to "talking on paper" and from there to more formalized written constructs. Though whole-class events and technological aids can assist in this process, it's the act of communication itself that concerns FYC, and that act, as Kelly realizes, starts with conversation. James Britton wrote over forty years ago that "in a good conversation, the participants profit from their own talking . . . , from what others contribute, and above all from the interaction—that is to say from the enabling effect of each upon the others."[27]

Keeping student tasks to small, discrete (though ultimately interconnected) units—with the teacher developing the tasks but staying one step ahead of the students completing them—can allow the instructor to use past activity in the particular classroom to scaffold the new, building on evident activity and interest. This approach also keeps the teacher from falling into assignment design based on convention— and it necessitates a continuing discussion involving instructor and students. A course designed in this way cannot run itself, that is, it does not unfold according to a script—but this flexibility is often just what is needed for students who are not already acculturated to academic writing standards.

As we work within our classrooms, we instructors also must be looking at forces outside, often running interference for protection of the learning process, refusing to use imposed grading rubrics or other tools that reduce student writing from acts of communication to quantifiable marks on sheets of paper. If we grade in the manner so often being asked of us for purposes of assessment and standardization, we once more push student personalities and needs out of the equation, reducing the effectiveness of our instruction and the likelihood students will remain motivated enough to complete their degrees.

In 1969, Neil Postman and Charles Weingartner presented an optimistic view of the teaching profession as an instrument of change, *Teaching as a Subversive Activity*. They argued that while institutions of learning may be hidebound and committed to preservation of the status quo, teaching does not have to be. They are right, but resisting the status quo is not so simple. There is plenty of room for self-delusion, making it easy for teachers to fall into smug self-satisfaction, convincing themselves that they are struggling *against* the institutions making their activities possible. Writing in the caldron of the sixties, Postman and Weingartner believed they could use cultural confusion as a springboard to change. Since then, unfortunately, too many in education have used the same reasoning as an excuse for inaction.

One of the intents of many FYC instructors is to create a "safe" space for students to express their opinions, a space that can accept all sorts of diversity. The problem, from the student point of view, is that this "safety" is prescribed by the instructor's own prejudices so is not really safe for all. Some students' concerns about homosexuality, for example, must be masked, creating an "unsafe" environment for them in order to create a safe one for others. The idea of safety, in other words, is a reflection of the understandings and biases of the institution with little respect for those of a diverse body of students. Factors like these affect students' attitudes toward expression, influencing each one differently—and such influences must be taken into account in course design.

What we have learned through teaching working-class students at City Tech is that each new group of students is different and that tactics for the semester must be developed in response to the particulars of the individuals. As a result, there are few specific tasks or procedures we can suggest, other than making sure one comes into the FYC classroom with as strong a grounding in the scholarship of composition as possible and a commitment to continuing participation in professional conferences and discussions. Beyond that, these are the only rules we can offer:

1.   Trust in your own judgment.

2.   Listen to your students.

3. Teach the class, not the rules.

4. Remain flexible, remembering George Orwell's dictum in "Politics and the English Language" that it is better to break any rule than to allow the barbarous.

Each teacher, like each student, is different, and able in distinct ways. We must recognize our own individual strengths and weaknesses, but in every case, we *must* make the individuals in each group of students the heart of each semester.

Effective FYC instruction, by starting with the students' own cultural subjectivities, can introduce students to writing processes that do draw on their passions and that can demonstrate to them the power of the written word under their own control—and that they *can* control their own writing. This should be our goal.

Notes

1. Alcoff, "Cultural Feminism."
2. New York College of Technology, "About City Tech."
3. New York College of Technology, "New York City College of Technology: Facts 2014–15."
4. New York City College of Technology, "New York City College of Technology: Facts 2014–15."
5. New York City College of Technology, "City University of New York."
6. Arum and Roksa, *Academically Adrift*, 191–99.
7. Ferster, *Teaching Machines*, 10.
8. Ibid., 3.
9. Dewey, *Experience and Education*, 73.
10. Shor, *When Students Have Power*, 17.
11. Boltanski, *Mysteries and Conspiracies*, 16.
12. de Certeau, *Practice of Everyday Life*, 188–89.
13. Shor, *When Students Have Power*, 17.
14. Ibid., x.
15. Virtanen, "Working-Class Students," 445–46.
16. Ibid., 455–56.
17. Ibid., 463–65.
18. Bloom, "Freshman Composition," 655.
19. Ibid., 656.
20. Moffett, *Teaching the Universe of Discourse*, 24.
21. Shor, *When Students Have Power*, 12.
22. hooks, *Teaching Community*, 93–94.
23. Ibid., 100–101.
24. Moffett, *Teaching the Universe of Discourse*, 15.
25. Ambrose, et al., *How Learning Works*, 15–16.
26. Freire, *Pedagogy of the Oppressed*, 120.
27. Britton, *Language and Learning*, 239–40.

4

CALIFORNIA DREAMS
Working-Class Writers in the California State University System

Cassandra Dulin

The US Department of Education has found that forty percent of students who set out to complete a bachelor's degree from a four-year institution fail to graduate in six years.[1] There are many reasons students leave college before they complete their degrees. A study conducted in 2009 found that working while going to school was the main reason students left before finishing their programs.[2] Juggling work and school is difficult and stressful. This same study also found that the students who dropped out due to strenuous work schedules admitted it would be too hard to reenroll. These students live with the reality that working is the only way they can survive, even if it means giving up on the opportunity to advance in their careers with a four-year diploma. Richard A. Greenwald and Elizabeth A. Grant suspect colleges are not prepared for the working-class student because they are seen as being a temporary population. In a lot of ways, the academy "demonstrate[s] a lack of compassion for and ignorance of the material realities of working-class students;"[3] colleges acknowledge there are differences in class among students, but they fail to recognize these differences as an institutional reality, which might possibly be the result of a lack of discussion on class in the college system.

Because the numbers don't show up in federal statistics, it is difficult to find information on students who enroll part time, reenroll after taking a break for a time, or transfer in from another college or university. Most of the information gathered on college students pertains to first-time and full-time students, which means institutional decisions about working-class students are haphazard and incomplete. Complete College America, from the Bill and Melinda Gates Foundation, recommends

DOI: 10.7330/9781607326182.c004

that states encourage colleges to focus on lowering student attrition rates and raising completion rates by attaching financial incentives to increase student graduation. Since the California State University (CSU) system enrolls a significant working-class student demographic, understanding the needs of this student base is a critical component to success.

The working-class population is not homogenous, and the problems they face are just as diverse as they are. These differences make it difficult to locate where working-class issues should be targeted and addressed. Since colleges and universities are dedicated to creating an environment where diversity can flourish equally and easily, a closer look at the working-class student is needed in order to make effective policy changes at the institutional level.

The CSU system is an expansive arrangement of twenty-three colleges spread out across the state and makes up one of the largest and most affordable university systems in the United States. It is responsible for supporting California's densely populated and diverse public school system through its education programs and state credentialing support procedures for teachers. The CSU system is also responsible for supplying the state's workforce with engineers, accountants, health care and hospitality workers, and agricultural scientists.[4]

Working-class student s make up a large portion of the student population in higher education. A 2003 study called *Diversity and College Admission* found that about 74 percent of colleges and universities across the United States have a commitment to student diversity that they make clear in their mission statements.[5] The working-class student comes to class with an array of perspectives and experiences different from other college students who come from more affluent backgrounds.[6] It is important that diversity is addressed in the discussion of student development in education; however, issues that face the working-class student are complex and diverse and can range from an inefficient secondary education to cultural misalignment of school and home.

According to Jenny Marie Stuber, studies have been conducted on student achievement involving students who face multiple barriers to education[7]; however, there has been little effort to understand the obstacles students face, such as challenges created by social class differences. In my work, I hope to conceptualize a working-class pedagogy that supports those who are not necessarily ready for college and those who require a different way of thinking about student needs. For this research project, I used the Early Start program for the CSU system in California as a model for thinking about the programmatic structures in place for working-class students. I will first describe what the Early Start program was designed to do and how it works at the institutional level; then I will discuss the appropriateness of such programs for the growing population of working-class students, according to their specific needs.

EARLY START

In 2012, the CSU system created a program called Early Start to improve college readiness in English and math skills for incoming freshmen. Its creation was the result of various strategies developed since the 1990s to improve the performance of high-school students in English and math before they enrolled in college. Early Start requires new freshmen to complete readiness courses in the summer prior to their first fall semester if they do not pass the CSU placement exams in English and math.[8] The remediation of students has been a big issue for the CSU system since at least 50 percent of first-time freshmen enter the system needing help in English and/or math.[9] Various programs to make students college ready have been created throughout the system over the past ten years, and these programs generally take place in the summer. One such program, called the Summer Bridge program, provides remedial English and math courses to low-income and first-generation college students the summer before they begin their freshman year. Not all CSUs had a summer bridge program on their campuses, so in 2010, the CSU Board of Trustees enacted a policy that required all CSUs to adopt an Early Start program by 2012.

Each of the twenty-two campuses across the state, with the exception of the Maritime Academy, which does not offer an Early Start program, is required to offer its students some form of remediation "partly determined by campuses' philosophies on remediation," which provides each CSU the ability to craft a program that fits its local needs.[10] Two-thirds of the colleges offer students a one-unit course; these courses "are designed only to fulfill Early Start requirements and are not intended to remediate students fully or advance them to higher level."[11] Other colleges offer remediation that consists of three units over the summer before the students' freshman year is designed to help students advance their skills to the next level. This pedagogical divide is found more with programs offering English remediation; some colleges seek to fulfill the Early Start requirement for their college because they believe a separate summer class shortens the experience and isolates what students will eventually learn from the freshman writing curriculum, and others design longer summer programs to encourage remediation before the students enter classes in the fall.[12] Much of my research will focus on a study of the campuses that offer the one-unit Early Start program since this type of program is the one most commonly found throughout the CSU system.

The CSU campuses have varying student demographics and compositions. Some campuses' students require more remediation than others. The students who are required to enroll in the Early Start program are not indicative of the overall freshman population of the CSU system. About 57 percent of the students enrolling in Early Start programs across the state are Latin@, which contrasts with that fact that Latin@ student make up 41 percent of the entire freshman class. In addition, about 65 percent of all Early Start students qualify for financial aid, but only 51 percent of the total freshman population of the CSU system show evidence of needing help paying their tuition.[13] Some educators have mentioned that the mandatory remediation of the Early Start program negatively impacts low-income students who need to work during the summer in order to support their families.[14] This means the students who participate in the Early Start program have unique needs that must be considered when administrators make decisions that might affect these students' success in higher education.

DISCUSSION OF WORKING-CLASS STUDENTS AND EARLY START

The working-class student embodies many different qualities of interest to administrators and professors who encounter these students on a daily basis. The data collected for this research on the working-class student in Early Start programs is the result of six interviews conducted at CSU Bakersfield and CSU Stanislaus. These interviews involved two composition professors teaching in Early Start programs and four students who had participated in the 2014 summer program. Interviews were conducted during the spring semester of 2015. A variety of characteristics were discovered about the working-class student from this study.

One characteristic of working-class students is that they generally come from parents without college preparation. About 34 percent of students entering a four-year university are first-generation students and are seen to be more at risk for dropping out their first year; only 73 percent reenroll in their second year.[15] These numbers are an ongoing concern for college administrators as they look for ways to alleviate this attrition, which has been seen to be the result of working-class students' unfamiliarity with what to expect from college and the dominant culture of higher education.[16] Mike Rose posits that first-generation students come to college with expectations that are not aligned with academic reality, and they struggle to readjust these misconceptions during their first year.[17] An Early Start participant in this study confided that he was nervous about starting school because he was the first child out of five of his siblings who decided to go to college. His family was excited for him, but they could not offer him any advice on how to be successful because they went straight to work after high school. His dad is a cook in his uncle's restaurant, and his mother is a seamstress. First-generation college students face disadvantages because they lack a frame of reference when it comes to college matriculation.

Many of the students who enter the Early Start program are unprepared for the college-level writing necessary for them to succeed in a first-year writing course. According to an Early Start instructor, the one-unit Early Start course only provides students with fifteen hours of writing instruction and fifteen hours of reading instruction within a two-week period. This means that when students exit the program, they have not gotten the remediation they may have needed to enter a college-level freshman writing course and succeed in the coursework. Overall, many working-class students do not find themselves as comfortable in a college writing classroom as middle-class students do. Linda Adler-Kassner found that many working-class students get very little experience with composition in their secondary education and struggle as a result when they enter the college classroom.[18] They are aware that their writing expression is not the same as the academic expression expected of them by the university and their writing instructors. In order for some working-class students to learn how to write for the university, they need time to practice. One Early Start instructor mentioned that the one-unit Early Start course at her institution did not provide students with the experience in writing they needed. Students were typically given reading and writing exercises that walked them through the writing process, with which many students were unfamiliar, and they were given practice essays to compose in preparation for the final essay at the end of the two weeks. They were also required to spend seven to eight hours outside class during the two weeks completing reading and writing activities designed to support the writing they did in class. The overall writing experience students were exposed to in the program was not enough for them to get acclimated to the academic genres found in their college-level classes. Collectively, they completed a couple of essays that were helpful to students but were not enough, in many cases, to help them bypass a remedial writing class that following fall semester. The Early Start program begins the remediation process for the working-class students in the summer session but does not "remediate" them. Attending this intensive program in the summer is a hardship for some working-class students, and many of them are still stuck taking basic-skills classes in the fall.

Unfortunately, many working-class students take a succession of remedial courses before they enter college-level math and English, and this presents some hardships for working-class students with families and extensive responsibilities outside class.[19] In conjunction with enrolling in the Early Start program before the start of the fall semester of their freshman year, students must also take other basic-skills classes depending on their performance on the placement tests. In some cases, students may be required to take two semesters of basic writing before they can enter a college-level writing course. This requirement prolongs their time spent working on their degree and increases their risk of dropping out. Most of the students who completed the one-unit course in the Early Start program examined in this study still needed remediation upon entering their freshman year.

Another common characteristic that makes the college experience perplexing for working-class students is the volatile socioeconomic hardships they face on a daily basis. Many working-class students have previously enrolled in college and have dropped out due to divorce; they may have experienced layoffs from their jobs; and they may be forced to work one or more jobs to pay for living expenses to support their children and families. These responsibilities complicate the schedules we can expect working-class students to accommodate. One of the students in this study stated that he worked as a janitor for a local school district from 5:00 a.m. to 2:00 p.m. and helped out as a car mechanic with his father on the weekends and quite often during the week when he got off work. His mother was disabled, so he and his father worked to support her and help pay the mortgage on their three-bedroom house. He was excited to take night classes in the fall semester but worried he wasn't going to have enough time for the demands of college. He had been working for the school district for six years and wanted to lead his own class as a sixth-grade teacher at some point in the future. The only way for him to get out of his current employment was to go to college and get a teaching credential. He knew he needed to increase his reading and writing skills and that English was not his favorite subject when he was a high-school student several years previously. He realized that working fifty to fifty-five hours a week between both jobs and taking night classes would be difficult; he had reconciled that he would need to complete both at the same time if he was to move forward with his life.

The one-unit Early Start program requires that students dedicate two weeks, or eight business days, four hours a day, in order to fulfill the Early Start requirement. Students can choose from a variety of sessions that meet at different times during the day (9 a.m.–1 p.m., 1 p.m.–5 p.m., 5 p.m.–9 p.m.). For working-class students with unpredictable work schedules and babysitting needs, these choices may or may not fit their lives. They may be forced to take time off work in order to dedicate the hours needed to complete the Early Start requirement. One Early Start participant in this study confessed that she had to take four days off from work in order to attend the mandatory Early Start program. She worked about thirty-five hours a week as a server at two different local restaurants, the early-morning shift at one restaurant twice a week and the evening shift at the other restaurant five days a week. She enrolled in the morning session for the two-week Early Start program and opted to take time off at the restaurant where she works mornings twice a week in order to keep schedule complications to a minimum. She said it was the most convenient way to continue to participate in her decision to go to college and remain employed during that time to pay her rent. This study found that students were also expected to complete writing and reading outside class. This two-week period could become a real hardship for working-class students who need to recoordinate the operations of their daily lives.

Some one-unit Early Start programs offer their sections online for more time flexibility. This option can also pose challenges for the working-class student. One working-class student in this study stated that she had a very old laptop she couldn't always rely on for her homework. She had to regularly come to campus in order to use the computers in the library for her assignments. Sometimes she had to bring her children with her because her only free time came after she picked up her daughters from their grandmother's house. Technology poses some major problems for working-class students who don't have the technology they need to be successful in a classroom and need to shift their lives around because it is the only way to get the work done. Some working-class students are not as familiar with technology as other students simply because they haven't been exposed to it. Online programs can be beneficial to working-class students because they give the students the opportunity to complete their work in the spaces when they are fulfilling the other obligations in their lives; however, it can also be a burden and complicate their lives when they must accommodate for the lack of resources at their disposal.

A benefit of the Early Start program is that it can be found on each of the campuses with the exception of one. Each CSU regionally supports the surrounding population, and students can enroll in an Early Start program on one campus and officially enroll for fall classes at another. Once a student fulfills the mandated requirement at any of the campuses, the credit can be transferred to their home institution. The Early Start program is statewide, so it allows students the freedom to choose a program that works best for them. This meets the needs of working-class students because it provides them with options that support their work schedule and family life.

This study also found that a common characteristic of working-class college students is that many value the material gain of a college education in their lives. These students think carefully about their class choices and prefer to take only the ones that are necessary. Joanna Brooks and Fern Cayetano find that working-class students see higher education as a promise to a higher reward: a better job and more financial resources.[20] Their learning is tied directly to getting a better job. When working-class students decide to go to college, their dedication means they will give up time with their families and time that could be spent recuperating from their busy work schedules. This sacrifice means they expect these choices to produce some benefit for their future. If they are required to enroll in a one-unit, two-week Early Start program for thirty-two hours of their time, they want to see how it has helped them in some way. If they get through the program, in some cases at major personal expense, they want to know how this program is beneficial to their college career. This study found that many students who need significant amounts of reading and writing instruction to become college ready, and who generally score fairly low on the university placement tests, are placed into developmental writing courses in the fall semester following their Early Start participation. Sometimes they are required to take two remediation courses before they are allowed to begin college-level English. Their frustration might begin when they realize the two weeks they have just dedicated to the Early Start program didn't get them any closer to their goal of finishing the required college-level writing courses.

RECOMMENDATIONS

The Early Start program is a mandated requirement that forces each of the colleges in the California State University system to begin a conversation about the issue of remediation at the institutional, programmatic and classroom level. It ensures that each college has a summer program that targets students in need of basic skills, even if the program is only a one-unit, two-week introduction to reading and writing. This kind of initiative gets the discussion started, and that is a very good thing. Making college more accessible to a diverse range of students with varying skill levels means a system needs to be in place to accommodate students who need remediation. The Early Start program unites an enormous state university system in the same conversation about remediation. Not all who participate may find Early Start pedagogically effective, but it has been effective in getting all the CSUs to look at what students need to be college ready. Working-class students, however, still seem to struggle when their needs do not equate with the needs of traditional full-time students. The institution continues to make decisions derived from the traditional student population, and this negatively influences working-class students who follow different rules and live on different schedules.

Colleges and universities across the United States should consider assessing some of the programs they have in place that support the working-class student. It is important that institutional objectives align with what occurs at the programmatic level. If the institution has as its goal to support a diverse student population, it is imperative that programs operate with this philosophy in mind. The characteristics and values of the student population that will be involved with remedial initiatives like Early Start must be considered so the proper decisions about special accommodations for them can be put into action. If our goal is to promote increased graduation rates and reduce student attrition, guidelines or frameworks should be constructed as a way of viewing growing populations like working-class students. Such frameworks would increase the likelihood that these students will be successful.

The working-class student is not new to the institution of higher learning. This student has slowly become commonplace at colleges and universities across the United States. Economic and political changes have made it possible for working-class students to overcome some of the obstacles they normally face when becoming college students: being unprepared for college-level curriculum, facing financial restraints, having familial obligations and responsibilities, and feeling the urgency to enter the workplace to earn a living. These obstacles must be considered when looking at appropriate pedagogy for this diverse group of students. It is imperative that the needs of working-class students continue to be uncovered so institutional and programmatic goals and processes work to support their needs.

Notes

1.   US Department of Education, National Center for Education Statistics, *Digest of Education Statistics*, table 329.
2.   Rochkind and Johnson, "How Higher Education Can Support."
3.   Greenwald and Grant, "Border Crossings," 32.
4.   ICF International, *Working for California*. According to the CSU system website, the CSU system enrolls about four hundred and sixty thousand students a year, and the targeted students in many of their support programs are low-income and non-traditional students. The average age of a CSU undergraduate is twenty-four, and the average amount of time it takes for a student to graduate is six years (Johnson 2010). Thirty-six percent of undergraduate students work more than thirty hours a week ("Non-traditional Students Benefit from CSU Plan"). Two goals of the CSU system are to increase student access and support student degree attainment for its diverse student body by providing an array of support services (Johnson 2010). Many of these programs support the significant population of working-class students that enter the institution needing extra academic help.
5.   DiMaria, "Working-Class Students."
6.   Rose, *Lives on the Boundary*.
7.   Stuber, "Integrated, Marginal, and Resilient".
8.   Taylor, "Initial Review."
9.   Johnson, "Higher Education in California."
10.   Taylor, "Initial Review," 4.
11.   Ibid.
12.   Ibid.
13.   Ibid.
14.   Carmona, "Cal State's Early Start Program."
15.   Stuber, "Integrated, Marginal, and Resilient."
16.   Rose, *Lives on the* Boundary; Stuber, "Integrated, Marginal, and Resilient."
17.   Rose, *Lives on the Boundary*.
18.   Adler-Kassner, "Shape of the Form."
19.   Ferretti, "Between Dirty Dishes."
20.   Brooks and Cayetano, "(Dis)location of Culture."

5

THE WRITING SPACE AS DIALECTICAL SPACE

Disrupting the Pedagogical Imperative to Prepare the "Underprepared"

Jacqueline Preston

In most public and private universities, students are placed in one or another writing course based on scores from the ACT, SAT or another standardized assessment, such as Accuplacer. As it stands, most writing assessments used to place students measure primarily students' capacity to demonstrate knowledge of middle-class "Standard Written English" of the essayist bent. We know students of low-income families are likely to achieve lower scores on these aptitude tests. Not surprisingly, a high percentage of students of working-class origin fill basic writing (BW) and first-semester first-year writing (FYW) classrooms. At worst, many of these courses, as well as the students, are tagged *remedial*. At best, these courses are labeled *intro* or *developmental*, and the students enrolled are regarded as "underprepared."

In 1985, in his landmark essay "The Language of Exclusion: Writing Instruction at the University," Mike Rose provided historical context for examining the language of remediation that informs the field of composition and rhetoric and made a strong argument for abandoning what he referred to as a "troublesome metaphor."[1] As recently as the 2013 annual Conference on College Composition and Communication, in his session titled "Toward a Political Economy of Basic Writing Programs," Victor Villanueva implored us to stop thinking about students enrolled in BW and FYW classes in terms of deficit and "in need of being fixed."[2] Villanueva's call, some thirty years after Rose's, is a glaring example of how little progress we have made as a field in addressing this issue. I stand with these authors; however, I suggest that the problem cannot be fully addressed until we understand better how deeply rooted the

DOI: 10.7330/9781607326182.c005

language of remediation is in the writing theory that dominates our current curriculum, pedagogy, and, perhaps most insidiously, our assessments. As well intentioned as we are in our discussions of metaphor and its entailments, these discussions fail to acknowledge the role writing theory itself plays in situating students as underprepared. Until we take up a theory that rejects outright the notion of the culturally deficient subject or, more proactively, until we apply theory that situates the student writer otherwise, our attempts to unhinge ourselves from the deficit models that creep below the service of even our most liberatory approaches will be futile.[3] The work presented here joins those who struggle to approach the study of writing in a way that would frame the histories and individual biographies of students of working-class origin as assets rather than deficits to learning.[4]

I begin this chapter by exploring some of the exigencies underpinning current writing pedagogy to draw attention specifically to an idea so firmly held across disciplines that to suggest otherwise appears unreasonable, that is, the notion that writing is primarily a "technology of representation."[5] While I maintain that writing includes representation, I hope to demonstrate that it is highly problematic to build curriculum, pedagogy, and assessment rooted in the idea that what it means to write well is merely to represent ideas effectively and that what it means to study writing is to engage in practices aimed solely at improving one's capacity to represent those ideas. To highlight the ways language functions beyond representation, I turn to an ethnographic study that took place in a rural working-class community. This study includes analysis that examines up close the function of language in context in an effort to extend a more complex understanding of the important work that takes place in the writing space itself and to posit a theory of the writing space as a dialectical space of continuity and change. My hope is to bring to light the central role writing theory plays in our efforts to facilitate institutional spaces in which all students can engage acts of writing that are relevant and productive.

THE IMPERATIVE TO PREPARE THE "UNDERPREPARED"

At least since Shirley Brice Heath's literacy ethnography, *Ways with Words*, we've considered how discrepancies between a student's home community and the academic community can create challenges for some students more than others. Scholars of composition, particularly FYW and BW, often reference, with good intent, discourse-community models to emphasize how differences in values, customs, language, and style shared by members of a community situate students at a disadvantage in the university. Such models highlight the difficulties individuals face, specifically students of working-class origin and many minority students, as they make their way from what James Paul Gee describes as "primary discourse communities," the home, to "secondary discourse communities," the academy and workplace, for example.[6] While some contemporary models take pains to engage students in discussions of discourse communities and acknowledge multiple literacies, they neglect to create a space in which the biographies, experiences, and well-developed literacies students bring with them to the classroom are valued. Instead, these histories are brushed aside, treated as obstacles to overcome versus an essential and fertile resource from which to draw.

Our FYW programs, including BW, most often refer to discourse-community models fundamentally tied to an assumption that in order for student writing to be relevant and productive, it must resemble a style of imagined discourse, most often described as academic. The discourse community model as it has been taken up in FYW and BW classrooms has done little to inspire the kind of curricular change needed to upset the notion that students of working-class origin are somehow ailing. More often than not, a notion of an academic discourse community is used in the classroom to underscore a need for resemblance and in this way functions similarly to autonomous views of literacy to keep in place the idea that students are in need of a remedy.[7]

In the following section, I shift attention away from the student subject and the classroom to take up the arguments of posthumanists, such as Sidney I. Dobrin, Byron Hawk, and Raúl Sánchez, who insist on extracting the study of writing from the classroom to understand better the multiple functions of writing.[8] In line with this scholarship, I argue, like these authors, that only when we disengage the study of writing from the historical and disciplinary constraints associated with the teaching of writing can we offer a theory of writing that encompasses language and writing in all its complexity. My goal, however, remains in the end to serve students, particularly those who find themselves caught in a system that by all appearances works mightily to restrict access rather than extend it. This system is rooted in an ideology we have yet to fully extricate ourselves from.

As Roland Barthes justly argued some twenty years ago now, the success of any ideology and the practices born of it can be gauged by the degree of its naturalization, that is, the fact that it is generally understood as normal and natural.[9] The idea that writing is primarily and merely a technology of representation is one idea upholding a system of beliefs supporting the notion that the purpose of the FYW and BW classroom is to prepare those we regard as underprepared. The intensity with which this widespread and universally shared understanding of writing is institutionalized conceals its historically contingent nature. FYW and BW courses emerged, and many continue to be housed, in English departments. As numerous scholars have noted, the curriculum and pedagogy that constitute composition courses are generally driven by a notion of "good writing" as that which functions to represent ideas according to specific rules of discourse common to the discipline within which it is born. As has been well documented by others, the purpose and use of first-year writing as it has been conceived in the context of literature departments is to teach students a kind of essayist literacy common to the humanities.[10] Within this disciplinary context, we've come to regard writing as primarily representational, often overlooking the important work that goes on in the writing space itself. Based on an assumption that FYW and BW help prepare students for the writing they will do across the curriculum, to assume that the primary purpose and use of these courses is to teach students to represent ideas effectively is a claim with which few would argue. It is, however, in exploring what seems obvious and normal to us that we have a chance at disrupting once and for all the pedagogical and evaluative processes situating the writing student as culturally deficient and, as it were, underprepared.

RECALCITRANCE: A BURKEAN DIALECTIC
FOR THE WRITING SPACE

A common assumption carried forward in the theories of writing that dominate composition pedagogy is a that what is important about writing is its capacity to communicate an idea with accuracy and precision. As such, in the classroom, we've come to regard the writing space as merely a conduit for communicating ideas effectively. To make visible the potentialities afforded in the writing space at present mostly ignored, I draw from a three-year longitudinal rhetorical ethnography, which explores in detail the processes by which collective rhetorics emerge within community and are then carried forward. What is of significance to this essay is a question of how language functions in conversation among these community members to bring about significant sociocultural shifts in attitude. Referencing data collected as part of the study, and through analysis of talk that takes place between a group of college students and their parents, we see that while language and writing include representation, important generative work is taking place here, work too often overlooked, forsaken, if you will, for a focus on clarity, accuracy, and precision in word. Counter to the idea that language functions within communities to accurately represent an idea, we shall see that imprecision and inaccuracy function necessarily to bring about the sociocultural shifts members of this community deem, at least within the context of this conversation, as necessary in the face of change.

The conversation examined here takes place in the context of what Kenneth Burke refers to as "recalcitrance," a moment of crisis or a hiccup that threatens to upset the familiar and accepted. Burke uses the term *recalcitrance* in *Permanence and Change* in his discussion of "orders of recalcitrance," referring specifically to our physical reality—the process by which the materiality of the world kicks back to challenge a familiar worldview.[11] In a later treatment, however, Burke asserts that his use of the term encompasses what he refers to as "the subtle shifts that exist between the similar and the antithetical," insisting that his early definition was "ambiguous."[12] *In Attitudes Toward History*, Burke writes that recalcitrance refers not only to "the factors that *correct* a statement" but also "the factors that *substantiate* a statement" and "the factors that *incite* a statement."[13] In other words, recalcitrance pertains to any source, word, idea, or object that arouses in an individual the necessity to come to terms with a shifting conception of reality.[14] Burke's recalcitrance is most often treated as a correction only. Here, I reference Burke's fuller definition and treat recalcitrance as an inspiration, a stirring of potentialities, a coming together poised to produce an emergence of qualities that did not before exist. The term *recalcitrance*, meaning to act stubbornly or with resistance, draws its meaning from the word *calcitrate*, meaning to kick, so it carries with it not merely the idea of resistance but also a notion of kicking back. Within these moments of recalcitrance, language functions to not only express that which was and resolve that which is but also to produce that which did not exist before—that is to say, it cuts new rhetorical pathways. What follows is an examination of the mechanisms by which individuals use language to renegotiate and construct anew, an opportunity to look more closely at how language executes beyond representation.

As part of the larger study referred to here, I interviewed six college students (male and female) from Johnston, a small rural farming community in southern Ohio. Members of the community refer to their hometown as "traditional," "conservative," and "Christian." As is typical of many small rural communities, residents' families have lived in and around the area for generations. High-school graduates tend to stay in the community to raise families, and those who attend college away from home often return. Sociocultural change by all appearances is slow.

To understand better the collective rhetorics dominating the community and the means by which members adapt to changes in attitude that challenge traditional ways of thinking and being, I completed archival research, conducted field observations, interviewed participants, and arranged a focus group that included a small group of college students and their parents. These meetings occurred at the end of the students' first semester and again two years later. These conversations provided the opportunity to examine up close how language functioned to bring about a shift in attitude. The proceeding transcript is part of a conversation occurring during one of these events. This discussion takes place the summer following the students' completion of their first year away at college. Those present during the conversation include four college students and their mothers, all of whom identify as white, female, Christian, and heterosexual—long-term residents of Johnston. The conversation surfaced in response to a question posed to the group about students' experiences transitioning to college. The resulting analysis provides an opportunity to examine how language functions to mediate shifts in attitude, in this case attitudes pertaining to homosexuality and race.

To prompt discussion, I asked this group of mothers and their daughters to talk about their experiences encountering views different from their own either in the workplace or at college. One mother, Melody, spoke up when I offered, as examples, religious beliefs, issues of race, and sexual orientation. Melody initiated the conversation, interrupting my explanation by stating that sexual orientation was "not an issue" for her or her two daughters. As illustrated in the transcript, she explains that she works with two women who are gay, and these women are close friends of the family. The two women speaking are Melody and Jeanette. Melody is the mother of Jamie and Kay, and Jeanette is the mother of Sarah and Laney, all of whom are present.

> MELODY: I work with a lot of gay and lesbians and they're friends, and Jamie, and Kay [Melodies daughters] are exposed to them. We had lunch with them yesterday. So those conversations I guess don't even—If they happen are, "Oh. I figured that one out months ago. I can't believe you just caught on to that one."
>
> JEANETTE: Well that's the same type of thing with, you know, Joe's [Jeanette's husband] brother being gay.
>
> MELODY: Right.
>
> JEANETTE: This past weekend he brought his significant other, his partner to their wedding—

MELODY: Partners . . . Partners. That's what they call them.

JEANETTE: And so, I thanked him for that. I did, I thanked him for that— You know, my kids are so open to that. It's always been a part of their lives, and they [her daughters] are very defensive [of their uncle]— they don't make judgment calls. So when somebody else does, they, defend. I thanked him [her uncle] for that cause otherwise . . .

Before proceeding, I want to point out that a typical response when examining this conversation, particularly among academics, draws on what Paul Ricoeur refers to as a "hermeneutics of suspicion," that is, a concerted effort to unmask contradictions to reveal how language functions unconsciously to conceal the real.[15] If we were to take up what Ricoeur refers to as "a tactic of suspicion and a battle against masks" and use this tactic in conjunction with a discourse-community model, we might not only note discrepancies between the discourses used by members of this working-class community and the discourses familiar to the academy but also take pains to point out the falsity concealed within the conversation.[16] In contrast, my primary interest is not in uncovering discrepancies or revealing underlying attitudes, but rather I am adopting what Ricoeur identifies as a "hermeneutics of faith" or appreciation in the hope of avoiding a reductive interpretation and critique and instead bringing to light the mechanisms by which participants use language to necessarily and cooperatively sustain continuity while effecting cultural shifts.

A Burkean Interpretation

Burke describes the "dialectic" as a complex and dynamic space of continuity and change, a space not of representation but of overlap, ambiguity and imprecision.[17] In "Dialectic in General," from *A Grammar of Motives*, Burke writes, "By dialectics in the most general sense, we mean the employment of the possibilities of linguistic transformation."[18] According to Burke, language functions via a process of "merger and division," a kind of "spiraling development,"[19] quite literally as a "series of terms in perpetual transformation."[20] For Burke, the dialectic is a generating principle. As we shall see here, ideas and assumptions are carried into this space; they merge with other ideas, both familiar and new, to produce meanings and relevancies that did not exist before. Via the word, these ideas intersect, conflate, modify, divide, and redress the familiar ideas encountered there.

To fully recognize the conversation as a process in terms of recalcitrance and a dialectical space of the Burkean kind, it is necessary to consider the context in which the conversation occurs. Homosexuality, in this conservative Christian community, historically and culturally falls under the category of deviant sexual activity, an immoral and unacceptable act marking the homosexual as worthy of rejection in this community. The historical and social context in which the conversation between the mothers and their daughters takes place prompts those speaking to hold important, particular aspects of the conversation. In this way, this conservative, Christian community provides a fertile commonplace that ideas necessarily grow out of and work against.[21]

Early in the conversation, both Melody and Jeanette speak about being gay as a nonissue. Those present, as is evidenced by their talk, wish to maintain important relationships with people they know and care for, those who self-identify as gay—Melody's friends from work, who are also friends of her daughters, and Jeanette's brother in-law, a favorite uncle to her children. What can be observed through this analysis are the mechanisms by which language functions to resolve the tensions and open up the possibility of bringing into alignment conflicting beliefs and competing rhetorics in a moment of recalcitrance. Necessarily, members draw on the familiar rhetorics of home, overlapping and intersecting long-held traditional rhetorics, assumptions about what it means to be gay, with less familiar rhetorics, those encountered in the workplace and in the university. The mechanism by which this process takes place includes linguistic acts that function rhetorically to invert and restructure configurations of the social reality generally shared by members of the group. The transcript below outlines a series of important turns as the conversation continues between Melody and Jeanette. Here Melody and Jeanette take up language to remedy definitions of being gay that would place loved ones outside the fold.

MELODY: It's one more lifestyle.

JEANETTE: It is a different life style . . .

MELODY: It's like whether they're handicapped or whether they're gay or whether they're lesbian or whether they're black or. . . whether they're Hispanic.

JEANETTE: Yeah, it's just another . . .

JAMIE: Lesbian or Gay is one stereotype. you're not offended by it? So why would you be offended if we brought home a black person.

JEANNETTE: I wouldn't be.

MELODY: I am not offended.

JAMIE: [This is a problem we have with our family.]

MELODY: This is a problem and not with me, personally.

MELODY: I personally have to be the evil one to keep Jessie from being disowned by other members of the family; but I am not that way and you know that I'm not.

I want to begin with a focus on Melody's use of the term *lifestyle*. It bears mentioning that in contrast to socially conservative arguments in which the term *lifestyle* is used to support the view that homosexuality is chosen and not biologically determined, the term *lifestyle* functions here to resist familiar rhetorics that frame the homosexual as an outsider. In response to Jeanette's comment about her brother-in-law "being gay," Melody states, "It's one more lifestyle." Jeanette responds, "It is a different lifestyle." The statement "It's one more lifestyle" performs an action in its utterance, what J. L. Austin refers to as a "performative."[22] In the act of stating "It's one more lifestyle," "being gay" is recast as a subcategory of lifestyle. By repeating the claim "It is a different lifestyle," Jeanette calls attention to a rather significant action being performed: the act of reinterpreting the phenomenon of "being gay" via a kind of reclassification.

Melody's use of the term *lifestyle* as a category, under which race, ethnicity, and disability fall, would likely cause concern in an FYW classroom focused on representation; it might be labeled *inaccurate*, *imprecise*, and *offensive*. Through a rhetorical lens, however, that is, by treating language as a performance and not merely a technology of representation, we are able to see that it is Melody's peculiar use of the term that deems it an effective mode of persuasion and identification. It's a risk on Melody's part, one key to accomplishing what is being attempted here. By employing the term *lifestyle*, Melody induces cooperation from the group, nurturing an interpretive shift already in place, which is a reconfiguration of what it means to be Other in this community. The term *lifestyle* functions in this conversation to reclassify gay as acceptable other.

Though Melody is not explicit in stating how being black and Hispanic is like being gay, it's significant that she does not include in her list heterosexuality or whiteness, two categories with which she and the other participants identify. As such, she sustains a necessary kind of continuity among members of this community with regard to what counts as Other. At the same time, her list indicates an emerging rhetoric of the Other—a category of Other that includes a list of those her group all agree are different but acceptable, part of the fold. Just as Melody conjures up the familiar rhetoric of the Other, those who are different from, she interrupts it by introducing the term *lifestyle* as a means to denote those who are different from but acceptable. Via this terministic transformation, she induces others to agree that being gay is like being black and being Hispanic. Melody's use of the term *lifestyle*, though it rings imprecise, functions rhetorically to recall familiar rhetorics specifically for the purpose of constructing new ones.

As the conversation continues, a similar ambiguity of language is present as Jamie, Melody's daughter, enters the conversation. As we shall see, even as Jamie accepts her mother's use of the term *lifestyle* without question, she cuts new rhetorical pathways by purposefully introducing a term that functions both to substantiate and to correct her mother's statement. It's within this moment of social recalcitrance we see that language functions beyond representation to enact cultural shifts. Despite what seems an ambiguous use of the term *lifestyle* in the conversation above, Jamie does not challenge her mother's definition. She does not question the accuracy of the term but rather the practical application of the abstraction. In other words, what Jamie is concerned with is whether or not her mother's lived responses are consistent with the claims she makes. In response to her mother's claim that being gay is like being black, Jaime challenges what she sees as a contradiction, not in terms, mind you, but in practice.

"Lesbian or Gay is one stereotype," Jamie states, "So why would you be offended if we brought home a black person?" In this moment, Jamie introduces the term *stereotype*, a word perhaps drawn from one of Jamie's classroom discussions, a term, though used imprecisely, that carries with it the potential to challenge existing paradigms. It contains within it a powerful rhetorical motive, one that functions in this context to overlap the familiar with the unfamiliar. Jamie employs the term *stereotype* to mean the Other, overlapping her mother's use of *lifestyle*, weaving together and intersecting a stance or attitude familiar to this group with one less familiar. Within this particular cultural context, Jamie's use of the term *stereotype* cuts a new path and opens up potentialities, facilitating further shifts within this community as to what is acceptable.

The talk between these mothers and daughters has implications for the writing classroom and particularly for students of working-class origin in that it insists we, as instructors of writing, take seriously how language functions in both the conversational and the writing space beyond representation, in this case necessarily to sustain continuity while exacting change. While it is tempting from an outsider's perspective to focus on what the dialogue might say about working-class students' beliefs, what is of significance to this essay is what the dialogue tells us about language and writing. A notion that language's primary function is to represent ideas accurately is carried forward into the FYW and BW classroom, where curriculum and pedagogy often forward a notion that representation is language and writing's chief function. As argued early in this chapter, a theory of writing that situates writing as primarily representational situates the working-class student as underprepared and in need of a remedy. Pedagogy born of such theory fails students in that it fails to acknowledge writing's generative qualities. While certainly language involves representation, pedagogy rooted in theory that underscores the function of language as primarily representational, and proficiency as a matter of correctness, accuracy, and resemblance, ignores, at everyone's expense, especially the working-class student's, the complexities and the generative qualities inherent to language and writing. For students, far more important work is taking place in the writing space than merely communicating an idea. As in conversational space, it is in the writing space that individuals use language to exact shifts in attitude, negotiate transitions, sustain continuity, and intersect the familiar and the unfamiliar. In contrast to pedagogy underscoring writing as representation so often tailored to working-class students, a pedagogy of assemblage highlights writing's generative qualities.

A PEDAGOGY OF ASSEMBLAGE

Our understanding of how literacies develop and a recognition that language functions in multiple ways insist that we look for new theories of writing in which to ground FYW and BW pedagogy. We need a theory that regards the writing space itself as a complex dialectical space of continuity and change, one that underscores acts of writing as key to negotiating moments of recalcitrance and acknowledges the importance of recognizing writing as a space where students unavoidably take risks. We need models of writing for our classrooms that unleash the potentialities acts of writing afford all students. We need pedagogy that provides opportunities for students to treat the writing space as a place where resemblance and accuracy necessarily take a back seat to the more generative potentialities inherent in acts of writing. Theory and pedagogy that treat writing as more than representation reposition the working-class student as poised to engage with writing in meaningful ways and challenge assumptions that the working-class student is in need of a being fixed.

In 2014, I and a small team of researchers became committed to the idea that students placed in FYW and BW classrooms are not "underprepared" but instead fully furnished with the equipment needed to write in ways relevant and useful to them personally, the communities from which they come, and in their classrooms. We carried out a grounded theory study to examine the benefits of what I've come to refer to as a *pedagogy of assemblage.*[23] A pedagogy of assemblage as illustrated in the project-based course featured here approaches writing as a gathering of parts into one context poised for distribution. It places at the center of the curriculum individual projects relevant and meaningful to the assemblages that mark the student's everyday life, at home, in the academy, and in the workplace. Within the context of student-proposed projects—a collection of short stories, a weekend workshop, an after-school program, brochures, podcasts, websites, letters to the editor—writing is understood as representation but only so much as it helps to forward the overall assemblage, the project. This method is designed to help students see their writing as part of this and other assemblages, as necessarily constituted by many parts—their own experiences, literacies, beliefs, and ideas and the ideas and experiences of others. In the midst of this framework, the writing space emerges as a place where the familiar and the unfamiliar encounter one another to carve out new rhetorical routes, to generate culture itself.

Such a pedagogy incorporates methods and practices in the classroom that facilitate for students the capacity to experience writing as a thing that takes place always in a broader context, a whole constituted by many intersecting parts, the remembered past as well as the imagined future—parts whose interactions produce emergent qualities that would not be possible were it not for the unique exchanges the students bring to bear in the writing space. For instance, in reference to the group of students referred to in the analysis, the student who brings with her a familiar rhetoric and a history of growing up in a rural working-class community in which being gay sets a loved one outside the group brings with her a creative tension, an exigence for resolving competing ideas, responding to others' opinions, and incorporating new concepts into her existing realities. The core function of language includes adaptation to the shifting assemblages that make up our lives. A project designed by students that allows them to draw on these histories, beliefs, and experiences and intersect these with emerging ideas is an opportunity for the students to explore and resolve these tensions in the context of a meaningful project, within which their writing is embedded.

In the context of a project, writing functions beyond representation to resolve tensions; build and sustain working relationships; move a project forward; raise and answer questions; explore and extend concepts; reject, accept, and create new ideas; and carve new rhetorical paths for imagining what could not have been imagined before. Research involving secondary and primary resources in the context of such a project takes on new meaning. Writing is thus a kind of becoming, an exploration, an intersection, a dynamic dialectical space of both continuity and change, a space in which writers take ownership of their own learning in a ways that exceed their capacity for merely producing writing that resembles and represents.[24] While a pedagogy of assemblage does not exclude a notion of writing as representation or the importance of meeting an audience's expectations to adhere to traditional rules of Standard Written English, it does treat accuracy and precision as secondary. Attention to audience is not merely a matter of adapting one's discourse to resemble or meet the expectancies of a particular audience. Rather, audience plays a more immediate and essential role in helping students identify what experiences, ideas, and additional sources of information are relevant to a particular writing situation and the overall assemblage, the identified project. In the context of the writing project, students come to see themselves—their beliefs, experiences, and ideas—as foundational; thus, they find themselves well equipped as writers and well positioned to take part in the study of writing.

What Working-Class Students Gain

As part of the study, I explored students' reactions to assignments, their choices about topics, attitudes toward writing at the outset of the course, and shifts in attitude or orientation that occurred to them over the course of the semester.[25] My interest in completing this study was not so much to determine the effectiveness of the curriculum based on established criteria rooted in theories of writing as representation but rather to identify new criteria for what counts as effective pedagogy, based on students' responses to their experience in these classrooms. What I found most notable in interviews with students was their overwhelming reference to what best can be described as a shift in orientation to writing, specifically a move away from an emphasis on correctness and toward relevancy, focusing more attention on understanding how their writing fit into a larger scheme. In response to questions about what they gained, students interviewed commented on experiencing writing for the first time as "bits and pieces" linked to something larger—"something of value."[26] This shift inspired not only a change in attitude toward writing but also a renewed capacity for seeing themselves as competent and prepared writers.

One student, Hyram Scott, wrote in the context of a project associated with the local bike collective, of which he was a member. In his interview, Hyram described his experience writing in the context of a project he cared about. "It showed me that I can actually [write] all semester and have [as] an end result something that I'm really proud of. So it gave me more confidence within my writing and made writing applicable to my life . . . I didn't really care at all about writing before this class."[27] Once students were able to draw a connection between their writing and their histories, developing literacies, current interests, and imagined future, few saw themselves as unprepared to write. A focus on generating writing versus producing writing that merely resembles provides students of working-class origin opportunities to use their experience, literacies, and knowledge and to build on existing literacies. While students attended to local concerns in preparation for publication and were highly motivated to do so, these issues took a back seat to producing writing that helped them complete the project.

In this way, students came to understand writing as far more complex an undertaking than they had originally understood it to be. Understanding writing as a generative process affords students of working-class origin a better chance to take ownership of their writing and learning than an exercise in adopting the conventions of a particular discourse does. By inviting students to produce and then build on their existing writing as they access outside sources, interview experts, and conduct field observations, students have a chance to experience the writing space as a dialectical space, a space of both continuity and change. To illustrate, Alex, a student in the study who worked as a counselor at a substance-abuse center, chose a project associated with his work. The writing he completed in the course took place in the context of designing and developing a formal research proposal he would present to the organization he was currently employed by. Alex revised early written reflections on his own experience with substance abuse to introduce his subject matter. Building on previous writing, reflections, interview transcripts and reports, and annotated bibliographies, he was able to use the writing space as a means to extend and reconsider assumptions, modify and invent new ideas, and sometimes resolve conflicts between his interpretation of his experience and what the research suggested. In this context, Alex's orientation to writing, its worth and utility, and his opinions about his own capabilities as a writer began to shift.

Students like Alex who have been identified as underprepared and who may have been placed in "remedial" courses quickly assume a sense of competence and confidence in their abilities as writers and their ability to use writing effectively. The notion of a "remedial writer" begins to fall to the wayside when our pedagogies are committed to theories of the writing space as a dialectical space of continuity and change and not merely a space that functions to represent ideas.

CONCLUSION

As I have argued here, remediation as a "troublesome metaphor" cannot be fully addressed until its roots in writing theory are uncovered. Because so much of our current pedagogy is rooted in theory that regards resemblance and representation as primary, even our most contemporary pedagogies do little to inspire the kind of curricular change needed to upset the notion that students of working-class origin are somehow ailing. Our disciplinary history has given rise to a peculiar notion of writing as merely representation. Thus, it is outside the classroom that we have the best opportunity to regard writing as more than resemblance. By examining how language functions in conversation, in moments of recalcitrance, we can understand better the generative function of language. A close examination of how language performs to negotiate moments of recalcitrance has important implications for the writing classroom. It's here we come to understand that language, though often imprecise, functions necessarily to recall familiar rhetorics specifically for the purpose of constructing new ones. It's here we begin to see a need for new theories of the writing space and new models within which to ground pedagogy.

In the context of theories of the writing space unhinged from the historical constraints of a discipline designed to prepare the underprepared, we can begin to build theories and pedagogies for the classroom that recognize students of working-class origin as individuals fully equipped with experiences, literacies, ideas, and beliefs essential to engaging in meaningful and effective writing. A theory that acknowledges the complexities of writing understands the writing space itself as a dynamic dialectical process. While it acknowledges the role of representation, it defies the notion that the working-class student is in need of a remedy. In lieu of discrepancies in discourse, it underscores what of value and necessity working-class students brings with them to this space. My hope is that by forwarding a theory of the writing space as a dialectical space of continuity and change, and by exploring students' responses to pedagogy rooted in such a theory, we can begin to see the advantage of building pedagogy that provides opportunities for students to draw on their literacies, histories, ideas, and beliefs, of practice in the classroom that treats this experience as the necessary fodder for nurturing and inspiring the unknown emergent qualities inherent to the writing space. Through a new theoretical framework for understanding the writing space as more than a means to communicate, we position the working-class student differently, not merely out of compassion or in service to social justice but, more important, because we recognize that what students of working-class origin bring with them to the classroom is indeed of great value and necessity to their literacy development and their identities as writers. This repositioning of the student and a new understanding of how writing functions provide a foundation upon which scholars of writing can begin to build pedagogy that serves the working-class student, avoiding outright methods, practices, and assessment that stifle and undermine working-class students' capacity to take up writing in meaningful ways and to produce writing that has relevance to their everyday lives—personal, professional, and academic.

Notes

1. Rose, "Language of Exclusion," 357.
2. Villanueva, "Political Economy."
3. The idea that some students are culturally deficient grew out of the concept of a "culture of poverty," a phrase coined by Oscar Lewis in 1959. In his ethnography entitled *Five Families: Mexican Case Studies in the Culture of Poverty*, Lewis argued that some parents and the communities in which the children live do not instill the same values and experiences white middle-class families provide for their children. Scholars from across disciplines then argued some children could be identified as culturally disadvantaged and deficient. By 1971, however, anthropologist Eleanor Burke Leacock had challenged this hypothesis, arguing that the assertion itself contributed to sustaining poverty and that the idea of a culture of poverty was untestable.
4. In addition to Rose and Villanueva, see Mack, "Ethical Representation," Peckham, "Complicity in Class Codes," and Seitz, *Who Can Afford?*
5. Sánchez, *Function of Theory*, 3.
6. Gee, *Introduction to Discourse Analysis*, 174.
7. Street, *Literacy in Theory and Practice*.
8. Dobrin, Rice, and Vastola, *Beyond Postprocess*.
9. Roland Barthes, *Mythologies*, 143.
10. Farr, "Essayist Literacy"; Horner and Lu, "Working Rhetoric"; Brereton, *Origins of Composition*.
11. Burke, *Permanence and Change*, 255.
12. Burke, *Attitudes Toward History*, 47.
13. Ibid.
14. Prelli, Anderson, and Althouse, "Kenneth Burke on Recalcitrance," 97.
15. Ricoeur, *Freud and Philosophy*, 26. In this text, Ricoeur defines a hermeneutics of suspicion as a type of interpretive stance characterized by a distrust of language as a symbol dissimulating the real. Analysis is thus animated by a kind of skepticism towards the given.
16. Ibid.

17. In contrast to a more classical treatment of the dialectic, Burke's dialectic operates in the realm of both/and rather than either/or; the dialectic is, for Burke, the "margin of overlap," and it is in this overlap that worlds are both dismantled and expressed. See Williams, "Kenneth Burke as Dialectician," 17–18, 20.

18. Burke, *Grammar of Motives*, 402.

19. Burke, *Rhetoric of Motives*, 403

20. Ibid., 38

21. Preston, "Fertile Commonplace."

22. Austin, *How to Do Things*, 60–61.

23. See Preston, "(Project)ing Literacy," for a fuller treatment of the "pedagogy of assemblage."

24. See Deleuze and Guattari, *A Thousand Plateaus*, for more on the concepts of assemblage and becoming.

25. As part of this study, researchers conducted semistructured interviews with ten students enrolled in three separate project-based courses and seven faculty members who had taught at least one semester of the project-based course. Students who participated in the study all completed the course within a year of the study and received a passing grade. Researchers initiated the study using a grounded-theory method to examine what students and instructors stood to gain from a curriculum rooted in writing theory that, first, dismissed the pedagogical imperative to prepare students for their next writing class, and second, took up a theoretical framework focused on writing as assemblage.

26. Compiled from interviews with students participating in the research on project-based writing referenced here.

27. Hyram Scott, interviewed by Kevin Owen, Utah, June 2013.

6

CHANGING DEFINITIONS OF WORK AND CLASS IN THE INFORMATION ECONOMY

Edie-Marie Roper and Mike Edwards

Class changes. As coauthors, our own attitudes toward class differ in some ways and overlap in others. Edie-Marie worked as an undergraduate with federally funded TRIO programs for disadvantaged students but does not identify as working class, despite her dad having worked in a factory all her life and having worked in one herself. Mike served for four years as an enlisted soldier driving tractor trailers for the United States Army but does not claim a working-class identity despite that experience. As contributors to this volume, we have both been interested in the differences between our own experiences of class and those of our students. Class definitions are diverse and sometimes contested, as William H. Thelin and Genesea M. Carter note in their introduction to this collection, but their consistent use of the present tense in the definitional portion of their introduction indicates a synchronic perspective on class and the ranges and varieties of what it means at our present moment. The complexities we see in the ways we and our students understand class are diachronic: we focus our attention on those complexities across time, with their roots at least in part in the 1965 Higher Education Act that created TRIO and the 1944 Servicemen's Readjustment Act. Perhaps, then, we should instead begin by arguing that class has changed.

Such an assertion is unsurprising if one understands class as a cultural manifestation of economic difference. Technological advance brings about economic change, and the massive cultural reorganizations along class lines in the nineteenth century came out of the economic changes brought about by the industrial revolution. *Class* is a more common term today than it was at the end of the industrial revolution but a less common term than it's been in the half century since the Dartmouth Conference and composition's growth as a modern discipline, but we

DOI: 10.7330/9781607326182.c006

are again in an age of enormous technological and economic change. Today's class divisions are different from those of years past, and a significant part of our focus in this chapter is on the curious historical and generational shifts in overdetermined definitions of class. Some of those definitions, as we discuss in the remainder of this chapter, are in productive tension with characterizations of students as first-generation or low-income. If class demands definitional investigation, one component of that investigation should be to examine how instructors talk about class in ways that are different from how students talk about class, so part of our investigation here draws from the voices of students associated with the federal TRIO programs. Furthermore, we see a discourse on class in composition studies largely rooted in a conception of economy aligned with the growth of composition as a discipline after the Dartmouth Conference—an industrial economy and an industrial conception of class— so another part of our investigation traces broader historical trends in the use of terms associated with class.

While *class* has long existed as an overdetermined category of difference, its vexed definitional status is now complicated further by broader economic change. Because ideas about class often ascribe cultural meanings to economic difference, the shift from an industrial economy to an information economy has resulted in shifts in those cultural meanings ascribed to new forms of economic difference. Those new forms of economic difference are largely aligned with the effects of a shift toward a heterogeneous postcapitalist economy[1] based in part upon information technologies and digital environments deeply linked to the work of the composition classroom. The role those information technologies and digital environments play in the shift to a heterogeneous postcapitalist economy incorporate what Michael Hardt and Antonio Negri characterize as the "immaterial labor"[2] associated with computing and with affective and symbolic-analytic work. So class is taking new forms within the composition classroom as well as beyond it, and the changing experiences of class require attention to historical change.

Edie-Marie's history as a first-generation undergraduate student, graduate student, and composition instructor is related to both bootstrap narratives of generational uplift and downward mobility. She did not identify as working class until her first semester as a graduate student. Her analytical focus on the nature of these ideologies and identifying terms is fueled by her experiences with the federal TRIO programs for disadvantaged students. As a nontraditional freshman, Edie-Marie took an empowering required TRIO course that addressed the nature of first-generation students' experiences in college and particularly the relationship between retention rates and explicit attainment of cultural capital. TRIO relies on more definitionally clear-cut terms like *low income* and *first generation*.[3] For Edie-Marie, discovering the term *working class* as a graduate student opened up the possibility for a conversation about its diverse meanings and applicability in higher education while at the same time creating a felt need for a shift in that conversation because of the overdetermined and contested nature of the term.

Mike's scholarship and teaching both focus in part on the economic effects of digital technologies on the composition classroom. The experiences of the undergraduate and graduate students he teaches in courses on composition, rhetoric, and technology attest to the growing importance of economically valuable immaterial labor and the way that labor contributes to the production, distribution, use, and reproduction of economically valuable immaterial capital (e.g., intellectual property, ideas, human capital, cultural capital, experience goods) and technological capital (including not simply technological objects but the associated know-how and cultural systems of doing). Human labor, including that of composition students, continues to be disciplined by capital but also works with and against capital in complex relationships beyond the market paradigm, resulting in new possibilities for the appropriation of value not only by capitalist enterprises but also by the owners and distributors of labor.

The contested nature of the term *working class*, as Thelin and Carter have demonstrated in their introduction to this volume, exists in multiple ways along several vectors: wealth, wages, values, occupation, and relationships of power and control, exploitation versus self-determination. All those vectors are in part determined by economic factors or carry economic implications, and higher education is a site of presumed economic uplift along all those vectors. At the same time, working class is an aspect of identity that is changeable in ways other aspects of identity may not be. While higher education may have an effect on whether or not one claims the identifier *working class*, it does not have as direct an effect on one's being marked by identifiers of race, sexuality, ethnicity, gender, or ability. As we demonstrate in this chapter, *working class*, therefore, sometimes has the curious potential to obscure other identifiers and their positions in relations of domination. The identifiers associated with TRIO, however—*low income, first generation*—exist in a program designed to provide economic uplift for those marked by such identifiers. TRIO as a program is designed to make itself obsolete. In our scholarship and pedagogy, do we expect *working class* as an identifier of relations of economic inequality to become increasingly obsolete?

Economic inequality itself is not becoming obsolete, and the shift to a postindustrial information economy has been accompanied by increasing rather than decreasing economic inequality.[4] For that reason, we find it useful to extend Thelin and Carter's investigation of the definitional nuances of the term *class* and its relation to economic inequality before representing our findings about student identification with economic inequality.

In taking a historical or diachronic approach to considerations of class and its relation to economic inequality, we do not wish to suggest other scholars are thereby enacting dehistoricizing approaches but rather observe that they seem more focused on investigating the range of ways definitions of class operate at a particular historical moment. For us, however, the 1965 moment at which TRIO programs were created to provide social and economic support for first-generation college students and low-income students, and its historic intersection with the 1970 CUNY shift to open admissions, was a historical moment very different from today's economic situation. We find value in the formative influence of the research on the intersection of class and education cited by Thelin and Carter in their introduction, but we again find it belongs to an economic situation that has since changed considerably. Because class operates as the cultural manifestation of economic inequality, changing economic situations are accompanied by changes in class relationships.

We also find useful Thelin and Carter's observation that for the purposes of this volume, understandings of class "range from those based purely on the type of job a person holds (blue collar versus white collar) to those that see a systemic relationship between classes, determined by who controls the means of production,"[5] and their further considerations of distinctions between ruling classes and working classes, criteria of worker autonomy (both concerns relying on a fundamentally Marxist definition of class), and the notion of cultural capital. Like the editors, we see these definitions as sometimes contesting with one another but more often overlapping and contributing to an overdetermined sense of class.

Furthermore, class in nearly all of composition's literature is claimed as the authentic, individuated, and sometimes traumatic experience of that difference. In her introduction to *Teaching Working Class*, Sherry Lee Linkon observes that much of the scholarship in working-class studies has relied upon working-class academics examining their own experiences.[6] So, too, does Irvin Peckham note in "Complicity in Class Codes: The Exclusionary Function of Education" that the argumentative habit of foregrounding personal class histories is deeply characteristic of the discourse of working-class academics.[7] This is a rhetoric of authenticity, and as such, it carries affective value and performs in some ways the "immaterial labor" described by Hardt and Negri.

Rhetorics of experiential working-class authenticity and its affective consequences are widespread in composition's literature on class. In her response to Sharon O'Dair's criticism of critical pedagogy's attitudes toward the projected pedagogical "embourgeoisement" of working-class students, Leann Bertoncini uses her status "as a daughter of a steel-worker" to claim grave offense,[8] to which O'Dair responds with the authenticity claim, "I was raised in a working-class family, too, and I can assure you, as the daughter of a construction worker, that my arguments offend neither me nor my working-class family and friends."[9] No matter what one has to say about how class functions in the classroom, a working-class background stands as an experiential argumentative trump card that lends to the arguer irreducible affective weight.

Definitions of class that rely upon constructions of power and exploitation concern themselves with the degree of control students have over the circumstances of their educations and careers. This vocabulary of control comes out of Marx's concern with economic relationships of exploitation and the power inequalities that perpetuate and are perpetuated by those relationships: the bourgeoisie are those who control the modes of economic production, and the proletariat are those who do not.

Definitions of class that rely upon cultural capital or values suggest a deeper transformation of the economic into the cultural, as in Lynn Z. Bloom's list of cultural values that separate the middle class from "the super-rich and the very poor" in "Freshman Composition as a Middle-Class Enterprise," which include "thrift," "order," "cleanliness," "punctuality," and "critical thinking."[10] The assertion that these are what differentiate the middle class from those with more or less money seems uncomfortably close to class bigotry. Laura Micciche offers a similar translation of economic inequalities into cultural values in her account of how her own middle-class upbringing contributed to her teacherly conception of an ideal classroom where students interact with politeness and restraint, and how one working-class student's emotionally unrestrained behavior in the classroom disrupted that conception.[11] According to Micciche, "The expression of 'strong' emotions such as anger, rage, and sorrow are generally considered unacceptable in the classroom"[12] but can actually serve to spur certain forms of progressive change. However, despite the clear presence of economic concerns in the essay—Micciche describes how her working-class student is very late to one class meeting because of her job—that progressive change is considered only in "cultural and political"[13] terms, not in economic terms.

As Thelin and Carter demonstrate in their introduction, occupational definitions of class are fairly straightforward: one's job determines one's class. They are deeply familiar to Americans in the distinctions between blue-collar and white-collar work, but as such, they are problematic in that they rely on the occupational divisions associated with an increasingly superannuated industrial economy. Bennett Berger's 1960 *Working Class Suburb* is usefully representative in its reporting of the "almost unanimous opinion that a member of the working class was someone who worked with his hands . . . for an hourly wage, and usually in a factory."[14] Today, however, in the emerging information economy that relies more and more on flexible production and a casualized labor force even for white-collar jobs, it is as yet unclear who constitutes the new working class, and this concern manifested in the questions we posed to our informants, as we further discuss below.

The analytical stratification of classes by wealth and income is a common practice because of the easy availability and quantifiability of data, and we have relied to some degree on that easy quantifiability in this chapter. If one possesses or earns more or less than a certain amount of money, one belongs to a certain class. Those amounts of money by which class divisions are measured are definitionally arbitrary, as indicated by the often-invoked pseudostatistic that 85 percent of Americans consider themselves middle class, with the pseudostatistic usually framed in terms of wealth. One wonders: if 15 percent of Americans therefore do not self-report as middle class, can we assume that means the top 7.5 percent and the bottom 7.5 percent in terms of income level? If so, then according to 2013 US government statistics, about 24 million Americans are below middle class but 45.3 million Americans live in poverty.[15] While our example suggests the problematically arbitrary nature of such quantification, we do not dispute its power or its import: the recent economic work by Thomas Piketty[16] demonstrating the rapidly growing inequality of wealth is central to the concerns of this volume.

In fact, Piketty's insight is one of the core concerns of this chapter. Piketty represents his insight via the equation $R > G$, meaning that historically speaking, return on capital is greater than growth of income: investment always outpaces wages, and those who can buy or invest in technology will get richer, while those who must sell their labor will get poorer. Technological advance contributes to economic inequality, and as Elspeth Stuckey notes, "Literacy and economy are interdependent and . . . the basis of the economy is changing. Such is the case with lit-eracy—it is an unstable idea, despite our efforts to change it. The nature of the change concerns the shift from industry to information."[17] In that shift from industry to information, the work performed in the compo-sition classroom attains more value. Furthermore, "Literacy is, if noth-ing else, the condition of postindustrialism. A worker's possibilities are contained by his ability to negotiate subjects of capital. In contempo-rary capitalism in the United States, then, literacy and class are fused."[18] Emerging technologies have driven the steep increase in professional, managerial, financial, and service-sector jobs as well as the automation and subsequent elimination of many of the jobs associated with indus-trial production and manufacturing,[19] prompting the reconfiguration of old categories of class associated with occupation.

Those emerging technologies are aspects of capital, though today cap-ital is increasingly associated with digital technologies and massive flows of financial derivatives rather than the factory machines and stock offer-ings of an earlier economic age. Capital increasingly finds its way into composition classrooms, and as we understand from Marx, capital can-not idle: it seeks use, work. Work, as a component of today's information economy in the form of Hardt and Negri's immaterial labor, operates as an aspect of our overdetermined definition of class. Stuckey's remark about "information" suggests how digital technologies have deeply imbri-cated literate practices in the contemporary nature of work. Tony Scott also makes clear connections between writing instruction and the tech-nological work of late capitalism; he characterizes many of the students in his technical writing courses as working in "full-time 'white collar' jobs" and notes that "some already work as professional writers at some level."[20] In describing their work in those positions, he says, "Many of these students share personal work experiences that illustrate how they serve largely low-level, instrumentalist functions in their own positions as writers,"[21] so we see again the concern with self-determination and exploitation in our new postindustrial information economy.

Self-determination and exploitation are concerns of power and agency, and in many representations of contemporary capitalism,[22] human agency is ceded (we are quite intentional here in our use of the passive voice) to the invisible and unstoppable agentless agency of the economy. The message seems to be that the economy is beyond human intervention: J. K. Gibson-Graham describes the "shift from an under-standing of the economy as something that can be managed (by people, the state, the IMF) to something that governs society"[23] as an effect of the conventional wisdom that "the economy has been reduced to the market, and . . . it has taken hold of all manner of human interactions"[24] to the point at which the term *economy* has come to denote "a force to be reckoned with outside of politics and society, located both above as a mystical abstraction, and below as the grounded bottom line."[25] Students enter the university in part for economic uplift yet are figured with the rest of society as existing in situations of ongoing economic powerlessness.

That presumed economic powerlessness plays into conventional representations of class in the composition classroom, as well. Discussions of student class almost always understand the economic activity of class as either prior to the writing classroom (in the form of the student's family's occupational background) or subsequent to the writing classroom (in the form of the student's projected career) or simply outside the classroom (in the form of the jobs that compete with student hours spent in educational pursuits). However, we suggest that the immaterial labor associated with the composition classroom can and does have economic value beyond its exchange for a grade or for job skills. In an economy constituted by diverse forms of economic activity, labor, and enterprise, the classed work of the classroom is economically productive both in its local context and in the way it exists as a component of the broader macroscale economy. Our investigation, as we detail in the following sections, operates at both that macroscale of the broader economy and at the microscale of our respondents associated with the TRIO program.

The historic economic changes discussed above indicated to us a possible utility in examining the changes over time in the use of terms relating to class. To do so, we used Google's NGram viewer, which counts specified sequences of letters (n-grams) from Google's growing corpus of millions of scanned books and offers visually accessible graphs of those counts. Because our investigation is confined to a US educational context, we restricted our searches of terms to American English, for which Google currently has data going up to 2008. Furthermore, we find the etymological work of Raymond Williams particularly compelling in its dating of the emergence of the common usage of the terms *working classes* and *middle classes* from the 1840s and the industrial revolution's technological economic reorganization of social relationships, so we sought to verify the account offered by Williams against US historical usage with the Google NGram viewer, setting our start date several decades earlier.

That slightly larger historical view (figure 6.1) confirms the widespread use of *working class* as beginning around 1840. Subsequent large variations in use surround other political and economic shifts: note the

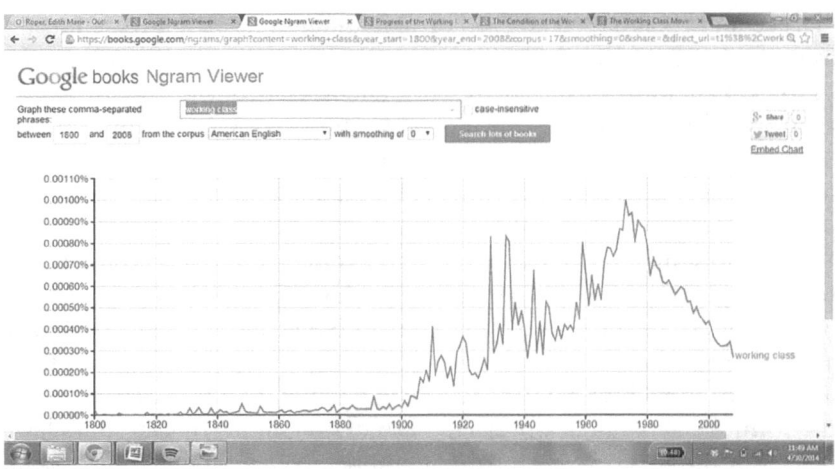

Figure 6.1. NGram Viewer of working class, 1800 to 2006

activity around 1929 and the economic shocks of major armed conflicts. Finally, there is a clear and significant decline in the use of *working class* from the 1980s to the present. That decline suggested to us that we might make productive further use of the Google NGram viewer, which we discuss below.

The broad assessment of class-related terms offers national and historical context for our investigation of working-class concerns in our classrooms, especially as they play out for our students in a changing economy. We thought it useful to focus on a portion of students in some way clearly and explicitly connected to some of the ways described above, and surveying current and prior students connected to the TRIO programs also intersects with our historical concerns, given the historical moment (1965) of TRIO's creation.

TRIO is a group of federal programs (eight total, but originally three) operated by the United States Department of Education's Office of Postsecondary Education that seek "to identify and provide services for individuals from disadvantaged backgrounds."[26] They define disadvantaged backgrounds in three specific ways: "low-income individuals, first-generation college students, and individuals with disabilities."[27] TRIO defines "low-income" annually according to standards relating to family income and poverty as set by the US Census Bureau and published by the Department of Health and Human Services.

If students' or parents' household incomes are below the numbers for minimum income listed in table 6.1, they qualify for participation in TRIO programs. The Washington State University Student Support

Table 6.1. Federal TRIO Programs: Current-Year Low-Income Levels

Size of Family Unit	48 Contiguous States, DC, and Outlying Jurisdictions	Alaska	Hawaii
1	$17,505	$21,870	$20,130
2	$23,595	$29,490	$27,135
3	$29,685	$37,110	$34,140
4	$35,775	$44,730	$41,145
5	$41,865	$52,350	$48,150
6	$47,955	$59,970	$55,155
7	$54,045	$67,590	$62,160
8	$60,135	$75,210	$69,165

Source: United States, "Federal TRIO Programs: Current-Year Low-Income Levels," https:// www2.ed.gov/about/offices/list/ope/trio/incomelevels.html.

Services Office maintains data on the other criteria for participation in TRIO programs.

In table 6.2, the term *first generation* has two possible definitions: first, a student whose parents never enrolled in any type of college for any amount of time, or second, a student whose parents did not complete a four-year degree. The TRIO Upward Bound, Student Support Services (SSS), and McNair Scholar programs, all of which have a presence at Washington State University, use the second definition. However, TRIO does not use the term *working class*, which led to Edie-Marie's early confusion about the term and our subsequent curiosity about how our TRIO respondents might feel about the term.

To investigate the overlap of working-class concerns with those of TRIO participants and index them against other identifiers, we designed and distributed an eleven-question anonymous survey.[28] The questions were:

1. Are you are participant in a TRIO program such as Student Support Services (SSS), McNair Scholars, Talent Search, or Upward Bound? (yes/no)

2. How old are you? (numeric answer)

3. What gender do you identify as? (male/female/other)

4. What race do you identify as? (Hispanic, Native American, Asian, Black/ African American, White)

5. Are you attending college now or will you attend college within the next year? (yes/no)

Table 6.2. Demographics for Washington State University's Student Support Services programs as of January 2015

Gender	
Female	107
Male	53
Race (participants select all that apply)	
Hispanic	74
Native American	0
Asian	11
Black/African American	29
White	54
Hawaiian/Pacific Islander	2
Eligibility	
First generation and low income	126
Low income only	6
First generation only	20
Disabled only	2
Disabled and low income	6

Source: Data received from Kristine Attao, email correspondence, Washington State University Office of Student Support Services, February 11, 2015.

6. Which of the following class categories, if any, do you identify your family of origin as being a member of? (Check all that apply: low income, lower class, working poor, working class, middle class, upper middle class, upper class, none.)

7. If you selected a category above, do you identify as being a member of the same class as your family? (yes/no)

8. Do you qualify for Pell Grants? (yes/no)

9. Do you identify as being a first-generation college student? (yes/no)

10. Which of the following identities do you most identify with? (Select one: lower class, working poor, working class, middle class, upper middle class, upper class, first generation, low income, none.)

11. In what ways does your identity affect your classroom performance? (open text answer)

Using Edie-Marie's network as a TRIO alumna and previous SSS counselor, we distributed the survey electronically and received a total

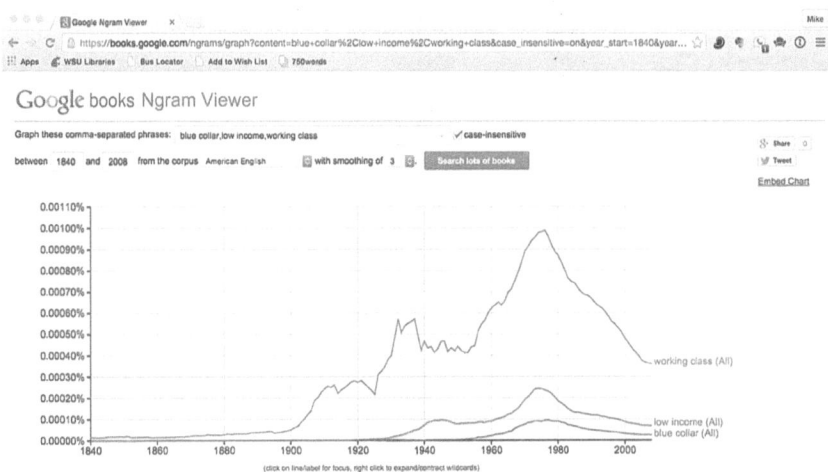

Figure 6.2. Blue-collar, low-income, and working-class designations, 1840 to 2000

of 116 questionnaire responses with 101 confirming TRIO participation and 93 confirming student status. We received 32 open-ended responses to question 11. Question 6 was intended to help us explore under-standings of class categories in the TRIO community but intentionally excluded the category *first-generation college student* because of its status as a contributor to or partial cultural descriptor of social class but not a class in itself and because of the question's focus on family background. Question 10, on the other hand, included *first-generation college student* because it referred to the respondents' own status and because it asked respondents to select what they considered to be a dominant identity. As we detail below, both the Google NGram investigations and the survey responses provided sometimes remarkable findings.

We understand *working class* does not operate in terminological iso-lation, so we compared its usage to other associated terms from 1840 to the present. Clearly in figure 6.2, *working class* is more widespread than *low income* or *blue collar*, which exhibit similar peaks and declines in their usage, raising questions about how Americans more generally discuss concerns of economic inequality. At the same time, we point out a decline in the use of *working class* as a popular term during the life-time of today's students: use of the term is now lower than it has been since 1929, a milestone date in economic history and class history. We also notice the peak of the usage of the term *working class* in the early 1970s (occurring at the same time as the OPEC oil embargo and the

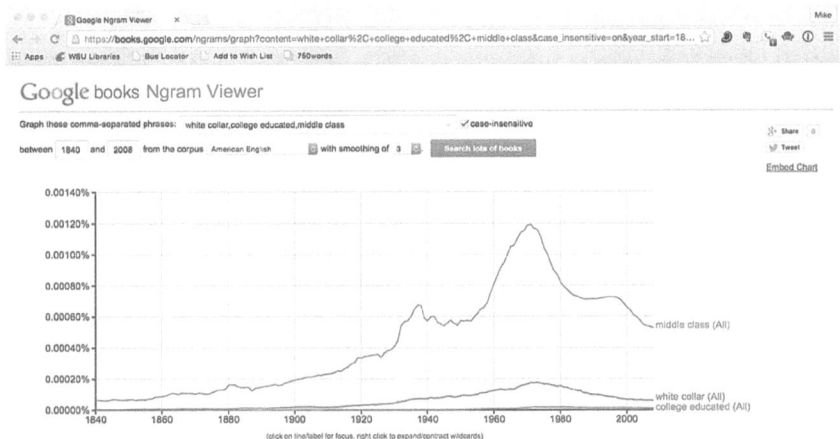

Figure 6.3. White-collar, college-educated, and middle-class designations, 1840 to 2000

dissolution of the Bretton Woods system, often characterized as the moment that marked the end of the golden age of American capitalism) and its subsequent decline.

To verify that the peak and subsequent decline of the use of the term *working class* and its associated terms were not merely idiosyncratic, we also investigated terms on the other side of the divide: *middle class, white collar,* and *college educated* (figure 6.3).

The peaks and declines are less prominent but still noticeable and similar in shape. We draw from these initial examinations a confirmation that the American conversation about class, regardless of definitional concerns, is in decline, as well as a broader national and historical context for our TRIO survey.

Some of the findings from our TRIO survey seem at first glance uncomplicated. When asked to select among class-linked socioeconomic identifiers (low income, lower class, middle class, working class, working poor, upper middle class, or upper class) no survey respondents identified as upper class. When asked what their dominant identity was using the same categories but adding first generation as an option, 31 percent selected working class as their primary identifier, 25 percent selected first generation as their primary identifier, 16 percent selected low income as their primary identifier, 15 percent selected middle class as their primary identifier, 10 percent selected working poor as their primary identifier, and 3 percent selected lower class as their primary identifier. However, when we look at those numbers in conjunction with other information, more complications emerge.

Those concerns of economic inequality are linked in interesting ways to our TRIO respondents' racial identification. Of the respondents who checked one or more boxes for question 6's identification of class background,

- 31 percent identify as white and working class but not working poor or low income;
- 15 percent identify as white, working class, and working poor or low income;
- 15 percent identify as white, working poor, low income and/or lower class, but not working class;
- 22 percent identify as not white and working class;
- 23 percent identify as not white and not working class.

In other words, white respondents were twice as likely to select working class as their only class identifier as they were to select additional class identifiers, whereas nonwhite respondents were almost equally likely to select working class as an identifier as they were to select other class identifiers. This indicates to us a degree to which working class as an identifier may crowd out other economic markers for white respondents and thereby problematically contribute to a felt fragmentation of class along race lines.

Of the respondents to our TRIO survey, 31 percent selected working class as their primary identifier (question 10). TRIO programs use the terms *low income* and *first generation* as selectors, and those terms can sometimes but not always overlap. First generation was selected as the primary identifier by 25 percent of our respondents, and low income by 16 percent of our respondents, for a total of 41 percent. While their responses are almost certainly influenced by their connections to the TRIO program, they offer a useful view of demonstrable (and sometimes ambiguous or problematic) class identification by people explicitly linked to concerns of economic inequality.

A small portion of our respondents—8.5 percent—identified as both working class and middle class. Furthermore, 53 percent of respondents checked multiple boxes as economic or class identifiers in response to question 6. Of the remaining respondents, in a survey connected to a program designed for economically disadvantaged students, 23 percent selected a middle class identity as their sole identifier. Is this choice of identity a form of what Marxists would challenge as false consciousness? What does working class mean to the rest of the participants, or to those who identified as both working and middle class? These complexities and questions point to an overdetermined and ambivalent class identity felt at a location (higher education) frequently identified with narratives of class change and economic uplift. The fact that 25 percent of our respondents answered no to whether they share their family's class background (question 7), thereby indicating that their own class statuses have changed, further contribute to our sense of an overdetermined and ambivalent class identity among a population identified as economically disadvantaged.

That sense was reinforced by the 32 of our 116 respondents who elected to answer the open-ended question, "In what ways has your identity affected your classroom performance?" (question 11). Four respondents stated in some way that their identities had no effect on their classroom performance. One respondent replied that identity brought about empathy for others, particularly in a racially inflected way, but did not elaborate. Six respondents offered answers connecting identity concerns to bootstrap narratives of uplift, including some remarks about race and ethnicity, as from the respondent who said, "Being Hispanic it makes me want to do better since I wish to help my family." Another respondent offered, "[I'm] proud to be a first generation college student from a low-income family and it has had a positive influence on my performance in school. Being a part of TRIO and knowing the sacrifices my family has made to get me here pushes me to be the best student I can be." These answers carried a generally positive emotional valence.

Negative emotional valence in relation to the intersection of identity with higher education seemed more common. Nine connected identity to feelings of not belonging at school. Race was one factor, as in the following response:

> As an African American attending an institution in which the overwhelming majority of the faculty and staff are white, I find it hard to reach out to them when I am struggling with family or life situations. Getting to know quite a few of them, they do not come from the same background as I do, thus when I share some of the issues that I'm enduring they just sit there with a blank stare because they have no idea what I'm going through. Not being able to reach out to faculty or staff during times where I have family issues affects my performance in the classroom in that I am so pre-occupied with trying to figure out how to deal with these situations that I am unable to focus in class, efficiently complete assignments, or adequately prepare for exams.

Other responses brought up concerns more directly connected to the economic inequalities we had asked about elsewhere in the survey and were perhaps skewed in that direction by those other questions. One respondent described feeling less prepared and less qualified than fellow students with more wealthy backgrounds. I have a very difficult time envisioning a successful career in my future. Even with a degree I have difficulty believing that I could ever be more successful than my parents. I was taught that poor people are always poor people and all of my adult role models while growing up were poor. Because of this, I tend to give up easily in class.

For such students, the narrative of ongoing economic inequality becomes a self-condemning prophecy.

Most common were the answers (ten in total) connecting identity to the obstacles and discomfort presented by the material concerns—time and money—presented by economic inequality. One respondent stated, "The only way that my identity affects my classroom performance is that at times, I may not have the amount of money to pay for books or materials that are needed for the class on time." Another noted the frustration caused by expenses in addition to tuition: "It makes me feel like I'm not rich enough to be in the program and excel." Another noted conflicts over allocating time between work and school: "I have to be at work and I need the money to pay for schooling and housing. My focus is not always in the classroom but at what I can do at work and how I can make money to complete my degree." For students vexed by such impediments to economic success, school becomes its own obstacle.

Finally, the historical shifts in usage of the terms *middle class* and *working class* indicated by the Google NGrams alerted us to a possible generational component to attitudes about class. When we split up our respondent cohort according to median age (twenty-one) and mean age (twenty-six), we found in both cases that more younger respondents identified as working class than did older respondents, in roughly the same proportions.

- Median younger identifying as working class: 34.5%
- Median older identifying as working class: 27.6%
- Mean younger identifying as working class: 32.0%
- Mean older identifying as working class: 27.5%

Given the economic shift away from manufacturing jobs and positions historically associated with working-class identities, these splits wherein more younger students than older students identify as working class are surprising. Furthermore, while 82 percent of all respondents answered yes to being first-generation college students, 11 percent of respondents who identified as being first-generation college students also identified as middle class rather than working class, and 30 percent of respondents who identified as **not** being first-generation college students selected working class as their dominant identity.

On the one hand, these findings indicate that more younger people than older people identify as working class, although we suspect that asking a forty-year-old about the characteristics of a working-class individual might generate descriptors radically different from those offered by a twenty-year-old. On the other hand, we wonder whether identifying as working class is increasingly associated not just with jobs in manufacturing (so-called blue-collar jobs) but more generally with low-paying and unrewarding jobs with minimal autonomy: in other words, with the entry-level jobs one might associate with younger respondents. The apparent contradictions between claimed family class background and claimed family college background seem harder to us to resolve, although if one measures class position by individual income, many college students certainly qualify as working class.

If *class* as a term and marker is declining in use and definitionally vexed, then why use it? The term *first generation* claimed by 82 percent of our respondents seems more definitionally precise and less likely to be contested or cause offense, and as the TRIO program itself indicates, might be more useful in directing specific groups of students toward helpful resources. At the same time, there are many students in at-risk populations that TRIO does not always help, both within and beyond first-generation populations. Still, given the class consciousness the term *first generation* generates, without the ambiguity or volatility of terms like *working class*, we find it to be a more useful marker.

As our survey responses indicate, economic inequality carries a racial component and a gendered component. The class markers historically associated with "blue collar" and "white collar" positions extended into "pink collar" positions, and the emergence of the information economy following the end of capitalism's golden age included the growth of what Ursula Huws characterizes as a "gendered *cybertariat.*"[29] The virtualization of work into Hardt and Negri's immaterial labor does not divorce us from our gendered, raced bodies—in many ways, it exacerbates inequalities of gender and race—but it makes those gendered and raced bodies less visible. We worry that the discourse of class, with its homogenizing effects, has played a similar role in the elision of economic difference even while ostensibly calling attention to it.

We see here interesting possibilities for pedagogy in contrasting the ways TRIO discourses and working-class discourses represent and respond to economic inequality. TRIO sets clear definitional criteria for students it seeks to help and then works to educate students placed into TRIO programs about the parameters of economic inequality in order to attempt to help them succeed. Part of TRIO's approach involves creating a critical consciousness (certainly there is considerable overlap here with the approaches of Freirean critical pedagogy) and calls attention to underacknowledged forms of cultural capital. As indicated by this volume, working-class definitions and pedagogies are rather more diffuse and contested and represent working-class identity as something one holds onto and something one maintains: betrayal of working-class identity can be viewed as an inauthentic false consciousness. TRIO's approach, to some working-class pedagogues, may seem crudely instrumental and may contribute to a sense of Richard Sennett and Jonathan Cobb's "hidden injuries"[30] or class violence. There are also historical tensions here as we wish to avoid dehistoricizing or romanticizing a monolithic working-class past that no longer exists. Today's situation is no longer the age of three big automakers and three big networks we associate with the golden age of monolithic capitalism and its factories and manufacturing careers that helped a working-class consciousness develop. We also see here a potential point of intersection in that working-class pedagogies can treat the experience of economic inequality not as something to be left behind but as a reminder that one's material past experience contributes to and shapes one's experience in the classroom.

Such reminders ought to operate as much for instructors as they do for students; Edie-Marie found that her TRIO experience affected her own pedagogy, much in the way Mike found his experience as an enlisted soldier affected his pedagogy. Classroom attention to the economic value of the immaterial labor performed therein helps foster not only student critical consciousness of economic difference but instructor critical consciousness of economic difference as well. Instructors' acknowledgment of systemic economic inequality, their locations within that system, and the heterogeneous forms of immaterial labor that allowed for their advance within that system can allow for the development of a common language of economic difference shared by instructors and students.

That common language of economic difference reflects the situation of the 53 percent of our respondents who selected multiple identifiers of class. The overlapping and contradictory forms of middle-class and working-class experience are heterogeneous in ways that work against the notion of class itself as a homogenizing concept and term. We see important uses for composition studies in coupling Gibson-Graham's notion of the diverse economy and Hardt and Negri's notion of immaterial labor.[31] These concepts together allow for not just capitalist and market forms of labor, transaction, and enterprise but also noncapitalist and alternative capitalist forms as well. Taken together, they also allow us to attend to the ways students and instructors alike participate in the production, distribution, use, and reproduction of immaterial capital, with the appropriation of value occurring in diversely measurable and quantifiable ways at multiple locations in that economic cycle. The quantification we undertake in this chapter serves as one attempt to do so, following TRIO's model, by using responsible and carefully historicized methods of data collection with an investigative vocabulary that is simultaneously precise and permissive of definitional difference.

Notes

1. We find the work of political economist J. K. Gibson-Graham particularly helpful in understanding this shift, but the shift has been addressed in depth and with considerable rigor by many ideological positions in the discipline of economics.
2. Hardt and Negri, *Empire*, 290.
3. US Department of Education, Office of Postsecondary Education, "Federal TRIO Programs—Home Page."
4. As we demonstrate below, Google's NGram viewer shows that the high-water mark of the usage of the term *working class* coincides almost precisely with the end of the golden age of capitalism in the early 1970s brought about by the collapse of the Bretton Woods system and the OPEC oil embargo.
5. Introduction to this volume, 4.
6. Linkon, ed., *Teaching Working Class*, 1.
7. Peckham, "Complicity in Class Codes," 265.
8. Mayers, Bertoncini, and O'Dair, "Two Comments," 561.
9. Ibid., 563.
10. Bloom, "Freshman Composition," 654–75.
11. Micciche, "When Class Equals Crass," 24–36.
12. Ibid., 31.
13. Ibid., 35.
14. Berger, *Working Class Suburb*, 83.
15. United States Census Bureau, "Poverty."
16. Piketty, *Capital in the Twenty-First Century*, 25.
17. Stuckey, *Violence of Literacy*, 57.
18. Ibid., 19.
19. US Department of Labor, US Bureau of Labor Statistics, *Occupational Outlook Handbook*.
20. Scott, "Writing Work," 229.
21. Ibid.
22. For an examination of representative examples in composition's economic discourse, see Edwards, "Economies of Writing."
23. Gibson-Graham, "Economy," 96.
24. Ibid.
25. Ibid., 94.
26. US Department of Education, Office of Postsecondary Education, "Federal TRIO Programs Current-Year Low-Income Levels."
27. Ibid.

28. We received Washington State University Institutional Review Board (IRB) permission for research on human subjects for this survey. Documentation is available upon request.

29. Huws, *Making of a Cybertariat*, 152–76, italics added.

30. Sennett and Cobb, *Hidden Injuries of Class*, 159, *passim*.

31. Gibson-Graham, *Postcapitalist Politics*, 53–78; Hardt and Negri, *Empire*, 290.

PART 2

Pedagogy in the Composition Classroom

7

TELLING OUR STORY
College Writing for Trade Unionists

Rebecca Fraser

A liberal arts college program solely devoted to tradespeople and their interests is a radical idea; after all, why spend money, time, and effort to educate people in the liberal arts who are going to be doing some form of construction for the rest of their lives? When I was nineteen, a professor challenged us with these questions: Should bus drivers go to college? Shouldn't we leave them well enough alone to drive their buses? Why give them the tools that might make it possible for them to imagine another life when all they are going to do is drive a bus for the rest of their lives? We need bus drivers, he continued, and I remember being a bit outraged at his argument (which might very well have been to evoke a response from us). Thirty-five years later, I am teaching in such a revolutionary program, one perhaps only imagined by that professor all those years ago. The United Association of Plumbers, Local 1 (UA1), and the International Brotherhood of Electrical Workers, Local 3 (IBEW), in New York City pay for their apprentices to get college degrees. The Harry Van Arsdale Jr. Center for Labor Studies at SUNY Empire State College (HVACLS) is one of very few liberal arts college programs that exist solely for trade unionists in the United States.

Harry Van Arsdale Jr. imagined the center into existence. According to a brief biography of Van Arsdale, "As Central Labor Council President he began a drive to establish a Labor College in New York City. After many trials and negotiations with the State University and Cornell University a labor college was born in September 1971 as part of the newly established State University of New York, Empire State College."[1] The SUNY Empire State College website states that "the New York state legislature created [the] Empire State College . . . Center for Labor Studies . . . to ensure that wage-earning adults had an opportunity to

DOI: 10.7330/9781607326182.c007

earn a college degree in a learning environment that celebrates their achievements and recognizes their distinctive needs.[2]

But why require these construction apprentices to go to college and read works like Tim O'Brien's *The Things They Carried*, Whitman's *Leaves of Grass*, or even Melville's *Moby-Dick*? One answer is simply to enrich their lives, to engage their imagination for what is possible, to challenge their notions about how the world works and why it works that way.[3] Another answer is that requiring students, over the course of eight courses, to engage in critical thinking will make them better electricians and plumbers. They will, almost necessarily, read blueprints with a new eye, confront wiring or plumbing challenges with a mind open to a wider variety of solutions. In addition, Pam Belluck, in "For Better Social Skills, Scientists Suggest a Little Chekhov," reports that a scientific study at The New School "found that after reading literary fiction . . . people performed better on tests measuring empathy, social perception and emotional intelligence."[4]

Finally, and most important, the instructors of our courses provide students a chance to tell, reflect on, and retell their stories—stories that if not told by them will get told by others who won't get it right. These stories—presented in assigned papers and told daily in our courses— are juxtaposed with, are enlightened by, and enlighten the stories of famed authors; the students' stories are particularly celebrated when they are published in our annual anthology of student writing and art, *Labor Writes*—an anthology used as a text in our College Writing course. The South African writer Imraan Coovadia writes about both color-coded and class-coded societal challenges. In quoting Jacques Ranciere, Coovadia points out that "'democracy is . . . a specific regime of speaking [writing, saying],'" and it is a refusal of a "'natural order' that destines specific individuals and groups to occupy positions [either] of rule or of being ruled.'"[5] *Labor Writes*, and the curriculum for College Writing then, are democratic practice; in both the anthology and in the course, students come to understand that to write is to actively learn democracy.

THE SET-UP

The Program

SUNY Empire State College associate-degree students must earn sixty-four credits to graduate; at HVACLS, they earn thirty-two credits from their apprenticeship and thirty-two credits in liberal arts classes they take with us—eight four-credit classes: College Writing; Texts and

Interpretive Strategies; Literature and Society; US History; Global Civilizations; Labor and Public Affairs; Class, Race and Gender; and Labor and Economics (taken, roughly, in that order). Our program is writing-and-reading intensive across the curriculum. About the program the dean writes, "Faculty, staff, students and institutional partners work together to develop and strengthen labor studies as a perspective on our world and as a means to ensure the best possible society for us all."[6]

A few of my goals, as coordinator of the writing/reading program and as a College Writing instructor, are

- to engage the voices of our students;
- to stretch their imagination by requiring them to read well-written fiction and nonfiction about work;
- to think critically about work, especially as it is perceived and constructed by our society and our culture;
- to write their own stories and make those stories available to the public;
- to inspire them to recognize the intelligence they use on their jobsites;
- to encourage them to examine and reflect on their work lives;
- to provide them the opportunity to explore the dynamics of complicated job sites and job responsibilities.

These goals are meant to engage students with the power they have, not only in their ability to wire a building but also in their ability to flip the switch in their brains. Included in this chapter are selections from student writing, writing that emerged in College Writing classes where they are asked to write about their jobs and the specific tasks they do on the job.

There is no question where HVACLS stands when it comes to workers' rights. Central text choices communicate clearly our perspective, sometimes even challenging students' ideas about the place of work and unions in society. Many of our assignments are designed to encourage students to engage in these matters and to make the connections to their own workplace and work circumstances.

The Students

A part of one student's story comes across in a letter written to me at the end of a semester of College Writing. It had been a tough semester for all of us, with many students quite vocal in their reluctance to complete assigned work. But we made it through, and L. wrote this note to me at the end of the semester:

How you doing? It's me L. your student that started this class disliking writing. Now this class is coming to an end, and I can sit back and remember how you changed the way I feel about writing. Now, I feel totally different about writing. I see writing as a form of expression. Before, I would get writing assignments from other classes and feel like "not this again." Thanks to you, I don't feel that way and now I can sit down without a problem until my hands fall off. Another thing I got from this class was the way I look at life. . . . You made me a smarter and wiser person. Thank you for changing me and most of all thank you for all your hard work and for being so understanding.

L. is fairly typical associate-degree student at HVACLS; an apprentice with the IBEW Local 3, he works with journeymen electricians during the day, and at night he takes classes toward an associate degree—an electrical theory class and at least one other class each semester. The union requires that he get an associate degree and the union pays for it; in addition, L. will receive a bump in his meager apprentice pay for each semester he finishes successfully. HVACLS administers the non-electrical liberal arts courses these students take, and sometimes they come to class covered in debris from their worksites or with a bad case of "hard-hat hair."

L. characterizes himself as the "working poor" and expresses a desire to hold on to that identity no matter what success he may achieve in his life. And while he owns this identifier, he also yearns for his daughter to have an easier childhood than he did—a childhood he says ended when he was about seven or eight and began hanging with the big guys on the street, hustling money, making a name for himself, trying to escape the confines of the small and run-down family apartment.

Students like L. often come into our program thinking of themselves as "just" laborers, or construction workers, or even "union thugs." These identities are worn sometimes as a badge of honor, sometimes as a stigma, and sometimes as both. Many of our students choose to go into a trade instead of going to college—then they find out that the union they just entered requires them to get a college degree in labor studies. That pill isn't always easy to swallow. Many of them, especially at the beginning, consider this requirement a burden rather than a benefit; after all, they have chosen a trade over college—often because they have been unsuccessful and unmotivated students.

The students in College Writing are 95 percent men, and many of them haven't succeeded in college and probably not in high school. They may have tried, may have taken a few courses at a community college and partied too much or worked too much; they might have a learning disability, or perhaps they just can't stand to be in a classroom for very long. Their average age is twenty-seven, and they cross racial lines. They are African American, Latin@, Asian, Caucasian, and more. Many of them worked any number of jobs before their current one, probably stood on line for hours to receive an application for the apprenticeship, and likely waited two to four years to get called to take the tests to get into the program. Many have taken deep pay cuts to join the union, to start from scratch, even with families to support. They may or may not know a lot about unions—some have come with a specific desire to have a union job, which they view as secure. Others come knowing little about what it means to be in a union. They learn about that as their apprenticeship unfolds—in college, in their theory classes held by the union, on their jobs, and at the union hall. One thing they all have in common, all these men and a few women, is that they are working hard from very early in the morning to late in the evening when they have classes. On the job they are slinging BX, bending conduit, climbing ladders to do wiring or plumbing overhead, or kneeling down to do work close to the ground. They are working with experienced mechanics to learn the practical tricks of the trade. And they get dirty. And while they may be extremely proficient in their jobs, even as apprentices, when they enter the classroom, many become insecure and uncomfortable.

Michael Kimmel and Bethany Coston write that "working-class men are the male equivalent of the 'dumb blonde'—endowed with physical virtues, but problematized by intellectual shortcomings. . . . He exempts himself from scrutiny because he clearly isn't capable of such deep analytic thought."[7] And Lisa Kirby notes that "it seems working-class men are generally portrayed as one-dimensional. Such representations are problematic, to say the least, because they place the working-class male in a troubling position of bumbling idiot, a type of comic relief that everyone else views as lacking in both intelligence and ambition."[8]

Our students have absorbed these portrayals and stereotypes, sometimes with awareness and sometimes not. At times, it seems as if there is a deep anti-intellectualism that runs through our student population. However, just as soon as I begin to believe that anti-intellectualism exists, a student or a group of students proves me wrong with their writing, a heated and well-informed debate, or a thoughtful discussion. The truth is that our students run the gamut, as they would in just about any other associate degree program. They come into College Writing with a variety of fears, expectations, and experiences. Some, like L., come with a dislike of writing. And a few come with anticipation to write their stories.

THE COURSE

College Writing classes at HVACLS are three-hour classes that meet once a week for thirteen weeks, as do all our associate degree courses. We divide the three hours into smaller chunks, shifting activities often, so students aren't doing one thing for too long. After all, they've already worked a long day, often starting work at 7 a.m., and our classes run from 4:30 to 7:30 p.m. They are tired when they sit their Carhartt-clad bodies down at a desk that might be a bit too small for them.

College Writing is one of the first courses required of our apprentices; in their first year they take College Writing and Texts and Interpretive Strategies—half of an incoming class in the first and the other half in the second. These two courses are foundational to the remainder of our program. Instructors share a common syllabus within their courses. I have written a College Writing syllabus that changes each semester, following instructor feedback. While the class is quite similar to College Writing courses at other colleges and universities (the writing process is engaged, writing coaches are taken advantage of, and there are texts that serve as both models for writing and discussion platforms), it is quite different in both its population of construction trade apprentices and in its focus around the topic of work they do, which directs the reading selections and much of the discussion and writing throughout the semester.

One motivation in creating the curriculum for our College Writing class is to assist these construction apprentices in becoming acclimated to the experience of being in a college classroom. Many of our students come to college with a great deal of both resistance and reticence. One recent student told me that simply sitting in a classroom makes him anxious and fidgety. "I'm not sure what it is, but I feel trapped when I'm in a classroom and I just can't stay there for very long," he explained to me when I inquired about his frequent trips out of the room.

A number of students chose a trade because they feel most comfortable on their feet, working with their hands, engaging their brains in visual problem solving. While they are very verbally oriented and great storytellers, it turns out (not surprisingly) when we informally test them that they are mostly visual learners. Many of them are more comfortable building, bending, threading, or fixing something than they are reading or writing. As one student wrote apologetically on his placement essay, "I don't write. I work!!!" In reflecting on this statement, the student's instructor, Sophia Mavrogiannis, wrote, "I was, however, very bothered by the phrase, 'Sorry you had to read this. I don't write. I work,' because in eight years of teaching, no student had ever apologized for their writing as a whole. Sure, I've gotten e-mails apologizing for inappropriate language, but this was the first time a student apologized for writing—not for his ideas or his language, but his writing as an action, as if to imply he had no business writing in the first place because he's a working guy."[9]

The Writing

An early assignment in class asks students to create a primer with as many job-specific terms as they can come up with, terms an instructor probably wouldn't know, that anyone who doesn't work as an electrician or plumber might not know. In fact, what we are asking them to do is not unlike Walt Whitman's unpublished *Primer of Words*. Of that *Primer*, Justin Martin writes, "[Whitman] even compiled a dictionary, full of slang like *bender, bummer, spree* and *shin-dig*, picked up from coach drivers and blacksmiths and stevedores. Though never published, Whitman's *Primer of Words* was intended as an update to Noah Webster's landmark work."[10]

Students are shy at first, not believing we are really asking them to do this, not really sure that they can gather together, or even access, these words outside the jobsite. So we ask them to begin with whatever task they worked on that day—what did they do? What tools did they use, what hazards did they have to be aware of, what problems did they encounter? Then we get them into groups to brainstorm the words, to start a running list. Sometimes we challenge them by telling them that since we've been teaching in the program for a number of semesters, they might have a hard time finding words we don't know. They dig a bit deeper to come up with more terms like *pencil rods, Alamacs, Mae Wests, channel locks, Kindorf,* and *mongo.*

Take, for example, Paul Allen's essay "Action, Reflection and Practice as an Electrician" from *Labor Writes 2013.* He writes:

> As an electrical apprentice, it is important to me that my work looks good, not just because it should, but as a person, I like to do everything to the best of my ability. . . . For example, when I am installing receptacles, there are usually three wires to connect to the receptacle. Once they are connected, they are usually stuffed in the electrical box any way they fit, and the receptacle needs to get screwed in. I always make sure that all the wires are trimmed and at an even length. Then, I splice them onto the receptacle and curl them all in a clockwise position, so none of the wires are crossing each other and look neat.[11]

Allen not only writes of the pride he takes in his work, a common theme in our students' writing, but he also talks about a work process with which most of us are unfamiliar in a way that makes it accessible. Not an easy task.

Bringing these words, these stories, into the classroom also does what many literacy theorists discuss—it brings together differing discourses into the same place at the same time (see James Paul Gee, Glynda Hull, and Susan L. Lytle for discussions of discourse, cultural scripts, and acquisition versus learning discourses). As I've said, most of our students are not comfortable in the classroom or with "academic" speak. Even when I believe I am being most colloquial, even when I attempt to avoid dense academic terminology, I can get blank looks from students. Bolder, more confident students ask what the word I used means, while most students simply remain passive and quiet, perhaps not wanting to display ignorance in the faces of their brothers and sisters. We do the primer exercise precisely because I know they may be intimidated by the language I use. I want to put myself in their position of lacking knowledge of terminology, and I want to put them in the expert's seat and teach me what they know that I know nothing about.

In his "Preface to *Proletarian Nights*," Jacques Ranciere discusses the words of the "*other*," the "*other*" being the "bourgeoisie (bosses, politicians, judges)" in relation to the voice of workers. Ranciere is speaking of those workers who made the sacrifice to spend their nights reading, writing songs, putting together newspapers, and writing poetry. He states that "if worker emancipation is to possess a human face, if workers are to exist as subjects of a collective discourse which gives meaning to their multifarious assemblies and combats, those representatives must already have made themselves *other* in a double, hopeless rejection, refusing both to *live* like workers and to *talk* like the bourgeoisie."[12] Likewise, our students and their writing exist in this kind of liminal space that is neither colloquial nor academic, but, in that double rejection, both. Student writing in *Labor Writes* is exactly the kind of collective discourse in which our students speak as workers, even as they, in their acts of writing, refuse to "*live* like workers."

Listen to student Joseph Difino discuss the complicated relationship he has with his father, who is also an electrician. In his essay "My Life as an Electrician," Difino writes:

> [My father] told me many times he always wants me to be better than him. He says that in each generation the son should always make better than the father did, and so on. . . . That's where the problem comes in. I want to make better than him. . . . [And] maybe I should go to work on Saturdays when my father asks me to work, instead of going out with my friends, spending money or something. The workers on the job look at me like I should be the one sitting back doing nothing. But they don't know. If my father saw me not working, oh man forget it, he would scream and yell at me. He would be all over me.[13]

I don't know about you, but I can hear Joe's voice in this writing, just as I can hear L.'s voice in the note he wrote me. I am happy for students when they are able to break down the perceived academic wall separating them from their voice. I feel like Ken Macrorie when he wrote in *Uptaught* forty-five years ago about how his students managed to stop writing "Engfish."[14]

Since the vast majority of our students will never pursue a degree beyond an associate degree, imposing "academese" on them seems to be beside the point. This does not mean we don't desire our students to be articulate and intelligent; rather, it is to recognize they are already intelligent and extremely articulate. They are master negotiators if nothing else! I was struck recently, when rereading Wordsworth's "Preface to Lyrical Ballads," by his (albeit romantic) desire to replicate the everyday tongue of humans: "The principal object, then, proposed in these Poems was to choose incidents and situations from common life, and to relate or describe them, throughout, as far as was possible in a selection of language really used by men. . . . My purpose was to imitate, and, as far as possible, to adopt the very language of men."[15] Students at HVACLS don't have need "to imitate" the "very language of men" as they speak it and write it in the essays they write in our program. "Incidents and situations from common life" are the topics of the essays they write, as well as the stories they love to tell each other whenever they get the chance.

The Reading

The two main texts in College Writing are the current issue of *Labor Writes* (our annual student anthology of writing and art) and *The Things They Carried* by Tim O'Brien; we treat these texts with equal importance—spending the same amount of time with each, working not to privilege one over the other.

Labor Writes goes a long way toward validating our students' writing and creative and intellectual skills. Each year we solicit writing from all the courses we offer; last year we had over 130 submissions and published more than half of them. This anthology, then, becomes the initial text in the semester; students are asked to read the anthology, section by section, and respond to both the content and to the writing skill displayed. Some students are intimidated, but most are encouraged to see that the sorts of things they would like to write about are included in the collection—in particular, there are usually a number of "How I Got Here" essays, which is the first writing assignment of the semester. Students are relieved to see they don't have to write about major, earth-shattering events but can instead write about the ordinariness of their existence (which they think is boring but is often quite fascinating, as we saw in the Difino excerpt).

Labor Writes essays serve two purposes—they instigate discussions of what it is like to be a trade apprentice, what the students are doing on the job, and how they are learning the skills they need to become a journeyman with an A card. Conversations range from the best way to do the daily coffee runs for the journeymen they work with to job safety and how to handle unsafe situations as apprentices. Later courses spend much more time on what it means to be a union member, and essays on related topics are in the anthology; these provide an important inroad into discussions about what responsibilities come with being a union member. We point them toward the perspective our dean articulates in his statement on the center's website:

> The best possible society, from the perspective of labor studies, is one in which everyone who wants to work can, and everyone who does work is paid enough to live a good life as a respected member of the community. Learning how to ensure these desires, which are well expressed by the traditional labor movement slogan, "a fair day's wages for a fair day's work," is the guiding purpose of a labor studies degree."[16]

We discuss what social unionism is and get them talking, writing, and imagining the ways their unions do and could contribute to the communities where they are located.

The second text in the course is *The Things They Carried*, with which we take time to consider the work of the soldier. The first chapter of the book, titled "The Things They Carried," is a catalyst for a discussion of what the apprentices carry with them on the job—what tools do they need daily, what tools can they leave behind? Are there tools unique to individuals on the job? What are those, and why do they need those specific tools? These kinds of questions lead to a discussion of the intangible things they carry on the job, just as O'Brien weaves those intangible things in and out of his description of the physical items the soldiers carry.

The second essay assignment for the course is to write an essay titled "The Things I Carry," and students write about their tools and their keys and phones, as well as about immaterial things they carry with them, like worry and love. Student C. Del Sole writes:

> One thing I always carry with me is my union card. Not because I have to, but because I take a lot of pride in having one. I am proud to be a Local 1 member; I am proud to represent the men and women who provide an incredible skill and service to the people of this city. Sure, the card is a

small plastic inanimate object that can't really do anything by itself. One thing it can do is allow me to get up and go to work every morning with a great feeling that I am part of something special and bigger than myself."[17]

In contrast, Ikari Shinji writes in his essay, "Of all the things I carry, the heaviest of these is responsibility. As an apprentice I am expected to go to work five days a week, go to school two nights a week, and attend any other meetings the union requires of me. I also have a responsibility to represent positively my union and its brothers and sisters, as anything I do to negatively represent the union affects all of its members."[18]

The most discussed and disturbing chapter of O'Brien's book is probably the least violent chapter, "How to Tell a True War Story," in which O'Brien reveals that any war story you believe is probably just a pack of lies. It is at this point that students begin to recognize deeply that the book in their hands is a *novel*, a fictional account of a character named Tim O'Brien who went to Vietnam and fought in the war, just like the author of the book did. O'Brien, the narrator, tells the reader, "In war you lose your sense of the definite, hence your sense of truth itself, and therefore it's safe to say that in a true war story nothing is absolutely true."[19]

This shifting of perspective is disorienting for our students and sometimes angers them, as they feel they've been duped. They find it hard to believe the book is "simply" a novel, and this incredulousness leads to a deep discussion about the nature of truth in storytelling. How much truth is there in the version of a story you might tell a friend about the dent in the car versus what you tell the policeman or the insurance agent? What happens to that story over time? Why does it change with audience and time? And what about exaggeration—is that truth telling or lying? Voices in these heated discussions are raised, students talk over each other, and a level of engagement is reached that surprises all of us.

In the end, however, the nature of stories having been explored as exhaustively as it is in the O'Brien book, students are more prepared for the key line in *The Things They Carried*, the last line of the novel. O'Brien, the narrator, tells us that in telling these stories, Tim was trying "to save Timmy's life with a story." And here we are at the very root of why we tell stories, why we ask students not only to tell stories in class but to write them down on paper in response to assignments. We could not get to that place if we did not read *The Things They Carried*; this last line causes all of us to look back on all the stories we've told and read over the course of the semester. Just how have those stories saved our lives? we ask our students and ourselves.

THE CONCLUSION

Mike Rose asserts, "It is hard work to teach creatively in the intersection of the academic and the vocational. . . . It means developing classroom activities that authentically represent the intellectual demands of the workplace. . . . It means seeking out the many literate possibilities running through . . . people's lives."[20] We do everything we can to highlight, engage, provoke, and challenge the intellect our students express at work. We explicitly bring their workplace into the classroom, as you saw in the exercises sketched out above.

At HVACLS, I also hope we succeed in engendering a culture of labor literacy—reading, writing, thinking, and talking about labor—that changes the unions the students are members of and that begins to bring about change in the labor world. Mike Rose asks us to

> consider, then, an observation by labor journalist John P. Hoerr: "Since the early days of industrialization, a peculiar notion has gained ascendancy in the United States: that wage workers and their representatives lacked the competence to handle complex issues and problems that required abstract knowledge and analytical ability." This sense of deficiency is in our cultural bones, and it affects and distorts the specific economic responses we develop, from education and job training to the way work is organized.[21]

Karen Hansen, a student, unwittingly contradicts Hoerr when she writes:

> I listen to my foreman describe our task. Immediately I am engaged. I pull up the filed skills I have acquired and integrate my new vocabulary of hardware, techniques and modalities. . . . Today we will be engineering a support system for a 16-foot fixture. This system not only needs to safely suspend this lighting over people's heads, but also needs to be mechanically sound, straight, plumb, and integrated into the carpenter's work. . . . I find it hard to understand why the work of a person who uses their mind and their body to the extent that I do would not be considered intelligent.[22]

Providing the space for students to tell their stories, to write about their work, to talk about their "ordinary" experiences is the job I put forward for myself and for the other instructors who teach College Writing. Placing a student essay alongside a story by Tim O'Brien gives students the experience of being emancipated in the ways Ranciere talks about; students have a voice of authority in our College Writing classrooms because who knows better than they do what it is like to be an apprentice in the trades? How else would I know about Stephen Ferguson's experience? He writes:

> Despite poor pay and hard work, working with the men and women of Local 3 makes it easier to go to work on a daily basis. Feeling like you

truly belong to something that is greater than just the task at hand is truly satisfying. The fact that I'm the "gofer" for a group of guys and still feel like I am an integral cog in a giant well-oiled machine says a lot about the importance of working with a sense of purpose. . . . At the start of my apprenticeship, I took a serious pay cut, but working toward a goal keeps me focused.[23]

I can echo Ferguson's words, could say them myself in fact. If my students feel like "an integral cog . . . working with a sense of purpose," I too can say the same. Working at a college designed especially for trade-union apprentices gives me a sense of purpose I might not have at another college. Working with a group of students who love to "shoot the shit" with the best of them is a privilege and not a burden. As my trade vocabulary expands and I learn more from my students, I am better able to elicit the stories that will save the lives of both my students and me.

Notes

1.   *Harry Van Arsdale Jr. Memorial Association Biography.*
2.   Merrill, "About the Van Arsdale Center," https://www.esc.edu/labor-studies-cen ter/labor-studies-program/.
3.   Ibid.
4.   *Well,* "For Better Skills Scientists Suggest a Little Chekhov," entry by Pam Belluck, October 3, 2013, https://well.blogs.nytimes.com/2013/10/03/i-know-how-youre -feeling-i-read-chekhov/?_r=0."
5.   Coovadia, *Transformations: Essays,* 170.
6.   Merrill, "Why Trade Unionists."
7.   Coston and Kimmel, "Seeing Privilege," 97–111.
8.   Kirby, "Cowboys."
9.   Mavrogiannis, introduction to *Pipe Dreams,* 1.
10.   Martin, *Rebel Souls,* 36.
11.   Allen, "Action, Reflection and Practice."
12.   Ranciere, *Preface to Proletarian Night.*
13.   Difino, "My Life as an Electrician."
14.   Macrorie, *Uptaught.*
15.   Wordsworth, *Preface to Lyrical Ballads.*
16.   Merrill, "Welcome to the Van Arsdale Center," https://development.esc.edu/labor -studies-center/message-from-the-dean/.
17.   Del Sole, "Things I Carry."
18.   Shinji, "Value of the Things I Carry Daily."
19.   O'Brien, *Things They Carried.*
20.   Rose, *Mind at Work,* 191–92.
21.   Ibid., xix.
22.   Hansen, "My Blue Collar Skills."
23.   Ferguson, "Reflection of Work."

8

EMOTIONAL LABOR AS IMPOSTERS
Working-Class Literacy Narratives and Academic Identities

Nancy Mack

By teaching writing I am asking students to buy into an academic identity and to learn to write like a member of what I have sarcastically called the *discourse community country club*. I also know that teaching this prestigious discourse to working-class students places them in a subordinate status to those who have been privileged by the academy.[1] Language is a class marker that can expose inferiority with one error in punctuation, word ending, or pronunciation. Conversely, hearing, speaking, or writing one small turn of phrase from my working-class roots can be ethically satisfying.[2] Language is so powerful that its use creates us as uncomfortable outsiders or welcomed insiders. Language contains a shifting terrain of ideologies we cannot talk ourselves out of. We both speak and are spoken to by language. Unless I address how learning academic language can make working-class students feel like imposters or traitors, I am denying the potential social injustice embedded in my job as a writing teacher. And teaching the literacy narrative presents the possibility of critically analyzing the emotional labor that cannot be separated from academic identity formation.

Like most teachers, my approach to teaching literacy narratives began with trial and error. I have taught variations of this assignment in several courses from first-year to graduate level. Fortunately, I quickly gave up asking students to write a history of their school experiences, which I believe boxes students into composing predictable glosses. I began problematizing the way I taught literacy narratives at Wright State University to working-class students, assisted by my readings from critical theories about identity and emotion. The first section of this chapter discusses the life process of identity formation in order to establish the significance of narrative writing. The next section describes the imposter phenomenon

DOI: 10.7330/9781607326182.c008

and offers suggestions for encouraging working-class students to critically analyze their responses to past language conflicts. The third section advocates increasing self-efficacy through a problem-solving approach to the emotional conflicts students will most likely experience while writing for the academy. Next, student agency is considered for forming a hybrid academic identity. The last section points to the ways other teachers have expanded upon the literacy-narrative assignment to foster identity formation. The pedagogical goal is to help students perceive literacy more critically, increase control over their writing, and gain agency in their emotional labor as they develop their own working-class academic identities.

IDENTITY FORMATION AND CRITICAL NARRATIVE WRITING

Identity labels are largely social constructs that fall apart under close scrutiny and have a seedy past of promoting oppression. However, these labels have a long life, and those who are labeled by others must decide how they feel about the labeling.[3] The working class is an equal-opportunity group with which most anyone can be identified in one way or another; however, most Americans would rather self-identify as belonging to the middle class.[4] Conflicts may arise when we perceive that others are judging us as less than them. I caution that students should be permitted to select and name the particular identities they wish to investigate without being essentialized by the instructor. In rereading Mary Soliday's foundational article advocating teaching literacy narratives to basic writers, I was reminded that she concentrates the assignment on the changing identities of her students: "In focusing upon those moments when the self is on the threshold of possible intellectual, social, and emotional development, literacy narratives become sites of self-translation where writers can articulate the meanings and the consequences of their passages between language worlds."[5] My contention is that rethinking the larger concept of identity can influence pedagogical decisions about designing writing assignments and their supportive activities. Specifically, a more complex notion of identity can affect how we teach narrative writing so it becomes more relevant to the life process of identity formation. A brief outline that follows lists the important features of identity theory that make it possible to privilege the teaching of critical narrative writing.

1. Multiply conflicted: we have many identities to which we must answer, and these each have different needs and desires that position them to conflict with one another.

2. Culturally and historically interpreted: identities are taught to us through many sources; thus, we are socialized by media, family, and school to know what is normal, expected, and forbidden. We cannot escape epochs of history that have defined and delimited all identities.

3. Ontogenetically developmental: each of our identities has a life history as we first become conscious of our cultural designation, critique the stereotypes of that identity, and make decisions about how we will conform to the expectations of others.

4. Locally situated: although identities are defined by the larger culture, local contexts bound by geography, community, workplace, school, or family exert influence to create variations in identity that may be somewhat unique.

5. Socially relational: identities are never isolated; we enact our identities through the many ways we relate to others whether we interact socially or observe silently. Consequently, we consider what others might think before we decide how to act.

6. Performed in everyday life: we perform our identities in all we do whether or not we are aware we are capitulating to cultural expectations.

7. Embodied in experience: experience provides a powerful, physical reality that may hurt, distress, or disturb us. If the memory of an identity conflict is troubling or comes to mind much later, we can reconsider how we originally interpreted that experience.

8. Emotionally managed: experience provokes reactions that can be almost instantaneous. Our emotional responses to identity conflicts may even be surprising to us. If we wish not to respond in a particular manner, we can choose to mask, control, or change our response.

9. Endlessly revisable: emotional responses can be changed through reflection, intention, and action. In this way we can take agency in the ongoing construction of our identities.

10. Mediated through image and language: we can compose our identities through the images we author in fashion, art, music, dance, poetry, drama, stories, narratives, and memoirs.

Narrative writing has the potential to be significant for identity formation through problematizing the meaning of experience. The past becomes an object of reflection refracted through the critical lens of the present in order to project a possible future. Thus, a critical narrative is less about past experience, somewhat about present reflections, and more about its meaning for future agency. As we learn by narrating our stories, the truth is all in the telling. In youth we discover the powerfulness of lying, and in old age we understand the importance of retelling an enabling fiction. It takes time and lots of critical thought to construct meaning out of the events that happen in our lives and to reconsider what is implied by the narratives we tell. Marxist philosopher Madan Sarup reveals how identity is hidden or assumed within a narrative: "When we are talking about ourselves, we tend to emphasize what happened and what we did, we focus on the concrete effects rather than the possible 'theoretical' causes. Nevertheless, these issues are implied in the story."[6] To some extent, time offers us distance from experience so the picture of what happened can enlarge to take in more of life—we can see patterns we could not perceive at the time, and we can observe connections to history and our location at that moment. We can choose to valorize an experience as a dramatic turning point in our lives or as the motivation to make a positive change. Of course, narratives can also be a dysfunctional means to cope, compensate, deny, or even lie to oneself. In his discussion of literacy-narrative pedagogy, Bronwyn T. Williams points to the importance of critical analysis for supporting changes in identity: "If we begin to make students aware of the kinds of identities they adopt when writing these narratives and how they might be able to change them in print as well as in their lives, we offer several important opportunities for student writers."[7] Critically examining and narrating experience will hopefully grant students agency in how they decide to author their futures. If they take no critical agency in how they compose their narratives, students may only reinscribe the limited narratives culture has written for them. Indeed, in a well-documented examination of the success of different cultural groups in the United States, Amy Chua and Jed Rubenfeld point to the negative effects of the well-known cultural stereotypes of inferiority projected upon African Americans and Appalachians.[8] The narratives for working-class lives are narrowed to only a few stereotypical choices, making it imperative for students to understand that narratives should be problematized. Sociologist Beverley Skeggs has studied working-class images in British reality television programs. Skeggs argues that the "resources for telling, representing, displaying self are not equally available" to the working class.[9]

Most critiques of the literacy narrative fault a lack of critical analysis in how students portray their identities as successes, victims, and prodigies[10] or heroes, rebels, and victims.[11] If the goal is to have students write more critically analytical literacy narratives, we must open issues of identity and literacy for investigation rather than dropping narrative writing altogether—as seems to be the trend in several high-school[12] and college writing programs in which argumentative writing dominates as well as at recent CCCC conventions.[13] Not unlike narrative writing, argumentative writing taught poorly can serve to reproduce hegemonic reasoning and cultural scripts. The difference lies in engaging students in thought processes that produce knowledge from critical reflection. The literacy narrative should serve an epistemological function for the students to create new knowledge. Fortunately, there are those composition scholars who are invested in finding a place in the composition curriculum for meaning making through some type of narrative writing, whether it is the personal essay, personal narrative, critical personal narrative, critical memoir, creative nonfiction, I-witnessing, life writing, lifestory, critical autobiography, autoethnography, academic storytelling, or chapbook.[14] Narrative writing is important for identity construction and is particularly significant for working-class students as they struggle to change their narratives by continuing their education. Nevertheless, it would be pretentious to believe working-class students are not already engaged in critical analysis of their daily lives. My role as a teacher is to further the development of students' critical thought processes in their writing so they can authorize their own meanings from experience.

I first revised the literacy-narrative assignment to focus on a critique of limited cultural definitions of literacy by asking students to itemize their many literacy practices both inside and outside school. I forwarded that literacy is wider than school literacy and that limited definitions of literacy benefit some groups more than others. Students narrate diverse life experiences, such as spouting basketball statistics from a game program to impress classmates, crafting greeting cards to cheer a father after chemotherapy, collecting cookbooks to read ravenously, and watching a teacher cry while reading aloud the last chapter of *Where the Red Fern Grows*. J. Blake Scott recommends that students construct three timelines for literacy: at school, at home, and in the community or with peers.[15] As might be expected, my students favored writing about experiences that were not school assignments.

After students had begun writing literacy narratives about a wide range of experiences, I added invention activities focusing on identity formation. I modeled drawing overlapping identity circles and shared my own changes in awareness and ownership of my cultural roles. I suggested a list of about twenty different identity types. Students drew their own identity circles and picked one or two identities for which to chart changes over time. During these invention activities, the class read critical literacy narratives by previous students. Tim Barnett defines critical literacy narratives as having "characters who use language to grapple with subject formation and create change."[16] In addition, students individually selected other student and published models to read from a pool that featured diverse identity groups. Students repeatedly expressed admiration for readings that contained identity conflicts similar to their personal experiences.[17] Next, students listed struggles, conflicts, and changes that connected language practices to identity issues. Students considered times when language or literacy caused them to feel like an insider or an outsider, hurt or soothed their feelings, helped them take a stand or speak up for others, negotiated peace, was silenced by others, and was most meaningful to them. Students chose one significant conflict to narrate. For instance, students wrote about passing notes in middle school to make friends with an outsider, relating as a gay adolescent to mistreated Native American characters in cowboy novel, and hearing a mother's repressed anger after she opened a letter from her judgmental parent. Even though they were doing a good job of detailing identity conflicts, I focused my attention on helping students generate more critical analysis within their narratives.

THE IMPOSTER PHENOMENON AND EMOTIONAL LABOR

While constructing identities as academics, working-class students will most likely experience conflicts related to feeling like an imposter. Feeling like an academic imposter can engage a number of contradictory behaviors based on a fear. Fearing exposure from failure can manifest in perfectionism, workaholic tendencies, saying yes to all opportunities, and being overly charming. Fearing exposure through success might lead to self-doubt, procrastination, avoiding risk, and not applying for rewards or advancement. Rather than naming these feelings the *imposter syndrome*, implying an individual illness, the preferred psychological term is the *imposter phenomenon* (*IP*). Psychologists have theorized IP in several ways. Some depict IP as intrapersonal, a discrepancy between one's public and private image.[18] Others categorize IP as interpersonal, the perception that one is different from others—since being a charlatan or sham carries no shame unless one cares what others think.[19] The institutional emphasis on retention has contributed to a recent interest in how the IP affects marginalized groups of students such as first generation, working class, racial minorities, ESL, and so on. Postmodern theory has enabled scholars to move away from the popular notion that emotions are involuntary, irrational, individual feelings to a more critical perspective that envisions emotions as part of our cultural subjectivity we are expected to perform. Owing much to performance theory, sociologist Arlie Hochschild is credited with having coined the term "emotional labor," which represents how emotions are managed in order to display those that align with corporate and organizational goals. Educational theorist Diana Zorn has contributed significantly to theorizing IP. Instead of labeling the person as *dysfunctional*, Zorn emphasizes the local contexts in which emotions are performed and perpetuated. Zorn defines emotion as enacted, embodied, and embedded in the local historical environment, characterizing emotion as a process of diffuse emergence, codetermined by both self and other, and mediated through the discourse of social formation. My belief is that the discourse of emotion colors all learning experiences so that when we learn anything, we also learn our place within the social hierarchy in relation to that knowledge. In other words, our expected emotional performance is communicated to us with every skill we learn, and those expectations are based on cultural stereotypes of identities. Thus, culture tells some to fear failure in certain skills more than others. And because language, written or spoken, is a class marker, first-generation college students develop a great apprehension about their language skills. Researcher Ann M. Penrose investigated college students' reasons for dropping out at a large state school. She found that first-generation students' self-assessment of their reading and writing abilities plummets after they arrive at college even though their performance indicates otherwise.[20]

Academic success can also be an emotional burden for working-class students. Allison Hurst studied successful working-class students and classifies them into three categories: loyalists to their roots, renegades who desire acceptance by a more elite group, and double agents who try to circulate between both groups. The emotional labor of feeling like an imposter, traitor, or outsider to both groups never completely goes away for working-class academics, and to expect students to stop feeling this way is unrealistic. Because this type of emotional labor jeopardizes the development of an academic identity for working-class students, a critical analysis of emotion and identity formation should be given attention in writing courses.

To examine identity issues, Williams proposes asking students to analyze the identities of all the characters that are and are not involved in their narratives, as well as to narrate the event from a future success identity.[21] To expand reflection, Kara Poe Alexander recommends teaching students how to include causal argument (past and present perspectives) and evaluation within their narratives.[22] My approach has been not to condemn or authorize master narratives but to engage students in a cultural historical analysis of their responses to experience. I asked students to construct layers of analysis for their chosen conflicts. My heuristic required students to situate their response to their experience within a time and space continuum, based on Ira Shor's matrix.[23] The prompts below were designed to help students reflect on their reactions at that time, in the present, and in the future as well as on influences from their location outward to other spaces and cultures. Students selected two or three of the prompts for a brief freewrite.

Create Layers of Analysis

1. Describe how you felt when this experience was happening to you. List the different thoughts and reactions going through your mind.

2. Tell how you felt immediately after the experience was over.

3. List the responses of outsiders who would disagree with your response or might misinterpret the event. Tell who they are and how and why they would disagree.

4. Explain how you view this experience differently now after you have had time to think about it and reflect on its significance to your life.

5. List three or more different responses that could have been made and how those responses would have changed things.

6. Explain who might have benefited from your reaction to this experience, either monetarily or through increased social status.

7. Determine how that specific context or location created the situation due to the habits or rules of an institution or a group.

8. Connect this experience to other regional and national events, especially US cultural preferences.

9. Name another cultural group and describe the ways their responses would have been different from your response.

10. Explain connections between this experience and your sexuality, gender, class, or wealth.

11. Explain connections between this experience and your ethnicity or race.

12. Explain connections between this experience and your choice of politics, religion, academic interests, or career.

13. Project this experience into the future and tell what advice you would give others who might face a similar conflict.

14. Explain how this experience relates to the type of person you want to be in the future.

By focusing on identity conflicts and adding a critical reflection activity to expand analysis, some students wrote essays that made connections across time. One student writes about how her escape into reading provided emotional comfort for surviving the conflicts first between her parents and later with her husband.

> Before I have time to consider or dwell on the events of the night, I sink down onto the back porch and welcome the familiar feel of cold concrete on my back and legs. I eagerly open my book to the page marked by my antique silver bookmark, a gift from my grandmother, and begin devouring the story. Soon I am no longer sitting outside my house. I am riding through the Sylvan Forest with Drizzt and Cattie-brie, who are in search of the rest of their adventuring party. Drow elves are lurking in the forest and preparing an ambush for the heroes. Everything else melts away into the background as I read on, hoping that they realize in time that they are being followed.
>
> It's twenty years later and yet here I am again, sitting outside on my porch with my book, hoping to escape the constraints and unpleasantness of my current situation. My husband and I have just had another argument, and I have retreated outside to my refuge. I have spent the last hour visiting some of my favorite characters and sharing in their adventures, giving myself time to prepare for the inevitable return to my responsibilities, with one notable difference. This time I have a lifetime of experience and wisdom to accompany me, none more notable than the knowledge that reading will always lead me back onto my true path. It led me to my decision to abandon a droll existence in computer programming and brought me instead to the pursuit of teaching of literature, writing, and language arts. I now have much more control over my life and much more faith that things will always work themselves out for the better. And in the event that things begin to spiral out of control, I know that my book will be waiting for me, ready to transport me temporarily away from my troubles and bring me back calm, collected, and determined once again.

This student ends her essay by making connections to her recent decision to take agency in her life and change careers to become a teacher. Although the student presents an optimistic future, she endured many hardships in order to reach her goal. Teachers are with students for such a brief time; we seldom know about the many struggles they face before and after they are students in our classes.

Although some did increase the amount of critical analysis in their writing, other students related their experiences with little reflection. They complained they did not know how to work reflection into their papers. So, I added an activity, which expanded upon the minilessons I was already doing about action, dialogue, sensory details, and inner thoughts. Before revising their writing, students read "Stupid Rich Bastards" by Laurel Johnson Black, marked, and discussed her use of critical reflection. The excerpt below comes from a first-generation college student whose narrative begins with a dialogue with her mother, who expresses relief that the student's boyfriend will be living with her for protection in the big city. The narrative continues by mentioning the boyfriend's potential deployment and their economic decision to marry. Two years later, the narrator makes a New Year's resolution to "read for fifteen minutes and journal at least three positive things each day." The narrator reflects on her difficulty in coming up with positive things to write about and her increased escape into reading her current novel. Upon later reflection, she realizes she wants a divorce, and a dialogue is included in which she confronts her husband. The essay concludes with a reflection about her current circumstances.

> "Divorcing" at the age of twenty years young is not easy. My mother cried more when I told her Seth was moving out than the day she did when she was moving me into that cramped apartment. Financially, I was distraught. I was the single tenant of a two bedroom house with my dog, Bentley; therefore, I was working two jobs to pay rent and bills. Although I felt alone, I reminded myself that this was not a time for mourning. It was a time to be twenty. A time to find myself.
>
> While indulging in my most current novel, my mind begins to wander. What if I had decided to run for fifteen minutes and record my calorie intake as my new year's resolution? Would I have become aware of my monotonous unhappiness? Would I have found the courage to be selfish? I cannot imagine an alternative outcome of events that followed the new year of 2015. The best years of my life did not begin when I walked into the student union of my university in the fall of 2013. The best years of my life began with the touch of a pen to a leather-bounded, wide-ruled, vacant book.[24]

When asked to write about which activities helped her compose her essay, this student cited the identity circles, the teacher's willingness to take a risk to share her own identities, reading the student essay excerpted above, and Black's essay. On the whole, I believe that increasing the use of activities and models related to critical reflection improved students' writing. It is all too easy to require critical analysis without taking class time to demonstrate what it might entail and how to work that information into a text.

SELF-EFFICACY AND SELF-CONTROL

Although feeling like an imposter is based on past cultural perceptions and can provoke much felt anxiety in the present, these fears are primarily vested upon future performance, which is probably why procrastination or self-sabotage are appealing. Self-efficacy is a form of task-specific self-projection. Experts in cognitive psychology Albert Bandura and Frank Pajares define high self-efficacy as believing in advance that one is competent to achieve a given task. These scholars make the distinction that self-efficacy is not the same as self-confidence, self-esteem, or self-concept. Bandura has established that self-efficacy directly affects a student's effort, persistence, interest, and achievement. In his review of numerous empirical studies, Pajares contends that self-efficacy is more predictive of writing performance than apprehension or other motivation variables. As with the imposter syndrome, even direct evidence of academic success can be unlikely to change entrenched negative perceptions of ability. This may explain why marginalized college students tend to attribute their success to their teachers and to blame themselves for failure.[25] High self-efficacy involves self-regulation, or the ability to exercise control over thoughts, feelings, and actions rather than reacting out of fear. Self-efficacy can be understood in terms of perception, control, and agency over emotional labor.

The previous two sections of this chapter emphasized perception by focusing on critical awareness of literacy and emotion. For increased self-efficacy, working-class students also need to cultivate a sense of control over the experience of writing. Having strategies for problem solving stress about writing can foster a feeling of control. Prior to the writing-process movement, little class time was spent on the specific tasks that are part of writing. Writing-process strategies can help students control their writing experience, but these strategies may be viewed as busy work. Students can be forced to prewrite, but that requirement does not mean they will ever choose to do so when attempting another writing assignment—even during the same course. So, I used numerous metacogntive reflection activities before, during, and after the process to get students to articulate the ways a particular strategy was or was not effective. Occasionally, students even requested more invention activities for a later assignment, but more strategies did not necessarily mean those strategies transferred to other courses. Metacognitive reflection is extremely important, but because emotion is connected to self-efficacy, what has been missing is more reflection about emotion. Students' emotional barometers should be checked frequently because composing meaningful texts can be an emotional roller coaster for writers. The goal is to emphasize that writers can problem solve this emotional distress. Contrary to the belief that writing is jinxed when talked about, I have learned that discussing my process can lead to solutions or just tolerating the stress, to knowing I will eventually work through the problem—a realization indicative of high self-efficacy. Writers don't have to complete the task stress free; they just need to know they have or can locate the resources that will help them to do so.

People like feeling in control, with some of us needing more control than others, especially for tasks we perceive as difficult for our identity groups.[26] Many diverse strategies can have both calming and focusing effects for writers. Mindfulness practices and meditation are beginning to be incorporated into writing classrooms for this purpose. If a strategy is effective for some writers, teachers should consider sharing it. Many of us have a preferred time of day, place, or beginning routine for writing. These routines, no matter how odd, can provide a sense of control. Control issues may be the reason some students hold on to the five-paragraph theme structure or other overgeneralized rules about writing. Such strategies persist because they still have an emotional use-value for the writer (and teacher). We must remember that teachers who forward these strategies have the best of intentions—to help students pass through the system. However, as Lisa Mahle-Grize questions, do we want to define success according to the business model as the only end product? We are experiencing a growing pressure on all fronts—legislators, the public, administrators, colleagues, and students—to speed up the time to a degree. We find we must do both things—give some pragmatic, easy-to-remember solutions to surface-level writing problems and engage students in learning how to critically analyze institutional and cultural constraints. For working-class students, cultural critique is not a polite parlor conversation; it is a survival skill.

In addition to critiquing general concepts like literacy, education, and success, teachers might help students to critique specific limit situations, such as difficult writing assignments and/or instructional practices of their future teachers. I am considering preparing final-exam questions that are scenarios for students to problem solve: (1) your professor assigns a paper topic on the first day of class and never mentions it again; (2) comments on your first essay read like personal attacks; (3) the teacher takes off for usage errors on timed essay exams; (4) you absolutely hate the topic given for a research paper; (5) your draft is two pages, and the paper must be twelve; (6) the teacher has explained the assignment, but you still have no idea what they want; (7) your professor does not permit the use of *I* in papers, but you want to include a relevant personal experience. A similar gambit might be for colleagues to conjecture what to do about various types of comments from editors. Both faculty and students need multiple strategies for coping with the emotional labor connected to academic writing.

The self-efficacy of working-class students is not a discrete issue and therefore must be investigated and supported on numerous fronts. Writing centers must be permanent fixtures that welcome students and provide outreach programs for teachers. Writing-across-the-curriculum programs should support faculty and students with consultation and assistance from experts in writing pedagogy. Composition faculty staffing, job permanence, and workloads must be improved if scholarship is to expand for assisting specific populations of marginalized students. In addition, the institution must provide adequate support for working-class students' economic emergencies, including food banks, transportation, counseling, and legal services. Problems of self-efficacy should be considered as cocreated by the larger institution and culture. National and state politics dictate funding, admission, placement, years to degree, and loan financing, all of which preserve the status quo. The longer I teach working-class students, the more I realize how much these social issues matter for writing pedagogy.

A HYBRID ACADEMIC IDENTITY

The previous section about self-efficacy concentrates on the perception/projection of future performance and feelings of control while engaging in the tasks of writing. This last section addresses the hope that working-class students can gain emotional agency for the construction of their own academic identities. Micalinos Zembylas, in *Teaching with Emotion*, suggests that increasing critical awareness of emotional labor can assist in resisting cultural normalization of emotion. In this way, Zembylas envisions emotional labor as potentially positive or negative depending upon how emotion is used to negotiate subjectivity. The goal isn't to eradicate, mask, or replace emotions but to imagine what can be done to change the situation so one can feel differently. Zembylas and Fender relate Foucault's description of care of the self to question institutionalized assumptions and discourses about emotion in order to govern, rework, or resignify oneself through individual agency. Therefore, emotions are intersubjective and cocreated and can be conscious, rational, and ethically answerable to our social relations with others.

All writing constructs discursive identities. When students compose narratives in which they critically examine, revise, and rewrite their responses to experiences, they are rehearsing new forms of emotional agency and subjectivity. Critical narratives about literacy can bring into question identity formation and the possibility of consciously constructing a hybrid academic identity. Mary Soliday explains the connection to agency: "When they are able to evaluate their experiences from an interpretive perspective, authors achieve narrative agency by discovering that their experience is, in fact, interpretable."[27] However, I do not believe it is possible for working-class students to simply adopt an elite academic identity—or invent a university for that matter. I am hopeful they can begin the process of creating a hybrid, alternative academic identity not based on a rejection of their other identities—which Keith Gilyard terms "cultural suicide."[28] In a study of her students' literacy autobiographies, Donna LeCourt establishes how a critique of academic discourse is essential for the creation of a hybrid identity: "For these students to begin seeing the possibility for 'speaking the hybrid subject,' they must first be able to recognize academic discourse's exclusionary practices and its role in constructing the very self/Other relations they, then, seek to undermine."[29] Wisely, LeCourt wants students to accomplish much more than learning or even critiquing academic discourse. LeCourt places her hopes on changing academic discourse itself: "As such, agency operates almost as another version of Foucault's care for self. Rather than orchestrating a need for identification *with* academic discourse, however, 'care' comes to be understood as the preservation of difference *within* academic discourse."[30] My own desire to speak difference within academic discourse became more important as my writing and education progressed. LeCourt hypothesizes that graduate students recognize this loss more acutely than basic writers.[31] As students continue their coursework at the university and pursue majors and careers, their academic identities continue to develop and change. Charles Bazerman describes how students who are new to an academic discipline go through a process of trying on, trying out, and faking academic discourse on their way to becoming discursively socialized by their discipline.[32]

Teachers must realize how emotionally charged academic identity formation is in order to provide ethical writing experiences that invite working-class students to take agency in forming a hybrid academic identity. Taking individual agency over identity formation necessitates a cultural and social understanding that does not rule out collective agency. Thus, a critical awareness of identity formation can both lead to and generate from collective agency. In an extensive treatment of writing and identity centering on academic discourse, Roz Ivani concludes that "critical awareness of relationships between writing and identity gives students a sense that there are alternatives available, that they have a degree of freedom in this respect, that their writing is part of a wider struggle between competing subject-positions within the academic community as a whole, and that by their choices they might eventually contribute in some small way to social change."[33] Working-class and/or first-generation college students frequently feel they are representing their families and communities by entering academic life. This feeling of representing a group larger than ourselves can empower the stories we tell and our desire to make changes not just for ourselves but for others as well.

When encouraging the construction of a working-class academic identity, teachers must remember that narratives express different cultural values. Skeggs has completed three major studies of British working-class life and describes how working-class members of society struggle to narrate themselves as persons of value in a culture that devalues them. Skeggs points out that the narratives that have value in the larger culture are the ones ascribed to the middle class that advance the liberal humanist values of individuality, competitiveness, self-investment, and future orientation.[34] Skeggs reports that working-class values are more relational than middle-class ones. Working-class narratives stress the importance of care, loyalty, and affection performed without utilitarian motives. Skeggs claims economic insecurity and precariousness orient working-class persons toward investing time and energy in friends and family and "keeping an eye out for others."[35] Through these relationships, working-class people develop a shared understanding of injustice and are most resentful of snobbery and pretentiousness. When I applied these working-class values to the literacy narratives my students had written, I recognized similar themes in their essays. Many of their narratives related experiences in which literacy affected their relationships with others.[36] Students wrote about many emotional responses to literacy conflicts involving loved ones, parents, family members, neighbors, friends, enemies, strangers, and so forth. The majority of working-class students were narrating language experiences that examined their relationships rather than their accomplishments. However, I do acknowledge my bias as the teacher; I share those same values since I grew up in the same working-class town where I teach. All writing does indeed display values. It behooves teachers to recognize the differences between middle- and working-class values.

When reading literacy narratives, students should discuss the values displayed in the texts as well as how those values are connected to the biases of writers. Daniel Mahala and Jody Swilky extend Linda Brodkey's central metaphor of bias from her article with the same title. Rather than characterizing writing as something to avoid, Mahala and Swilky characterize it on the bias as "the result of a long reflection on and struggle with the cultures that impose on and work through the writer."[37] Students must be granted authority over their own experiences, particularly the values they wish to valorize and analyze. Writing about personal experience opens up a space for marginalized students to inhabit in the classroom. As Deborah Mutnick insists near the end of her chapter about rethinking the personal narrative, "For working-class, African American, Latino/a, and other students whose lives have only recently been reflected in the curriculum, there is an even greater need for opportunities to explore and document their own experience, illuminate the borders between the academy and their communities, and make conscious choices about how they will position themselves in their professional and civic lives.[38]

EXPANDING THE LITERACY-NARRATIVE ASSIGNMENT

Teachers can open the literacy-narrative assignment to multiple genres, multiple perspectives, and hybrid formats. In "Freedom, Form, Function: Varieties of Academic Discourse," her CCCC chair's address, Lillian Bridwell-Bowles encourages teachers to enlarge our definition of academic discourse: "As my title suggests, I want to know how the various forms and functions of academic writing have anything to do with educating ourselves for our whole lives, and by this I mean all of our multiple identities and our multiple dreams for ourselves. To be successful, we need to teach students conventional forms and better analytical skills, but also we need to encourage them to dream, to think in new cycles and to have visions for the future that are hopeful."[39]

Bridwell-Bowles relates her own critical literacy narrative that incorporates her connections to political, historic, classed, racial, geographic, gendered, religious, literary, musical, educated, educator, scholar, and professional identities. Bridwell-Bowles's call for experimentation reminds me of two former graduate students who have taken up the literacy-narrative assignment and improved it for their students. Dani Eller has generated a series of assignments featuring the investigation of rival hypotheses to students' initial literacy narratives. Eller draws from Linda Flower's community-building theory by assigning students to seek out and interview individuals whose identities, values, and/or assumptions rival the ones in their own literacy narratives in order to better understand that person's context. Stephanie Thompson takes an ESL approach to the literacy narrative that casts students' multilingual abilities as an asset. Thompson invites her students to reflect on the role of English and their other languages in their lives, particularly the influences of those languages on their identities. Thompson's assignment is similar to ESL teacher Gloria Park's assignment that she calls a *cultural and linguistic autobiography*. Park lists a series of prompts for students that ask them to narrate experiences with family and early education, assumptions about immigration to the United States, learning English, and educational goals. Other teachers have transformed the literacy narrative into a technological autobiography and a multimodal production. Digital storytelling gives students access to their rich vernacular literacies and makes use of evolving cultural spaces and contexts for expression.[40] Teachers and students will certainly appreciate two digital resources: Cynthia Selfe's *Digital Archive of Literacy Narratives* and Ana Ribero's multilingual collection *Global Voices*. In his analysis of the remediation narrative from *Pygmalion*, Patrick Berry both demonstrates and suggests that writing should be more than simply selecting one modality and should cross genres, media, and time.

Of particular interest are teachers who have expanded the literacy narrative into a whole-course examination. James Zebroski explains that the primary content of a course should be to encourage students "to arrive at a more explicit and conscious 'theory' of writing that can guide them to understand their own writing process."[41] Zebroski provides several outlines for course themes as well as a last assignment in which students invent a metaphor for their theory of writing.[42] I particularly like how Zebroski requires students to publish their literacy narratives and then use them to critique cultural literacy practices, citing their peers as evidence. Since many of the graduate students at my university have had problems finding a way to connect the literacy narrative to the traditional assignment of the textual analysis, I have enjoyed reading about the innovative course structure detailed by Anne-Marie Hall and Christopher Minnix. Hall and Minnix's basic writing curriculum follows the literacy narrative with a rhetorical analysis and then a contextual analysis of published literacy narratives prior to a revision and analysis of the students' original narratives. A writing studies course proposed by Elizabeth Wardle and Doug Downs, which has become a popular textbook in the field, contains a plethora of assignments and alternatives, highlighting students as researchers: ethnography, activity analysis, rhetorical analysis, autoethnography, portrait, survey, discourse analysis, and definition. Another textbook with a literacy theme is *The Elements of Literacy* by Julie Lindquist and David Seitz. This textbook includes several activities in chapters about literacy's relationship to mind, culture, class, work, and technology. To help students explore how literacy is implicated in the marginalization of some groups, LeCourt privileges studying public debates about literacy prior to students' returning to their literacy autobiographies. LeCourt also recommends that a critical analysis of literacy be aimed at discourses and assignments in students' majors.[43] Nancy DeJoy describes a sequence of assignments that traces literacy from personal experience to history, culture, and discipline, culminating with a revision of the first narrative, which projects their literacy into the future.[44]

Literacy narratives have a life larger than as an assignment given by a teacher in a composition course. Numerous professionals have felt compelled to reflect on their working-class experiences with literacy, and those writers give insight into the emotional labor that comes with the pursuit of academic identities. In particular, several anthologies provide a close examination of the specific conflicts working-class academics endure.[45] My students might well wonder why someone would complete the assignment to write a literacy narrative were they not doing it for a grade. Narrative writing can offer the writer some degree of ethical integrity—to bear witness to a powerful emotional experience. As a genre, witnessing entails a narrative, spoken or written, that is important to the writer for self-preservation or self-formation. These narratives often describe struggles against cultural limitations and injustices. Witness narratives may be shared as a means to seek solidarity with others. Kelly Oliver has written extensively about witnessing and underscores the significance of witnessing for establishing subjectivity and agency: "Without an external witness, we cannot develop or sustain the internal witness necessary for the ability to interpret and represent our experience, which is necessary for subjectivity and more essentially for both individual and social transformation. And if subordination is taken to the extreme of objectification, then the possibility of address, of witnessing, is destroyed and with it the possibility of subjectivity. Only when someone listens to me can I listen to myself."[46] The potential significance of narrative writing is crucial for marginalized students who are most at risk for alienation, especially in their early coursework at the university. I agree with Howard Tinberg, who in his hopeful article about literacy narratives asserts that students may need to heal by theorizing their lives.[47] To welcome working-class students to academic writing with grammar exercises or argumentative essays about hackneyed controversial topics is to deny their life experiences and identities and by default replace them with offensive stereotypes.

For inspiration about how to revise the literacy-narrative assignment, we should look to the work of Chicana and Chicano education scholars and their use of the Latin American genre of the *testimonio*.[48] In a special issue of *Education and Equity in Education*, the editors provide an over-view of *testimonio* as involving critical reflection, affirming a source of knowledge, and empowering social change.[49] Dolores Delgado Bernal, Rebeca Burciaga, and Judith Flores Carmona stipulate that "*testimonio* transcends descriptive discourse to one that is more performative in that the narrative simultaneously engages the personal and collective aspects of identity formation while translating choices, silences, and ultimately identities."[50] Narratives that speak for both the singular and the collec-tive may be constructed by their authors because their experiences are difficult for outsiders to comprehend. The audience's lack of compre-hension may be based upon cultural difference, discomfort with power-ful emotional expressions, and/or entitlements. Designing classroom practices that make room for students' many identities means accepting another person's worldview. Entitlement prevents people from seeing, hearing, understanding, and empathizing with the cultural alienation others endure, which is why oppositional behaviors make no sense to the outsider. We fail to understand students who refuse to participate in class or prefer to take a zero on an assignment. Telling one's stories requires the perception of an audience capable of listening.

Writing assignments should leave room for writers to create ethical relationships among their identities. From what topic to write about to how to punctuate a sentence, writing is never devoid of cultural hier-archies. Puzzling through how best to foster the academic identities of working-class students is much more difficult than just giving writ-ing assignments. As I make room for working-class students to create their own ethical academic identities, am I willing to listen to platitudes that are important to them but that critical pedagogues would consider naïve? Do students have the right to espouse meritocracy, rugged indi-vidualism, upward mobility, or education as the great equalizer? As a working-class academic, have I ever made myself a hero in my own lit-eracy narrative or the rebel in my imposter narrative? I argue that in many cases, students have the right to construct themselves as successes, victims, or rebels, not simply because they have the right to be naïve or because I am a generous teacher but because sometimes these narratives have a use-value in oppressive contexts. Janet Bean makes precisely this point in her chapter about the narratives of her working-class students.

> Before we judge students' narratives of upward social mobility as evidence of a failure to think critically or simply dismiss them as bad writing, how-ever, we might consider the possibility that the very persistence of these narratives, their use by thousands and thousands of individuals, signals a more complex relationship between writer, cultures, and power than is

readily apparent. In focusing on how the master narrative supports hegemony, we may be forgetting to ask an essential and pragmatic question: how are individuals making use of narratives of meritocracy?[51]

Necessarily, platitudes about success are consciously constructed and intentionally revived in times of great stress and despair. Hope is an enabling fiction. Critical pedagogues and students alike want to believe that getting a college education will make their lives better in large and small ways. Teaching the critical literacy narrative is less important than finding ethical ways to support working-class students as they struggle to form the identities, academic and otherwise, they wish to enact in their daily lives.

Notes

1. France, "Assigning Places"; Stuckey, *Violence of Literacy*.
2. The concept of code meshing as forwarded by Vershawn Ashanti Young values students' home languages as a linguistic asset. Students must be able to incorporate their home languages in their academic writing. Encouraging the use of dialogue in narrative writing is one means for teachers to demonstrate respect for students' rich language resources.
3. Mack, "Being the Namer."
4. Fussell, *Class*.
5. Soliday, "Translating Self and Difference," 511.
6. Sarup, *Identity Culture*, 15.
7. Williams, "Heroes, Rebels, and Victims," 344.
8. Chua and Rubenfeld, *Triple Package*, 175–80.
9. Skeggs, "New Formations of Spectacular Selves."
10. Kara Poe Alexander, "Successes, Victims, and Prodigies."
11. Williams, "Heroes, Rebels, and Victims."
12. The Common Core State standards privilege argumentative writing. The standards only list three modes of writing, in this order: argumentative, informative, and narrative. Argumentative writing is repeated from grades six to twelve.
13. Garcia, "The Tyranny of Argument."
14. I prefer the term *critical memoir* (Mack, "Critical Memoir"). Teachers tend to describe assignments using the modes of writing: expository, descriptive, narrative, and argumentative. I have found that genre terms like *memoir* communicate more effectively with students and are more specific. Placing the word *critical* in front of other terms for writing may be overdone, but it does place an emphasis on academic analysis. After writing this essay, I may revise the name for this assignment to *literacy conflict memoirs* to differentiate it from a *literacy history*. However, in this chapter, I have used *literacy narrative* because it is the name commonly used for this assignment.
15. Scott, "Literacy Narrative," 110.
16. Barnett, "'Love Letters,'" 21.
17. Mutnick, "Rethinking the Personal Narrative"; Corkery, *Narrative and Personal Literacy*.
18. Leary et al., "Impostor Phenomenon."
19. Probyn, *Blush: Faces of Shame*.

20.   Penrose, "Academic Literacy Perceptions and Performance," 457.

21.   Williams, "Heroes, Rebels, and Victims," 344–45.

22.   Alexander, "Implicit Response."

23.   Shor, *Critical Teaching*, 164–66.

24.   I have used pseudonyms for student examples.

25.   Clark, "'Cooling-Out' Function."

26.   Aronson and Steele, "Stereotypes and the Fragility."

27.   Soliday, "Translating Self and Difference."

28.   Gilyard, *Voices of the Self*, 161–62.

29.   LeCourt, *Identity Matters*, 202.

30.   Ibid., 199.

31.   Ibid., 163.

32.   Marjorie Coffey advocates reading and writing literacy narratives for writing-in-the-disciplines courses to help students develop professional identities.

33.   Ivani , *Writing and Identity*, 340.

34.   Skeggs, "Imagining Personhood Differently."

35.   Ibid., 506.

36.   Very few of my students' narratives were about individual achievement or other middle-class values. This is dissimilar to Alexander, who analyzed students' literacy narratives. The heuristic activities and the models I share promote identity conflicts rather than achievement. The student examples I have included mainly describe conflict, although the conclusion projects future success.

37.   Mahala and Swilky, "Telling Stories, Speaking Personally," 366.

38.   Mutnick, "Rethinking the Personal Narrative," 91.

39.   Bridwell-Bowles, "Freedom, Form, Function," 47.

40.   Burgess, "Hearing Ordinary Voices."

41.   Zebroski, *Thinking Through Theory*, 17.

42.   Ibid., 41.

43.   LeCourt, *Identity Matters*, 207–17.

44.   DeJoy, *Process This*, 124–25.

45.   See Collins et al., *Class Lives*; Dews and Law, *This Fine Place So Far from Home*; Oldfield and Johnson, *Resilience*; Muzzatti and Samarco, *Reflections from the Wrong Side of the Tracks*; Tokarczyk and Fay, *Working-Class Women in the Academy*; Welsch, *Those Winter Sundays*.

46.   Oliver, *Witnessing: Beyond Recognition*, 88.

47.   Tinberg, "Theory as Healing," 287.

48.   Reyes and Rodriquez explain the history of the *testimonio* genre and provide a helpful bibliography. For more information about *testimonio* pedagogies, see Benmayor, "Digital 'Testimonio' as a Signature Pedagogy for Latina Studies"; Cruz, "Making Curriculum from Scratch"; Gutiérrez, "Developing a Sociocritical Literacy in the Third Space"; and Saavedra, "Language and Literacy in the Borderlands."

49.   Delgado Bernal, Burciaga, and Carmona, "Chicana/Latina 'Testimonios.'"

50.   Ibid., 364.

51.   Bean, "Manufacturing Emotions," 103.

9

WE'RE ALL MIDDLE CLASS?
Students' Interpretation of Childhood Ethnographies to Reflect on Class Difference and Identity

Liberty Kohn[1]

Lynn Bloom has argued that first-year writing functions not to address social class differences but to instill critical thinking as well as middle-class decorum, efficiency, language use, and related middle-class standards in students.[2] Linda Adler-Kassner argues the same of the college essay, for in the essay "disjuncture between students' values and the values implicit in the essay can pose a difficulty for some in the composition classroom."[3] This disjuncture can situate first-year writing as a "dumping ground for the problems of the academy and a fertile site for investigating academic and student literacies."[4]

Composition has responded to social class as disjuncture and opportunity in a variety of ways. Various approaches include analyzing the representations of the working class in popular culture,[5] writing literacy narratives that include class background,[6] critically reading ethnography,[7] sharing working-class life with classmates and participating in community writing projects,[8] using students' genealogies of family occupation and education as an entry point in connecting their past to their present,[9] and using English courses to introduce the structure of the university "to empower [students] and demystify the conditions of [working class students'] learning."[10] Simply put, the above approaches address entrance into academic or mainstream culture by considering the personal history of the student and/or the student's engagement with institutions, local communities, or media. My hope is that this chapter will add a new wrinkle to discussions of social class in the first-year writing classroom by evaluating students'—mainly, working-class students'—responses to readings on how the operations of social class during childhood can affect adult circumstances, opportunities, and cultural capital.

DOI: 10.7330/9781607326182.c009

AN ASSIGNMENT TO FOCUS ON CHILDHOOD AND SOCIAL CLASS

In fall 2012, my first-year writing classroom's reading and writing assignments included sociologist Annette Lareau's ethnographic research contrasting children's daily activities and social interactions in working-class and middle-class homes. Lareau's research outlines differences in the amount and type of language exposure in the home, entitlement to negotiate with adults, families' sense of entitlement to negotiate with institutions such as schools, and the number and type of social activities that lead to a fluid identity. Lareau's ethnography is also a highly engaging ethnography students enjoyed reading.

My interest in assigning Lareau was to shift discussion of social class toward childhood and away from university or adult life, allowing students to temporarily move away from stigmas easily attached to working-class adults. As I designed the assignment, I was aware of Steve Parks and Nick Pollard's results when attempting to have working-class students share life stories or explore local working-class geographies: Parks and Pollard, despite best intentions, found that middle-class students' response to working-class peers was silence or, at best, sympathy, but without an agentive shift or identification with the working class.[11]

With this in mind, I assigned sociologist Lareau's research on social class, which was undertaken through her own and her graduate students' thick ethnographic observation over hundreds of hours with volunteering families. The following bullet points are based upon Lareau's own summaries, which my students read, of how parenting strategies affect children and therefore affect opportunities and agency with institutions. Lareau's research indicated that

- Both "white and Black middle-class parents engaged in practices of *concerted cultivation* . . . [P]arents actively fostered and assessed their children's talents, opinions, and skills. They scheduled their children for activities. They reasoned with them. They hovered over them and outside the home they did not hesitate to intervene on the children's behalf. They made a deliberate sustained effort to stimulate children's development and to cultivate their cognitive and social skills."
- Working-class parents "viewed children's development as unfolding spontaneously, as long as they were provided with comfort, food, shelter, and other basic support."
- "As a result [working-class] children had more autonomy regarding leisure time and more opportunities for child-initiated play. They also were more responsible for their lives outside the home. Unlike in middle-class families, adult-organized activities were uncommon."
- "Instead of the relentless focus on reasoning and negotiation that took place in middle-class families, there was less speech . . . in working-class

and poor homes. Boundaries between adults and children were clearly marked; parents generally used language not as an aim in itself but more as a conduit for social life. Directives were common."

- "In their institutional encounters, working-class parents . . . turned over responsibility to professionals; when parents did try to intervene, they felt that they were less capable and less efficacious than they would have liked."[12]

Early in her book, Lareau outlines the importance of the above differences, arguing that these differences lead to what Lareau terms a "transmission of differential advantages" wherein middle-class children have "development of greater verbal agility, larger vocabularies, more comfort with authority figures, and more familiarity with abstract concepts. Also important, children developed skill differences in interacting with authority figures in institutions and at home."[13]

Irv Peckham translates Lareau's findings into the potential effects of social class in the composition classroom, suggesting that for middle-class children, language is play, including double entendre and irony, giving them an advantage in exposure to rhetorical forms, multiple perspectives, and statements as arguable, not infallible. Peckham also suggests that desirable literacy strategies such as reading against the grain would be, for working-class students, "talking back," or negotiating with authority, which is uncommon to working-class culture but desired by the university.[14]

METHODOLOGY: USING LAREAU TO EVALUATE WORKING-CLASS ADULT LIFE

In fall 2012, at Winona State University, my first writing assignment began with students reading one working-class and one middle-class ethnography as well as Lareau's summary of her findings. Lareau's ethnographies were followed by an essay examining the restrictive Taylorist managerial strategies of current service-sector jobs.[15] A final reading was a chapter of Deborah Brandt's *Literacy and Learning*, an ethnography on the professional, middle-class workplace highlighting autonomy, on-the-job learning, expert conceptual knowledge, and the importance of writing and communication in the information age.[16] The latter essays represent aspects of service-sector, adult working-class and middle-class occupations, respectively.

I asked students to seek overlap in the three essays, and to evaluate how class-based behaviors encouraged or discouraged during childhood linked to the literacies and subject positions of service-sector and professional-sector employment. This in-class compare and contrast activity became the basis of their first formal writing assignment, but students were to conclude the paper with a connected two-page reflection on how the criteria they chose to compare and contrast the three essays corresponded with their own childhood, adulthood, and personal perspectives on social class.

I gave the aforementioned assignment to two sections of first-year writing. I asked all students to retain copies of rough drafts prepared for workshop and turn them in at semester's end for my study. Thirty students did include the rough drafts in their final portfolio, and these thirty students became my study sample. I chose rough drafts, not revised drafts, because my feedback pushed students toward a higher level of engagement with the material that would have altered my interests in a "raw" capturing of initial perspectives on social class.

To be coded for this study, a paper needed to contain a claim with elaboration through such evidence as personal experience, anecdote, hypothetical scenario, or incorporation of or response to a claim from a course reading. I did not count the number of appearances of a claim but only the number of papers that contained such a claim. Recording the number of instances of a particular claim was not a goal; rather, I was interested in what positions students were adopting and how they were framing their own class backgrounds. Students often offered contradictory explanations of social class in a single paper, in which case I tallied both the initial claim and the countering, modified, or hedging claim.

RESULTS

The results of my study will be exemplified and unpacked through best-case representation for the remainder of the chapter. Due to space constraints, I will discuss students' reflections on childhood but not how students used their teenage work experience to frame their class backgrounds and conceptualize class operations in the United States.

I. Response to Childhood Ethnography

1. Acknowledged and elaborated on how the differing cultures of social class in childhood affect people's adult opportunities 30/30

2. Argued for bootstraps/meritocracy to overcome childhood working class circumstances 13/30

3. Self-identified as working class 4/30

4. Provided evidence of a mixture of working-class and middle-class identity in their autobiography 13/30

The results show I achieved one major goal: after reading Lareau, all students acknowledged the importance of childhood circumstances to adult opportunity; each student elaborated on the effects of social class to help or hinder one's path through educational institutions or a career. However, thirteen of the thirty students modified their acknowledgment of the power of circumstance through inclusion of a bootstraps narrative or meritocratic reasoning.

Only four students identified their childhood with the working-class parenting strategies defined by Lareau. The high degree of students' identifying as middle class is surprising, as my Midwestern, Division II, nonurban public university hovers predictably around 48 percent first-generation students (neither parent earned a four-year degree). That is, despite the odds that approximately fifteen of my thirty students would be working-class students, only four saw themselves as working class after reading Lareau. However, this discrepancy is not, in some ways, surprising. Even amidst the post-2009 economic woes, a majority of Americans with college degrees view themselves as middle class, and nearly half of those without college degrees view themselves as middle class, despite evidence to the contrary and the fact that the social class with the largest gains between 2002 and 2012 is comprised of the classes below middle class.[17]

Reading these results in relation to working-class studies, if one were to read students' narratives only as students' self-deluded belief in their own middle-class status, one would misread these narratives. Based upon my students' writing, working-class student identities may be more blurred, mixed, or fluid than research on a "static" working-class identity suggests,[18] at least when students are entering the university. Working-class students appear to construct a childhood and college identity with greater fluidity than their working-class background suggests, perhaps because students create a fluid proacademic identity to help them "fake it until they make it."

Thus, I agree with Nancy Mack's suggestion that definitions differentiating the middle class and working class, such as "competitive individualism" versus "connection, community, and place," or "becoming versus belonging,"[19] can be "problematic since they assume a fixed identity and will not help students deal with rapid change."[20] My student narratives, when read as students imagining or constructing a university identity, clearly challenge a clean delineation of working-class and middle-class home life. My students' writing in this chapter illustrates elements of Lareau's class differences but also of the construction of fluid student identities in what should be, according to research, a less fluid, working-class student population.

UNPACKING STUDENT VIEWS ON CIRCUMSTANCE, BOOTSTRAPS, AND SOCIAL CHANGE

"The bootstraps myth runs very deep in our culture,"[21] as does the belief in a classless society,[22] yet these beliefs collide with the very real challenges working-class students experience negotiating the four-year university for a variety of economic, academic, and institutional reasons.[23] This belief in bootstraps and meritocracy shapes our beliefs about work, education, and social change. Patrick Finn argues that "meritocracy demands no concessions from the free-market economy. There would be the same rules and the same roles, only different people might fill the roles. Meritocracy does not challenge social class; it simply gives affluent classes cover. They can blame the poor and working class for their apparent failure and congratulate themselves for their victory in a 'fair contest.'"[24] Finn's evaluation of the problem of meritocracy interested me deeply. I wondered if students' reading about the importance of one's social class in childhood might lead them toward a critique of meritocracy similar to that of Finn, in which an unfair playing field is cloaked by the idea of a meritocratic fair contest.

One example of student writing that acknowledges circumstance, then modifies the power of circumstance with a bootstraps argument, comes from the only student who stated that her own working-class childhood places her at risk in college academics. SB states that

> I agree with the fact that social class does have a lot to do with a child's development. Whether or not a child's parent is around to help guide them can have a huge impact on their personal development . . . . Parents can't rely just on school to teach kids . . . . As a child, my parents were always working and my brother and I were left home a lot so we were independent early on. My parents never made me work on my homework or helped me with it, if I saw my parents it was usually late at night or on the weekends. My mom and dad never read to me as a child and I fell like this affected me immensely today because I know my language use isn't as advanced as it should be and my student habits are horrible. Then again, I can't blame all this on my parents, and neither can Lareau. When children grow up a lot of this responsibility falls on them, like at my age I should now be teaching myself better study habits. Because of where I grew up, I do feel that I was able to get a job right away in high school and that my personal development throughout my childhood helped me to get that job opportunity.

SB was the only student to outwardly state she was working class, a product of natural-growth parenting strategies, and struggling with college because of these factors. Although SB initially recognizes herself as at risk as an adult in college, she veers away from critique of socioeconomic circumstances; instead, she moves toward a meritocratic rationale for her childhood turned adulthood: personal responsibility. This approach makes it possible for her to avoid blaming her parents, a very human reaction. SB understands that her family's economic situation created the natural growth of her childhood—her parents were only home late at night and on weekends—and in this she recognizes the power of socioeconomics upon her family circumstance, yet she doesn't critique socioeconomic phenomena such as her parents' working late hours. Her avoidance of socioeconomic critique implies that any critique of her childhood would tend toward critiquing her parents' childrearing strategies, not the free-market labor conditions that kept her parents away too often.

SB offers an important lesson for those using the classroom as a location for working toward social change: students may see themselves or family members as primarily responsible for circumstance. On the cusp of viewing her parents' long hours of work as a problematic working-class condition, SB instead shifts to bootstraps and meritocratic reasoning. I'd like to imagine that a working-class student would blame a system that keeps parents away when they don't wish to be away (i.e., Finn's unfair contest), but no student in my study offered an elaborate critique of this sort.

Similar to the example of SB, each of the other twelve students who included a bootstraps statement suggested themes of responsibility or choice to override an initial explanation of circumstance as connected to opportunities. SB doesn't necessarily "blend" social construction and choice. She clearly sees childhood circumstance as connected to her adulthood, but her adulthood is where circumstance and social construction suddenly lose their power and responsibility and personal initiative become the major determinants in success.

I'd like to provide a second perspective that acknowledges middle-class culture and that the student claims as his own while he simultaneously denies the working-class cultural operations identified by Lareau. SN writes,

> I believe that language use in early life shapes our view on the world as we grow older. Lareau believes that the child rearing strategy of concerted cultivation instills "a robust sense of entitlement." The child believes that, because of the open discussion and comfort with superiors, institutional settings should help to tailor their specific needs. I found this to be very true. I grew up in a family who believed that multiple activities, open discussion, with a set of parents who wanted me to not

be "excluded from any opportunity that might eventually contribute to their advancement." I believe that, regardless of the socioeconomic factors, it is up to the parents to let on to their children the traits to be successful later on in life. Lareau argues that these economic factors are what makes and perpetuates societies varying personalities. Poor and working-class parents teach their children to grow on their own while the middle class try to give their children every opportunity to reach their full potential. I believe this is a matter or readily available resources and how much energy the parent wants to give their child to help them. The financial factors are only a small part, it is truly the parents decision if they want to seek out activities for their child to grow or to allow them to roam free.

We see a strong use of Lareau to frame SN's own childhood, and SN quotes Lareau to explain his own family dynamic. Although he acknowledges the effect of available resources, he denies one major factor in working-class households—money—and replaces it with competing logics based in parents' lack "energy" spent on their child. Language, another major factor that determines educational success, also disappears. Also, economic circumstances and working-class parenting strategies are not applied by SN to explain people's limited opportunities. In fact, the socially constructed phenomena of natural growth and concerted cultivation become parents' *choice* by the final sentence.

Reading SN's contrary views this way, one sees that Lareau's research, despite being influential on my students' attribution of unequal childhoods, contains socially constructed parenting strategies that students often interpret as parental *choice*, which is deeply reminiscent of bootstraps and meritocratic logic. Of the thirteen students who both acknowledged and denied the effect of parenting strategies on individuals' success, all except SB included some type of statement in which their childhood's concerted cultivation and/or educational success was attributed to either their own or their parents' choice, not cultural phenomena knowingly or unknowingly occurring in middle-class homes.

Several implications can be drawn from this set of thirteen papers. First, students acknowledge the importance of childhood circumstance on later life success, access, and mobility, but *choice* is a tempting and available logic, particularly when discussing adult life. Second, in terms of teaching sociological research to persuade students that circumstances matter, any attempt to move beyond the competing narrative logic of choice/bootstraps/meritocracy should involve an explicit exploration of social construction in both working-class and middle-class culture as well, as a class discussion on the injustice of applying social construction to support one's views but denying its effects when convenient.

STUDENTS (MIS)READ SOCIOLOGY: SOCIAL
CONSTRUCTION AS OPINION AND STEREOTYPE

Because teaching working-class culture in a way that promotes social change entails understanding how students interpret readings on social class, I'd like to highlight several student misunderstandings. I'll begin with the basic misunderstanding from previous examples: that parents have or are aware of natural growth, and natural growth is a *choice*, not a socially constructed, naturally occurring phenomena.

In the following response, KK demonstrates a different problem with teaching sociological readings on class difference. KK states,

> I grew up in a middle-class home, but the atmosphere was very laid back, as in most working-class households described in *Concerted Cultivation*. . . . When I read *Concerted Cultivation*, I was slightly offended because from what I understand, her basic point was that middle-class children grow up to be more successful than working-class children based upon the way they were raised. From this perspective it is easy to see that Lareau is drawing solely from her opinions and lacks any sort of statistic to back up her claims.

KK challenges Lareau on the grounds that her viewpoint is subjective and improper and her evidence nonstatistical, which is noble in intent and reasoning for a first-year writing student. However, we see that students may read social theory and ethnography as nothing more than an individual's story or unsupported "opinion" as opposed to expert insight into and interpretation of hard-to-define cultural activities. KK was not the only student to contest Lareau's findings as biased.

We also see in KK mild resistance to the class-based typification of childhood, a not-uncommon theme among my students. KK's is a unique case in which a self-identified middle-class student claims some of the qualities of natural growth. KK's outrage is at the proposition that middle-class children—perhaps she herself—benefit from invisible privilege. We see parallels to the type of denial common in white-privilege discussions. KK seems to be "slightly offended" by the implication of invisible middle-class privilege. KK borrows a line of reasoning from white privilege in which oppression is agreed upon but anger arises from the idea that the invisible "may privilege me."[25] KK is likely offended because recognition of middle-class privilege in her success erodes an unflagging rationale of her hard work and meritocratic advance.

In a final example of disagreement with Lareau, we see another self-identified working-class student arguing—much like SB—that parents shouldn't be blamed for essentially lazy children. HM writes,

While each of these authors have their own opinion, I have one too. . . . On some level, I am agreeing with Lareau. I too believe that in order to attain a wider vocabulary we need to be able to feel comfortable talking with adults. . . . I think its important for a child to feel like they have entitlement to do so, especially as they grow up. I do however disagree with her comment about concerted cultivation being an "essential aspect of good parenting." I grew up in a working-class family and although my mom didn't encourage me to be involved at school I made my own life choices to get involved. I don't think all the blame should be going to the parents. I believe it is the willingness of the child. . . . Sure parents play a key role in motivating us but I truly believe a kid can step out of their social class and become something more than just a stereotype.

Previously identified themes, such as acknowledging children's circumstances while simultaneously working toward a bootstraps logic, appear here. We also see another self-identified working-class student absolving parents from blame. Like SB, HM could have acknowledged the socioeconomics of working-class home life, which might have led HM to a critique of how socioeconomic structures inhibit parents' agency. Instead, HM illustrates a lack of critical commentary on working-class parents' socioeconomic situation and its relationship to parenting. One explanation for HM's targeting (or even blaming) children, not adults or socioeconomics, seems to be an absence of socioeconomic critique by students—students seem to discuss people, not structures, systems, and activities. A second explanation for working-class students' avoidance of parental blame may be, as Lareau's research implies, that working-class children are raised in an authoritative relationship with parents and wish to retain or defend this relationship in which the parent is the ultimate authority, even if presented with information suggesting that, in comparison with middle-class parents, their working-class parents have parented "wrong." It is best for working-class students to blame themselves, the children, to exonerate the authority, the working-class parent.

Most interesting is the final line; instead of outlining the process through which working-class children may be locked out of opportunities, HM interprets Lareau's social theory as delivering a stereotype. Like middle-class KK, HM resists the typification of childhood validated through sociological research. HM was one of just two students to claim that even children should be able to overcome circumstances. Most students (eleven of thirteen) argued that only adults should be able to overcome circumstances. It is interesting that the only two students to argue that children should be able to escape circumstances while still children were two of the four self-identified working-class students (SB and HM). (The other two self-identified working-class students did not address this topic.) This application of bootstraps logic to childhood suggests the deep rootedness of the bootstraps narrative for working-class culture, deep enough that both SB and HM use it to explain even young children's behavior and outcomes.

Also of note, we see a middle-class student, KK, resisting Lareau's middle-class typification of childhood because it implies middle-class privilege, and, conversely, we see a working-class student resisting Lareau's typification of working-class childhood because the student may not wish to be a "stereotype," yet both students use the same rationale for denying class typification—individualism—once again suggesting the rootedness of bootstraps rationale in all classes as an explanation for many outcomes.

SEARCHING FOR AND FINDING WHAT MAKES YOU MIDDLE CLASS

The next topic I'd like to address is students' own framing of their social class. When offering brief narratives and analyses of their own childhoods, nearly all students framed their childhoods through two behaviors of concerted cultivation: extracurricular activities and a language use in the home. Of the four self-identified working-class students, only SB does not reconstitute her childhood as habits of concerted cultivation. SB connects her childhood to the parenting strategy of natural growth.

> My parents never made me work on my homework or helped me with it, if I saw my parents it was usually late at night or on the weekends. My mom and dad never read to me as a child and I fell like this affected me immensely today because I know my language use isn't as advanced as it should be and my student habits are horrible.

Unlike SB, HM sees a large number of extracurricular activities, which is associated with concerted cultivation, as a dominant influence in her childhood. Moreover, she, not her mother, is responsible for these middle-class practices.

> I grew up in a working-class family and although my mom didn't encourage me to be involved at school I made my own life choices to get involved.

While HM claims social involvement as her evidence for a middle-class childhood, PD sees his use of language—another major difference between working-class and middle-class childhood—as equivalent to that of a middle-class childhood. PD was, indeed, a strong writer. We see in his response some acknowledgment of the lack of language use in his family but also a rationale that individuals are responsible for language differences and growth.

> Growing up in a not poor but not very well off family, I like to believe that
> I have still gained the knowledge to be able to use language in a way just
> as well as kids who grew up better off financially. In the case that language
> depends on your social class is only true when dealing with and compar-
> ing the two extremes of the spectrum. The individual's use of language is
> different from person to person.

PD's claim about language, while arguably valid, does contradict
research from Lareau and Heath about the similarity of language across
social class and family life. Interestingly, most students turned to extracurricular activities when framing their childhood within the parameters of concerted cultivation. PD, however, turns to language, his strong
suit, to frame his childhood as equivalent to a middle-class childhood.

HH, the fourth self-identified working-class student, similarly situates her childhood as one with extracurricular activities. Although she
doesn't comment on language in her home during childhood, she does
acknowledge that language will shape her future. HH writes,

> I would consider my family more working-class than anything, but I feel
> very blessed everything I ever had. I got a Catholic education, got to always
> be a part of sports teams, and always had a roof over my head, and food
> in my stomach. . . . I've always been interested in writing, so in Brandt's
> article, I was really interested in the different setback throughout the
> different paths taken. I feel as though by being able to express yourself
> through writing, there can be no limits, and with restrictions, you will be
> able to develop your own work, into something bigger, and better.

Like her self-identified working-class classmates, HH incorporates the
easiest aspect of concerted cultivation that one may read into one's
childhood—extracurricular activities—into her statement. She then
acknowledges the importance of language but references her future
professional language use and avoids discussing language use in her own
home during her childhood, leaving this latter aspect of working-class
homes untouched in her reflection.

What we do not see in any of these four working-class students' statements are the other elements of concerted cultivation—children negotiating directly with authority, parents negotiating with school faculty
or administration, or parents directly coaching interactions with adults.
To be fair, none of the thirty students offered direct stories on parental
intervention with regard to educational or other institutions. However,
SB and HM were the only two students of the thirty to openly state that
their parents did not intervene, negotiate, or participate in their K–12
experience. In terms of the study, this finding means no students offered
evidence of parental intervention, but two of the four self-identified
working-class students did comment on the *lack* of parental intervention

without any prompting by the assignment description. While this finding must be taken lightly because of the small sample size of only four students, the finding does demonstrate students' awareness of a lack of intervention that correlates with the information these students received from reading Lareau, even if neither SB or HM uses this and other elements of Lareau's study to frame their working-class background as a powerful circumstance that will continue to affect them in adulthood.

WHEN WORKING-CLASS STUDENTS AREN'T WORKING CLASS

Only four of twenty-six students announced themselves as working-class students, despite the facts that my university is approximately 50 percent first-generation students and that 28 of the 30 students had held service-sector, minimum-wage jobs. The numbers don't add up, and many students who were clearly in the working class (which I could see from enrollment percentage and as I learned more about them) did not see themselves as in the working class. These students typically referenced the same two aspects of middle-class childhood to support claims of a middle-class childhood. They constructed a childhood that included a fondness for reading and talking with parents, which they equated with concerted cultivation, or cited participation in sports or extracurricular activities during their K–12 years that equated with Lareau's negotiation with authority. What follows are two first-generation, working-class students who didn't claim working-class status.

PA, whom I identified as a working-class student based upon the family history I learned from him over the semester, offers a great example of how most students saw concerted cultivation as the dominant parenting method in their family. PA writes,

> I was born in Bosnia and if my parents stayed there during the war my chances of going through natural growth would have been high because of the lack of organized activities in Bosnia compare to the United States. I would of ended up like the working-class children and spent my leisure time playing with other children outside. Moving to the United States gave me an opportunity to experience concerted cultivation. Growing up my parents encouraged me to read books. . . . The activities that my parents enrolled me in were basketball and soccer. I am glad that I was raised in the middle class because it has put my language at an advantage and developed me into a college student .

The most interesting aspect of PA is that in contrasting his potential Bosnian childhood with his US childhood, US K–12 education and its routine extracurricular activities automatically become middle-class

concerted cultivation. Like many students, PA references parents' encour-
agement in terms of books and extracurricular activities as automatic
signs of a middle-class childhood.

WK, whom I knew to be a first-generation student from a small rural
town, and who told me toward semester's end that she was leaving college to enroll in cosmetology school back home with her best friend,
demonstrates the power the discourse of parent-child love has to cancel
out information on class difference and analysis of one's home life, even
if the purpose of such analysis may help one reconcile family history and
potential risks when entering and negotiating the university.

> I believe what most impacts you is how you were brought up, not neces-
> sarily how many activities you were in, although that would be a plus, but
> how good of a loving relationship you have with your family members and
> friends. . . . Those brought up in a loving environment are also going to
> achieve higher grades in school, because their parents care about them
> enough to sit down and help them through a difficult math problem or
> help them with that weeks spelling test.

WK largely discounts one of Lareau's staples of concerted cultivation,
the influence of highly structured social engagement in multiple networks. If students previously used choice to disavow social construction
and the effects of social class, WK uses love as disavowal here, perhaps to
protect herself and her home life when analysis of her home life threatens to reveal literacies and attitudes different than those desired by the
university or middle-class life.

Naturally, it is hard to know what exactly happened in each students'
childhood home, and the dividing line between concerted cultivation
and natural growth may be mixed in many homes or at least situational,
not systematic. Equally true is that autobiographical reflection in the
form of a literacy narrative has the potential to distort people's reflection in terms of what they wish had happened—to remember the positive, to employ their lives toward their ultimate goal of graduating from
college, or to shift away from troubling critiques of their lives. Eileen
Ferretti's analysis of working-class mothers' identification with working-
class life is similar to my own students'. The working-class mothers in
Ferretti's study agreed with an essay on the effect of gender stereotypes
on women's educational opportunities, but the women "exempted
themselves from the group of women" the article discussed,[26] much as
my students often didn't recognize themselves in Lareau's rich ethnography. On a discourse level, Donna Dunbar-Odom suggests that literacy
narratives often use the metaphor of literacy as "passport,"[27] and in my
students' narratives, we see a number of forms of passport—middle-class

language, extracurricular involvement, and children using their own bootstraps—to create narratives perhaps not so much analyzing their childhood as creating a discourse to create an identity that points to a successful academic and professional future.

BLURRING THE LINE BETWEEN THE WORKING CLASS AND MIDDLE CLASS

If we choose to believe, not doubt, students' discussion of their childhood as representative of their home and social class, we then see an equal mix of working-class and middle-class strategies in depictions of childhood. For instance, HM depicts her mother's practicing natural growth, but HM claims she practiced concerted cultivation on her own as a child; KK, who was "slightly offended" by Lareau's findings, claims to be from a middle-class family that practices a laid-back parenting approach with lots of free time, not structure. PA, who emigrated from Bosnia, is a first-generation student and immigrant who produces evidence for himself as the product of a middle-class US home, despite the challenges his parents would have had adopting middle-class concerted cultivation strategies so quickly upon arriving in the United States. In all, thirteen students offered narratives that, in light of my working knowledge of their personal histories and/or their own autobiographical statements, resulted in their mixing a working-class and middle-class existence. The remaining seventeen students focused on their teenage and college employment, not their childhood, when reflecting on their own social class, or I simply did not know enough about them to see a clash in their narrative construction of self as middle class. Still, many students appearing here whose background I did know, working-class students such as HM, PD, HH, and PA, even middle-class KK, all write narratives blurring social class affiliation.

CLOSING

Although these students' writing suggests a number of insights I've outlined, I'd like to close with several large conclusions. First, by reading and responding to ethnography on class differences in childhood, students did acknowledge and elaborate upon social class's ability to remain a hindrance in childhood and adult life. This acknowledgment provides a pedagogical direction to Parks and Pollards' dilemma of getting students to move beyond sympathy for working-class adults and toward acknowledgment of class differences, particularly recognition of class differences' ability to provide or remove obstacles in an individual's educational advancement or social change. However, a number of students offered bootstraps narratives, which shows reading childhood ethnography alone will not undo popular meritocratic assumptions. Reading and writing on social class's influence from childhood to adulthood is a beneficial pedagogical tool, one that situates social class as the norm and bootstraps as the counterargument, not bootstraps as the primary logic and model of cultural or democratic operations.

A second conclusion is that students often create personal histories that are passports toward academic success, further blurring the lines between working-class and middle-class identities. If an instructor's goal in using readings on working-class childhood is to help students potentially identify themselves as at risk, that goal may not be easily attained. Students appear resistant to labeling themselves as working class or, even if no label is required, students do not perceive themselves as participating in the complete set of behaviors defined by Lareau as working-class *natural growth*. Most students imagine they are primed for college success, even when presented with reading assignments that suggest obtaining a college degree will be for them a road of many unknown challenges.

However, if we read social class autobiography as not a biased or slightly fictitious passport and identity constructed toward academic success but as an authentic representation of social class in childhood and the home, many students' lives are a mixture of the behaviors dichotomized by Lareau as *concerted cultivation* and *natural growth*. Consequently, my student data simply reiterates the fuzzy lines separating social classes. However, this fuzzy line can also contribute a space where people can productively see themselves in relationship to both the working class and middle class as opposed to thinking in terms of a dichotomy that may seal off identification with one or the other. If we can learn something from my students, it is that many Americans are a little bit working class and a little bit middle class. This includes many of my first-year composition students, and this includes myself, a working-class, first-generation college student who finally finished a degree at the age of thirty, receiving both bold family support and much accidental discouragement at times from my late teens through my midthirties—high school through grad school. Perhaps we must recognize that many people, through a powerful, oftentimes conflicting mix of personal history, hope, and imagination, are a little bit working class and a little bit middle class. In helping people recognize this powerful mixture of their own lives and so many others' lives, we could avoid forcing people to choose a side (likely the middle class). Perhaps acknowledging that many people, perhaps including oneself, are a little bit working class and a little bit middle class will suggest some identification with working-class life, and class inequality and social change will become ideas and ideals owned by many.

Notes

1. *For Mom and Dad, who helped me find everything I needed.*
2. Bloom, "Freshman English," 658–71.
3. Adler-Kassner, "Shape of the Form," 92.
4. Ibid., 88.
5. Beech, "Redneck and Hillbilly Discourse."
6. Dunbar-Odom, *Defying the Odds.*
7. Seitz, *Who Can Afford?*
8. Parks and Pollard, "Emergent Strategies."
9. Heathcott, "What Kinds of Tools?"
10. Renny, "New Working-Class Studies," 218.
11. Parks and Pollard, "Emergent Strategies," 481–83.
12. Ibid., 236, 238–39.
13. Ibid., 5.
14. Peckham, *Going North Thinking West*, 79.
15. Scharf, "Scripted Talk."
16. Brandt, *Literacy and Learning.*
17. Dugan, "Americans Most Likely."
18. Lareau, *Unequal Childhoods*, 238–39; Heath, *Words at Work and Play*, 9–11; Bernstein, *Class, Codes, and Control*, 10.
19. Mack, "Being the Namer," 337.
20. Ibid., 337.
21. Powell, *Retention and Resistance*, 86.
22. Aronowitz, *How Class Works*, 17–18.
23. Sternglass, *Time to Know Them*, 203.
24. Finn, *Literacy with an Attitude*, 167.
25. Ratcliffe, *Rhetorical Listening*, 7.
26. Ferretti, "Between Dirty Dishes," 81.
27. Dunbar-Odom, *Defying the Odds*, 31.

10

PEDAGOGIES OF INTERDEPENDENCE
Revising the Alienation Narrative for Cultural Match

Holly Middleton

In 2007 I moved to northern New Mexico to teach at New Mexico Highlands University (NMHU), an open-admissions federally designated Hispanic-serving institution. At the time, an anti-DUI public service campaign (PSA) was underway appealing to the cultural values of young Hispanic men. In this series, the effects of DUI are dramatized as a threat to families—not to those of the victims of drunk driving but to the families of those who drink and drive. The one I want to single out is called "Mi Mijito." It opens on a young Hispanic man leaving the house for a night out as his *abuela*, or "grandmother," reminds him to be careful. He tells her he loves her and kisses her goodnight, and then we see him leave the bar, drive away, and get pulled over by the police. A jail door then slams behind him. While this is happening, his grandmother is praying the rosary and looking at his old pictures, telling us in the voiceover: "Mi mijito, he's a good man. But sometimes he just makes bad decisions. I tell mijito 'cuidado,' be careful, you might hurt someone. He doesn't listen." When the young man calls his grandmother from jail and implores her to bail him out, the grandfather takes the phone from her hand and says, "Leave him in jail." The PSA ends with a split screen of the young man in jail and the grandmother at home, each with their backs up against a different wall. Despite her repeated warnings and their obvious love for each other, the young man's actions have driven the beacon of love and sympathy in Hispanic families, his own grandmother, to abandon him. Not only that, but the pain of serving time in jail is peripheral to the pain he is inflicting on his grandmother for being there. This message is clear: Hispanic men who love their grandmothers don't drink and drive.

I begin here because PSAs draw on their audience's cultural identities to shape behavior, and this one provides a snapshot of how the state

DOI: 10.7330/9781607326182.c010

of New Mexico understands its target audience's relation to family. As extended familial relations are typical not only for the self-identified Hispanic population of New Mexico but also for many of Latin American descent, the dynamic between the young man and his grandmother may also be familiar to teachers of Latin@ students. In New Mexico, my students' grandparents were as central to their lives as their parents. It is important to note that this network—cousins, aunts and uncles, godmothers and godfathers—of a Hispanic or Latin@ student's extended family often provides the kind of social and economic support that for other populations would constitute a public or privately delivered service. Yet to non-Latin@ instructors, this network can also seem disruptive if absences begin to accumulate and capable, apparently ambitious students stop showing up after midterm simply due to—what may seem to the instructor—a minor family obligation. In this way the interdependence and familial obligation that characterizes many Latin@ students' lives can conflict with the university's norm of independent achievement. Teachers working with students at the nexus of Latin@ ethnicity and low socioeconomic status (SES) must strategize pedagogies that deal productively with this tension.

In this chapter of *Class in the Composition Classroom,* I join a conversation among scholars addressing what Donna LeCourt calls the "alienation narrative," the well-known tension between working-class background and the middle-class expectations of the university that can arise for working-class students. I want to specifically join the call to change the institution to fit students rather than focus on assimilating the student into the institution. But how do we enact or imagine this daunting task? I propose one way is to develop pedagogies of interdependence designed to harness the generative potential of this tension. In a course and pedagogy I called Writing as Advocacy, students adopted the subject role of advocate and were asked to read, write, and act on another's behalf. In this way the classroom became a community that privileged and enacted interdependence rather than independent achievement.[1]

For this particular student population, ethnic identity intersects with working-class status. According to 2008 data, at that time, 51 percent of NMHU undergraduates were from families with incomes below $45,000, and 18 percent came from families with incomes below the federal poverty level.[2] Fifty percent of our 2008 first-time freshmen were first-generation college students, so it is important to consider how our students' ethnic identities intersect with class. Yet these numbers on household income and first-generation percentages do not capture what "class" means at NMHU—or anywhere else, for that matter.

In their work defining class in the introduction to this volume, Thelin and Carter draw on Michael Zweig, who urges us to look not at household income or the jobs we hold, but the roles we play:

> Class is not a box we "fit" into, or not, depending on our own personal attributes. Classes are not isolated and self-contained. What class we are in depends upon the role we play, as it relates to what others do, in the complicated process in which goods and services are made. These roles carry with them different degrees of income and status, but their most fundamental feature is the different degrees of power each has.[3]

Thelin and Carter conclude from Zweig that "autonomy, then—the level of our ability to control aspects of our lives, especially those involved with work—is a large determinant of our class standing."[4] Zweig locates the "role we play, as it relates to what others do" distinctly in the realm of "goods and services," but I would add that one's autonomy at work is affected by the roles one plays outside of it. A man who can depend on his cousin next door to care for his children is less subject to his conditions at work than a man whose only option is an expensive daycare. A woman whose mechanic father will keep her car dependably running— and take her to work until it is fixed—experiences more autonomy than a woman who, without that kind of support, looks for work closer to home or skips meals to pay for a new transmission.

Note also the distinction between *independence* and *autonomy*: while both are synonymous with *self-governing*, Merriam-Webster's definition of *independence* includes "freedom from outside control or support" within its purview, making receiving "support" the action of a dependent.[5] The routine cultural denigration of dependence belies the ways the interdependence of a kinship network can increase autonomy for its members. As student loan debts climb and economic safety nets shrink for working-class (and middle-class) students, sustained commitment to individual academic achievement can be seen as a kind of naive refusal to reckon the short- and long-term value of a kinship network as safety net. Independence, an American cultural ideal and university norm, locates itself outside that network (or above it) and constitutes a rejection of that network that paradoxically erodes autonomy for working-class students. If we return to consider Latin@ working-class students' reliance on family alongside the lack of economic safety net often noted for working-class populations, we must acknowledge that a safety net woven by interdependence on others is—and here I do not mean to privilege the concept, only acknowledge it—a quite rational expansion of one's autonomy. We have a lot to learn from these values that conflict with academic achievement.

Promising new research suggests that a university's shift from independent to interdependent norms can narrow the achievement gap between first-generation and continuing-generation students. In the multi-institutional study "Unseen Disadvantage," researchers found that when university cultures emphasized independence over interdependence, first-generation students experienced a "cultural mismatch" that predicted poor academic performance for the first two years of college. Stephens et al. note that all college students recognize independence as a shared US cultural ideal. However, only for continuing-generation students is it an ideal that matches their prior experiences in their families and communities. These students experience a university's message of independence "as relatively normative and as a seamless extension of their prior experience."[6] While first-generation students, on the other hand, recognize independence as a US ideal, it is not an extension of their prior experience: "Their prior experiences in their local working-class family and community contexts are likely to have been guided by norms of interdependence (Stephens et al., 2011; Stephens et al., 2007). As a result, first-generation students are likely to experience the university culture's focus on independence as a cultural mismatch—as relatively uncomfortable and as a clear divergence from their previous experiences (cf. Lubrano, 2003)."[7]

The distinctions between independent and interdependent norms will be familiar to readers. Stephens et al. identified university norms by asking university administrators to complete several tasks; here I offer one task as an illustrative example: given a list of twelve expectations, 261 university administrators were asked to select the five that best represented their university's expectations for students. The expectations reflected either independent norms ("learn to express oneself") or interdependent norms ("learn to listen to others"). After analyzing the results of this first task, researchers concluded that 84 percent of the administrators characterized their university norms as independent.[8] Incoming college students were then surveyed to identify whether their motives for attending college were independent or interdependent. Much like the university administrators, these incoming students selected from a list of items that reflected either independent ("expand my knowledge of the world") or interdependent ("help my family out when I'm done with college") norms. Stephens et al. found, as they had hypothesized, that class background predicted motive, and motive predicted academic achievement. For example, first-generation students with a household income of less than $60,000 selected twice as many interdependent motives as did continuing-generation students.[9]

A cultural mismatch between a student's interdependent motive and a university's independent cultural norm predicted poor academic performance during the first two years of college.[10] In subsequent studies, researchers found that the cultural mismatch could affect students with a single message. For example, the researchers gave first-generation students two welcome letters expressing different norms. The students who read the welcome letter with independent norms performed significantly worse on a cognitive task than those who read the welcome letter with interdependent norms.[11]

The findings of "Unseen Disadvantage" indicate that small interventions can have a measurable impact, and the findings direct us away from conversations about students' "capacity" or "preparedness" and instead toward what we can do to improve "fit" or "cultural match" for students. Along with the research on stereotype threat, this body of current research illuminates how university contexts such as welcome letters, test instructions, and classroom design can have a significant impact on student success.[12] Far from initiating working-class students into middle-class culture, then, Stephens et al. propose changing the institution to fit them:

> Although social class achievement gaps are often thought to be the product of differences in students' intellectual abilities or academic skills (cf. Pascarella et al., 2004), our findings suggest that the gap in performance between first-generation and continuing-generation students is, at least in part, a product of the predominantly middle-class cultural norms of independence that are institutionalized in many American colleges and universities.[13]

It is becoming more possible to imagine how faculty, staff, and administrators can change the institution to align with the values of students from working-class backgrounds, creating a context that can make pedagogies more effective.

STUDENT IDENTITY AND SUBJECT ROLE

In "Class Affects, Classroom Affectations," Julie Lindquist proposes a pedagogy of affect wherein teachers perform empathy through surface acting in order to eventually feel empathy through deep acting and become the person their students need them to be. Lindquist proposes deep acting as a strategy to help students navigate the paradox of the affective space between nostalgia and ambition that characterizes working-class culture: Lindquist writes that "an important part of developing a more affective pedagogy of class is genuinely to treat 'class culture' as a set of affective positions defined by investment in historical cultural practices, on the one hand, and social and economic aspirations, on the other."[14] Lindquist draws on the work of anthropologist Douglas Foley to define working-class experience as "constituted by the struggle to place identity formation between a nostalgic, imagined authenticity and the possibility for the invention of a forward-looking, more public voice."[15]

Lindquist is extending Amy Robillard's argument that we need pedagogies for working-class students that engage memory and ambition.

> Since, as Foley points out, class culture is by nature a tension, an "unpredictable synthesis" of the old and the new, a volatile mix of sacred and profane, such tensions can't be treated as rational problems to be solved, but rather as affective positions to be engaged. If this is true, then one begins to recognize that the implications extend not only to *what teachers need to do* in order to engage these positions, but also to *who they should be*.[16]

Lindquist proposes that literacy educators listen to their students to learn who their students need them to be in order to teach them. But this is a consideration we can extend to students: who should they be? This question of identity is a pressing matter for working-class students experiencing a cultural mismatch between the person they know how to be, the sum of their prior experiences, and the person they believe the university wants them to be. I propose that advocate is a role students can play, a way for them to be, that can help them negotiate the tensions between their prior and current experience. The advocate is an affective subject position wherein a student can invent what Lindquist calls a "forward-looking public voice" but one that speaks on another's behalf. By fulfilling the familiar obligations of interdependence, the advocate does not have to conflict with either the historical practice of working-class culture or the deep networks of Latino@ families. It can channel arising tension into action.

In fall 2009 I framed a basic writing course as Writing as Advocacy. My course description defined writing as a way to act on another's behalf and a feature of community leadership and responsibility. We began the semester with a discussion of students' own community leaders and what made each of them a leader. Interestingly, while Stephens et al. identify leadership as an independent norm, students identified their priests, ministers, and parents of friends as leaders in their community.[17] In other words leaders, to them, were mentors and advocates, those acting on interdependent motives and out of obligation to others.

Asking students to assume the role of advocate led to embodied strategies for reading, writing, and peer review. Our required textbook was William Robinson and Pam Altman's *Integrations*, and each writing assignment was a case study: students were given a real-world scenario with supporting documents, and their assignment was to write a recommendation for action using evidence from the supporting documents. Assuming the role of advocate made students better able to read the scenario and its documents for how they pertained to the situation and its implications for the individual embedded within it. While adopting the subject role of advocate made them assume an overtly moral stance, it also helped them achieve the kind of critical distance valued in academic writing. The class also included a visit from the director of a local Court Appointed Special Advocates (CASA) office and a final project that asked them to create a public-awareness poster for a local man who suffered heavy-metal poisoning at work.

Let me offer an example of how advocacy shaped this course.

The first assignment was the following writing scenario from *Integrations*: Denise Liu is a fourteen-year-old freshman who wants a job because all her friends have jobs. Her mother doesn't want her to work because she's afraid Denise's grades will suffer; her father opposes it because he thinks she should be at home helping her mother. The supporting documents were interviews with college students who worked in high school; there were also two articles on the effects of work on teens: one that supports it and one that does not. The student had to write a recommendation for whether Denise should work or not; if the student thought she should work, they had to spell out the conditions under which Denise should work, and why.

It sounds simple, but this scenario was complicated for my students because their initial response was to simplify it too much. We had discussed advocacy, and I had framed the course in terms of advocacy, but it was in applying advocacy to the case studies that it took shape. In other words, to do this assignment well, students had to be good advocates for Denise. To be good advocates, students had to

- respect the person or organization's wishes by considering what they wanted and how they felt (respond accurately to the rhetorical situation/writing assignment);
- suggest resources that could help the person or organization (use appropriate and relevant evidence);
- recommend a course of action in the best interest of the person or organization (develop a thesis).

Framing the writing task as advocacy helped clarify the purpose of the writing assignment. For instance, in their drafts, students tended to be dismissive of Denise's reason for wanting to work: because her friends have jobs. They were either openly contemptuous of her motive or they mapped their own reasons for getting a job onto Denise's situation. In this way, they weren't responding appropriately to the rhetorical situation. Responding to them as students, I might treat this as a misreading and return to the text. But responding to them as advocates changed my own orientation to one of context: even if they didn't like Denise's reasons, they had to withhold judgment and take them seriously in order to advocate for her. In this way, the pedagogy also repositioned *me* and brought new possibilities and strategies into relief, rendering others inappropriate. Students assessed the relevance of personal experience and textual evidence and evaluated their own and their peers' drafts through this lens. It lent the writer a concrete role in relation to others that was flexible enough to carry through the semester and the writing process. For their final group project, students made posters raising awareness of environmental health risks, and their posters were exhibited at the annual literacy fair.

A local man named Alex Trujillo had become very ill after installing custom countertops for his family's business. It turned out that the material used to make the composite was contaminated far beyond legal limits, and he sustained severe brain and nervous-system damage that was diagnosed as heavy-metal poisoning. A neighbor had told me about the Trujillos specifically because the family wanted others to know the risks, so I contacted Alex's mother Shirley before the semester started to discuss the possibility of my students making public-awareness posters to be exhibited at the literacy fair. Together we set the parameters of the assignment, and I assured her that one of the goals of the assignment would be to respect the wishes of the family.

I interviewed Shirley and Alex's wife Lucy about how Alex got sick, the care he now required, and their struggle with his insurance company during Alex's diagnosis and treatment. I converted our interview into a sound file and gave the sound file to each group of students. They had to listen to the interview and as a group choose to increase public awareness about one aspect of the case. The case was complicated—Shirley and Lucy discussed environmental and industrial toxins, heavy-metal poisoning, healthcare and insurance, alternative medicine, medical training, corporate crime, and federal regulation. Ultimately, though, they wanted people to know that even at legal levels, there were enough toxins in the environment to make people sick. In their groups, students created posters that told Alex Trujillo's story and then shared data on the health risks of industrial chemicals, heavy-metal poisoning, and the lingering effects of environmental disasters. They all conformed to the family's wishes, in other words. It is worth noting here that again, in adhering to the course's working definition of advocacy, I had to withhold what would have been my own preferred emphasis—enforcing federal regulations—because it did not conform to the family's wishes. They wanted the public informed about health risks, not corporate malfeasance.

This pedagogy was developed for the student body at one institution, and each institution is unique. How effective was it? I don't have a data-driven answer to that question. I do know that at NMHU attrition was so high that a successful pedagogy was one that simply motivated students to keep coming to class. And this class had solid attendance and a high passing rate. Discussions about the readings were lively and engaged, and more students tended to complete the readings. I also noted a higher level of comfort with the academic essay, which was the final form all recommendations had to take. I acknowledge the excellent scaffolding of the textbook *Integrations* while adding that playing a familiar role helped increased students' comfort and fluency with the form.

Scholars have argued that the essay reflects middle-class values, and in "The Shape of the Form," Linda Adler-Kassner traces our investment in and the origin of the essay to Progressive Era values: "Mastery of the essay's form has long been integrally linked to assimilation of cultural values that [early twentieth-century compositionists] consider to be reflected in and perpetuated by the form of the essay. If students come to that form with different values, it might seem far less 'natural' to them than it is to students who already participate in those values."[18] Continuing-generation students from middle-class backgrounds have more experience in self-elaboration through language, and this elaboration is a value reflected in the essay form. However, I believe students who took on the role of advocate and elaborated a thesis/evidence/conclusion form were more able to see the essay as a communicative form that reflected interdependent values.

TOWARD INTERDEPENDENT NORMS

Adler-Kassner notes that even if our emphasis on citizenship is not explicit, our jobs are contingent on preparing students to participate in academic culture.[19] Much as my NMHU students redefined leadership through interdependent norms, the citizen here does not have to embody middle-class values but can be reconfigured as an interdependent prosocial actor. Once again, I turn to recent research on class difference and the role of independence in the "compassion gap." In a recent study on the link between social class and unethical behavior, researchers concluded that wealthier people may be less compassionate as a result of their independence from others, reversing the conventional wisdom that working-class individuals are more likely to engage in unethical behavior to "increase their resources or overcome their disadvantage." Instead, Piff et al. found that "increased resources and independence from others cause people to prioritize self-interest over others' welfare and perceive greed as positive and beneficial, which in turn gives rise to increased unethical behavior."[20] If part of our job is to transform the student into the citizen, then promoting a conception of the citizen as an independent actor may work against even that larger long-term public interest.

Universities have long been sites of cultural production that reproduce social inequalities. Whether they can serve working-class interests is an old question taken up again in the *College English* special issue on class. Donna LeCourt articulates the "rock and hard place" of the alienation narrative: "Either we deny economic mobility or we perpetuate a change in worldview to the detriment of our students' abilities to maintain their social relations and sense of self. This is the crux of the alienation narrative. Such a narrative, however, relies upon a central premise, that economic and social mobility are in constant conflict."[21] The issue here for LeCourt is that the alienation narrative renders not only class culture but also the institution static. LeCourt continues, "However, by painting the picture with broad strokes—by presuming an a priori existence of working-class and middle-class academic discourses—we neglect how much messier and more complex the relationship among class positions can be while students are experiencing it, and thus we neglect opportunities for configuring the relationship differently."[22] I believe Latino@ students' kinship networks offer a model for reconfiguring the relation between working-class and academic discourses, of adapting the university to students.

All writing instructors can benefit from considering how interdependence functions (or does not) for their students. In *Coming Up Short*, Jennifer Silva found in interviews with working-class adults in their twenties that rituals of adulthood—college graduation, home ownership, marriage—are rendered unobtainable when the burden of risk disproportionately shifts to individuals. This persistent failure to reach landmarks and the lack of choice in shaping their own economic conditions—their lack of autonomy—led the young people in Silva's study to think of adulthood as something achieved through emotional self-regulation, a form of self-discipline marked by distrust of institutions and relationships. Working-class students have a lot to teach us about what happens when institutions do not adapt to them, when a student takes on all of the risk (in student loans, deferred income, and so on) but receives none of the benefits of higher education. Pedagogies that enact interdependent norms can make the university and its classrooms welcoming places by assuring students no one is expected to go it alone.

Notes

1. My interest in interdependence began as I got to know my students and recognized interdependence in reading about the Puente Project in California. The program was created in 1981 to increase academic success for Mexican-American and Latino@ students in California community colleges. Barbara Jaffe writes that between 1996 and 2001, the program increased passing and retention rates for Hispanic students by 20 to 25 percent through a three-pronged attention to counseling, mentoring, and writing. In basic writing classes, instructors assign students to peer writing groups called *familias* to cultivate the personal skills of interdependence and accountability. See Jaffe, "Changing Perceptions, 169–90.
2. Hill, *New Mexico Highlands,* 13.
3. Zweig, *Working Class Majority,* 11.
4. Thelin and Carter, introduction to *Class in the Composition Classroom,* 6.
5. *Merriam-Webster Dictionary,* s.v. "independence," accessed June 29, 2015, https://www.merriam-webster.com/dictionary/independence.
6. Stephens et al., "Unseen Disadvantage," 1189.
7. Ibid., 1181.
8. Ibid., 1183–84.
9. Ibid., 1186–89.
10. Ibid., 1189.
11. Ibid., 1190.
12. Examples of this kind of research include studies on how affirming a minority student's adequacy improves performance on a writing assignment while confirming a negative stereotype undermines performance on the same task. In another study, objects stereotypically associated with computer science were removed from a computer-science classroom and replaced with a nature poster and phone books, resulting in more women becoming interested in the subject. Cohen et al., "Reducing the Racial Achievement Gap"; Cheryan et al., "Ambient Belonging."
13. Stephens et al., "Unseen Disadvantage," 1193.
14. Lindquist, "Class Affects, Classroom Affectations," 187–209.
15. Ibid., 193.
16. Ibid., 193.
17. Stephens et al., "Unseen Disadvantage," 1184.
18. Adler-Kassner, "Shape of the Form," 99.
19. Ibid., 92.
20. Piff et al., "Higher Social Class."
21. LeCourt, "Performing Working-Class Identity," 31.
22. Ibid., 32

11

NEVER AND FOREVER JUST KEEP COMING BACK AGAIN
Class, Access, and Student Writing Performance

Missy Nieveen Phegley

As a high-school teacher in the mid-90s, I often integrated technical writing into the curriculum for my *non-college-bound* classes (a label used by the school administrators to differentiate from the *college-prep* classes), which were mainly populated with working-class students who planned to enter the workforce immediately after graduation. Consequently, I frequently asked these students to create documents using a computer. On one particular occasion, after introducing a new assignment, I asked my class whether they had any questions, and I received the usual *Are you gonna make us type this?* As I answered, a tall white student nicknamed "Fro" for his 70s-style blonde afro slammed his fist down on his desk and complained loudly, "You can't make me type this! I'm not rich enough to have a computer!" Slightly taken aback, I assumed an authoritative voice and gave the teacherly response, stating that he had access to the two computers in my room (to be shared by twenty-five students during a fifty-minute class period) as well as the lab, which he could use during study hall and lunch and before and after school. Even though I knew he was not satisfied with my response, I used my authority to indicate the discussion had ended. However, my ending the discussion did not eliminate many of these students' lack of access to technology, which often led to incomplete or altogether missing assignments and, eventually, poor grades in the class.

Time passed and these stories continued. While teaching as an adjunct at a community college in the early 2000s, I regularly took my composition classes to the computer lab to work on their writing. The first time each class used the computer lab was usually a challenge as students adjusted to software and computer settings. At one point during

DOI: 10.7330/9781607326182.c011

a summer session course, I began circulating around the room as my students started working on their papers using the computers. When I finally reached Kendra,[1] about twenty minutes later, I saw that her monitor was black and she was nervously fidgeting. I asked whether she had a problem, and she said she could not get the screen to work. Because she did not want to draw attention to her inexperience, she chose not to ask for help from either me or nearby students. I moved the mouse to "awaken" the computer, helped her open the word-processing program, watched her get started, then moved to check on another student. While speaking with the other student, I observed Kendra's lack of keyboarding skills and realized she would never complete the writing task in the given amount of time. Even though I knew Kendra was a nontraditional student attending school to create better job opportunities for herself, I had assumed she would have some experience with typing even if she had little experience with a computer. She managed to turn in most of her work during the semester, but she just barely passed with the minimum required grade.

Now, nearly twenty years later, Fro and Kendra's experiences are repeated, maybe with different words and attitudes, but the message is often similar. Just recently, I was speaking with a coteacher for one of our university's online dual-credit sections. (My institution, Southeast Missouri State University, has begun offering online dual credit to rural schools that do not have faculty with the appropriate credentials to teach dual credit in the high school. A university instructor teaches the course online, and the high-school teacher provides supplemental instruction in the classroom.) She mentioned that several of her students had missed a couple classes for extracurricular activities, and she was concerned they would be penalized for not completing the assignment on time. I assured her that they could complete and submit the assignment from home, as it was not due until midnight the following day. She responded almost sheepishly, "A lot of our students don't have Internet at home." In a later conversation with the dual-credit university instructor, he remarked that when the high-school teachers offered students access to the Internet and computers in the evenings and weekends, their students typically had better grades at the end of the semester.

According to Cynthia L. Selfe and Gail E. Hawisher, we know that the very nature of the university system can marginalize those students whose backgrounds are not middle class, and we also know the technology itself reflects the values of the white-collar professions.[2] Audrey Watters pulls no punches when she states, "Despite our talk about meritocracy, it's a racially segregated, class-based system of education, one that technology as easily entrenches as subverts."[3] In this chapter, I will first discuss data collected from five years of student scores on writing-proficiency exams. With the assessment data in mind, I will then examine whether a technology-enhanced composition curriculum facilitates an environment that further marginalizes working-class students, possibly even creating a new category of marginalized students.

EFFECT OF SOCIOECONOMIC CLASS ON WRITING PERFORMANCE

As with many colleges and universities, my institution has embraced writing assessment as a means to determine the effect of curriculum and instruction on levels of performance in key areas. We administer a variety of writing-proficiency exams, and the assessments are used to place students in the composition course best suited to their needs, to monitor the effectiveness of their writing experience, and to ensure that all students who graduate from the university have basic writing competencies. For the purposes of this research, I will only discuss the WP002 and WP003. These writing-proficiency exams are administered at the end of Composition 2 (WP002) and again after students have completed seventy-five credit hours (WP003). Each exam consists of two parts. The first part is a forty-five-minute expository essay on a general-knowledge topic. The second part is a sixty-minute argumentative essay on a topic related to the part 1 topic; the student is provided with source material and asked to incorporate those sources into the essay to support the argument.

Given the anecdotes at the beginning of this chapter, one might assume that students from a lower socioeconomic class background and with less than ideal access to technology would not perform well on a writing task, particularly as composition courses rely more and more on technology to facilitate and disseminate instruction. However, as demonstrated in table 11.1, data from five years of writing-proficiency exams show no consistent correlation between family income and assessment scores.

Based on this evidence, I believe we can safely conclude that student performance at the completion of the end-of-sequence composition class and again after completion of seventy-five credit hours does *not* correlate with family income. However, we can observe some interesting trends in the scores. The gradual dip in WP002 scores correlates to a gradual increase in class caps for composition courses, which saw an increase from twenty-five to thirty during that time (an observation that warrants much more discussion than this chapter can provide). Despite the possible impact of class size on student performance, this appears to even itself out by the time students take the WP003.

Table 11.1. Average writing proficiency scores by family income

WP002 Scores by FISAP Income					
FISAP Income	AY11	AY12	AY13	AY14	AY15
< 20k	8.07	7.90	7.68	7.99	7.27
> = 20k and < 30k	8.04	8.01	7.96	7.89	7.42
> = 30k and < 40k	8.17	8.01	8.04	7.93	7.30
> = 40k and < 50k	8.04	8.17	7.84	7.89	7.26
> = 50k and < 60k	8.13	8.14	7.96	7.85	7.50
> = 60k and < 70k	8.20	8.14	8.04	8.00	7.54
> = 70k	8.23	8.16	8.13	8.02	7.55
WP003 Scores by FISAP Income					
FISAP Income	AY11	AY12	AY13	AY14	AY15
< 20k	7.94	7.91	7.84	8.08	7.15
> = 20k and < 30k	8.08	8.13	8.18	8.21	7.62
> = 30k and < 40k	8.01	8.22	8.13	7.95	7.94
> = 40k and < 50k	8.21	8.19	8.24	8.24	7.56
> = 50k and < 60k	8.32	8.25	8.24	8.07	7.73
> = 60k and < 70k	8.49	8.36	8.08	8.35	7.85
> = 70k	8.29	8.27	8.25	8.31	7.86

Source: Test scores from Writing Proficiency exams, WP002 and WP003, are for tests taken within the academic year. Income is FISAP income from FAFSA for the year (data are only available for students completing FAFSA). Southeast Missouri State University Institutional Research, February 2015.

The other interesting trend is the significant drop in average test scores for AY15. I can hypothesize about various factors affecting the scores—we are reporting only one semester of data rather than a full year, students taking the WP002 in the fall did not have the advantage of testing at the completion of back-to-back semesters of writing instruction, and students taking Composition 2 in the fall more likely received Composition 1 credit in high school or failed Composition 1 and had to retake it. Nevertheless, there is one factor that affected all students who were assessed. Starting in fall 2015, the administration of the exams went fully online for both the WP002 and the WP003. Prior to this round of testing, all face-to-face sections of Composition 2 administered the test during the final exam period. Students were given a booklet with instructions and the exam prompts, and they wrote the exams by hand. In spring 2014, the WP003 was offered online and face to face, and students could choose test dates according to their preferred testing method. In fall 2014, the WP003 was offered primarily online, and the only students who had the option to write by hand were those who required testing accommodations and those who missed their original testing date and rescheduled the exam with Testing Services.

Students taking the WP002 in fall 2014, which is also the final exam for their Composition 2 course, were given a forty-hour window in which to complete both essays, starting at 8 a.m. on a Friday morning and ending at midnight on the following Saturday. Students were reminded to start the exams in plenty of time prior to the close of the testing window, as any in-progress work would be submitted at midnight. Finally, students were advised to use a stable Internet connection because a dropped connection would end their exam. With the change in test structure, issues of access now came into play. Students without adequate personal access had to schedule time to make use of public access, which created an additional layer of complication. However, this complication was not significant enough to affect overall student performance.

Clearly, more data is necessary in order to draw firm conclusions about the correlations between test scores and the test structure, but the initial data seem to indicate that digitizing the test affects the performance of all students, regardless of socioeconomic background and varying levels of access to technology. Issues of access may certainly complicate a working-class student's ability to take a writing exam online, but the consistent drop in scores among the income ranges indicates there are additional factors that can influence student performance. However, the results of this study also lead us to safely conclude that students who may start at a disadvantage are still able to demonstrate a level of performance, upon completion of their writing requirements, that is on par with students who have experienced a greater, more consistent level of access.

WORKING-CLASS STUDENTS AND ACCESS

With the above assessment data in mind, instructors must still remain cognizant of the complexity of access and its role in working-class students' ability to learn in a technology-infused environment. Despite assumptions that "everybody" has a sense of basic keyboarding and computer functions and "everyone" knows how to use a smartphone, I have found many students, when asked to complete a writing activity on the computer, are unable to complete their work adequately because the technology poses a challenge, with many students either resisting the use of new technologies or struggling with them as they complete their work both in and out of the classroom. Many of my students have shared, through writing or in person, their lack of experience with or lack of access to technology. One student wrote that she felt "handicapped without a printer." Another student shared, "I am becoming acquainted with the Internet and more computer techniques as I am not very computer literate. Sometimes these aids are frustrating." A current graduate assistant in the English department lives fifteen miles from town, but her only option for Internet is through a satellite provider. As a result, Internet access is dependent upon the weather, and so far this month, she has had Internet access only two out of three weeks. In each case, these students were faced with technology and access issues that, at times, were beyond their control or their means and, more important, took their attention away from their writing and research processes.

Other instructors have shared similar anecdotes with me.[4] From their personal experiences, they have tried to identify those students who seem to have the most trouble with technology. Their various responses include the following: women who do not use computers on a daily basis; African American student athletes; urban students who do not own computers; nontraditional African American females; nontraditional students working to retrain for another career; students from working-class backgrounds; and those who come from "poor" schools, with urban students being less technologically savvy than rural students. These instructors have identified problems students encounter with technology as lack of keyboarding skills; a general phobia about using the Internet; and difficulty with basic word-processing functions, often despite proficiency with advanced technologies.

Lack of personal access to a computer, lack of consistent access to the Internet, difficulty in composing with generally accepted yet unfamiliar software, and late assignments due to any of these reasons can result in lower grades for working-class students. Unfortunately, instructors can easily jump to equating lack of experience or access to technology with a lack of skill in composing an essay, particularly when assignment and course grades might confirm this assumption.

Stories of working-class students who face challenges with technology take on greater significance as the integration of technology into our composition curriculum becomes a permanent fixture for many of us. Despite my excitement about the range of possibilities that open up for both my students and me, I worry that, as composition instructors, our assumptions of students' capabilities are shaped by our own middle-class experiences and our expectations of the potential for their experiences.

Claims put forth by state and federal initiatives make it easy for us to assume our students come to us proficient in the use of technology, particularly when those claims suggest there is a computer in every classroom—and often a device in the hands of every student—and that no child has been left behind. However, is this a warranted assumption? If not, how are our students affected by our assumptions about their proficiency with technology?

Ultimately, the issue at the heart of these questions is access, and we must recognize access is a function of wealth. Charles Moran asserts that despite reluctance to admit our nation is divided by wealth and social class, the wealth gap makes the technology gap dramatically visible, especially in our writing classes.[5] I am sure we can think of numerous situations in which students who had access to better computers created nicer, prettier documents whereas those who did not have the same level of access produced work not nearly so visually pleasing. The seemingly simple solution for closing this gap tells us that more opportunities for public access should be created, as evidenced by the number of initiatives to provide more public access. However, as Moran points out, there is a firm distinction between public and personal access, and the two cannot be considered equal levels of access.[6]

Public access includes labs in schools, libraries, college dorms, campus buildings, and so forth. These labs are available to the entire public or certain sectors of the public. Unfortunately, there are many drawbacks to using public labs. Students must travel to and from the lab, plan their schedules to allot enough time to maximize their use of lab computers, and remember to bring all necessary tools and information with them. In addition, because students are using computers that belong to an institution, they must abide by that institution's rules regarding time limits, consumption of food or drink, computer settings and software set by the institution, printing capabilities, and freedom to listen to music. Depending on the time of day or even the time of year, access may be limited because students may have to wait in line to use the computers during times of peak usage or they may have to work within imposed time limits. At the same time, the number of computers and the type of access available to students also varies from institution to institution.

Despite these drawbacks, the availability of access is necessary for students who wish to learn about and make use of current technology. Fortunately, allocation of funding at both the federal and state levels has been creating opportunities for access for almost twenty years. In 1997, the US Department of Education created the Technology Literacy Challenge Fund, which was a five-year, $2 billion fund to provide formula grants to state education agencies to support grassroots efforts at the state and local level to meet the four national technology goals for schools: modern computers, high-quality educational software, trained teachers, and affordable connections to the Internet. These funds were awarded to all fifty states and outlying areas according to the ESEA Title I formula.[7] In 2001, President Bush unveiled a plan for enhancing education through technology in the No Child Left Behind Act. Bush's plan advocated that schools use technology as a tool to improve academic achievement and also emphasized that use of the latest technology in the classroom should not be an end unto itself. The proposal expected to accomplish this goal by sending more dollars to schools for technology, reducing paperwork and increasing flexibility, allowing funds to be used for Internet filters, focusing funds on proven means of enhancing education through advanced technology, and offering matching grants for community technology centers.[8] And now, President Obama's fiscal year 2016 budget asks for $200 million for Education Technology State Grants to support models for using technology to help teachers and school leaders improve instruction and personalize learning.[9]

While these initiatives have created a great deal of change and continue to seem promising, I realize, from personal experiences as a teacher at both secondary and postsecondary levels, that students who do not have regular personal access and are unfamiliar or uncomfortable with technology may attempt to avoid using it even when its use is required. I have observed high-school students spend considerable time attempting to find and open a word-processing program and then simply giving up. I have overheard both high-school and college students ask a fellow student proficient in computer use to do their computer-based work for them. I have observed students working on collaborative projects elect to do activities that did not require them to use either a computer function or program with which they were unfamiliar. Recently, a student refused to do anything beyond basic word processing, claiming she was going to be an elementary teacher and she had no need to learn anything about other programs because she would never have to use them again. Students have even asked me to text them when assignments were due because they seldom sat down at a computer and read their e-mail or looked at the class website. While these anecdotes do not necessarily relate only to technology and writing instruction, they do illustrate the kinds of challenges we may face with our students when we require a certain level of digital literacy as they compose.

Despite the promise of federal initiatives for technology in education and our assumptions about widespread access, figure 11.1

Figure 11.1. This infographic demonstrates how the Internet is important in various aspects of our lives, who the disadvantaged users are, why they do not use the Internet, and how we can work to improve disparities (Siefer, Internet Is Important, *2013).*

demonstrates the continuing disparity in access to the Internet and use of technology.

While much has been done in providing greater opportunities for public access, many external issues surround public access; therefore, personal access seems to be the ideal. Obviously, the prime benefit of personal access is the ability to use the computer anytime the student chooses and for as long as a student chooses. Moran identifies other benefits of personal access including the ability to create a workspace that is comfortable and meets a student's personal preferences for a work atmosphere and for computer settings.[10] There are still drawbacks, though. Clearly, the capability for private access is dictated by wealth, and, unfortunately, wealth influences more than a student's ability to own a computer. Because technology is advancing at such a high rate, a student's personal system and software may be "outdated," which can become problematic if students must use technology in a classroom setting that does not align with their personal system and software. Moreover, even though a student has a computer, he or she may not have access to all the necessary components, such as Internet access, a printer, or even commonly used software programs.

Unfortunately, contemporary society's general concept of access is limited, which also limits our understanding of this phenomenon in regard to the role of technology and the need for access. Thomas Reynolds and Charles Lewis quote President Bill Clinton's remarks in Westland, Michigan, on September 17, 1996, to illustrate the overly simplistic understanding of access:

> If we hook up every classroom in America to the Information Superhighway, what it means is this: that in the poorest inner-city classrooms, in the most remote rural classrooms and all the classrooms in between, for the first time in the history of our country, all of our schoolchildren will have access to the same learning at the same level of quality, in the same way, in the same time as the students in the richest schools in America. That is achievable and we must do it.[11]

This Clinton-Gore vision of technology in education based on naive assumptions about "inside" and "outside" classroom spaces is problematic in that it configures the conditions of computer "access" as a twofold system of absence or presence, and while this perspective may seem dated, it is still widely prevalent. Reynolds and Lewis believe these assumptions echo a similar lack of writing teachers' awareness regarding the material conditions of students writing with computers.[12]

Regrettably, contemporary society's general concept of access assigns it binary value—access is either present or absent—and when concerns are raised about access, those concerns are addressed by attempting to eliminate the absence of access. As instructors of composition, we are directly affected by this simplistic concept as well as guilty, at times, of perpetuating it. Despite the continually increasing number of composition courses that are held in computer-equipped classrooms that require frequent access to the university's learning management system, that use e-books rather than print textbooks, and/or that are offered as hybrid courses or completely online, students still spend much of their time studying and completing writing tasks away from the classroom, making use of either public or private access. Beth Hewett states that "nationwide survey participants rated students' ability to read and write lower in importance for being adequately oriented for OWI [online writing instruction] courses, suggesting that these skills are considered less critical than technology orientation and time-management skills in a text-heavy environment."[13] Unfortunately, we have moved into an era of presumed universal computer access, and we expect our students to meet our requirements easily due to the perceived abundant access to technology in both public and private spaces and a perceived level of digital literacy. In truth, as Reynolds and Lewis contend, universal access is a "moving target" because as technology evolves, so must the access available to our students. As a result, those students with greater resources are more likely to be able to keep up with the evolution of technology while those students with fewer resources are often trying to catch up.[14] While we can make some generalizations about socioeconomic class and access, the issue of access is too complex to link it solely to financial resources. Simply put, access cannot be defined as the mere presence or absence of technology. Some of the complexities we must consider in our understanding of access are specific conditions of access, composing processes in relation to access, and class-based perceptions of the role of technology.

CONDITIONS OF ACCESS

In *Literate Lives in the Information Age: Narratives of Literacy from the United States*, Cynthia Selfe and Gail Hawisher identify four gateways through which people have typically gained access to technology: schools, homes, community centers, and workplaces. Through their research, they found that the more of these gateways that are open to people, the more likely people are to "acquire and develop a robust set of digital literacy practices and to value digital literacy"; nevertheless, they also contend that "the relative importance of these gateways in the lives of specific individuals varies according to the needs and motivations of the people who use them; the historical contexts in which people exist and are motivated to use computers; their material and economic circumstances; and the social circumstances that both shape, and are shaped by, their actions."[15] Because factors like race, class, interest, motivation, timing, and opportunity all affect access, they also affect the ways people develop their technology skills through the identified gateways. Selfe and Hawisher identify several conditions of access that affect at what times and in what ways people acquire their technology skills and whether they even choose to acquire those skills; these conditions are

> fit, or match, between their needs and the capabilities of available computer hardware and software; the motivation, or personal stake, they had for learning to communicate in online environments; the resources, financial and otherwise, they had available to devote to computers; the immediacy and convenience of computer access; the availability of technical support in a form that fit their particular learning style; and the safety, security, and general ambience of the computing environment they had available for use.[16]

Expanding from these general conditions and based on observations from interviews I conducted with a range of students,[17] I was able to identify several specific conditions of access that impeded or facilitated these students' ability to acquire literacy with technology. Specific conditions of access include software compatible with the school's, necessary hardware such as a printer and USB ports, access to the Internet, and time for unrestricted exploration of computer functions and the Internet.

On the surface, it is easy to assume students with a personal computer have a functional level of access; unfortunately, there are additional costs and expectations for access not immediately apparent. For many students, the convenience of a personal computer is complicated by software that is not compatible with the school's. As Shantelle, one of my student interviewees, indicated, she does not have the word-processing program provided in the school's labs, and she considers this "a big problem." While she has found ways around this, such as e-mailing herself any text written in class, she finds it takes time to reformat the work and make changes caused by problems with incompatibility. Purchasing compatible software is an option, but for many, the cost is prohibitive. For instructors, software incompatibility can also be a challenge. As Reynolds and Lewis suggest, this incompatibility can serve as a rationale for students to remove or at least marginalize themselves from the classroom community by skipping class or choosing not to work on their writing when given time in class.[18]

For some students, possessing and maintaining appropriate hardware, such as a printer or USB ports, can also become a challenge to sustaining adequate access. Even though Daniela owned a laptop computer, she had neither a printer nor functional drives. For her, the lack of necessary hardware made her personal computer useless for any writing other than personal journals because she had to use the school's labs to type and print her papers. Eventually, she was able to save up to purchase an external drive and later still a printer.

Access to the Internet has quickly moved from a convenience to a necessity. While students who live in residence housing at most universities have ready access to the Ethernet or Wi-Fi, many students live off campus or commute from distant homes. For some, the cost of Internet access puts it out of reach. Because Daniela has a child, she chose to live off campus, but she was unable to afford an ISP account. Whenever she needed to conduct research on the Internet, she had to schedule time to go to campus so she could access the Internet from one of the university's labs. When she went home for the summer, she again did not have Internet access. Working and caring for her child consumed much of her day, and scheduling time to spend at the library checking her e-mail was low on her priority list. This lack of access can be detrimental, as Teresa Redd notes in "'Tryin to make a dolla outa fifteen cent': Teaching Composition with the Internet at an HCBU [one of a number of historically black colleges and universities]." Redd argues, "College students from homes without Internet access rarely have had time to learn what other students with on-demand access have learned from unrestricted exploration. They are still novice users, and it is precisely here—in the gap between novice and experienced users—that the digital divide is the widest."[19]

Also an issue of access is the amount of time spent online. Redd cites Jeffrey Cole, head of UCLA's 2001 study of the digital divide, who identifies significant differences between those students who have been online more than five years and those who just recently went online. Cole distinguishes the skills that come with experience, stating that novices know how to surf the Internet to find entertainment, but experienced users know how to put the Internet to work for them, executing tasks such as banking online and making purchases. From her own observations, Redd extends this notion, suggesting that experienced users are more adept at finding and exploiting online resources, downloading and installing programs, and navigating and participating in virtual classrooms.[20] I have also found that students with more online experience are much more proficient at online research, as they have become skilled at using a variety of academic databases to learn about their subjects while novices tend to rely on general search engines such as Google.

Although access to the Internet is available for those who live on campus at this university, students still encounter complications. Our College of Education has recently provided iPad integration for all undergraduate education majors, which has caused a significant strain on bandwidth, causing slowdowns and occasional server interruptions. In addition, for commuter students who live in rural areas, widespread Internet access is not always available. While Internet service providers are increasing their coverage areas through cable, telephone, and satellite, many students still do not have consistent home access.

Another significant factor of adequate access is time to explore the computer and its various functions. As with any skill, reaching a level of proficiency requires time to practice, and the same is true with developing technology literacy. For many students, finding ample time to practice using and learning about the computer can be a challenge. If they do not have personal access, their time available to spend using public access often allows them only to complete a specific task, whether that includes researching a particular topic or typing an essay. For Bethany, scheduling her own time on the computer was often difficult, as she had to share it with five other members of her family. However, each member of Foster's family had their own Wi-Fi-enabled computer to use at will. Foster's situation confirms an assertion by Laura Brady, an English professor and writing center director, who says, "Those who *already* possess higher income and education levels also possess the greatest access to technology."[21] While both families have personal access, Foster's family has provided significantly greater access for each member than Bethany's family has been able to provide. This greater access occurs as a result of his family's ability to obtain personal computers for each member and because that number of computers allows for unrestricted exploration of computer software, games, and the Internet.

An important component of students' time spent using technology is their perception of the availability of public access. As public access becomes more commonplace, we tend to assume access to technology becomes easier for a greater number of people who do not have personal computers and/or ISP accounts. Some students who have a personal computer may still find it necessary to use public access because they may lack various components such as hardware, software compatible with the school's, or a stable Internet connection. While Foster is positive about public access when he must to use it to access the

Internet, he does find that lab hours can be inconvenient, particularly when he needs to use the lab during early-morning hours. Daniela, on the other hand, is much more negative in her opinion of public access. She feels that even though the university provides computers at the library and various other labs, "it's like a waiting list for a body part." Quite evident in this statement is her frustration with wait time and non-functioning computers that, in her experience, are endemic to public access. Knowing she has a computer at home that does not meet her needs makes these challenges even more frustrating.

When students must make use of public access, their perception of that access can be affected by the number of time constraints they have. Because Daniela has family responsibilities and no extended family nearby to assist her with childcare, she has little flexibility in scheduling her time to use public computer labs. She must use public computers when she has time available. If she must spend time waiting for an open computer (and this time can be considerable, particularly when computers are down or the labs are busy), she has less time to complete her work. On the other hand, Bethany, who also has family responsibilities, perceives public access as being much more available. However, she is established in her community with extended family and friends close by to help occasionally with childcare. She also has reliable transportation to travel to public access sites, and she realizes she has other options for public access available to her in addition to the university's labs. She frequently uses computers at the local elementary school or public library, and these sites have much less traffic than the university's public labs, so she does not have to wait the length of time to use a computer that Daniela often does. Traditional students without family and work responsibilities that demand much of their time perceive public access as being much more available. Foster saw time waiting to use public access as an opportunity to socialize. Several other interviewees often returned later if they could not access the computers immediately, and this delay posed fewer problems for them than for nontraditional students.

While the majority of our students may be capable of performing the computer tasks we ask them to complete in the composition classroom, the early and consistent exposure they had to computers affects their level of confidence in completing those tasks. Because technology often serves as an entry point to our students' learning, those students with more experience and confidence in using technology likely meet learning objectives more quickly. At the same time, technology may impede the learning of students with little or no computer experience, particularly when they encounter access-related challenges.

TECHNOLOGY AND COMPOSING PROCESSES

Varying conditions of access can have a range of effects on our students. One of the more significant factors affected, as it relates to writing, is the composing process. From the people I interviewed, I learned that student's composing processes relate to their particular conditions of access. For students with consistent personal access, the composing method of choice was to compose while typing on the computer, but for students with inconsistent personal access, the choice was to compose with pen and paper. We can acknowledge a lack of personal access as a reason a student may choose to compose by hand simply to make more efficient use of time. Because both Bethany and Daniela had inconsistent personal access and added responsibilities of being parents, they seldom had the luxury of spending several hours in one of the school's computer labs composing their papers. For them, it was more effective time management to come to the lab with a draft in hand and type it as quickly as possible. In addition, the environment for public access may not be compatible with the students' most effective method of learning or working. Janie states that she does not like to be around many people when she is typing because they distract her, causing her to complete her work much more slowly. Many students accustomed to composing by hand tend to choose this method in class (if the instructor gives them a choice) even when they have immediate access to a computer; they are more confident with the composing method they use most frequently and feel more comfortable employing it while away from their home learning environment.

Several interviewees who compose on the computer mentioned their distaste for messy, handwritten drafts with arrows to notes in the margins and crossed-out sections. They much prefer working with the clean look of typed text on the computer. In contrast, those who compose by hand feel they do not produce the same quality of work when they compose on the computer because the polished appearance of typed text on the computer screen makes their draft seem complete, and therefore additional revision seems unnecessary. Bethany illustrates this when she says, "I'm less apt to go back and mark out a word or change a word, you know, because it's already there. It's already printed and it's already typed nicely in black and white."

These composing preferences can provide a variety of challenges for composition instructors, particularly when their classrooms are filled with students with opposing preferences. Whether or not the students have access to computers in class, instructors may encounter students who are uncomfortable when asked to compose during class. However, this discomfort does provide an opportunity to begin a conversation about composing preferences and the nature of those preferences. These kinds of conversations may function as metacognitive activities for students as they begin thinking specifically about their process and the components of that process that make their journey of composing work for them. This growing awareness of their individual processes can lead to better control of their writing as they step back from composing, particularly when they reach a point at which they are struggling, and apply what they know of their process to move through that moment. In addition, instructors can ask students to experiment with their methods of composing through in-class writing activities, urging them to move beyond their composing comfort zone and employ different strategies. In asking students to experience different composing methods, instructors are enabling discussions about the composing process and the technologies students use while providing an opportunity for metacognitive reflection about what "works" for students and why that method is effective or ineffective. At the same time, this kind of reflection may give working-class students exposure to new strategies for composing instead of defaulting to those strategies with which they are most comfortable.

Another factor that affects composing preferences is students' confidence in their typing skills. Students who feel their typing skills are strong are more willing to compose on the computer, claiming they can type faster than they can write and, therefore, are more able to get all their ideas down, particularly when the words start flowing quickly. Foster, for example, feels he can type quickly, and when the words start flowing, he is able to run with an idea. When he composes on paper, he feels the stopping and starting involved with crossing out and erasing often disrupt his thought process, sometimes even causing him to lose his idea. Georgia voiced the same notion, saying, "When I'm on the computer and I'm thinking of so many things, I type faster than I write, so it's easier for me, and if I have so many things on my mind and I'm trying to write them all [by hand], I forget some of them." Those who feel they type slowly believe they are much better at writing their ideas down on paper because they do not have to concentrate on pressing the right letters on the keyboard. Shantelle believes composing on the computer slows her down. She says, "I have yet to learn how to type without looking at the keyboard," and her concern about her typing skills becomes evident as she frequently mentions them in relation to her writing. As instructors, we also must recognize that facility in typing on one device does not translate to facility on another device. Students who are highly proficient at texting may struggle when using a standard keyboard in class.

CONCLUSION

If we presume our working-class students have appropriate levels of access, either through public or personal access, and that they are proficient in using technology, we risk making a false assumption that may result in negative consequences for our students. In her article "Fully Online and Hybrid Writing Instruction," Hewitt states that "technology access alone may be insufficient because fluency with online gaming and social networking does not equal education-based computing and interpretive skills."[22] We must recognize that our working-class students are affected by many factors that go beyond the mere presence or absence of technology, and we must work to expand our concept of access in order to accommodate its complexities and better serve our students' needs as we deliver our instruction.

While it is apparent that varying levels of access have a direct effect on working-class students' digital literacy and their composing processes, and that these issues may at times impact their course grades, we must also recognize that working-class students are capable of performing at the same level as their peers who have experienced more thorough and consistent access. As instructors, it is imperative that we pay attention to the complexity of access and its role in working-class students' ability to learn in a technology-infused environment, holding ourselves accountable in providing sufficient time and space for our students to concurrently develop writing skills and digital literacy skills.

Notes

1. Student names from this point on have been changed.
2. Selfe and Hawisher, *Literate Lives.*
3. Watters, "Is It Time?"
4. These anecdotes are the results of an informal query posted to the WPA listserv. Thirteen people responded, providing information about the types of students who have trouble with technology and the respondents" instructional approach with those students who experience difficulty.
5. Moran, "Technology."
6. Ibid.
7. US Department of Education, "Technology Literacy Challenge Fund."
8. US Department of Education, "No Child Left Behind."
9. *Homeroom*; "The 2016 Budget: Improving Opportunity and Affordability in Higher Education," Homeroom US Department of Education blog entry by Melissa Apostolides, February 2, 2015, accessed February 20, 2017, https://blog.ed.gov/2015/02/the-2016-budget-improving-opportunity-and-affordability-in-higher-education/.
10. Moran, "Technology," 203–23.
11. Reynolds and Lewis, "Changing Topography."
12. Ibid.

13. Hewett, "Fully Online."
14. Reynolds and Lewis, "Changing Topography."
15. Selfe and Hawisher, *Literate Lives.*
16. Ibid.
17. I interviewed thirteen students to gain insight into these individuals' perspectives on literacy and access to technology. The anecdotes that follow reflect their experiences and their responses.
18. Reynolds and Lewis, "Changing Topography."
19. Redd, "'Tryin to make a dolla.'"
20. Ibid.
21. Brady, "Fault Lines."
22. Hewett, "Fully Online," 202.

PART 3

What Our Students Say

12

SOCIAL ECONOMIES OF LITERACY IN RURAL OREGON
Accounting for Diverse Sponsorship Histories of Working-Class Students in and out of School

Cori Brewster

Drawing on a subset of interviews conducted with fifty-two students from rural Oregon attending eleven public two- and four-year colleges across the state, I focus in this chapter on the diverse sponsorship histories of seven rural, working-class students and the social economies of literacy in which these students participate.[1] I include occasions in which students have been sponsored as well as occasions in which they have served as self-sponsors and actively sponsored the literacies of others. As Kim Donehower, Charlotte Hogg, and Eileen Schell have argued, the "rhetoric of lack" through which rural experience is so often read in public discourse may blind us to the opportunities students *have* had and to students' agency as marshals of literacy and educational opportunity themselves.[2] Likewise, assumptions of rural homogeneity may prevent cultural outsiders and insiders alike from recognizing the multiple axes on which the literacy histories of students coded *rural* and *low income* vary across both time and place. While it remains important to acknowledge economic and other disparities faced by many rural schools and communities in the United States, it is even more important that blanket assumptions not become warrants for furthering such disparities, as I discuss below, or prevent us from learning more about the shifting networks of literacy opportunity in which rural students on our campuses participate.

The study on which this chapter is based emerged from two overlapping sets of conversations. One was with faculty and administrators on my regional public campus about the lack of meaningful data on the kinds of writing students had done either in or out of school before enrolling in

DOI: 10.7330/9781607326182.c012

college. And the other conversation was with faculty and librarians on the statewide Oregon Writing and English Advisory Council about increased state and national pressures to identify common outcomes and accelerated paths to proficiency, again absent any clear or shared understanding of the diversity of students' literacy histories or the different literacy "incomes" with which students on different campuses start out. With little more than standardized test scores, financial-aid data, and high-school grade-point averages at our disposal, it was becoming increasingly difficult to persuade policymakers and higher education administrators that one size does not fit all: for example, efforts to push first-year composition down into the high schools were unlikely to serve all students well; performance-based funding models must not overlook significant social and educational inequities; and decisions about placement and curriculum should remain at the institutional, not the state, level. The lack of detailed information on rural students' literacy experiences was especially troubling in this context, as "rural and regional need" were frequently cited as primary justification for significant changes to policy and programming but typically with little direct local evidence or input from the actual communities such changes were meant to serve.[3]

While many faculty could respond to blanket proposals by talking about individual students and schools with whom we had worked, and though we had some scattered information from student literacy narratives and in-class surveys, few had ever made a systematic practice of collecting information on students' prior literacy experiences in school, let alone the range of opportunities they had had to write outside school settings or the ideas about writing they carried with them into college classrooms from those encounters. While many writing faculty espoused an ideological approach to literacy, in other words, we would have been hard pressed to describe in any detail the social or ideological contours of incoming students' literate lives, much less bring that knowledge to bear in political or administrative circles. In an effort to better document the diversity of rural Oregon students' literacy experiences and identify areas in need of further research, I proposed a preliminary multi-institutional qualitative study to be conducted during the 2013–14 academic year, modeled on the work of Deborah Brandt and drawing heavily on Brandt's notions of literacy sponsorship and literacy opportunity.

As Brandt has defined them, "sponsors" can be understood as "any agents, local or distant, concrete or abstract, who enable, support, teach, and model, as well as recruit, regulate, suppress, or withhold literacy— and gain advantage by it in some way."[4] As an analytical tool, Brandt argues, sponsorship can clarify for teachers how students in their classrooms are differentially subsidized in their literacy learning. . . . Because sponsorship focuses on the many factors that create and deny literacy opportunity, it moves our sights beyond the socioeconomic profiles of individual families toward broad systems of resources for literacy operating in students' worlds.[5]

This approach is especially useful in describing the diversity and complexity of rural students' literacies across the United States, as it shifts attention from broad geographic categories to the ways both individuals and communities participate in and are positioned by multiple, dynamic, often ideologically fraught systems of exchange.

This approach also helps foreground ways in which "contexts and people are mutually constituted," as Marjorie Faulstich Orellana argues, and recognizes "that when people move between discourse communities they bring their contexts with them, fundamentally altering the nature of the new spaces into which they move."[6] This perspective is particularly critical in studying economies of literacy in small, rural communities in which individuals routinely play multiple roles within and across multiple social institutions, and in which the ideological convergence of some sponsors may be especially powerful and the conflicting imperatives of others especially pronounced. Orellana's attention to ways in which contexts for literacy overlap, constitute, and change is also useful given the increasing mobility of working-class families across communities of all sizes and in considering the different ways students' literacies and identities actively shape both our institution's and our own.

Working from these assumptions, I arranged one- to two-hour-long face-to-face semistructured interviews with fifty-two students from twenty-one Oregon counties on their home campuses during the fall 2013 and winter 2014 quarters.[7] I then returned to each campus for shorter follow-up interviews with twenty-four of those students during the spring quarter of 2014. Major interview areas included students' prior reading and writing experiences both in and out of school; students' memories of how their writing has been assessed in different domains and by different sponsors; how students are involved in the literacy learning of others; how students see their prior literacy experiences connecting (or not) to the writing asked of them in college classrooms; and how students think about "rurality" in relation to identity, opportunity, and school.

All but one of the seven students whose experiences I discuss here are first-time, traditional-aged students. All intend to earn at least a bachelor's degree, and all attended public high schools in Oregon, representing towns ranging in size from 150 to 22,000 in seven rural counties in different parts of the state. Four of the seven are native English speakers, two are native Spanish speakers, and one was raised in a bilingual Spanish-English household that had shifted almost entirely to English by the time she left home. Though they wouldn't necessarily identify themselves as working class, all but one are first-generation college students, and none have parents employed in the kinds of professional fields they hope to enter themselves.[8] Students' families include truck drivers, agricultural workers, technicians, and sales clerks, with one family member on disability for mental-health issues and two on permanent disability as a result of physical injuries at work. Two of the seven students attend community college in the same town in which they attended high school, four attend four-year universities (one online and the other three on campus), and one is dual enrolled, earning most of his credits at a community college but taking one class per term at the university in order to keep his scholarship and remain involved in marching band. While there is of course much to say about the experiences of the older and middle-class students I interviewed as part of the larger study, my hope is that the narrower selection here helps focus attention on important differences and similarities in the sponsorship histories of rural, working-class students entering college in Oregon at approximately the same time and same age.

In the following sections, I describe in detail the kinds of writing students in this smaller sample did both in and out of school before enrolling in college and the range of literacy sponsors with whom they engaged. In the process, I emphasize critical areas of convergence and conflict among students' primary sponsors and the ideas about writing, schooling, and assessment these students have carried with them into college classrooms at least in part as a result. In their own ways, students' experiences help illustrate how access to particular literacies is both situated and stratified in rural contexts and how different degrees of convergence between different sponsors further privilege some students in some capacities and further disadvantage and dislocate others. They highlight too how students make sense of shifting expectations for literacy and actively leverage their prior experiences as they move from one context to the next. In closing, I turn to implications for instruction and policy, including how students, faculty, and other higher education decision makers might work more meaningfully together to both identify and respond to diverse, shifting, and locally specific rural and regional needs.

PAUL, DOUGLAS COUNTY, UMPQUA COMMUNITY COLLEGE

Like many of the rural, working-class students I interviewed on campuses across the state, Paul (born 1990) moved so many times growing up he can't remember all the schools he's attended. What he does remember is never wanting to go, having "a little problem with authority," and being suspended repeatedly from the Seventh Day Adventist academies his increasingly religious single father enrolled him in. "They didn't like some of my ideas," he laughs, "so they threw me out of there."

> There was this one time that I was up for evaluation or whatever because I had been bad. And they wanted me to do like an interview to see if I was ready to go back to school there or whatever. And they asked me who my hero was at the time and I was like ten and I was like, "Ozzy Osbourne, who else?" They're like, "That is not a good answer." Like, "Ozzy Osbourne, not Jesus? But Ozzy?" "Yeah, sorry." This other kid, he got in, and he said Martin Lawrence.

An avid reader of all things Beat and 1960s counterculture—Jack Kerouac, Tom Wolfe, Hunter S. Thompson, Ken Kesey—the white, twenty-three-year-old college sophomore from timber-based Douglas County enrolled full time at Umpqua Community College five years after earning his GED, bored with washing dishes for minimum wage and watching friends from high school filter in and out of the justice system for minor drug infractions.

Most typical perhaps of our field's representations of young white working-class men, Paul experienced reading and writing in school as a series of conflicts and restrictions. "They used to tell me that I couldn't read," he says. "Like when I was in elementary school, I liked reading. But, they would never let me read the books I wanted to read. They always said, 'That's not in your reading level,' or whatever, 'so you're not allowed to check that out.' Or, 'If you're in this grade, you can't check out a book for like sixth graders' or something like that. And that would always tick me off." As for writing assignments, he explains,

> I didn't do them until I started college. And then when I started college I trudged my way through them. I just try to get it done and do it as good as possible so that I get a good grade and then I don't have to do another writing class again. . . .
> I'm just like, I can talk to somebody in a conversation and I can articulate my point fine. But every time I write it down on a piece of paper, they'll find one hundred million things wrong with my essay and they'll give it back to me and be like, "Oh, this is shallow," or, "This is a biased statement," or something like that. I'm like, whatever, you asked me to do it. It's like, what do you want?

When asked about the criteria used to assess his writing in college composition, he is not sure; though it's been just a few months since he took the first of three first-year writing courses required for his associate of arts transfer degree, he mainly remembers the instructor looking for plagiarism and running essays through Turnitin.com.

Outside school, Paul had no occasions to write that he can remember. Moving so often kept him from participating in any sports or other extracurricular activities, as did his father's religious concerns. The one exception was a short stint in Pathfinders, where he made soap-box cars and learned outdoor skills. It was just like Boy Scouts, he jokes, but "with good, wholesome Seventh Day Adventist people teaching us instead of those regular Sunday Christians." He felt like an "outcast" there too, however, and "never got too involved." Today, he has an e-mail account he uses only for shopping online, and he reads but generally does not post to Facebook. The only time Paul remembers being asked to write at work was to sign that he understood company policies, most of which he had not read.

ABBEY, COLUMBIA COUNTY, OREGON STATE UNIVERSITY

A junior studying chemical engineering at Oregon State University, Abbey's sponsorship history stands in stark contrast to Paul's, reflecting a very different set of relationships with school officials and a far wider range of opportunities to use writing in ways she considered meaningful both in and out of school.[9] Like Paul, Abbey (born 1993) was raised primarily by her father, moving from place to place in search of work before settling in a town of 2,200 in the Coast Range when she was in the sixth grade. "I've been to, like, five different elementary schools. I don't remember all of them," she says. Responsible for her brother and step-brother most evenings while her father and step-mother worked the night shift forty-five minutes away, Abbey threw herself into sports, Honor Society, leadership, and other school-sponsored activities during the day. At home, she read and wrote: rigging a pulley system to exchange notes with a next-door neighbor; complaining about her stepmother in her diary; writing letters to a boyfriend in the military; and reading fantasy novels "because they're different from what I'm experiencing every day." Mostly, she says, "I just followed whatever my friends were reading because I don't know how they found out about what you should read. I just never saw a big poster anywhere." Like many rural students, she attributes much of the reading she did outside school to boredom: after both her house and her school were destroyed in a catastrophic flood her first year of high school, her family lived on their property in a trailer with no electricity, and there was not much else to do.

Although Abbey believes she was at a slight disadvantage not having advanced placement courses available in her school, she counts her close connections with her teachers as a major advantage over college students from bigger places. "In a small town," she says, "everyone's friends. Like even your bus driver you know and so you joke with him and your teachers and stuff like that. . . . And so, talking to your teachers [in college], I think it's a little bit easier for me just because I'm used to it. I mean, I babysat for half of my teachers. And so you are so close to your teachers. Especially my basketball teacher. I mean, we hung out. His grandson was in my grade so I went over to his house when he was there. So there's just that closer community feeling." After the flood, coaches and teachers often helped Abbey financially, paying for basketball shoes and sports camps and giving her access after hours to the school. "My sophomore, junior, senior year, we had all kinds of complications," she explains, "because after they raised the house we got abandoned by our contractor. So we were just nine feet off the ground with no insulation or anything. And so all our pipes froze and busted and so then I asked my coach, would he let me stay after class or after practice and shower and brush my teeth before I went home."

While Abbey notes that she was asked to write often in school and that teachers regularly helped revise scholarship essays and draft speeches for school clubs, it was her experience as "a poster child basically for someone who was in the flood" that led to her most meaningful opportunities to write before coming to college. As she describes it, "My senior year my superintendent approached me and asked me to start doing speeches for our school to make a bunch of rich people cry and kind of write us checks so we could get a new school." The superintendent "just verbally told me, 'This is kind of what we're looking for,' and then I took it from there, wrote it, and obviously I had my teachers proofread it before I gave it." The speaking engagements allowed her to skip school and meet "cool people from all over Oregon, governors and senators and stuff": "Like, one day I skipped an entire day of school to go to Hillsboro and talk to a bunch of rich people and it was really fun." Her contributions have been recognized with a plaque on the wall of the new high school, and she now sees herself as an ambassador for education, particularly for poor, rural schools.

Important to note, it was these same experiences that helped Abbey advocate for herself financially on campus and that have led in turn to more meaningful contexts for the professional writing classes she is required to take for her degree. Employed in precollege programs, she explains that her supervisor "is one of my professors and my advisor. And I came up to him one day, [and] I was like, 'I don't have a phone. People won't hire me,' and at the time I couldn't afford to get a phone and find a job. And he said, 'Give me a week and I'll see what I can do,' and a week later [I had this job]." She now spends part of the summer traveling to rural communities to facilitate science camps and organizes Lego robotics and other outreach activities in schools near campus throughout the year. Whereas Paul has little sense that the writing courses he's taking connect to any of his interests or to his future career as a music teacher, Abbey sees all the writing and rhetorical analysis she's done in her college courses as useful now and in the future, preparing her to write grants for her campus job, promote educational opportunities for rural students, and find a job eventually as a chemical engineer.

JUSTIN, UNION COUNTY, LINN-BENTON COMMUNITY COLLEGE AND OREGON STATE UNIVERSITY

Abbey's experiences and approaches to school are mirrored in important ways by Justin's, a white first-year student (born 1995) from a town of five hundred in northeastern Oregon, dual enrolled in Oregon State University and Linn-Benton Community College nearby. Like Abbey, Justin identified strongly with his K–12 teachers, coaches, and advisors, participating in band, sports, student government, Future Farmers of America (FFA), and 4-H. FFA and student government in particular provided regular opportunities to speak publicly and to write for real audiences and purposes. As chapter historian for FFA, he kept the club scrapbook. As an officer, he learned Robert's Rules of Order and "helped to type thank-you letters to all the people who donated for the banquet. And then senior year," he says, "I was our vice president and we did this thing called POA. It's the Program of Activities and it's . . . our budget, our calendar, our code of ethics, code of conduct, requirements, everything . . . I had to write all that out and kind of structure that and it's like . . . forty-seven pages." Even more influential, competing in public speaking and livestock judging at regional, state, and national levels gave him practice in oral reasoning, audience analysis, and organization and gave him a reason to stay current on agricultural issues, which he read about regularly online and in the *Capitol Press*.

As it has for generations of rural students, participation in leadership, 4-H, and FFA also brought explicit expectations for allegiance to sponsoring organizations' values and for particular attitudes toward school, industry, and authority, both of which were ritualized and reinforced through written texts as well as public events. Recalling a speech he made as outgoing senior-class president the week before he left for college, for example, Justin explains how important it remains for him to be a positive example and show respect.

> So I basically said, you know, "Step it up, be respectful, don't take advantage of the teachers. You know, you're here to learn. . . . If you're not going to take it seriously then drop out and get your GED because we don't want you here." I probably shouldn't have said that, but the intent was, you know, step it up. . . . There's always those times when you're going to like turn off for a second and be like oh, crap, okay, got to turn back on, got to be the example. I didn't want to be . . . I guess *cocky* in lack for a better word, but I always try to be elite, I think I should say, in terms of school work.

This allegiance to dominant school and community values has in fact served Justin very well, earning him thousands of dollars in scholarships from FFA, 4-H, agricultural honor societies, and private foundations as he has composed his identity again and again in scholarship essays according to sponsoring agencies' codes and goals.

Unlike many of his peers—and unlike common representations of rural, working-class young men—Justin explains that his house was full of books and talk about books growing up. His father read regularly to Justin and his brother when he wasn't gone driving a truck—*Goosebumps, The Boxcar Children, The Great Brain, Flip*, the Bible—and his mother, who works in a Christian supply store, often read books he and his brother recommended after they read them in school.

> We'd always say, "Hey, Mom, you know, you should read this book or read this book," and . . . if she ever got into it, she would just sit there for hours and just read like half of it. But she bought the first *Harry Potter* book [herself]. That's like her favorite movie of all times, the first one. I don't know why, but she read that, and then she bought *The Great Gatsby* and she read that. Or she's reading it now. . . .
>
> So I'm reading for my [college] history class *The Source* by James Michener. . . . And I told her, "You're going to have to read this because it's really interesting." She said, "Yeah, I will," . . . so I'll probably just leave it at home for Christmas break.

The whole family often sits down at the kitchen table for impromptu Bible study when Justin and his brother are home, picking a section to read together and discuss. "Psalms is a big one; Jacob, John, really anything," he says. "We'll be like oh, well, 'What do you think, what does this mean to you, you know . . . what do you think we should do or how should we live our lives,' . . . kind of deciphering what it meant." Justin's ability to transport texts, identities, and practices across all the domains important to him prepared him well for the transition to college and first-year composition, he believes, as no doubt has the repeated public assurance that he has both the authority and the duty to speak.

Together, Paul's, Abbey's, and Justin's experiences highlight in particular how literacy opportunity is both socially and ideologically patterned in the rural communities in which they grew up—following in some ways along social strata like family income, race, gender, and parental education but differing significantly according to ideology and identification, with Paul's access to literacy reflecting the distance between his beliefs and those of his most powerful institutional sponsors, while Abbey's and Justin's opportunities continue to overlap and expand. Although Abbey's positioning as the "poster child" for poor rural students would seem to complicate her identification with middle-class sponsors to some extent, she does not view it as problematic, and in fact, it has opened the door to many more "authentic" writing opportunities she would not otherwise have had. For Justin, the strong identification with organizational and corporate sponsors through Future Farmers of America has been and will likely remain critical in funding his education and providing the "identity kit" necessary to enter veterinary school and establish a successful large-animal practice in some similarly constituted agricultural place.[10]

JULIA, WASCO COUNTY, OREGON STATE UNIVERSITY

The next two students I discuss in this chapter also attend Oregon State: Julia (born 1991), a junior studying human development and family sciences, and Carla (born 1994), a first-year prelaw student majoring in philosophy. For Julia, who grew up in a predominantly white agricultural town in the Columbia Gorge, the intersecting challenges she faced as a working-class student of color and nonnative speaker of English have led to a strong interest in early-childhood education and a desire to return home after college to serve the growing Latin@ community there. One of few lower-income, Spanish-speaking students enrolled in a monolingual Catholic school from kindergarten through the eighth grade, she says, "I felt kind of like at the time, [Spanish] was . . . well, not necessarily prohibited, but like . . . it just wasn't . . . necessary."

> At times I wouldn't feel smart, and . . . when it came to comparing our grades and stuff, like, that was something I would never want to share.

And [my classmates were] just like, "Oh, well, my mom helped me out
with a project last night," . . . and then I was like, "Oh, well, my mom's a
working mom and she takes the night shift," you know, like, "I don't get
help from my parents."

I couldn't really relate to . . . stuff that they had at home or going out
and buying stuff. It was just different, and so I would keep more reserved.

This sense of isolation was compounded by the difficulty Julia had with
reading, which she says grew more frustrating from year to year: "I remember by middle school I would just read the beginning and then maybe just
like towards the middle and then towards the end because it just got to a
point where, like, I just can't do this . . . I don't even want to read."

Although Julia's parents encouraged her to do well in school, she
identifies her older brother as her main source of academic support.
"Both my parents are from Mexico and my mom reached up to the
third grade of elementary," she explains. "My dad never had an education. . . . Well, he barely knows how to write his name, so he doesn't know
anything beyond that like reading."

I remember at times [the three older children] would sit at the dinner
table and have like our homework time and yeah, we would help each
other out. . . .

And then now the two youngest ones, one is eleven and the other one
is four. . . . I guess we were the parents now and we wanted [my sister] to
succeed and get that education that we never had. And so we encouraged
her to read and like, "Oh, be sure to get your homework done and then
you can watch TV." And so she's been really successful and we're really
proud of her just because she's . . . something that we've always wanted to
be, like, we can see it in her now. So it's really neat to see her actually not
struggle compared to when we were growing up.

Julia says she got more involved in school activities when she transferred to the public high school, participating in sports and MEChA
(Movimiento Estudiantil Chicanx de Aztlan) and helping translate
material for club and community events. Learning to read and write
in Spanish in high school came easily, she says, because at that point
she "already knew how to read and write in English." Critically, it also
opened up successive opportunities to volunteer without having to take
a leadership role.

This linguistic currency further increased in value at Oregon State,
helping land both her campus job, which requires a great deal of translating and writing in Spanish and English, and her internship as a bilingual family-outreach coordinator for local public schools, which she
loves. Working from a developing ideology of literacy that has been
informed as much by her own experiences as by her college courses,

Julia says, "We're trying to facilitate events and organize like any work-shops for the parents so that way they can become aware that, you know, it's important that your children start reading at a young age because this is what they're going to be doing throughout high school and then maybe even college."

CARLA, MALHEUR COUNTY, OREGON STATE UNIVERSITY

While Julia identifies strongly with programs for first-generation and Latin@ students at Oregon State, Carla, who was recruited and men-tored through these same programs, does not. A first-year student from a far more diverse agricultural community on the eastern side of the state, Carla explains she is often asked to write and talk about her expe-riences in ways that don't match her own perceptions. Program coordi-nators will ask, for example,

> about, like, our racial identity, our personal history. And sometimes the kids will go around the room and be, like, "Oh, well, you know, when I first came to the United States or, like, in high school, like, this happened. My counselor said this, and it really hurt my feelings," and all this stuff. And it'd get to me, and I'd just be, like, "Well, I come from . . . , and a major-ity of us are Hispanic. I didn't experience that. Like, my teachers and my counselors are, like, "Yeah, like, go, you know, apply to Oregon State, apply here." Like, "Yeah, you can take those classes." Like, our school just offered honor classes and a few AP classes and a few [community] college credits, and, like, I took those classes just 'cause.
>
> Coming here, I've met people from Kazakhstan, people from Pakistan. I've met people—this kid from Asia. I've met other Hispanics. I've met people from, like, Arabia. I've met tons of people, and I'm just, like, "Well, I haven't experienced that back at home or here, and . . . then they're just kind of, like, "Well, you know . . . this is the safe circle. You can tell." And I'm just like, "I am telling." Like, I'm proud to be Hispanic. I'm proud. Like, you know, my family and I, like, we do the whole culture stuff. We speak Spanish at home all the time. I speak Spanish here. But, I mean, I haven't felt like Oregon State is somewhere I don't want to be because of racial discrimination. Like, I love the way we deal with it. . . . So it's kind of hard when they . . . ask you about your personal stuff. 'Cause I'm just like, "I don't have anything bad." But I can tell you good stuff.

Like fellow Oregon State students Justin and Abbey, Carla was highly active in school-sponsored activities in high school, serving as the secre-tary for leadership as well as volunteering at a local after-school program, developing Sunday-school lessons, and participating in liquor-commis-sion patrols with the police, all of which provided multiple opportuni-ties to read and write for audiences and purposes both immediate and authentic. As secretary, she says, "I had to write reports, like who did what, how we all contributed to the project, how the project went, how we would do it differently, and then put it all in a folder for the next . . . person to take my spot." For the liquor commission, Carla and her friends were trained on writing consistent, detailed reports that would hold up in court and then sent in to try to buy alcohol underage at businesses around the county. She was trained to write reports for the after-school program as well, occasionally filling out standardized forms on behavioral incidents to share with parents and keep on file for liability reasons.

At home, Carla journaled and read, encouraged by her mother, who earned her GED as an adult in the United States after completing fourth grade in Mexico. "My family and I, we practice our faith and our religion," she explains. "We believe in God, so my mom will send me books like, 'Hey, read this book, listen to this girl's story.' And it's just like paranormal based, how she worshipped the devil and how all that just kind of took an impact on her life." Her sister and her best friend also love to read, though her dad and other siblings hate it, she says, typically reading only the end of a book if she tells them first what the majority of it is about.

Strikingly, while Carla felt she was adequately prepared for college writing and spends a significant portion of time in her campus job writing e-mails and drafting reports, she doesn't think of herself as a writer, nor—like Paul and most other working-class students interviewed for this project—does she know how her school writing is assessed. She remembers the number she had to get on the state writing rubric in high school in order not to have to rewrite a paper but not what the criteria associated with that rubric were. Similarly, she remembers skimming over the rubric in her first-year composition course before turning in papers but not at all skimming what was being assessed. By contrast, she says, her campus job has taught her a lot about audience awareness, which has translated directly into the way she thinks about her essays for school: "So [now] when I actually, like, write my papers . . . I'll read it so they know what I'm getting at, and I know what I'm getting at. 'Cause when I write, I know what I mean. I know what I'm going to say. But when you read it, it could mean completely different to you. So that has helped a lot. . . . Rather than just, 'Oh, like, this is my paper. I can write however I want it.' 'Cause that was my mindset before."

Like Julia, Carla's goals are linked closely to her family and her home community, though she had little sense of what she might study before taking a career-exploration course her first term. When career inventories suggested she would be well suited to law, she says, it didn't fit: "Because when I think of lawyers, I think of super-duper 'up there,' you know, big city, stuff like that. So I was like, 'Uh, no. I want to keep my small city, my community with the people I know.' And I told my advisor that, and she's just like, 'Well, you can do that. You can have your own little practice in your small town.'" After testing the idea on her family and her friends at home, Carla began to convince herself that it was possible, recalling that she had always enjoyed persuasive writing and mock debates in school. The strongest motivator, however, has been watching her parents' legal battles with their employers over serious on-the-job injuries that have left both of them unable to work. "Going home and witnessing that has just made me, like, 'Wow, I really need, you know, to start planning.' Like, I really need to focus on being here [in college]. As much as I don't want to be here, in the end, it's the best thing that's going to happen. . . . I'm being positive about it. I found [in law and philosophy] something I like. And in the long run, I hope it happens."

MARCO, CLATSOP COUNTY, CLATSOP COMMUNITY COLLEGE

The last two rural, working-class students I introduce in this chapter exemplify perhaps most clearly how students forge connections across seemingly disparate contexts, actively leveraging prior literacy experiences to create wider access and opportunities for themselves. Attending community college in his rural coastal home town, Marco (born 1995), for example, credits Internet evangelist Paul Washer and conversion to Pentecostalism in the tenth grade with a complete reversal in his attitude toward school and significant improvements since in his abilities to read, evaluate evidence, and write. A first-generation college student and multilingual oldest son of Mexican American dairy workers, Marco explains, "I discovered that men are supposed to be the main support of the family and take care of the family and kind of be the main headship but also not abuse that power. . . . And learning that I also figured out that if I want to be a good husband or a good man when I grow up, I have to first focus on my grades and be a good student." From that point forward, he says, with the help of tutors in the federally funded Upward Bound program he signed up for, he made fast progress: "In the beginning I was a writer who was having struggles even developing sentences. By the end of senior year [in high school] I managed to go into honors English and pass with an A."

While Marco's desire to be a particular kind of man and husband someday more strongly motivated him to succeed in school, he is also clear that his religious conversion provided important new context for writing and English classes he hadn't recognized before. He has been especially pleased to find that his first-year writing courses focus on textual analysis and formal reasoning, skills he uses regularly both in school and out. His composition class has proven a great aid in debating scripture with friends and family members, for example, and he is looking forward to taking more literature courses, which he feels provide good practice in exegesis along with important "insight into the human condition" and what makes people good or bad.

Unlike many of the working-class students I interviewed who wrote no more than two- to three-page reports in high school on topics such as favorite cars and future jobs, Marco was assigned a wide variety of research- and experience-based papers, both before he joined honors English and after. Significantly, he also remembers many opportunities to write for local audiences and purposes in high school, including a year-long senior project in which he researched improvements to the city aquatic center and presented his proposal at a public meeting. Though he cannot remember what criteria were used to evaluate his writing in high school or college, he talks about writing effectively as a process of using appropriate evidence and adapting to one's audience, something he has learned through his many public opportunities to testify and persuade—opportunities sponsored by his school and his religion, as well as increasingly by himself.

DENISE, GRANT COUNTY, EASTERN OREGON UNIVERSITY

Attending Eastern Oregon University online from a timber town of 1,700 in Grant County, the final student, Denise (born 1983), has still different stories to tell about the diverse contexts in which she read and wrote before enrolling in college and the tangle of family, community, and institutional sponsors that both supported and constrained her developing literacies. One of eight in her graduating class and the only one to attend college, Denise believes the weekly letters she wrote to her mother in prison throughout elementary school gave her a leg up on other students in English class. "It was important for me to express myself" in those letters, she says. "Like, express, you know, complete sentences, proper punctuation and, you know, legible writing so . . . we could connect. . . . I feel like if I wouldn't have had that foundation before . . . I started junior high and high school, that I would be different. I would have been different. My other peers, they just did the bare minimum to get by because it was required. They [didn't] use it every day."

After her mother was released from prison, Denise's family moved from Portland to a relatively remote town of 150 to run a restaurant, which she worked in before and after school and managed beginning her junior year of high school. Thirteen years later, a junior in college, a part-time medical assistant, and a mother of three with credits accumulated from four different two- and four-year colleges, she is particularly attuned to stereotypes about rural students and to reductive assumptions about place and class. "I'm the first in my family to go to college," Denise explains, "the first in my family to not be, like, welfare dependent and to actually graduate high school"—so when she received an e-mail from an online writing instructor that accused her of asking for handouts and choosing online classes because they were "an easier cop out," the insult was profound. "The word *podunk* was in there, and *inbred*," she says. "I would give anything to quit my job and move my family and go to college on campus. I mean, it would be a dream. . . . I wanted to better myself and wanted to finish my education so that's the path I had to choose. I have a good job, my husband has a good job, you know, we have insurance and my kids are stable. We have a good network here. So it's working. It's not because I think it's easy, because I don't."

Like most of the students I interviewed, Denise actively sponsors others' literacies in and beyond her home community, from teaching her children to journal, to encouraging friends and neighbors to enroll in college, to helping fellow students navigate learning-management systems and faculty expectations. In Freirean terms, that is to say, Denise serves as both student-teacher and teacher-student in school and out: a key broker of literacy in her community and, like Abbey and Julia, a vocal advocate for rural and working-class students' needs.

CLOSING: ACCOUNTING FOR THE DIVERSITY OF RURAL LITERACIES, OPPORTUNITIES, AND NEEDS

If these seven students represent a very small sample of the rural college-going population in Oregon, their experiences begin to amplify nonetheless a number of important themes. At a minimum, they speak to the wide diversity of students' literacy histories and values, which both defy easy categorization and challenge the broad, sometimes ill-informed assumptions about rural and working-class students that still so often surface in legislative, institutional, and classroom contexts—as Denise's experience with her online writing instructor for one attests. At the same time, these students' stories highlight the concomitant social and ideological patterning of literacy opportunity among students differently positioned within and across small communities and in relation to family, school, employers, social institutions, and the

state. As Brandt has argued, "By looking at the day-to-day efforts of literacy learners and their day-to-day contacts with public institutions and
other social infrastructures, we can see more explicitly how economic
inequality connects to outcomes in literacy and literacy achievement."[11]
We can also see how widely opportunities for literacy learning vary both
across and within contexts, and how students' literacies are differently
valued, shaped, and supported by the different communities and institutions in which they participate.[12]

Though the critical question remains how much students want their
instructors to know about them or attempt to draw explicitly upon their
prior experiences in college, it does matter that faculty have a nuanced
understanding of where students on our campuses come from, where
they imagine themselves going, and what implications both might have
for pedagogy and program policy. At the most fundamental level, the
student experiences described here and throughout this volume should
remind readers of the importance of regularly checking and challenging blanket assumptions about rural and working-class students, communities, and schools. Where meaningful local "data" doesn't exist,
efforts must be made to collect it. However politically expedient it may
prove to generalize in particular settings about what large swathes of
students lack or need—securing a new course or instructor line, for
instance, by playing into faculty and administrator perceptions that rural
schools are uniformly deficient or that some students "just can't" or "just
don't" write or read—it should go without saying that broad, unchecked
claims like these carry real consequences for students: from the ongoing
cultural indexing of *rural* to *illiterate*, to poor student self-perceptions of
ability and belonging in college, to lowered expectations in the classroom, to state- and institution-level decision making about education
funding and the kinds of degrees and curricula best suited to meet rural
and regional needs.

For writing faculty, the diverse experiences of the rural, working-
class students profiled in this chapter seem to offer a number of more
specific program- and classroom-level recommendations as well. One,
clearly, is to continue thinking about what constitutes an "authentic"
context for writing in college classrooms, considering the diverse social
economies of literacy in which both rural and nonrural students already
participate. Though it has become increasingly common to advocate
that composition courses provide students opportunities to write for
real audiences and purposes, the "real" and "public" contexts imagined in many popular textbooks, programs, and assignments very often
remain highly generalized, on the one hand, and tied to predominantly

white, language-majority, and middle-class forums on the other. How might such assignments be recrafted to recognize the diverse social networks of which students are currently or are becoming a part? How, for instance, might assignments create wider openings for students to discuss their work in progress with friends, family members, former teachers, coworkers, and others outside the classroom with and alongside whom they do, or might more actively do, school? How might assignments better recognize and/or examine students' future roles in their communities or more consciously position students as sponsors or brokers of literacy and information themselves? Thinking about the experiences of students like Marco and Denise, in what other domains or contexts might students be more directly supported in translating the knowledge and practices a given assignment affords?

A second key reminder emerging from these interviews is to be explicit with students at all levels about assessment criteria and the value systems and structures different criteria both reflect and support. This explicitness is important not simply in increasing rhetorical knowledge and promoting transfer—as has been advocated in many venues (and as would no doubt have been useful to students like Paul and Carla, who have little sense of how or why their school-based writing has been assessed)—but also in rendering more visible the roles differently interested sponsors have played in students' understandings of writing, calling attention to the way different literacies are valued in different contexts and encouraging students to consider both critically and creatively where potential areas of conflict and convergence lie and why. As Donehower, Hogg, and Schell have argued, "The idea that there are different systems of defining, valuing, and practicing literacy must become a central concept of the composition classroom."[13] Without access to a more critical "metalanguage of literacy," as David Barton calls it,[14] it will remain difficult at best for students to situate their experiences within the wider politics of literacy, let alone advocate publicly for their communities, members of their family and social networks, or themselves.

At the same time, it is increasingly necessary for writing faculty to find ways to support legislators, governors, board members, and other higher ed decision makers in developing a nuanced understanding of literacy learning and the wide range of experiences, opportunities, attitudes, and abilities with which students arrive on our diverse campuses. As more public colleges and universities in the United States move toward performance-based funding, and as decisions about placement, remediation, dual credit, institutional degree offerings, and other matters once entrusted to faculty shift increasingly to politicians and other state-level decision makers, it is more important than ever that we can speak compellingly about who our students are, why context matters, and how we might work more effectively together to sponsor rich and varied opportunities for learning designed to serve diverse students from diverse communities of all sizes well.[15]

Notes

1. Brandt, *Literacy in American Lives*. As I explain further later, I rely heavily in this chapter on Brandt's concepts of literacy sponsorship and opportunity to describe the diverse "economies of literacy" in which rural, working-class students both participate and are produced.

2. Donehower, Hogg, and Schell, *Rural Literacies*, 14.

3. Efforts to reduce degree expectations for dual enrollment teachers is one example. Decisions to eliminate majors in the liberal arts at rural-serving public institutions and expand vocational programming under the guise of meeting "regional needs" is another.

4. Brandt, *Literacy in American Lives*, 19.

5. Ibid., 44–45.

6. Orellana, "Moving Words and Worlds," 126.

7. Although I aimed to recruit as diverse a group of students as possible, the study sample is neither random nor necessarily representative. Constraints of time and the challenges of working across nearly a dozen different campuses led me to work from a convenience sample, relying on faculty, students, and administrators on each campus to help solicit student participation. For the purposes of recruiting students, I used definitions of *rural* established by Oregon Governor Ted Kulongoski when establishing the Office of Rural Policy in 2004: students who had lived for the majority of their K–12 years at least thirty miles by road from an Oregon town of fifty thousand or more. Older and returning students who grew up elsewhere but lived at least thirty miles by road from an Oregon town of fifty thousand or more for five years prior to enrolling in college were also eligible. The study group is relatively consistent with the racial and economic makeup of rural Oregon, with students representing "rural" towns of less than five hundred to forty thousand from all parts of the state.

8. Two have parents with elementary-school educations; two have parents who earned GEDs after leaving school in elementary and high school; and two have parents who attended some college before the students were born. Just two have a parent with a bachelor's degree, one of which was earned after the student left home.

9. Despite, notably, attending high school in a town ten times smaller than Paul's "rural" community of twenty-two thousand along a major freeway.

10. Gee, *Social Linguistics and Literacies*, 155.

11. Brandt, *Literacy in American Lives*, 185.

12. There are of course many less visible sponsors I have not yet addressed here: publishers, for example, curriculum developers, testing companies, Internet providers, lobbyists, policymakers, powerful advocacy-oriented foundations like Carnegie, Lumina, and Gates. I have also said very little in this chapter about the specific political and economic contexts of students' hometowns, or about broader regional, national, and global changes that bear on the dynamic social economies of literacy in which students participate. With the exception of Paul and Julia, I have spent

little time on the way even the youngest students' literacies are differently valued across contexts or how they are likely to continue gaining, losing, and changing value over time. For Denise, for instance, it is very unlikely she would be hired for a medical position comparable to the one she holds now in a bigger community in which the labor pool includes more people officially credentialed to do the same work. For Abbey, a bachelor's degree is the minimum she will need to apply for the kind of work her father does now for a computer-chip manufacturer, one of the last employees hired based on his military experience in the early 2000s. What will her bachelor's degree be worth another ten years from now? How will or won't it provide opportunities to return home or to continue advocating for rural students and schools? These are critical questions as well, inseparable from analysis of larger political economies of literacy and the ideologies of place, identity, and schooling on which they depend.

13. Donehower, Hogg, and Schell, *Rural Literacies*, 167.
14. Barton, *Literacy: An Introduction*, 145.
15. I owe many thanks to the students, faculty, and staff across the state who shared their time, insights, and offices for this project. I am indebted as well to the Oregon Writing and English Advisory Council and the Oregon Agriculture Foundation, without whose support this study would not have been possible.

13

RETHINKING CLASS
Poverty, Pedagogy, and Two-Year College[1] Writing Programs

Brett Griffiths and Christie Toth

The educational impact of poverty on working-class students often goes unexamined in disciplinary conversations about composition pedagogy and theory. This elision reflects a long-standing national rhetoric that simplifies interactions between social classes and hails a middle-class identity so persuasively that most Americans self-identify as middle class, regardless of their economic bracket, material affordances, or social interests.[2] As a result, narratives about education and social uplift tend to obscure many of the lived realities of students experiencing poverty.[3] In first-year composition courses, where many students first encounter the linguistic and cultural expectations of a middle-class professoriate, examining the relationships between class and literacy becomes essential. As a discipline that has sought to help acclimate students to the linguistic and cultural expectations of a predominantly middle-class professoriate, composition studies has an intellectual and, in our view, a moral imperative to examine the relationships between poverty, socio-economic class, and literacy learning. Such examination is particularly important in two-year college settings, where students from low-income backgrounds are most likely to enroll and where class effects can create additional barriers to upward mobility.[4]

Our chapter presents a dialogic analysis of two case studies examining two-year college composition instructors' responses to the phenomenon we call *poverty effects*: the combined social, emotional, and material impacts of poverty that can disproportionately influence the behaviors, learning, and academic performances of working-class and working-poor students. Our studies took place in two very different geographical, racial, and cultural contexts. The first study examines three colleges in the postindustrialized Midwest United States and the second a tribally

DOI: 10.7330/9781607326182.c013

controlled college system on the Navajo Nation.[5] Taken together, our findings demonstrate that faculty face what we describe as *routine crises* of poverty effects in their composition classrooms. The language participants used to describe such conditions varied, as did the particulars of their pedagogical responses. However, all dealt with poverty effects through individualized, ad hoc negotiations they sometimes found logistically and emotionally taxing. While these responses were empathetic and occasionally went well beyond what many might expect from a college professor, they were often insufficient or unsustainable given the pervasiveness of student poverty; the colleges themselves seemed to have few programmatic strategies for understanding and responding to poverty effects in classrooms. These findings suggest that two-year colleges—and other access-oriented institutions where students experience routine poverty-related crises—should consider developing program-level responses to these conditions. In order to enable such programmatic conversations and decision making, we argue that composition studies must itself develop a better critical vocabulary to help department colleagues discuss poverty effects in the writing classroom.

DEFINING OUR TERMS
Poverty

As we discovered over the course of our research, the term *poverty* is freighted with complex ideological and rhetorical baggage: too often, it carries stigmatizing and moralizing connotations, particularly through politicized theoretical constructs like "the culture of poverty."[6] While we recognize that economic experiences of material scarcity contribute to social and psychological effects that can themselves perpetuate economic poverty,[7] we strive throughout this chapter to distinguish between economic conditions and interrelated social and emotional effects. We attempt to be rigorous in our use of the terms *chronic* and *episodic poverty* as economic classifications derived from the United States Census Bureau definitions,[8] in which "chronic poverty" refers to the condition of living below the poverty line (in 2014, an annual income of $23,850 for a family of four) for three years or longer[9] and "episodic poverty" is defined as living below the poverty threshold for two or more consecutive months in a two-year period.[10] For the 2004–2006 period, nearly one-third of the US population experienced episodic poverty, roughly twice the official measurement of chronic poverty.[11]

Economist Michael Zweig has argued that poverty is a condition that occurs cyclically and affects working families for which wages are low and/or episodic.[12] Pointing to this cyclicality, labor historian Jack Metzgar has emphasized the need for a more grounded conception of poverty as an episodic threat to working families and communities.[13] Thus, we take the term *poverty* to include both chronic and episodic poverty, recognizing that both conditions threaten the educational aspirations of many, perhaps a majority, of working-class and working-poor students, who are most likely to enroll at two-year colleges.[14]

Pedagogy

The term *pedagogy*, which arguably unifies our various professional locations and positions as compositionists, is often taken for granted in our scholarly literature. It often refers to attitudinal and theoretical orientations to teaching, as in Gary Tate's *A Guide to Composition Pedagogies*, but it just as frequently (and often interchangeably) refers to what instructors do in the classroom that evidences those orientations.[15] The term *pedagogy*, then, refers to the theorized teaching decisions and the rationales that support those decisions as faculty move between theory and practice. As Shari Stenberg and Amy Lee put it, "Theory and practice necessarily function in interplay, and pedagogy encompasses both."[16] As we have thought about the relationships between socioeconomic class and pedagogy in our respective research sites, we have wrestled with the immensity of conceptualizing pedagogy in relation to poverty. Are we referring to how instructors' theoretical orientations and teaching philosophies shape their responses to student poverty effects? Are we examining how instructors respond to the specific exigencies poverty presents through curricula? Through articulated course policies? Through direct interactions with students? In a word, *yes*. However, as we will discuss, our studies suggest the need for more theorizing of the dynamic interactions between practice (classroom interventions, course policies, and curricular innovations) and theory—that is, philosophies, structural analyses, and perhaps even a (re)definition of pedagogy that extends beyond the classroom to the program level.

Program

Jeff Klausman argues that "most two-year colleges . . . have a collection of writing classes, not a program."[17] He explains that although composition makes up the bulk of their courses, English departments at two-year colleges have usually not thought of themselves as writing programs. As Klausman asserts, a program "is characterized by an explicitly expressed coherent curriculum with integrated faculty development and assessment. Lacking that, we have only classes loosely related by too-often unspoken and, most likely, conflicting assumptions about aims, means, and purpose."[18] In other words, a *program* involves a conscious effort to cultivate theoretical coherence across an institution's writing curricula and a common conceptual vocabulary—with a concomitant degree of shared pedagogical understanding—among its faculty. Distinct from *major*, program cultivation depends upon engagement among faculty with one another and with current disciplinary knowledge in order to define and express coherent curricular practices revised and enacted through departments. Pedagogical responses to poverty effects are generally also left to individual instructors' "too-often unspoken" and "conflicting" assumptions about socioeconomic class, teacher roles and responsibilities, and standards for "college-level" performance. We see the growing movement to develop writing programs that meet the distinctive conditions and needs of two-year colleges as an opportunity to theorize programmatic responses to this structural reality.

COMMUNITY COLLEGES, STUDENT POVERTY, AND COMPOSITION COURSES

Articles examining pedagogical responses to poverty effects in first-year college writing courses are scarce. In fact, a review of the scholarly and popular literature suggests that educators most often introduce poverty as a "subject" for study *by* college students. Scott Seider, Samantha Rabinowicz, and Susan Gillmor, for example, describe service learning as a pedagogical strategy to help students understand the causes and conditions of poverty.[19] Similarly, Steck et al. describe changes in beliefs and attitudes about poverty experienced by students at a private college who participated in a one-night "poverty simulation."[20] We recognize the importance of teaching students about poverty, its complex causes, and its far-reaching social impacts. We agree with Ira Shor[21] that class-conscious teaching approaches, especially among two-year college writing instructors, may help students face their own unfamiliarity with the class structures that shape their experiences and opportunities. Indeed, James Valadez's qualitative exploration of the experiences of students living in poverty[22] suggests that unexamined assumptions about education, work, and access can lead such students to pursue educational paths that actually impede economic mobility. Nevertheless, programs like those described above may inadvertently position poverty as something students have to "go to" rather than something they may well have experienced or, for that matter, *be* experiencing. Such exoticization reinforces ideological constructions of poverty as a static economic state experienced by "others" and, in particular, "others outside college."

In the few studies that do explore the experiences of two-year college students living in poverty, researchers often point to the complexities of managing the physical expectations for course attendance and the intellectual habits of learning alongside childcare, family responsibilities, inconsistent housing, and unreliable transportation.[23] Neither two-year colleges themselves nor governmental aid systems have been able to sufficiently recognize and address these concerns. For example, initiatives aimed at limiting "dependence" on welfare by recipients, such as the Personal Responsibility and Work Opportunity Reconciliation Act of 1996 (PRWORA), have the net effect of cutting benefits for students attending college because educational activities are not defined in terms of work or work-seeking behavior. Yet, small, nonprofit community organizations like Iowa's Beyond Welfare have demonstrated the importance of systematic support for these students. For most two-year-college students, however, no such supports exist.[24]

Ronald Weisenberger asserts that the lack of recognition and support for community college students living in poverty stems from the lack of support for community colleges themselves. He explains,

> Community colleges were created to be flexible in order to meet workforce demands such as the absorption of a surplus labor force and retraining. In attempting to meet these demands the colleges make promises that they can guarantee a better life for their students, especially the poor and working-class ones. However, they have little control over the factors that cause economic displacement, and are in fact subject to them. When economic downturns and changes in the tax structure restrict the moneys available to the colleges they are left without adequate resources to meet even those societal expectations that they might be capable of fulfilling, and then are subject to being scapegoated for a failure to fulfill their mission.[25]

The first decade of the twenty-first century has borne out Weisenberger's analysis. Following a decade of cuts in government subsidies in higher education, 2009–2010 saw state funding for two-year colleges decline as much as 15 percent in some states, even as enrollments surged in the midst of recession. Unlike other colleges and universities, which can offset cuts in government appropriations by shifting costs to individual students in the form of tuition hikes, two-year colleges have had to drastically refigure their operating budgets. Over the last ten years, this has resulted in funding declines of 10.7 percent for instruction and 13.6 percent for academic support, including tutoring services, writing centers, and so forth.[26]

College writing courses are nearly ubiquitous requirements at two-year colleges, and they constitute a crucial variable for measuring student progress and educational attainment.[27] Studies from a variety of institution types suggest students' experiences in writing courses directly inform their decision to remain enrolled, their perceptions of college, and their choice of major.[28] As such, writing courses constitute an important site of intervention for improving the higher education outcomes of students most at risk of discontinuing their studies. Current scholarship indicates that class identity plays an important role in the writing identities students take up and that this knowledge should inform composition pedagogy.[29] However, our research suggests that the poverty effects students experience can complicate two-year college instructors' various and often already competing pedagogical goals, including preparing students for transfer and the workforce, cultivating civic engagement, and maintaining academic standards.

METHODS

This chapter offers a dialogic analysis of two semester-long ethnographic case studies examining how writing faculty at two-year colleges responded pedagogically to their institutional contexts. Brett's study focused on community colleges in an area disproportionately affected by the recent recession—the sprawling manufacturing economies in southeast Michigan. Christie's study was situated in a two-year tribal college in the southwestern United States. We designed and carried out our studies separately, and neither of us originally framed our research as an examination of poverty effects in the classroom. Indeed, we should state from the outset that we were not—and are not—engaged in what Eve Tuck has called "damage-centered research," "intent on portraying neighborhoods and tribes as defeated and broken."[30] We have both written elsewhere about the rich pedagogical, political, and cultural work we have witnessed in our studies, and we have both struggled throughout the writing of this piece with the concern that focusing on the effects of poverty on students' academic experiences might obscure students' determination, resourcefulness, and resilience, which we have regularly witnessed through our teaching and research. However, our ongoing dialogues over the course of our data collection and analysis suggested striking parallels in the ways instructors experienced, discussed, and responded to student poverty effects across the two sites. Taken together, we believe our findings offer important insights into how instructors negotiate these pedagogical challenges. Here, we compare the results

Table 13.1. Overview of quoted faculty participants

Instructor	College	College Setting	Class Background	Ethnicity
Clarisse	Corner College	Urban	Middle Class	White
Callie	Corner College	Urban	Middle Class	White
Robin	Ridgeway College	Semirural	Middle Class	White
Roxana	Ridgeway College	Semirural	"Recently middle class (grew up in a below-poverty-level household)"	White
Sadie	Silver Lake College	Suburban	Upper Middle	White
James	Tribal College	Rural reservation	Working class	White
Patrick	Tribal College	Rural reservation	Low income	Diné
Lily	Tribal College	Rural reservation	Low income	Diné
Barb	Tribal College	Rural reservation	Working class	White

of our individual analyses and identify common themes. Table 13.1 provides an overview of the institutional affiliation, class, and racial/ethnic background of the faculty quoted in our findings section. All faculty members who participated in these studies had the opportunity to review and provide feedback on early drafts of this chapter, we integrated that feedback into the final version. Before presenting our findings, we offer a more detailed discussion of our individual research sites and methods.

Case Study 1

Brett's study examined the teaching expectations, opportunities, and constraints identified by composition instructors at community colleges in southeast Michigan. The participating instructors included six women and four men, all of whom were white. Seven participants self-identified their class backgrounds as "middle class," one as "below poverty"; two chose not to respond. Instructors hailed from three colleges: five taught at Corner College, three at Ridgeway College, and two at Silver Lake College.[31] Corner College serves an urban community with high levels of unemployment and "official" 2009 poverty estimates around 16 percent. Ridgeway College serves a semirural community where the official rate of poverty was 39 percent. Silver Lake College serves a predominantly suburban community with an official poverty rate of 11 percent, one of the lowest in the state. This brief overview necessarily oversimplifies variations in enrollment demographics, especially as they pertain to race, educational attainment, and job opportunities in this postindustrial crescent outside metro Detroit, where socioeconomic class and racial demographics are imbricated in a context of urban manufacturing, renewal, and immigration.

For this study, Brett collected course syllabi, classroom observations, and instructors' written feedback on student writing. She conducted one-on-one interviews with instructors about each set of data in order to identify and understand instructors' teaching choices and rationales. A total of ten instructors participated in this study, and seven participated in all three task-focused interviews. Brett used HyperResearch software to open code and organize a constant comparative analysis[32] of transcripts from twenty-five one-hour interviews. This chapter presents the findings of a secondary analysis of those data, using the categorical codes of *poverty* or *class*, and category codes of *student characteristics* and *teaching adaptations* from her primary analysis to identify passages in which instructors described teaching challenges associated with students' poverty levels and class dispositions.

Case Study 2

The second case study presents findings from Christie's research with four writing faculty and sixteen of their students at two campuses of a tribally controlled college serving the Navajo Nation, whose 27,425-square-mile reservation homeland is located in the Four Corners region. The Navajo Nation is highly rural, and road quality and access to electricity, running water, mobile-phone coverage, and broadband Internet varies from community to community. As long-time tribal college English instructor Kay Thurston observes, "Probably the number one reason for the high attrition among Navajo students is financial. While it would, of course, be incorrect to suggest that every Navajo student struggles financially, the fact is that poverty on the Navajo reservation is so widespread it's the norm."[33] Nearly a third of households have incomes of less than $15,000 a year, and 38 percent of tribal members and 44 percent of children are considered to be living in poverty.[34] Official unemployment rates are higher than 20 percent in many communities, and in some places exceed 50 percent.[35] These conditions are a function of the history and current racialized structures of US settler colonialism, which seeks to control Native American lands, resources, and people for the benefit of the settler state.[36] The tribal college was founded to provide reservation access to postsecondary education that would help maintain Diné language and traditional knowledge while also fostering economic development and political self-determination on the Navajo Nation.[37]

In discussing poverty effects in this context, Christie is leery of perpetuating the invented image of the "degraded or reservation Indian," a "degenerate and impoverished" ideological construct that has served settler colonial projects for centuries.[38] Contra this racist misrepresentation, Christie has seen a great deal of love, laughter, and resilience, spiritual and intellectual engagement, and pride in Diné identity and heritage in the communities where she has researched and taught. Furthermore, understandings of "poverty" and "wealth" are always shaped by local histories and values. While most Diné people Christie has met want stability for their families and opportunities for their young people, that vision of prosperity extends beyond just material well-being to encompass cultural, physical, and spiritual vitality, environmental restoration, and the fullest possible measure of tribal sovereignty and self-determination.

For her original study, Christie conducted and analyzed four longitudinal interviews with each participating instructor and student and weekly observations of one composition section taught by each instructor. She also performed textual analysis of course documents such as syllabi, readings, and assignment handouts. These analyses were supplemented by Christie's own experiences teaching composition as an adjunct instructor at the college. The participating instructors included two men and two women: two were Navajo, and two were white/Anglo. All four instructors came from working-class or low-income backgrounds themselves. The sixteen students in the study included ten women and six men, all of whom were Diné. One student also identified as African American, and two had additional tribal affiliations. Like Brett, Christie used HyperResearch to open code and organize constant comparative analysis[39] of interview transcripts, observation field notes, and course documents, and in this chapter she also presents secondary analysis of the instructor interviews using the categorical code *faculty responses to student socioeconomics* to identify passages in which instructors described students' socioeconomic status and their reactions and/or pedagogical responses. She also draws on her primary analysis of student interviews, focusing on passages coded *challenges*, defined as "difficulties and barriers that sometimes undermine students' success in college."

FINDINGS

In this chapter, we highlight four key themes we identified through our dialogic analysis: poverty effects in the classroom, instructors' vocabulary for discussing poverty, pedagogical responses to poverty, and the ideological tensions present in those pedagogical responses. Across both studies, we found clear evidence that the effects of poverty on students' behaviors, learning, and performance shaped teaching conditions in composition classrooms. In interviews, however, instructors did not seem to share a critical vocabulary for describing poverty and its effects among their students. Rather, they employed a variety of terms reflecting their observations and interpretations of students' experiences. In some cases, instructors adapted course policies and teaching approaches to accommodate the needs of students experiencing poverty. However, this adaptation typically occurred on an individual, ad hoc basis, leaving the challenge of supporting students to individual instructors, their resources, and their understanding of poverty effects. Furthermore, we identified persistent ideological tensions in instructors' responses, particularly among their empathy for the poverty-related barriers students encountered, the value they attached to student agency, and their perceived obligation to uphold what they considered college-level "standards." Based on this analysis, we argue such tensions might be better and more fairly negotiated at the program level rather than treated as a matter of individual pedagogical decision making.

Poverty Effects and the Composition Classroom

While differing in method, both studies showed that poverty effects could negatively impact students' behaviors, learning, and performance in their composition courses. Consistent access to reliable transportation was perhaps the most pressing challenge for many students, particularly at rural campuses like those at the tribal college and Ridgeway, where public transportation was limited or nonexistent. Ridgeway instructor Robin explained, "I would say the general population here is just, they're struggling just to get here sometimes. Gas money . . . I mean even to take the bus . . . we're out in the middle of nowhere really." Many students could not afford to own vehicles, leaving them reliant on relatives, partners, or friends for transportation. These arrangements were not always stable or predictable, particularly over the long four-month arc of the semester: vehicles break down, get damaged or repossessed; employment statuses or work schedules change; relationships sour. Even those students with access to a vehicle were vulnerable to breakdowns, accidents, and difficulties affording gas or making payments. Several students in Christie's study described hitchhiking to and from campus, in some cases after dark, an unreliable and potentially dangerous set of circumstances.

The ever-present demands of child- and eldercare also constrained some students' ability to attend class or complete coursework on time. Tribal college students often relied on extensive family networks to meet these needs, but when those networks fell through, students had few alternatives to missing class. Likewise, several tribal college students described unexpected absences because their children or other family members suddenly got sick, requiring travel to and long waits for treatment at clinics or hospitals. Health conditions associated with poverty further complicated these issues, as many of these family illnesses were related to poverty conditions and/or environmental racism—that is, diabetes, workplace injuries, ailments caused by substance abuse, and cancers related to occupational exposure to carcinogens.[40]

Unstable housing situations also affected some students' learning and performance in their writing classes. One student in Christie's study, a single mother, faced eviction in the middle of the semester, causing her to miss a week of class. Likewise, shared family living situations could be crowded and, in some cases, precarious. Instructors in Brett's study identified both periodic and persistent homelessness as challenges to students' most basic educational agency: textbooks, pens, and USBs could not be reliably stored on the street or even in shelters. Sadie, a Silver Lake instructor, described feeling overwhelmed by the recent influx of poverty-related disruptions: "I mean the stories these students bring me for why their lives are the disasters that they are. I mean I used to get the dead grandmas . . . this is what happens, but you know I was mugged? the bus? homeless?" The nature of even stable housing could present challenges to studying and completing assignments. Many tribal college students lived in homes heated with wood-burning stoves, and some did not have running water. Thus, time-consuming chores like chopping wood and hauling water could sometimes constrain the time available for coursework.

In many cases, long-standing patterns of episodic or chronic poverty had also shaped students' preparation for college-level work. For instance, frequent family relocation in response to shifting economic conditions had repeatedly disrupted students' attendance at (often under-resourced) K–12 schools. This legacy of childhood poverty meant some students faced significant academic challenges as they transitioned to college-level reading and writing. Underpreparedness could extend to a lack of familiarity with certain writing technologies. Instructors in both studies indicated that some of their students arrived with little computer experience. This inexperience resulted in a lack of core logistical knowledge, such as how to manipulate a keyboard or a mouse, as well

as situated knowledge about how to conduct online research or to effectively use word-processing software. In short, a longstanding legacy of
limited access contributes to learning challenges for students living in
and cycling through poverty over time. Furthermore, given that access
to resources like computer labs largely depended on reliable transportation and access to child- or eldercare, multiple poverty effects could
compound barriers to student learning.

As all these points suggest, a lack of financial resources created logistical challenges and limited the flexibility of students experiencing poverty. This lack made even the relatively small, routine costs of a college
writing course—such as purchasing textbooks, printing out readings
or drafts, and acquiring a USB drive to save written work—difficult for
some students. Furthermore, pressing financial concerns could force
students to deprioritize schoolwork or class attendance. Sudden unemployment or other financial emergencies within households—episodic
poverty—could change the delicate equations that enabled students to
attend college. The semester was a long commitment for students in
precarious financial situations: a lot could go wrong over the course of
four months. When push came to shove, some students had to choose
short-term income opportunities over their long-term educational goals.

Faculty brought diverse explanations, emotional reactions, and pedagogical responses to these poverty effects. However, they generally
agreed about the consequences of poverty effects on student learning:
relatively high levels of tardiness, absence, and late or missing assignments; instructional challenges related to technology and inconsistent student attendance; and, in the longer run, high rates of course
withdrawal, dropout, or failure. These conditions were almost taken
for granted at colleges with high student poverty rates. As James put
it, "That's part of life at a tribal college. You just have to work around
it . . . the challenges are so routine." The ubiquity of these challenges
leads us to think of them as the "routine crises" of poverty effects in two-
year college composition classrooms.

Talking about Student Poverty

One of the most resounding findings across both our studies was how
consistently faculty described effects associated with economic poverty without actually using the word *poverty*. In fact, one of the major
challenges of this dialogic analysis was determining when faculty were
"indexing" economic poverty using other terms or descriptors and when
they themselves were having trouble identifying whether the sources of

students' difficulties were academic, material, social, psychological, or some complex combination thereof.[41] In some instances, instructors described symptomatic material effects of poverty, such as "homelessness," "transience," and "economic difficulties," to refer to students' material conditions; on other occasions, they referred to challenging life experiences that are correlated with economic poverty and can be problematically conflated with it. For example, Corner College instructor Clarisse explained, "They're coming out of bad lives, a lot of them. . . . There's abuse, there's homelessness, there are those types of things that you don't usually think about that students come to us, and they don't do well in the classroom because they slept in their car and they haven't had anything to eat for a day." Here, Clarisse begins by using "bad lives" to capture an overall landscape of difficulties students face, both economic and social. She connects those experiences and conditions to barriers students face as a direct result of material scarcity: poor sleep and hunger. In this way, "bad lives" indexes the economic conditions we understand as poverty and the social and emotional complications we are calling *poverty effects*. Our analysis of several participant interviews and our own interrater examination of codes proved that encompassing phrases like *bad lives* seemed to index a broad network of associated poverty effects that had the potential to blur educational, economic, and social barriers to student learning.

Instructors often remarked that students had "complex" or "complicated" lives, that students had "stuff" or "things happening in their life," that they had "personal issues" or "problems," came from "dysfunctional families" or "homes," or were experiencing "other factors" that seemed to encompass a range of economic, family, and physical and/or mental-health issues that might affect students' academic performance. The terms faculty used to describe students' challenges suggested they often had difficulty distinguishing between issues of "motivation, "commitment," or "study skills" and poverty effects that were beyond students' control. Patrick's description of his tribal college students' difficulties meeting paper due dates encapsulates this tension: "The work ethic thing—students have a difficult time with time management and being able to do things. I really think that they need other skills besides writing skills, like time management, for example. Of course there's other things that they have with their own life. I think those things that you don't see contribute to that as well." Although Patrick begins by framing late work as a matter of individual student character and academic preparation—an explanation that foregrounds student responsibility and agency—he ultimately acknowledges that students face significant external challenges faculty cannot always see or understand. Several faculty similarly indicated that the conditions of students' lives affected their academic performance in ways often complex and difficult to parse. As James said, "In many cases, the academic struggle and the life struggle are so intertwined that you just can't separate them." The disinclination to expressly identify these "life struggles" as poverty related may reflect instructors' own uncertainties about the interrelations between students' academic preparation or performance and their material, social, and emotional circumstances.

Across twenty-five interviews, only one instructor in Brett's study—Robin—used the word *poverty* in relation to her students' experiences. In this instance, Robin used the term to draw an explicit comparison between conditions at her rural two-year college campus and two other colleges in the region: "The difference though between those two schools and Ridgeway is the high levels of poverty here and extremely dysfunctional families. I have never seen anything like it . . . a lot of students here at Ridgeway are . . . oh, we have homeless students. We have students in just very dysfunctional homes. We have single parents with a lot of kids. Extreme poverty is the biggest difference right off the top of my head." Here, Robin describes two interacting life conditions, poverty and "dysfunctional" homes. There is copious research examining how economic poverty correlates with social and psychological effects that both derive from and contribute to an individual or family's economic circumstances. Robin identifies that these effects are interrelated causes of the difficulties her students encounter, although she does not articulate the nature of these relationships. Her declaration "I've never seen anything like it" underscores how overwhelmed she feels by the teaching dilemmas these students present and the lack of tools available to respond to such conditions.

Across all sixteen interviews with tribal college faculty, only one instructor, Lily, used the term *poverty* in relation to her students. She did so on two occasions: in both cases, she was discussing socioeconomic conditions on the Navajo Nation. For example, while describing the common themes in her basic writing students' essays, she said, "You have students that talk about their goals and desire, of going somewhere. Having a dream of leaving this world of poverty, the world of not successful idea that surrounds them, but through education, through college, there's hope." Lily discussed poverty as a set of conditions that impacted life on the reservation—her use of the term implies an understanding of poverty as social and intergenerational, and she sees students' awareness of these conditions as a strong force motivating them to pursue postsecondary education. The fact that Lily used the term *poverty* to describe broad social conditions students sought to *transcend* or *improve*, rather than as an analytic framework for understanding the challenges they faced in the classroom, further illustrates instructors' widespread disinclination to apply the term *poverty* directly to students.

In our view, this discursive tendency reflects two major issues that warrant further examination. If *poverty* is ideologically constructed as a stigmatized, deficit-oriented, and generally permanent *identity* category rather than an often episodic *situation* or *experience* that affects identity resources, the term might seem to discount students' resources and deny them agency or hope. Faculty may have been understandably, even laudably, reluctant to apply a term with such negative associations to human beings they cared about and who they knew possessed important personal resources and capabilities. This reluctance may have been particularly true at the tribal college, an institution explicitly committed to celebrating the richness of Diné knowledge and kinship and to encouraging students to understand their cultural heritage and identity as valuable resource they carry with them regardless of material conditions. Particularly for two-year college faculty whose commitments to teaching are fueled by a belief that education will enable students to improve their circumstances, the term *poverty* might seem to index an uncomfortable fatalism.

However, this avoidance of the term *poverty* reflects the second major concern emerging from our dialogic analysis, which was that instructors seemed to lack a shared vocabulary for discussing student poverty—chronic or episodic—and its effects on learning. This lack of critical vocabulary made it difficult to identify the *structural* nature of the personal and family crises that periodically disrupted students' educational experiences, regardless of their commitment and resourcefulness. As we discuss below, the inability to talk about these issues structurally—to discuss *why* poverty-related student crises are, in fact, routine—makes it difficult to address them on anything other than an individual, ad hoc basis.

Pedagogical Responses to Poverty

Faculty in both studies responded to poverty effects in their classrooms in a number of ways. We organize our discussion of these responses into three categories: inclusion, alleviation, and accommodation. At the tribal college, faculty sometimes sought to make composition courses more relevant to students and validating of their experiences by *including* poverty-related course content. For example, three of the faculty assigned readings that discussed issues related to either (1) the material conditions of poverty, such as homelessness or the logistical challenges of rural life when resources are scare or (2) social issues often linked to poverty conditions, such as substance abuse and domestic violence. Furthermore, all four faculty assigned writing tasks—reflective writing, personal essays, and/or research papers—that gave students the opportunity to write about poverty-related issues if they chose to do so. Finally, in class discussions, all four tribal college faculty made at least occasional reference to periods in their lives when they had experienced poverty conditions, demonstrating their familiarity and empathy with many students' circumstances, modeling resilience, and legitimating the claim that education can provide a pathway to economic stability. Although these forms of inclusion were not overtly grounded in structural critiques of capitalism or colonialism, they did help destigmatize experiences of poverty and frame them as subjects for intellectual and creative investigation.

Faculty across both studies also made pedagogical choices intended to *alleviate* poverty effects among their students. Some instructors made a conscious effort to minimize additional costs for students. Several instructors, for example, deliberately selected low-cost textbooks when allowed by department regulations to do so, and James used the same book across the entire required composition sequence so his students would not need to buy new books each term. Likewise, instructors in both studies took measures to reduce technology-related barriers for students. James, for instance, accepted handwritten essays from students who had limited access to computers; instructors at Ridgway, on the other hand, made extensive use of institutional technology infrastructure to provide students with access to digital resources and learning experiences they might otherwise be unable to afford or acquire. Every writing classroom at Ridgeway offered a laptop for each student, and all students had access to data storage via the college website. Some instructors began the lesson by having students print their papers from the classroom printer, and at the end of class they were reminded to save their work to their digital folders. As a result, students could arrive and leave empty handed but still have a stable record of their ongoing work. One evening student who came to class straight from his manufacturing job told Brett that having his materials typed for class would be impossible without this support.

Other forms of alleviation were meant to reduce the routine material and logistical challenges of poverty. At the tribal college, for example, James emphasized to students that children were welcome in his office—indeed, he kept a bag of lollipops in his desk for just such occasions. This gesture made it easier for students who were parents to seek additional help when they needed it. Likewise, Barb often brought fruit and other snacks to class, in part because she knew students might suffer from food scarcity in their homes. She also described efforts to connect students in crisis with campus resources and tribal agencies, although she expressed frustration with the limitations of these services. Perhaps the most notable example of alleviating poverty effects Christie observed involved Patrick. Six weeks into the semester, he discovered that one of his students, Morning Star, was hitchhiking thirty miles each way to get to his evening class on the college's main campus: the course section at a branch campus closer to her home had filled before she could enroll. Upon learning of this dangerous situation, Patrick unofficially transferred Morning Star to his branch campus section of the same course, allowing her to attend class and complete the coursework closer to home. He also connected her with a tutor at the branch campus to help her get caught up on the work she had missed early in the semester. This flexibility enabled Morning Star to pass a course she had been forced to drop on two previous attempts. Forms of alleviation were present at the Michigan community colleges as well, though sporadic and not always openly discussed. Sadie, for example, offered limited access to her faculty printer and copier to students she knew were homeless.

The most common pedagogical response to poverty effects, however, was *accommodation*, most commonly through flexible course policies. Some faculty had developed policies that explicitly responded to the routine crises their students faced. James had an official policy of accepting late work with no penalty up through the end of the semester, in part because he found tracking and penalizing late work cumbersome. Likewise, he was flexible about tardiness, thereby accommodating the routine crises that could affect student schedules. Clarisse also described the need for course policies that were sensitive and responsive to students' material circumstances: "I accept papers up to one week late, ten percent penalty, which is practically nothing, but you have to have something like that. You can't be—well, no, you'd have to have your life in order well enough to not have this problem. So many of them are parents. And their kids get sick and they have no healthcare." Likewise, Robin indicated she accepted late papers and offered flexible attendance and tardiness policies. She also sought to check in with students regarding their reasons for being late as a strategy for gaining insight into their life situations and identifying appropriately individualized responses. Indeed, several tribal college instructors noted the importance of keeping the lines of communication open in order to understand the circumstances affecting students' performance.

Other faculty sought to uphold more rigid policies regarding attendance and due dates, largely because they believed students benefited from clarity about college expectations. However, such efforts often failed to resolve the tension between responding to students' circumstances and maintaining those expectations. Callie, for example, had recently adapted her course policies.

> I feel really witchy about my new attendance policies and my new late work policies, but I'm still much more lenient than anybody around me. . . . We do have students who have no idea what . . . the expectations are. They're trying to work full time and another job and take care of kids and be active in their church and take care of their grandmother, and they try to do less than will be enough, so I'm just trying to give them really clear expectations, really clear rules, about what they have to do.

However, even those who officially maintained no-late-work policies sometimes made exceptions to accommodate students experiencing poverty-related crises. Barb, for example, granted assignment extensions in at least two instances: the first when a student faced eviction and the second when a student unexpectedly lost a parent in a substance-abuse-related accident. Likewise, Patrick had an official policy of not accepting late work, but, as his efforts with Morning Star demonstrate, he enacted a remarkable degree of flexibility when he believed the occasion warranted.

Across our studies, it was clear many writing faculty cared deeply about their students who were experiencing poverty effects. They empathized with the challenges these students faced, and they wanted to see their students succeed. Those instructors who came from working-class and low-income backgrounds themselves often identified strongly with their students and believed they had particular insights into their struggles. In many cases, their teaching was motivated by a commitment to make positive contributions to their communities (or to communities socioeconomically similar to the ones in which they had grown up). However, one significant theme that emerged across our studies was a sense that instructors' pedagogical responses to poverty effects in the classroom were almost always a matter of individual discretion rather than part of larger programmatic or institutional initiatives. There were a few notable exceptions: the technology infrastructure in Ridgway College writing classrooms, the tribal college's policy of administratively withdrawing students who missed three consecutive class meetings without notifying their instructors, the visit the tribal college's retention specialist paid to Barb's class to talk to students about the expectations for college work habits and institutional resources available to help them succeed. On the whole, however, the challenges of supporting students who were experiencing poverty seemed to fall on individual instructors and their abilities and resources for responding.

And these abilities and resources were often limited, particularly given the heavy workload two-year college faculty carry: nearly all the instructors in our studies were teaching at least five courses, most of them composition. The demands of teaching these course loads—particularly keeping up with responding to so many student papers—while trying to accommodate poverty effects could over time lead to 'empathy fatigue." In Christie's study, which included a series of interviews over the course of the semester, three instructors expressed mounting frustration with the logistical challenges of student absences and late work, and some seemed to become more inclined to frame students' explanations as "excuses" as their exasperation grew. James commented directly on how these demands impacted his teaching.

> I'm concerned about the fact that attendance characteristically isn't good. I'm also concerned about the fact that they're coming in late, as late as they're coming. . . . To be honest with you, that bothers me a lot. . . . I think, I just, I feel too scattered. . . . Late work is the biggest problem because sometimes I don't want to give them attention when they come in late. Sometimes I don't feel like I have the time. Sometimes I'm being maybe implicitly punitive, but . . . and you've done enough teaching to know that when you get these staggered papers out of sequence, you're not . . . you're . . . it's like being in a time machine. It's probably the biggest problem here.

In short, the unacknowledged and uncompensated "overtime" involved in accommodating poverty effects could tax faculty to the point that they were no longer confident in or satisfied with their own pedagogical work.

In some cases, these pressures impacted faculty retention. Sadie, Roxana, and Barb left their positions within a year of participating in our studies, citing "burnout" and a lack of institutional support. Roxana described herself as "burning out" in the middle of the winter semester of her second year. She was in many ways a model community college "teacher-scholar."[42] She drew on students' funds of knowledge to develop course content, consulted current literature on writing pedagogy to improve her teaching weekly, attended conferences to improve her understanding of language variation and student learning, and developed student feedback practices that were personalized and direct, with each student getting a narrated genre analysis of their work. She left the college after her third year. Roxana's experiences provide a glimpse into the kinds of emotional labor and commitment of personal resources demanded of instructors who we might say are "doing it right." It also points to one of our major concerns as authors: while we are, on one hand, developing an argument for stronger and more comprehensive supports for students living with poverty effects, we are mindful that, as workers and professionals, instructors at two-year colleges are often overworked, undercompensated, and insufficiently recognized or respected. In order for these faculty members to *do* more for students experiencing poverty, they need to *have* more—more resources, more time, and more programmatic and institutional support to develop responses that enable their students to succeed.

IDEOLOGICAL TENSIONS

Finally, throughout both our studies, we identified persistent ideological tensions between faculty's desire to support students experiencing poverty and a need to uphold their perception of "standards" for both the quality of student writing and the work habits associated with college. Sadie's comments illustrate these competing values.

> So we have to either decide, you know? . . . that we are going to give them a pass for doing work that is not college level work . . . I'm being shoved in two directions. I try to keep my ethics [about college standards] but . . . usually your ethics would sort of make you feel morally warm but, my little homeless girl shows up and she can't find her flash drive because she is homeless . . . I am going to give her an F? I am going to hold the standards? That is not what I want. I want to help this chick get a job, and a happy life, and house for Christ's sake.

As Sadie's conflicting impulses suggest, such tensions are often emotional and virtually impossible to reconcile. Instructors are tasked with the sometimes conflicting roles of *preparing* students to succeed in future college courses and *certifying* through course grades that students are, in fact, "prepared." Faculty often felt an obligation to maintain high expectations, or, as Barb put it, "keep the bar high, not lower the bar."

The drive to uphold such standards was fueled in part by instructors' sense that students were unlikely to encounter much flexibility if they transferred to four-year institutions. James, for example, was sometimes ambivalent about his responses to students' logistical challenges and described his efforts to make sure they understood that accommodations would not be the norm at other institutions: "Maybe it's good that I don't [make more accommodations], because I would be more accepting, because sometimes I harangue students about that. I keep reminding them that, 'this isn't going to work for you when you get to a four-year college.'" Instructors often hedged accommodation in this manner, letting students know they should not take such flexibility for granted. James, Patrick, and Lily were particularly concerned with equipping students in this way because they were keenly aware of the racist assumptions Diné students might encounter among off-reservation university faculty. Instructors in the Michigan community colleges expressed similar concerns about the identity positions of their working-class students, as well as the large community of second-language learners from the Middle East, who were also subject to assumptions based on their religion and styles of dress. Thus, although the specific racial, ethnic, and class markers varied, two-year college faculty across our studies shared a sense that their students came from socially marginalized backgrounds and were particularly vulnerable to stereotyping and discrimination. They therefore needed to be particularly well prepared to face the rigors of university academics.

This point relates to a third competing ideological strand that ran through many of our interviews: a respect for student agency, with a concomitant belief that students needed to take responsibility for their own education. Some faculty felt upholding expectations for attendance and due dates was a means of countering the infantilizing aspects of poverty, racism, and/or colonialism their students might have experienced. Barb, for example, repeatedly asserted that her students were "adults" who were responsible for establishing their own personal and academic priorities. Likewise, Patrick often expressed concerns about fostering "taught helplessness" among his students.

> To me, I think there's consequences if as a college student, if you don't turn the paper in. It's, what I was saying, are we teaching them to be helpless? Taught helplessness. Are they learning to helpless because we're teaching them to be helpless? . . . It's invisible, but it's a real just like anything else and a lot of people suffer from it. I think a lot of our students at [this] college suffer from it. Do I follow up on [missing work] with them? No, because of that. I don't want to teach them to be helpless.

Such statements reflect a sense that experiences of chronic or episodic poverty might hinder students' problem-solving abilities and their sense of agency. Many faculty asserted that an important part of college was learning to be self-sufficient and resourceful—a particularly important value in Diné society manifest in one of the tribal college's mottos: "If it's to be, it's up to me."

Some instructors saw upholding standards for attendance and due dates as furthering these learning objectives. Others, such as Callie, viewed choosing not to attend class—and accepting the consequences—as a reasonable and responsible choice available to students with multiple and layered priorities: "It's no great disgrace if you didn't get through college this semester because you were taking care of your grandmother. You know, that's what adults do sometimes." Indeed, many instructors' comments about upholding standards revealed an anxiety about the difficulty of distinguishing between unavoidable poverty effects that prevented students from coming to class or completing coursework and problems with "study habits" or "work ethic." Christie's conversations with both students and faculty suggested instructors were not always aware of when students' difficulties meeting standards were caused by poverty effects—students were not always forthcoming about the cause or extent of their challenges, and not all faculty felt it was appropriate to ask. As Patrick said, "You're here or you're not here and if you don't say anything about what your problem is, I don't know. I don't ask students, 'Is there something going on at home?'" In both our studies, the tension between requiring students to take responsibility for meeting standards and the reality that students experiencing poverty sometimes had little or no control over their circumstances was persistent and unresolved.

When it came to determining grades, some faculty indicated they were willing to adjust "standards" to account for students' life circumstances when they felt it was warranted. As James said of his own grading policies, "It's something of a sliding scale. The better I get to know them . . . I allow for [life problems], too, but good students can have something going on in their lives and still prevail. . . . Yeah, you have to be aware of these things, and you also learn to tell the difference between somebody who's milking that and somebody who's for real." Again, this statement reveals the ambiguity between "excuses" and "legitimate" crises, poverty related or otherwise, that are typically left for instructors to negotiate. Patrick's explanation of his decision to award Morning Star a passing course grade reflects a similar tension: "At the very beginning, there were some students that had these issues that cannot be fixed at the college. I feel it's my role, or they'll deal with the responsibilities to change some of the problems she . . . but, nevertheless, give her an opportunity. If she can demonstrate the minimum standards, I allowed her to go through." Patrick, who took a hard stand against "taught helplessness," struggled to articulate the fraught relationship between student responsibility, his own role as an instructor, and the larger structures beyond the control of either the college or the student. In the end, he, like many faculty, chose to err on the side of flexibility—of giving students more "opportunity" to "demonstrate mini-mum standards" so they could continue their education.

Such ideological tensions might be exacerbated by the relative status of two-year colleges and their faculty. As Howard Tinberg has described, two-year college faculty are "border crossers," translating between sec-ondary and postsecondary educations as well as between two-year and four-year institutions.[43] As professionals, their positioning is sometimes ambivalent and conflicted: are their open-admissions institutions "real" colleges? Are they "real" professors? In this space, the drive to defend a notion of "college standards" might also be a matter of defending institutional and professional identity. Patrick Sullivan observes that the "'college-level' writing" two-year college faculty are charged with teach-ing is, in fact, a contested construct difficult to define.

> It may very well be that these conflicts are irresolvable and that all stan-dards related to our students' written work must ultimately be local, determined at least in part by our response to the complex realities of the communities we serve and the individual students we teach. Any discus-sion of shared standards may require us to ignore or discount the very powerful political and social realities that help shape students' lives on individual campuses and in particular learning communities. . . . On the other hand, it may well be that our profession could benefit enormously from reopening a dialogue about this question. At the very least, as a matter of professional policy, it seems reasonable to revisit issues like this routinely—to open ourselves up to new ideas and insights, and to guard against rigid or prescriptive professional consensus.[44]

We share Sullivan's sense that the notion of shared standards often elides the "very powerful political and social realities that help shape students' lives," including, as we have shown, the effects of chronic and episodic poverty. We also agree that the profession would benefit from an open dialogue about the unresolved—and perhaps unresolvable—tensions that two-year college faculty experience between the obligation to uphold their sense of "the standards" and the material conditions of many of their students' lives. In part, such dialogue might mean shifting the burden for managing such ideological tensions away from individ-ual faculty and placing it within programmatic discussions grounded in a critical vocabulary that can better contend with the structural nature of poverty itself.

CONCLUSIONS

A recent study indicated that 14 percent of students enrolled in two-year colleges are homeless. Following a decade of calls to increase education attainment and "skilled-workers," this percentage is likely to rise.[45] Many of those students will be experiencing chronic or episodic poverty conditions that present challenges to their academic success. The findings of our case studies suggest that although two-year college composition faculty often make valiant efforts to meet such students' needs, these institutions are not yet equipped to mitigate students' poverty-related challenges, support sustainable pedagogical responses among faculty, or facilitate long-term, programmatic decision making about these issues within departments. As a result, a significant subset of students experiencing poverty effects may end up negotiating a system of inconsistent rewards and relief that do not enable them to achieve their ultimate goals: a college degree, more stable employment, and greater civic participation and ability to advocate for their communities.

We suggest that faculty can begin this project within their own departments by calling for increased programmatic awareness of the interrelation between poverty effects and apparent academic preparedness. We urge faculty to enjoin their departmental colleagues in focused deliberation about the critical terms they might use to discuss and respond to the systemic poverty effects their students face. Ideally, faculty would develop these terms so they engage and reinforce the disciplinary knowledge that makes programmatic cohesion possible. Further, we suggest that when faculty work together with clearly defined programmatic objectives and coherently articulated observations of students' poverty-related experiences, they may be able to move beyond emotionally taxing ad hoc responses and work with other colleagues, campus units, and college administration to develop structural responses to structural problems. For example, some two-year colleges, such as Brett's current institution, Macomb Community College, house food banks that serve the academic community of students and faculty. Others, such as Washtenaw Community College, Mesa Community College, and Austin Community College, have worked with public-transportation providers to ensure fair (if not free) bus fare and adequate bus lines to serve their colleges. Still others have raised specialized emergency funds to support students in need and counsel students on additional benefits available through government and private agencies. There are undoubtedly many other innovative programmatic and institutional initiatives faculty can imagine within their local contexts.

The success of such initiatives is, however, contingent on consistent efforts to make a continuously changing student body aware of what is available, which in turn depends on an informed, engaged, and stable faculty able and willing to connect students with these resources. We recommend faculty actively undertake discussions of poverty effects, identifying institutional resources available to students struggling with poverty and determining how to connect students to those services effectively while respecting FERPA rights. Furthermore, we suggest departments establish open and ongoing dialogue about their constructions of "academic standards" and the tensions they experience between upholding those standards and responding with empathy to students' material circumstances. While these competing values may never be entirely reconcilable, it seems fairer to both students and instructors to make such tensions the subject of collaborative, programmatic discussion rather than the internal conflict of individual faculty. Finally, we encourage administrators at two-year colleges to foster faculty discussions about students' poverty-related experiences. We urge administrators to support responsive instructional policies that will enable sustainable excellence in student-centered teaching at open-admissions institutions. This support includes recognizing and rewarding the often invisible labor of addressing student poverty effects in the classroom, providing support for programmatic responses, and investing in a professionalized and fairly compensated professoriate.

We have suggested that meaningful solutions to structural issues rely less on individual instructors' pedagogical choices—however critical and progressive those choices might be—and more on programmatic responses to material conditions beyond even the most "heroic" teacher's ability to address. Programmatic responses, however, demand coherent theoretical and empirical grounding. As a field, composition studies has undertaken rich discussions of academic acclimation and culturally inclusive pedagogy, but it has often elided or occluded issues of class, class effects, and particularly poverty. This omission—a theoretical weakness resulting at least in part from status differentials between institution types and the student demographics they serve—disproportionately impacts colleagues teaching in two-year college settings. Our field has failed to provide a critical vocabulary or robust theoretical framework through which to discuss the material conditions of two-year college writing instruction (although community college-based scholars like Barry Alford and Keith Kroll, among others, have worked hard to address this gap).[46] We believe one of the next big projects in composition studies must be to develop frameworks for discussing student poverty effects, particularly at the institutions where a *growing* majority of first-year writing courses are taught.

In an interview with Brett, Clarisse said, "The best definition [of two-year college instruction] is one I heard at a conference many years ago by people who were teaching in a community college in Appalachia. They said 'if we don't do our jobs well, children don't eat.' We're here to make sure that our students can support their families. That people who really come out of poor backgrounds, terrible schools and bad backgrounds, that we're giving them a chance to move into the middle class through what we do here." Clarisse's assertion may risk reinforcing the notion that, through access to higher education, working-class students can gain "a chance" to move into the middle class. Scholars have long debated the degree to which two-year colleges actually fulfill the democratic ideals of social mobility that are the US education gospel or merely imitate access while perpetuating existing inequities.[47] That question itself, however, may be a luxury many low-income and working-class students cannot entertain. Increasingly, a college degree is prerequisite for even buying a ticket to the "educational lottery."[48] If two-year college composition faculty are to help students experiencing poverty effects to take that "chance"—"warm them up"[49] rather than "cool them out"[50]—instructors must be theoretically, programmatically, and institutionally equipped to address material circumstances that obstruct literacy learning.

Notes

1. Throughout this chapter, we follow the Two-Year College English Association in using the term *two-year colleges* unless quoting or paraphrasing a source that uses different terminology. The *two-year college* designator includes community and junior colleges, as well as two-year tribal colleges, most technical colleges, and the growing number of state colleges that are primarily associate degree-granting institutions but offer a limited number of applied baccalaureate degrees.
2. Pew Research Center, "Most See Inequality Growing"; Zweig, "Six Points on Class"; Metzgar, "Are 'the Poor' Part of the Working Class?"
3. Brint, "Educational Lottery."
4. Cho, Jacobs, and Zhang, "Demographic and Academic Characteristics"; Cohen and Brawer, *American Community College*; Joshi, Beck, and Nsiah, "Student Characteristics."
5. We follow the tribal college's convention of using the term Navajo Nation to refer to the federally recognized legal and geographical entity and the term Diné (the People) as the ethnic/cultural designator of the people who have been called Navajo by colonizing Spanish and US forces. However, it should be noted that many Diné people refer to themselves as Navajo or use both terms interchangeably.
6. Harrington, *Other America*.
7. Haushofer and Fehr, "On the Psychology of Poverty."
8. United States Census Bureau, "Glossary—US Census Bureau," accessed February 16, 2017, https://www.census.gov/topics/income-poverty/poverty/about/glossary .html.

9. O'Connor, "Poverty and Paradox."
10. Anderson, *Dynamics of Economic Well-Being.*
11. United States Census Bureau, "Glossary."
12. Zweig, *Working Class Majority.*
13. Metzgar, "Are 'the Poor' Part of the Working Class?"
14. Provasnik and Planty, "Community Colleges."
15. Peary, "Hidden Ethos."
16. Stenberg and Lee, "Developing Pedagogies," 328.
17. Klausman, "Mapping the Terrain," 238.
18. Ibid., 239.
19. Seider, Rabinowicz, and Gillmor, "Changing American College Students' Conceptions."
20. Steck et al., "Doing Poverty Learning Outcomes"; "Genesee Community College Students Experience Homelessness."
21. Shor, "Why Teach about Social Class?"
22. Valadez, "Searching for a Path."
23. See, for example, Thurston, "Mitigating Barriers."
24. Bloom, "When One Person Makes It."
25. Weisberger, "Community Colleges and Class," 128–29.
26. Desrochers and Kirshstein, *College Spending.*
27. Bahr, "Educational Attainment as Process."
28. Cox, *College Fear Factor*; Sternglass, *Time to Know Them.*
29. Lindquist, "Class Affects, Classroom Affectations"; Peckham, *Going North Thinking West.*
30. Tuck, "Suspending Damage," 412.
31. To help protect participant identities, we refer to all colleges, faculty, and students using pseudonyms.
32. Corbin and Strauss, *Basics of Qualitative Research.*
33. Thurston, "Mitigating Barriers," 29.
34. Arizona Rural Policy Institute, *Demographic Analysis of the Navajo Nation.*
35. Navajo Nation Regional Partnership Council, *2010 Needs and Assets Report.*
36. Veracini, *Settler Colonialism.*
37. Stein, *Tribally Controlled Colleges.*
38. Berkhofer, *White Man's Indian*, 30.
39. Corbin and Strauss, *Basics of Qualitative Research.*
40. Samuel-Nakamura, "Uranium and Other Heavy Metals"; Ray, Holben, and Holcomb, "Food Security Status."
41. Johnstone, "Locating Language in Identity."
42. Buck et al., "Guidelines for the Academic Preparation."
43. Tinberg, *Border Talk*, vii.
44. Sullivan, "Essential Question," 2–3.
45. "Hungry and Homeless in College," *The Kresge Foundation*, March 14, 2017, http://kresge.org/library/hungry-and-homeless-college.
46. Alford and Kroll, *Politics of Writing.*
47. Brint and Karabel, *Diverted Dream*; Hagedorn, "Pursuit of Student Success"; Clark, "'Cooling Out' Function"; Deil-Amen, "'Warming Up.'"
48. Brint, "Educational Lottery."
49. Deil-Amen, "'Warming Up.'"
50. Clark, *Academic Life.*

14

RETROGRADE MOVEMENTS AND THE EDUCATIONAL ENCOUNTER
Working-Class Adults in First-Year Composition

James E. Romesburg

Every two years the planet Mars appears to temporarily stall in its direct or prograde motion across the night sky and reverse course, making a loop against the more stable backdrop of distant stars before resuming its long, steady trajectory eastward through the heavens. As seen from Earth, this looping or *retrograde* motion occurs over the course of weeks and months but has long been known to careful observers such as the ancients, who were troubled by the planet's aberrant behavior. Ptolemy theorized an elaborate system of "epicycles" to explain Mars's apparent motions within the ancient understanding of a geocentric universe, which positioned the earth at its center surrounded by planets attached to fixed, concentric spheres. Not surprisingly, from a modern astronomical perspective, observations of Mars's apparent motions consistently undermined theoretical explanations of its actual orbit for thousands of years.

Yet over the course of those many years, cumulative insights by thinkers such as Copernicus, Brahe, Kepler, Galileo, and Newton allowed astronomers to gradually work out the intricacies of our heliocentric solar system and to explain the complex *apparent* motion of Mars's orbit within that larger system. We now know that our own Earth's motion around the sun distorts how we see Mars's real trajectory, creating the optical illusion of backward motion when in fact both planets are moving along just fine in their orbits according to the gravitational laws that govern all celestial bodies. Thus, the system-bound perspective of our own orbiting planet distorts how we see a fellow traveler in that system, and as we gain insights into that other body's movements and existence, we gain knowledge of our own.

DOI: 10.7330/9781607326182.c014

Educators of adult students could learn much from the metaphor of retrograde motion, which might act as a corrective lens to the prevailing US cultural view of learning as primarily the domain of the young, revealing to those invested in formalized education—or at least those who care to look—that the perspectives shaping their own worldview will always distort how they see the directions other lives have taken. And while any teacher's focus is understandably on *schooling*, we are seriously limiting our perspective on *learning* by assuming it most often takes place in an institutional setting. In fact, the educational encounters occurring in school might be among the most the most limited and limiting types of learning humans undertake. And as a multitude of scholars[1] have pointed out, adults who return to school in order to escape their working-class positions are often viewed as "reprobates" who have forsaken their "natural" roles in the capitalist order.

INTRODUCTION: ADULT STUDENTS IN FIRST-YEAR COMPOSITION

> Professor/Researcher Q: *Can you describe for me a day in one of your first-year composition courses that was particularly useful or productive?*
>
> Student/Subject A: *No.*

First-year composition (FYC) courses pose a unique set of challenges for returning/older students. Typically populated by eighteen- to nineteen-year-olds, FYC courses at four-year schools are often seen as just one part of "the first year experience," which of course also includes adjusting to dorm life, rushing fraternities and sororities, bar hopping with fake IDs, and tailgating before the homecoming game. Lest we wring our hands and complain about these cultural realities, composition instructors and their writing program administrators should realize we are no less caught up in that academic culture with its seasonal cycles like welcome-back festivals, fall convocations, and an academic year punctuated by various ceremonies and commencements. Even closer to our disciplinary home, some of our field's proudest accomplishments, such as small class sizes and interactive, discussion-based pedagogical approaches, can seem like a hurdle to overcome for adults who are acutely aware of their *distinctions*, their class and age markers such as work uniforms, graying hair, or crows' feet; for these students, the anonymity of the darkened lecture hall crammed with two hundred or more students, each facing forward and silently taking notes, has its appeal. Still, because of our unique disciplinary practices, and because first-year composition is likely to be among the handful of courses adult students encounter early on in that crucial time when they are testing the waters of college life, getting a feel for academic culture, and trying to determine whether they should entrust the members of that culture with their limited time and financial resources, the field of composition studies has the unique opportunity—in fact a tremendous responsibility—to welcome such students into academic culture, and even to change that culture when necessary, if we are to fulfill an obligation that we can be, as Joseph Harris says, "a teaching subject."[2]

For all these reasons, the above student's elegant, one-syllable response, "*No*," resonates with me, as I suspect it might with many other composition instructors who have had the experience of teaching classes with mixed-generation student populations. Over the years I've wondered: What do older students in my first-year writing courses take away from those experiences? What are the implications of our culture's youth-oriented educational focus on first-year composition pedagogies? Are there steps writing instructors should be taking to ensure older composition students, who, by the definition I will argue for here, come overwhelmingly from the working classes, are not only getting the most out of those classes but are creating beneficial relationships with our more traditional-aged students in the process? Finally, how do the confluence of class, age, gender, race, and other "axes of inequality"[3] impact our nontraditional students' academic and personal lives? In this chapter I seek some answers to those questions as I explore the experiences of four so-called non-traditional-age students in first-year composition classes at a midsized urban university in the lower Midwest. In the end I will suggest ways instructors with mixed-generation classes might retheorize their pedagogy by not only taking into account the working-class pedagogies outlined in the present volume but also by adding a corrective lens from the *andragogical* theories of adult education so they might (1) listen to and *recognize* the needs of our working-class adult students and (2) help students of *all* ages meet their objectives in first-year composition.

BACKGROUND: EXISTING LITERATURE ON
NONTRADITIONAL STUDENTS IN FYC

Composition research on intergenerational classrooms reveals certain patterns of conflict and collaboration that cut across the age spectrum both ways. In fact, more than a few scholars have found that younger students are often intimidated by older students because the older students tend to be more outspoken in class and/or tend to spend more time outside class reading and writing; therefore, they are more prepared for class and get better grades.[4] Several studies also found a perception—among students of all ages—that adult students receive "special treatment" from their teachers, such as greater flexibility with paper deadlines due to conflicting "real-world" events.[5] As one adult student in Carol Kasworm's 2001 study said, "They [the faculty] seem to show—not that they are rude in any way towards younger students— they seem to be a little more deferential towards older students. They're adults dealing with adults rather than adults dealing with children."[6] A nineteen-year-old student in Mary Morrison's study elaborated on some of the intergenerational competition between students this way: "Oh, definitely [there is competition]! The traditional students see it as the older students [having] only . . . one or two classes to study for, but most of us are taking a full load, so they . . . have more time to study."[7] It is difficult not to wonder at this teenager's limited conception of a "full load" when reading what another adult student in Kasworm's study says: "We're playing with real houses. The [younger] students are worried about having fun."[8]

But this attitude should not be mistaken for condescension on the part of the adults. On the contrary, most studies found that older composition students genuinely value the chance to interact with younger persons in a context other than being "my friend's mom," and they use those sites of interaction to learn about the way a younger generation views the world.[9] A forty-eight-year-old student in Karen Uehling's study said, memorably,

> In the classroom the input from all age groups helps to bring the subject matter into better focus. I have enjoyed being with younger adults, with their fresh approach and carefree attitude, and sharing ideas with them. On the other side, the older adults have life experiences and wisdom to draw from. I would not like to see us without each other.[10]

Similarly, most of the adult students in Kasworm's study reported a "positive, respectful relationship" with faculty, believed faculty valued their presence in the classroom, and even thought instructors showed deference to the adults in their classes because they saw adults as being more serious about learning.[11]

CLASS AND NONTRADITIONAL STUDENTS

What these studies have not considered, however, is the *classed* experience of non-traditional-age composition students. Though it seems like a common-sense notion that older students do not come to our comp classes from wealthy backgrounds, any academic definition of *class* relying on common sense is treading on dangerous ground, so a few words of clarification on how I am using the term *class* is appropriate here. Central to Pierre Bourdieu's understanding of class is his concept of *habitus*, which is the set of internalized organizational structures by which we make sense of the world and our place in it.[12] Our habitus begins to form through our earliest social interactions and continues to shape, at an unconscious level, how we see the world around us, what we are disposed to like and dislike (our tastes), and also what we see as possible in our current and future lives. Habitus essentially informs us of our "place" in the world within the structure of power relations among classes, sexes, races, genders, and so forth, and this notion, formed early, retains such a powerful hold over our worldview that we not only carry it into adulthood but pass it on from one generation to the next through the process of socialization. Thus, from a Marxist perspective, our habitus makes inevitable our participation—albeit on an unconscious level—in "the reproduction of relations of production" of not only economic capital but cultural, social, and educational capital as well. Moreover, as Bourdieu says, "Position and individual trajectory are not statistically independent; all positions of arrival are not equally probable for all starting points."[13] In other words, in the context of this study, life trajectories that bring non-traditional-age students into our composition classrooms are unlikely to have had a middle-class childhood as their starting point. Had adult students been born and raised in a middle- or upper-class environment, they would likely have either gone to college when they were younger or else their habitus would have allowed them to see other possibilities for advancing their interests in the world, and that knowledge would likely have enabled them to utilize other forms of social and cultural capital available to them. They would have known the right people, said the right things, and had the right "feel for the game," to again use Bourdieu's language.

The four adult students profiled here have varying degrees of "feel" for the FYC "game" and for the game of higher education in general. I have no reservations calling these students *working class*, but I do concede up front that my comfort level in doing so is doubtless buoyed by the fact that I consider myself to have come from working-class roots, and as someone who experienced college as a non-traditional-age student, listening to Gene, Ann, Rhoda, and Mary talk about their FYC experiences certainly had a familiar *feel* to me.

INSTITUTIONAL BACKGROUND AND METHODOLOGY

This chapter presents results from one part of a larger project conducted at Columbus University, a large, urban, public, four-year institution in the lower Midwest.[14] Baccalaureate-granting metropolitan universities in the United States have historically offered working-class adults a comparatively inexpensive and accommodating alternative to two-year colleges, and research[15] has found enrolling in community colleges can be more of an *impediment* than an aid for those wishing to complete a four-year degree "because the cost of transferring can be burdensome and because four-year institutions can better help students to stay focused on completing the bachelor's degree."[16] Even worse for students from the working classes, a 2001 report by the National Center for Education Statistics (NCES) found that, while 21 percent of two-year college students from the lowest two socioeconomic quartiles expected to eventually complete their bachelor's degrees, only 10 to 14 percent of those students eventually do transfer to baccalaureate institutions.[17] For these reasons, urban universities have occupied an important place in the larger national higher education picture, meeting the needs of an older, less affluent student constituency.[18]

THE SURVEY

A survey instrument was designed to take a snapshot of the institution's nontraditional FYC student population and to locate subjects for follow-up qualitative interviews. Near the end of the spring 2009 semester, 23 percent (eighteen of the seventy-seven sections offered) of the English 101 and 102 first-year composition courses at Columbus were surveyed, and the resulting responses represented roughly 16 percent (three hundred of roughly nineteen hundred students) of all FYC students enrolled that semester. Because the purpose was to include as many nontraditional students as possible, this was not a random sample or systematic sample but a targeted one. Evening sections were targeted specifically with the rationale that older students could more easily accommodate those sections in their daily schedules. Still, to obtain a larger sample and an estimate of the number of nontraditional students in all FYC classes, I gathered surveys from sections meeting in most of the scheduled time slots in the weekly calendar: mornings, afternoons, and evenings.

Ten percent of all students surveyed were twenty-two-plus years old, while the remaining 90 percent fell into the university's definition of "traditional"-age students, seventeen to twenty-one years old. While roughly 46 percent of all students in the larger undergraduate population were older than twenty-two, the 10 percent figure is likely attributable to a combination of factors, such as the fact that FYC is a first-year course sequence and many of those older students transfer in with credit from other institutions.

Survey questions sought basic demographic information about students and asked a series of Likert-scale questions about their first-year composition course, their fellow students, their instructors, their assignments, and their general FYC "experience." Analysis of the survey data revealed conflicting results and offered few insights into the distinctions between the various demographic populations involved, with one exception: as the figures on the following pages demonstrate, some clear distinctions did emerge when data were analyzed by age group, particularly when it came to non-traditional-age students' forging relationships with their instructors and younger classmates.

The scale and resulting data are "Likert type" but not a measure of summated data in the way Rensis Likert devised (a method apparently rarely used or understood in the social sciences, in any event). From a statistical perspective, the most meaningful analysis comes from looking at (1) the distribution, (2) the measure of central tendency (for Likert scales, typically the mode and/or the median), and (3) the variability of the responses.[19] The statistical average, or mean, is less useful in analyzing Likert-type data since the scale employed is ordinal/sequential and not a scale of equidistant intervals (i.e., no one can respond 3.5 or 1.75, so finding an average of twenty "rarely true" responses and thirty "always true" responses does not produce a meaningful integer).[20] The mode and median, however, more accurately represent the respondent data, and examining the data's distribution around those numbers points to the direction in which the distribution is skewed. Thus, they reveal tendencies in the attitude of the group's responses.

Table 14.1 shows the mode responses for sections of FYC that meet the definition of a mixed generation, while table 14.2 shows the mode responses for traditional-age sections. While the difference between 3 and 4 seems minimal, the clear pattern is for higher perceived levels of commonality among students in the traditional-age classes than for mixed-generation classes, and the fact that the difference appears so clearly and consistently seems significant. Could the mix of ages be a causal factor in these scores? It seems likely, given the data in figure 14.2, which shows the distribution of responses to the same question from *all* individuals surveyed, with non-traditional-age students represented on the chart to the left and traditional-age students on the chart to the right. In both cases

7. Please rank the truth of the following statements on the following scale: 1 = Never true for me.
2 = Rarely true for me; 3= Sometimes true for me; 4 = Often true for me; 5 = Always true for me

	Never true	Rarely true	Sometimes true	Often true	Always true
I have much in common with most students in my English Composition class.	1	2	3	4	5
I am comfortable interacting with the instructor of my English Composition class.	1	2	3	4	5

Figure 14.1. Rating interactions with students and instructor

Table 14.1. Mixed-generation sections mode for questions 7a ("in common with classmates") and 7b ("comfort level with instructor")

Section	7a Mode	7b Mode	Section's % of Nontraditionals
A*	3	5	50
C	3	4	11
H	3	5	14
I	3	5	24
L	3	4	25
O	3	4	13
Q*	4	5	18
R*	3	5	55

Table 14.2. Traditional-age sections mode for questions 7a ("in common with classmates") and 7b ("comfort level with instructor")

Section	7a Mode	7b Mode	Section's % of Nontraditicnals
B	4	3 and 5	—
D	4	4	7
E	4	5	—
F	4	4	—
G	4	5	—
J	3 and 4	4	4.2
K	3 and 4	5	4
M	3	5	—
N	3	4	—
P	3	5	—

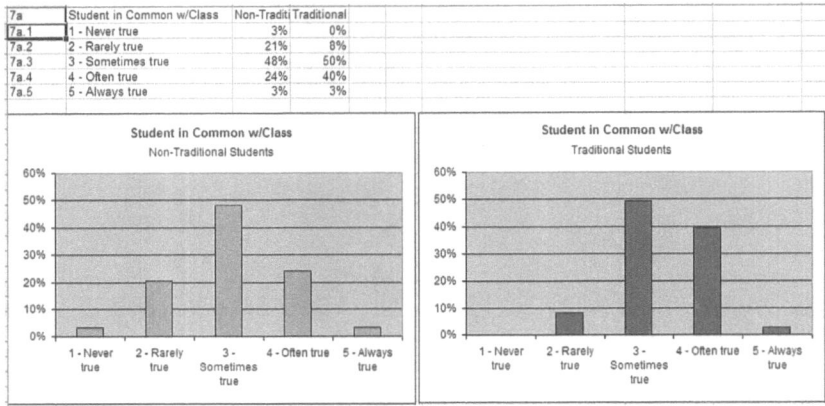

7a	Student in Common w/Class	Non-Traditi	Traditional
7a.1	1 - Never true	3%	0%
7a.2	2 - Rarely true	21%	8%
7a.3	3 - Sometimes true	48%	50%
7a.4	4 - Often true	24%	40%
7a.5	5 - Always true	3%	3%

Figure 14.2. Distribution of individual responses to survey item "I have much in common with students in my class" for non-traditional students and traditional students

the modal response is 3, but with traditional students the distribution is clearly skewed toward "often true" while the non-traditional student distribution resembles the classic bell curve of a normal distribution. Thus, the increased age affinity of younger students seems to be the force pulling up the modal numbers of traditional-age-only sections.

The quantitative data above provided a backdrop for gathering further qualitative data from interviews with four non-traditional-age students profiled below. Survey respondents were asked to provide a name and e-mail address if they were willing to sit down for a follow-up interview at the conclusion of the spring semester. Interview data were coded for age, gender, race, and socioeconomic issues; issues relating to formal educational backgrounds, composition classroom activities, and work and home life were analyzed; of particular interest, though, were the relationships these students formed with their classmates and their instructors. As their stories below reveal, having non-traditional-age students in our composition classes affords us great opportunities to practice reflective writing pedagogy and help us better understand how our classes function as writing communities.

LITERACY SPONSORSHIP FOR NON-TRADITIONAL-AGE FYC STUDENTS

Eugene Walker is a thirty-three-year-old army reserve private who enrolled at Columbus in the spring 2009 semester after returning from service in Iraq. Gene is engaged to be married and has two children

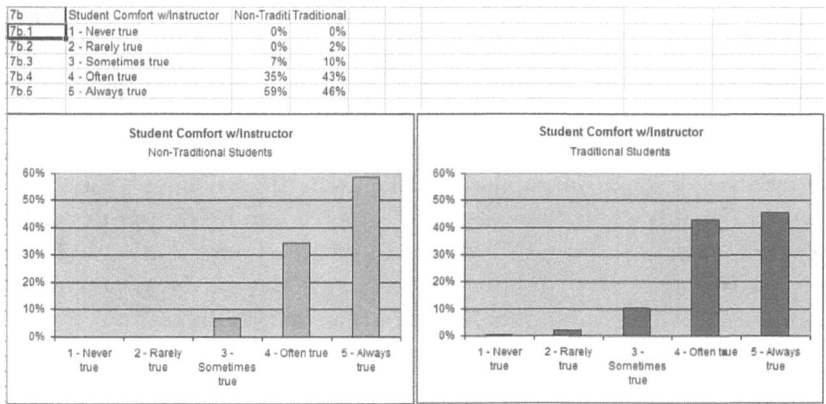

7b	Student Comfort w/Instructor	Non-Traditi	Traditional
7b.1	1 - Never true	0%	0%
7b.2	2 - Rarely true	0%	2%
7b.3	3 - Sometimes true	7%	10%
7b.4	4 - Often true	35%	43%
7b.5	5 - Always true	59%	46%

Figure 14.3. Distribution of individual responses to survey item "I am comfortable inter-acting with the instructor of my English composition class" for non-traditional students and traditional students

from a previous marriage, both of whom live in another state with their mother. This is a difficult subject for Gene to discuss, but he otherwise describes his home life as "fantastic."

> I have a wonderful fiancée, and she's real supportive. And when I came back from Iraq, she actually knew I was going to school . . . and in our little house there was this weird cubby hole in a random spot. She turned it into an office for me, set up a printer and all that other stuff. So . . . my home life was fantastic . . . very conducive to learning. She worked during the day, so I could study during the day and she'd come home at night and we'd get to spend time together. . . . I'd say the whole time I was in [school], I had no problems from home or work or anything.

Gene's tuition is funded by the Post-9/11 Veterans Educational Assistance Act of 2008, commonly referred to as the New GI Bill, which is making a measurable impact on the numbers of returning students in higher education, though it is certainly not comparable to the sea change triggered by the original GI Bill in the 1940s and 50s.[21] In this case, at least, the legislation seems to have helped Gene's family create a physical and intellectual space for study—a "distance from necessity," in Bourdieu's terms,[22] so crucial to the process of embodying the kind of cultural capital offered by higher education.

On the whole, nontraditional students—and working-class Columbus students of any age—have very little distance from necessity, but the New GI Bill and Gene's fiancée function together for Gene as what Debora Brandt has called "sponsors of literacy."[23] As Brandt describes them, sponsors are "usually richer, more knowledgeable, and more entrenched than the sponsored, [yet] sponsors nevertheless enter a reciprocal relationship with those they underwrite. They lend their resources or credibility to the sponsored but also stand to gain benefits from their success, whether by direct repayment or, indirectly, by credit or association."[24] In an immediate and intimate way, Gene's fiancée—who has already earned her bachelor's degree and holds a professional position earning sufficient funds to support the household while Gene attends school—stands to benefit once her future husband's degree is completed and he can contribute to a dual-earner household. In the case of the United States Army's sponsorship, the reciprocation is in one respect retroactive: you serve, then your education is sponsored. Still, the army gains considerable clout from the publicity attached to the New GI Bill, just as the GI Bill has certainly earned a favorable name in US history (and educational lore) as sponsor of all the World War II veterans who gained a college education and went on to essentially create the modern US middle class. Gene's educational pursuits, too, are historically situated, and as Brandt reminds us, sponsorship of his and all current veteran's literacy is the result of a political struggle: "The course of an ordinary person's literacy learning—its occasions, materials, applications, potentials—follows the transformations going on within sponsoring institutions as those institutions fight for economic and ideological position."[25] For the US military, facing recruiting challenges caused by over a decade of unpopular wars, the positive ideological implications of a New GI Bill far outweigh the capital necessary to finance such a program—especially when the military budget is always the last government program to be placed on the budgetary chopping block.

Ann Winfield is a twenty-three-year-old white female who transferred to Columbus from a community college after several semesters of part-time coursework. Ann has five years' experience as a clerical worker, but when she moved from a nearby rural area to her parents' home in Columbus, they provided the financial support necessary for her to leave her job and devote all her time to school for the duration of the spring 2009 semester: "I'm fortunate enough that my family has been supportive—*extremely*—of me getting my degree, so they've kinda allowed me to take the time." She understands the importance of her family's assistance, and from her description of the experience, Ann was more than slightly intimidated by the prospect of her first semester at a large university: "I was kinda nervous about getting back in school, and that whole [idea of] giving up a job that I had been working for quite a while that had good potential, and the whole idea of just getting back in school. I definitely wanted to get a good semester under, you know, underway before I started trying to work and include other elements into it." With Ann we see a firsthand example of the community college transfer hurdle and also examples of the kinds of support systems necessary to smooth and stabilize that transition. Higher education holds forth vague promises of a better future for such working adults, but giving up her own, self-reliant financial situation was clearly a traumatic experience for Ann. Many of her uncertainties seem rooted in her immediate, post-high-school attitude toward higher education.

> It's kind of interesting. I had a like, a full ride out of high school to come to [Columbus], but I wasn't ready to make the large university transition. I needed to go to community college to kind of get the feel for it. So, I did two semesters at [a local] tech college. And I liked it. I did. But I felt like a lot of things were kinda handed to you on a silver platter. It didn't really require you to think outside the box as much. So I decided it that probably wasn't for me.

For the teenage Anne, psychological barriers to university study trumped any financial barriers, and as a working-class teenager from a smaller town, the intimidation of leaving home to live on a large, urban campus—even though Columbus is less than an hour's drive away—outweighed the familiarity of a small school closer to home. Ann's language even mirrors Bourdieu's concept of having a "feel for the game," or the subconscious "bodily learning through repetition or practice" that benefits all of us when we are functioning in familiar social fields.[26] And we are all disposed to excel in new social fields most similar to those in which we have had considerable practice, so while Ann's decision to attend community college was surely based on several factors—proximity to home, commuting expenses, and so forth—she deliberately credits this familiarity of *field* with her conscious decision to attend community college rather than take advantage of the "full ride" to Columbus.[27] She wanted to get a "feel for" higher education at the community college before transferring to a university because she believed it would better approximate the scholastic world of her habitus, the academic world she had already excelled in, which at that point in her life had been the public school system.

Mary Hayek is a fifty-five-year-old Columbus administrative staff member who has worked for the university for thirty-four years and has been taking a class or two per semester for last the several years. Currently a junior at Columbus, Mary's educational goals are at once unconventional and straightforward: "To finally get a degree, no matter what age [laughs] in liberal studies." As someone who has been in the higher education environment for so long, Mary appreciates learning simply for the sake of learning. She is not pursuing a degree as the means to a professional end, yet she still has an enthusiasm for intellectual enrichment wherever opportunity presents itself: "I also take in a lot of lectures on campus. I can't necessarily do it during work hours unless it's on a lunch break. But I'll go to evening lectures, and some of the networks during lunch, during the day, just to get a broader perspective on certain topics." Mary's demeanor is thoughtful, patient, and articulate as she describes her degree program: "It's a step-by-step process, you know—checking off those classes. But not just checking them off, actually *learning* in each of those classes." As an employee, Mary's tuition is covered by the university,[28] as is her children's tuition, both facts that figure prominently in her long-term professional and educational goals: "The way I figure it, I don't know when I'll actually be able, financially, to retire, but I know I need to stay here at least until my two sons get their degrees because of that tuition remission. But in the end if I'm almost finished, but not quite, and I'm ready to retire, I figure I can just finish it up as a senior citizen, full time."

Broadly speaking, then, Columbus University is a key sponsor of the Hayek family's literacy and education, and Mary—whose Lebanese immigrant father earned a high-school diploma but whose mother dropped out—is grateful for her immediate supervisor's encouraging approach to her education: "He's really supportive of me doing this. And he knows that if it means I have to stay late, he knows I'll do that. I was here till 7:30 last night." Given Mary's long experience at Columbus, she knows how to navigate the individual personalities of a large bureaucracy, and she knows what, in her words, "will fly" and what won't: "Some supervisors are supportive, and others are sticklers. I've always managed my classes during my lunch break, or an extended lunch break, or an evening class. This [English 102] is my first 4:00 class, and I'm not sure that all supervisors would approve of that." Mary's supervisor is quite high up in the university's administrative hierarchy, however, and had not only the flexibility but also the authority to approve a three-week leave of absence for her to pursue an internship in Kenya the previous summer, part of a program that also earned her academic credit in her Pan-African studies minor. "I had to get a lot in order before I left, and do a lot of catching up when I got back," Mary says, and she makes it very clear that such flexibility is a rare and valuable commodity for Columbus staff members.

Mary, the oldest student profiled here, clearly has different educational goals than the other nontraditional students I studied, a fact that should warn us about the perils of generalizing too much about any demographic group in our writing classes. Yet the fact that she is a single mother whose educational sponsorship is essentially limited to her employer, the university itself, has led to a more protracted undergraduate career than those other students' and is a powerful demonstration of Sayer's argument that what we call *class* actually happens through a complex interweaving of "axes of inequality" such as socioeconomic status, gender, race, and so forth.[29] Mary's gender, marital status, socioeconomic standing, and lack of a more intimate sponsor such as Gene's fiancé, Ann's parents, and Rhoda's (profiled below) husband, have compounded her disadvantage, and Mary has been afforded precious little of the "distance from necessity" Bourdieu asserts is crucial for acquiring the type of cultural capital provided by a university education.[30] Based on the limited information I have, I do not know whether Mary's educational goals are a result of her class trajectory or vice versa. We can recognize, however, that her educational trajectory leaves her in a different place with different options once she graduates than the other students in this chapter will experience, and that her class—the powerful coming together of axes of inequality—has severely limited her available options.

STUDENT-STUDENT RELATIONSHIPS

Lest Gene's narrative paint too rosy a picture of his FYC experience, his discussion of small-group interactions with his younger classmates clouds this image considerably. His assessment of peer-review sessions, in particular, is bleak. Gene's class met in a classroom equipped with networked computers for each student, and his instructor relied rather heavily on wiki-based student interactions, both in and out of class. One group project required members to read and post a three hundred-word response to each group member's draft. But, "They didn't do it," said Gene with a mildly disdainful chuckle.

> They didn't do it, right? So . . . I said [my instructor] has a certain perspective . . . but what about other people? We all have different perspectives, and I never got that other perspective from my group. We never exchanged writing ideas. . . . I never got to read their two [papers] and they never read mine. So, in my experience it [peer review] was kind of useless because they didn't do the work.

Part of the problem seems to have been poor timing since, as Gene recalled, this project came late in the semester and the instructor commented that "the peer reviews seemed to fall apart" for every group, not just Gene's. However, part of the problem, in Gene's assessment, was clearly a lack of effort on the part of his group members, both of whom were in their teens.

Gene grouped himself with the same two students most of the semester and says the "in-class groups were okay, but the things that actually mattered, as far as the response [assignments that were] on the syllabus, which were pretty, I figured, pretty important, it just fell apart. Didn't work well at all in my opinion." Gene is hesitant to impugn the age or maturity level of the younger students in his class as a whole, but he believes a lack of focus was definitely an issue for his group members:

> In this particular case, obviously their focus wasn't Comp 101. I mean their focus was football, which is understandable. They have pretty busy schedules. And, the other guy, although a super nice guy, um . . . whether he was overloaded . . . I didn't really see his schedule . . . he always kinda seemed to be forgetful as far as, like, "When is that due?" And I'm like, "It's due today, brah." And he was like, "Oh, goddammit!" And then he has to go talk to [the instructor], who was very, I thought, was pretty flexible. He wouldn't let you fail . . . if you wanted to do it he'd let you make it up. But [the group member], he just didn't seem to really care, so I'm assuming it was age. There's people that are that age that are button-down, and can do, like, five different extracurricular activities and, you know, like eighteen [credit] hours and still make good grades, and make time for everybody. I couldn't tell you what the exact cause [was] between those two guys, though.

Needless to say, such sentiments do not bode well for positive "generational encounters." However, Gene's experience has given him the wisdom to take a more realistic, philosophical approach to his younger classmates:

> I see a lot of how I was in them, and, um . . . I don't offer unless asked, as far as guidance . . . if they're messing up, it's not my place to say, "Hey, you're screwing up, blah, blah, blah." I don't counsel them unless they want to be. So, if they say, "Hey, man, I don't understand this." I'm like, "Oh, it's just X, Y, and Z." But if they come to me with questions, then I'll give them the answers that I think would help them out. But I don't just offer counsel. Like "Hey, bro, this is a great opportunity" because I didn't listen, and I'm sure they [won't] either.

Gene is not too surprised that no younger students sought out the "wisdom of his age," but what he describes here is closer to what Etienne Wenger had in mind when he described how learning occurs through *generational encounters*. Wenger considers the generational encounter to be a crucial part of the learning process because it is "not the mere transmission of a cultural heritage, but the mutual negotiation of identities invested in different historical moments."[31] But in a classroom setting where the teacher is the only older person present, the "generational encounter" is impossible because teachers function as "representatives of the institution and upholders of curricular demands, with an identity defined by an institutional role."[32] However, a classroom in which older and younger students interact as peers is more likely to create a context wherein such encounters occur, possibly benefiting all students. Wenger's "communities of practice" are something like Bourdieu's concepts of field and practice, in which older, more experienced members lead by example. Practice, according to Wenger, "is not an object to be handed down from one generation to the next."[33] Rather, "older generations share their competence with new members by a version of the same process by which [those competencies] develop."[34] In other words, younger members of the community learn by sharing the *field*, and for Bourdieu and Wenger, the field in this case would be the classroom, with older members of that community as younger members practice. By this reasoning, Gene should not be too disappointed in his younger peers since they did at least share that field with him *as* he practiced, and they might have learned far more than he can know.

However, we all have reason to share Gene's pessimism in the following passage:

> But nobody asked me anything other than, "What did you do in the military? Did you kill anybody?" That's basically the only question I get, you know? And I'm like, "Okay, whatever." Yeah, nothing to do with organization, or like, "Hey, how do you stay focused?" Nothing like that, because I don't know if they even knew that I was so serious about school. They just knew I was a student too. I don't even think that they had the perspective to know that was my goal: to be a good student.

Gene is clearly and justifiably resentful of his fellow students' limited understanding of his war experience. Of course, only veterans of war can know what other veterans have gone through, and I did not ask how his classmates' inquiries made Gene feel. However, the lack of intellectual curiosity on the part of the younger students about what was going on *then*, in that English class, and how Gene focused or performed as well as he did—that lack of curiosity reflects poorly on the younger students themselves.

A thirty-five-year-old white female, Rhoda Folsom, is currently a junior pursuing a bachelor's degree in history and has been taking one or two classes per semester since 2003. Rhoda delayed enrolling in FYC because she could only afford to take a limited number of courses at a time and wanted to concentrate on major-specific classes. After losing her job in the fall of 2008, she enrolled full time and completed English 101 in the spring 2009 semester; at the time of her interview, she was enrolled in a summer term English 102 with the same instructor. Her experiences in

FYC have been radically negative when compared to Gene's, Ann's, and Mary's. According to Rhoda, those bad experiences are mainly attributable to her classmates, and she ascribes some blame to their youth. A large share of the blame could also be laid at the feet of the university, the athletic department, and—in a more problematic way—her FYC instructor. Rhoda is the student quoted at the beginning of this chapter who responded with a simple no when asked whether she could describe a "useful or productive" day in her FYC courses. Knowing her instructor, I had a hard time comprehending this reply, and given the acerbic quality of some of her responses, I debated whether to include Rhoda in this study at all. As I analyzed my qualitative data more deeply as a whole, however, it was clear to me that Rhoda's story *must* be included. She certainly had strong opinions, and they often leaned negative to the point of sounding personally embittered, but even if her commentary contains exaggerations of what occurred in her FYC classes, it is a contextually relevant commentary because Rhoda's are the complaints of a working adult who has taken those classes for credit alongside exclusively traditional-age students, and hers may reflect the experiences of other older students who are in an otherwise exclusively traditional-age composition class and thus do not have the built-in, older-student support system Gene and Ann had.

After losing her administrative job at the start of the Great Recession, Rhoda's husband encouraged her to enroll full time and finish up a degree she had been building in piecemeal fashion for six years. Like Gene and Ann, Rhoda does have a familial support system: "My husband said, 'Don't go find another job in our industry, because you are miserable. Go back to school and get your degree.'" But Rhoda is *herself* a "support system," as the mother of two teenage children, president of their high-school PTA, and head of a soccer program for seventy-five local public-school students. She cites these responsibilities and "time" as the biggest obstacles to her education, which she wants to continue through the PhD level to become a history professor. Her multiple leadership roles outside college give her a very different perspective on the "kids" with whom she attends class.

Rhoda describes her current English 102 course as "ridiculous," largely due to the fact that she is enrolled with what seems like half the university's student-athletes.

> This semester, I was in a group with two football players and a football hanger-on, and it was ridiculous. . . . We have four freshmen basketball players and at least two kids from the football team and all the freshmen baseball players in the class. And my classmates, when we are supposed to

be in groups discussing work, and I try to engage them and ask them questions about their classes, they are talking. One of the players informed me that all of his classes are like [this], which kind of scared me, and then [he] said that one of his classes all they have done is a gone on a scavenger hunt and colored. So we really don't have much to talk about.

Needless to say, Rhoda has not developed the kind of working rapport with her classmates that Ann did—though there are clear echoes of Gene's experience with his irresponsible groupmates. Rhoda continues in further detail:

I think in the 101 class my group actually did at least exchange papers and check each other's papers. But in the 102 class, the basketball players don't take their headphones off and they text messaged the whole time. My group only discusses the task far enough to make sure that I have done whatever work it is that we are supposed to turn in for them, and then they go back to their text messaging and talking about their Saturday nights. They come to class only because they want to make sure that the football guy sees that they are there, but there is not really any work being done. There is no work. Maybe for them there is but I don't see how.

I did not ask Rhoda to elaborate, but the "football guy" is presumably one of the athletic department's academic support personnel, who at Columbus regularly check in to make sure their student athletes are making satisfactory academic progress. From Rhoda's account, the fact that so many athletes are in one class has done neither those athletes nor the few nonathletes in the class any favors. In the context of this study, it seems to have reduced this adult student's FYC experience to one of a disgruntled babysitter: "I just think that I haven't learned anything, so it has just been a big waste of my money and time."

STUDENT-INSTRUCTOR RELATIONSHIPS

Whereas Gene was literally a role model—showing his younger classmates by example how to be a successful college student—and Ann played the role of willing participant, a friend to the younger students and older students alike (all the while learning from those older students), Rhoda withdrew from her classmates as much as possible, finding instead a mentor in her instructor. "She understands," says Rhoda, "that I'm coming from a completely different situation than most of these kids." Generational encounters were clearly happening in Gene's and Ann's classes, but generational warfare was more typical in Rhoda's classes—that is, until Rhoda stopped attending class altogether with the intention of completing English 102 on an independent-study basis, with the blessings of her instructor, of course: "Her and I have a great rapport, and she understands. And she lets me turn in papers so that I don't have to continue in this imaginary class. So we have had a good relationship." Rhoda and her instructor have worked out a solution, but from a utilitarian perspective, it hardly seems to benefit the class as a whole. Rhoda benefits in some ways since she no longer has to put up with her classmates' shenanigans. The slacking athletes benefit because they must now do their own group work. The instructor benefits since she does not have to hear Rhoda whine about "these kids." But as a whole, everybody loses in this highly dysfunctional environment, nobody getting the FYC experience they could have had with a more balanced enrollment: with fewer traditional-age students, fewer athletes, and more adult students, Rhoda's classes would have been better for all involved. The dysfunctional environment is the university's failing—and the failing of the athletic department's academic advising staff for funneling so many athletes into one section of English 102 (which, in my experience, is a fairly common practice at Columbus). In the end, although the university let her down, the instructor could have made the best of a bad situation by holding all students accountable—the younger students and Rhoda alike—for the role they have in making the class a success.

Having said that, I must add that Rhoda's instructor did show the type of flexibility teachers of mixed-generation composition classes should be willing to have, and that instructor was not alone among Columbus's composition teachers. A significant point of convergence in the testimonies of the seven instructors interviewed for this study is that nontraditional students have complex relationships with their teachers, and often their mere presence in the classroom forces us to reflect on our pedagogy in new ways. On a practical level, if a composition instructor actively tries to bring about the type of interactions that will foster positive generational encounters, non-traditional-age students in FYC can offer a wealth of knowledge and experience for their younger classmates. On the other hand, it is also apparent that negative experiences for some or all participants are possible if an instructor does *not* foster such interactions. Most constructive generational encounters, as Wenger employs the term, are not explicit moments when an older student instructs a younger peer on a particular assignment or "life lesson," and in fact those exchanges are likely to foment resentment on the younger student's part, as one instructor noted: "They would feel like [older students] were sort of condescending to them . . . some of the nontraditional students tend to take on almost a parental role in their relationship with some of the younger students." On the contrary, positive generational encounters are more likely to occur when older students model the behaviors and habits of successful students, such as diligently completing the assigned work on a daily basis and being rewarded for that diligence. Likewise, students who do not complete their work, especially in group situations such as peer-review sessions or teamed writing assignments, should be held responsible in some way that makes up the offense to their groupmates. Had Gene's instructor held the younger students accountable for not doing their part in peer-review sessions, perhaps they would have been more inclined to ask Gene questions like "Hey, how do you stay focused?" and not just the ubiquitous question of war veterans: "Did you kill anybody?" It sounds simple, but as a teacher who is not exactly a disciplinarian in the classroom, I know how tempting (not to mention easier for me) it is to let seemingly small matters "slide." But fostering mutually rewarding relationships in a mixed-generation classroom might require defusing potential conflicts before they occur, like those that were so destructive in Rhoda's "nonexistent class." The presence of nontraditional students in FYC classrooms complicates and pluralizes instructors' understanding of who their students are and how they might be taught. Experienced FYC teachers must rethink their well-worn teacher habits, and less experienced teachers must develop new, different teacher habits that accommodate more than just the typical classroom full of teenagers.

CONCLUSION: RETROGRADE, NOT RETURN

Much of the data gathered from the students and teachers in this study reinforces previous scholarship on adult students in higher education. For example, Gene's return from the Iraq War and Ann's broken engagement were significant, life-changing transitions in their lives that coincided with their enrollment at Columbus, and such moments of transition have long been cited as prime factors motivating adults to continue their formal educations.[35] Likewise, once adult students are enrolled they (generally) have a reputation for being among the hardest-working and highest-performing students in class.[36] Adult students' reputation for hard work and excellent results is also a major point of convergence in the qualitative data from my study. As the following quotations reveal, most older students take their FYC class more seriously, put in more effort, and often produce better work than their younger classmates.

- They tend to be, on a whole, as a group, very dedicated to the course and very dedicated to their education. And they tend to be really good students. Now every once in a while I'll have problems with some of them, like missing classes for work-related things. But even if

they do, they still turn in their work and it tends to be exemplary stuff.
It's obvious that they've devoted a considerable amount of time to it.
(Floyd, twenty-nine-year-old PhD student comp instructor)

- They seemed like they really wanted to learn how to write well. And
I used them as models for the younger students in that class because
they *didn't* seem to care. Older students . . . [are] almost always
completely prepared, as far as homework or writings that need to be
turned in. I find that a lot of them write earlier in the process because
they have to budget their time, because of children, or whatever.
(Daniel, thirty-six-year-old contingent faculty comp instructor)

- They tend to read the assigned text more, as a general rule. . . . I'll
see the ones who are outside waiting for class to start . . . the older
students will tend to be reading the text, whatever it is. The younger
students will tend to be *not* reading the text, whether they're on their
phone, or laptop, or whatever. . . . Maybe it's an issue of respect, or
even common sense or logic, like, "I spent the money for this book.
I'm gonna get my value out of it and actually read it and engage with
it more than just buying it because I have to buy it." (Lonnie, thirty-
three-year-old PhD student and comp instructor)

- I would say that most of the nontraditional students tend to see more
value in having an education, and I think that probably comes from
life experience and knowing what it's like to be out in the world and
not have an education. (Eve, twenty-seven-year-old PhD student and
comp instructor)

It is important to remember that these instructors are reflecting on
many experiences teaching mixed-generation classes, and while some
comments reveal specific students in specific courses, others are more
general impressions. Nevertheless, their observations reinforce much
of the existing statistical evidence from studies such as Carol Kasworm
and Gary Pike's, which showed a significant positive correlation between
age and grade point averages (GPA), and Shawn Carney-Crompton
and Josephine Tan's, which not only showed the same age/GPA correlation but also less grade variation within the older student population.[37] According to Kasworm and Pike, "The performance within the
Traditional group was more varied (grades ranged from 54% to 92%),
whereas the performance within the nontraditional group was more
consistent (grades ranged from 74% to 90%)."[38]

This evidence seems particularly significant in light of the fears students in this study expressed about returning to school and in fact supports Erich Fromm's assertion in *The Sane Society* that college might
be more appropriate for adults than it is for children.[39] The idea of a
returning student, a phrase prevalent in education literature and popular usage, is itself problematic because as even eighteen-year-old adults
quickly learn, no college student is in fact returning to any previous

educational experience but is moving into a different educational/cultural environment unlike what they experienced in their primary and secondary schools. And this is the distinction between retrograde movements and returns: in the latter case, the movement is *actually* backward, while in the former case, the movement only *appears* to be backward from another's ideologically situated perspective when it is in fact a movement into new territory. The myth of the return is ideologically powerful, dominating our conceptual model of adult learning because it is based on the dominant model of educational trajectories. Louis Althusser famously demonstrated that we move in linear paths through the educational system, just to the point where we are "ejected" into productive life in the capitalist system, with "a certain amount of 'know-how' wrapped in the ruling ideology."[40] Or as Samuel Bowles and Herbert Gintis said, "By the time most students terminate schooling, they have been put down enough to convince them of their inability to succeed at the next highest level. Through competition, success, and defeat in the classroom, students are reconciled to their social positions."[41]

It is a wonder that *anyone would want* to return to such a system! But life in what Althusser called "production" (today, more likely in the service economy) being what it is—dreary, humiliating, filled with terrifying uncertainties—millions of US working-class adults are willing to give formal education another chance since it offers hope of improving their lives. How many more might do the same if they understood college as a *path forward* rather than a step back into the "competition, success, and defeat in the classroom" they remember so well from their primary and secondary schools? Advocates for adult learning opportunities must offer a competing narrative to the ideology of returning students. I am not necessarily advocating use of the term *retrograde*, which probably has enough negative connotations attached to it already, but I do offer the idea of retrograde motion as a different conceptual model for educators who find Althusser's model a compelling yet ultimately paralyzing way of seeing the educational encounter.

Althusser described education as it *exists*. The retrograde model describes adult learning as it *might be*, which I see as more in line with hopeful educational theories such as Paulo Freire's. Hopeful educators do not see the "truth" and "lay the truth bare" before their students, asking them to adapt to a particular situation. They move first to their students' realities and see the world from their students' perspectives; the retrograde model affords the students' truth the dignity it deserves, which seems particularly important when teaching adult human beings who have spent a lifetime *coming* to that truth. Adult working-class students are awash in a culture that belittles their intellect because of a perceived lack of educational achievement, but over and over in my study, students and instructors spoke of how much the knowledge nontraditional students bring to class enriches the FYC experience for everyone involved. If educators of adult learners could do a better job articulating this fact to the public, we could combat the many common misperceptions about adult learning that foster the anxiety students in this study expressed about "going back" to school.

Notes

1.   See, for example, Quinnan, *Adult Students "At-Risk"*; Schon, *Beyond the Stable State*; and Gold, "Improving College Access."

2.   Harris, *Teaching Subject*.

3.   Sayer, *Moral Significance of Class*.

4.   See, for example, Bay, "Twists, Turns, and Returns"; Kasworm, "Adult Student Identity"; Morrison, "Old Lady in the Student Lounge," 29; Uehling, "Older and Younger Adults"; Warren, "Grandmothers in the Classroom."

5.   Kasworm, "Adult Student Identity," 13; Morrison, "Old Lady in the Student Lounge," 31.

6.   Kasworm, "Adult Student Identity," 13.

7.   Ibid., 29.

8.   Ibid., 10.

9.   Ibid., 14.

10.   Uehling, "Older and Younger Adults," 2.

11.   Kasworm, "Adult Student Identity," 13.

12.   Bourdieu, *Distinction*.

13.   Ibid., 110.

14.   A pseudonym.

15.   See, for example, Clark, "'Cooling-Out' Function"; Ganderton and Santos, "Hispanic College Attendance"; Pincus, "False Promises of Community Colleges."

16.   Ganderton and Santos, "Hispanic College Attendance," 115.

17.   Ibid., 114.

18.   Johnson and Bell, *Metropolitan Universities*.

19.   Clason and Dormody, "Analyzing Data."

20.   Mogey, "Evaluation Cookbook."

21.   Greenberg, "New GI Bill," 56.

22.   Bourdieu, *Distinction*, 6.

23.   Brandt, "Sponsors of Literacy."

24.   Ibid., 557

25.   Ibid., 177.

26.   Sayer, *Moral Significance*.

27.   Ibid., 26.

28.   Prior to the fall 2008 semester, tuition remission was available for employee spouses as well, but the university discontinued the practice in yet another move that put increased downward pressure on the enrollment of nontraditional students.

29.   Sayer, *Moral Significance*, 73.

30.   Axes of inequality line up in particularly devastating ways for single US mothers. The US Census Bureau figures for 2007, before the onset of the Great Recession,

reveal that the poverty rate for custodial mothers (27 percent) is more than twice the rate for custodial fathers (12.9 percent). For more, see Grall, *Custodial Mothers and Fathers.*

31. Wenger, *Communities of Practice.*
32. Ibid., 157, 275
33. Ibid., 276.
34. Ibid., 102.
35. Ibid., 102.
36. Merriam, Caffarella, and Baumgartner, *Learning in Adulthood.*
37. See, for example, Carney-Crompton and Tan, "Support Systems"; Kasworm and Pike, "Adult Undergraduate Students"; Kevern, Ricketts, and Webb, "Pre-Registration Diploma Students"; Makinen and Pychyl, "Differential Effects."
38. Kasworm and Pike, "Adult Undergraduate Students," 693.
39. Erich Fromm, *Sane Society.*
40. Althusser, "Ideology and Ideological State Apparatuses."
41. Bowles and Gintis, *Schooling in Capitalist America,* 155.

15

"BEING PART OF SOMETHING GAVE ME PURPOSE"
How Community Membership Impacts First-Year Students' Sense of Self

Genesea M. Carter

I learned that discourse communities not only help shape who you are, but also lead you on the path of the next discourse communties you could join. What you do today helps you determine who you will be tomorrow, and your discourse communties [sic] help lead the way for you to make those decisions.

—Nick, English 101 student[1]

College instructors who wish to help first-year working-class students transition from high school to college are often tasked with teasing out the array of intentions working-class students have for attending college. Working-class students attend college for a variety of reasons that have been well documented,[2] and supporting them in the classroom is not necessarily easy. Academia, as a well-oiled discourse community, can be inflexible and unforgiving toward new members who may not be prepared for the expectations therein. Students who are academic insiders already know how to "process, comprehend, and respond to existing knowledge—in short, making it their own—and make new knowledge," write Carolyn Boiarsky, Julie Hagemann, and Judith Burdan.[3] Those who are "academically literate," they explain, come to campus already knowing the college campus is a discourse community. In addition, academically literate students know "that *their job* is to become a member of that community"[4] because middle- and upper-class students have been groomed for such an academic identity.[5] Conversely, working-class students are not prepared for such a role in academia.[6] However, Hagemann notes, it is over simplistic to define them as "unprepared." Simply put, working-class students are prepared for a different

DOI: 10.7330/9781607326182.c015

community, and they do not often have the same sense of purpose for academia that middle- and upper-class students do.[7]

Teaching working-class students how to become members of the academic discourse community can be challenging, as working-class adults are marked by what Sue Ellen Henry calls the "'body as machine'" metaphor. Henry explains that working-class adults view their bodies as machines for making a living, caring for family members, and keeping up their homes."[8] Working-class college students, although not specifically named by Henry, also live within the "body as machine" metaphor, as most working-class students have extensive work experience that shapes their perspectives about their bodies as machines. Obvious within Henry's metaphor is the point that working-class students and adults do not view themselves as intellectual bodies. Missing the intellectual component complicates working-class students' purposes for being at college, as most working-class students view college as a means to an end.

The transition to academia includes another challenge: many working-class students' lives have not been conscientiously cultivated in the same way middle- and upper-class students' lives have. Annette Lareau writes that middle-class parents, as part of their "concerted cultivation," teach their children to negotiate and reason with authority so they learn to navigate the world around them.[9] As a result, middle- and upper-class students arrive at college with skills, such as agency and self-efficacy, that "have often been shown to correlate with successful adjustment to the demands of the university."[10] In sum, to bolster the success of working-class students in academia, an emphasis on cultivating working-class identities—that is, the ability for working-class students to "know themselves" and how they fit into academia—may be worthwhile in the composition classroom.

In this chapter, I explore how my English 101 Discourse Community Identity Profile can support working-class students' transition to higher education by encouraging them to explore ways in which their discourse communities cultivate their identities. As Nick, whose words I quoted in the epigraph, so eloquently wrote in his reflection, teaching working-class students to examine their discourse-community membership in relation to their identities can help them learn to conscientiously shape their own identities. Middle- and upper-class parents' concerted cultivation of their children's lives encourages a self-actualization and self-reflection many working-class students are not exposed to. As a result, working-class students often lack the skills to "know themselves," particularly in relation to higher education, in the same ways as their middle- and upper-class classmates do. Peripheral student populations who have not experienced the same cultivation may experience additional difficulties in their transition to college.

The Discourse Community Identity Profile assignment teaches students to reflect—perhaps for the first time, or more deeply—upon their own concerted cultivation of self. Working-class students can, and should, be taught how to reflect upon and cultivate their identities. In the profile, assigned in my University of Wisconsin–Stout fall 2014 English 101 course, students self-selected a discourse community they were insider members of and explored ways in which their communities shaped their identities and literacies. The profile is meant to create self-awareness at a number of levels: students must unpack what it means to have an identity and grapple with how their discourse communities have shaped their identities.

Because of my commitment to aiding working-class students' transition to academia, discourse-community membership is the overarching theme we explore in my first-year writing courses. While the discourse-community framework is useful to all students regardless of background or class standing, it is particularly beneficial for working-class students because it teaches them how to reflect on and evaluate the constellation of communities that intersect their lives. A large part of this conversation is helping them understand how communities shape their identities and question what kinds of identities they want to cultivate. Such conversations are particularly important, as the nuances of academic-community membership can be quite confusing and frustrating—or perhaps not even on their radar yet—for working-class students. In my classroom, these topics are woven into class discussion and every course project as throughout the semester students engage with a variety of discourse communities through a number of assignments: a Digital Literacy Map, a Discourse Community Identity Profile, a Campus Discourse Community Profile, and a portfolio of revised work.

There are three trends that emerged from my students' profiles and reflections: (1) students learned to reflect upon the cultivation of their identities, (2) students noted that discourse-community membership creates a sense of purpose for them, and (3) students choose their communities because of the family-like relationships within. Generally, students overwhelmingly acknowledged that the profile taught them more about themselves. This point is critical. For first-year students on a new campus, transitioning to college life is key to their academic success.[11] However, many working-class students perceive course content as "irrelevant to their experience, culture, and interests. The perceived (or actual) disconnect between academia and their lives may cause working-class students to begrudgingly accept an identity that will be constructed for them, or an identity that they will be alienated from."[12] Working-class students do not know how to "freely cross" between these two worlds—the "real world" and academia, write Richard A. Greenwald and Elizabeth A. Grant.[13] While it is imperative that first-year students learn how to navigate academic and social discourse communities, they cannot effectively do so if they do not know how to reflect upon their own identity construction.

First-year working-class students—and all students—need to learn how to evaluate their own selves, who they are, and who they want to be. Their self-actualization process is one way in which they learn to "find their place" on campus and in the classroom. Irvin Peckham writes, "One's vision of the world influences the social world in which one lives."[14] An additional challenge in helping working-class students transition to campus is that many believe they do not belong[15], or they are resistant to learning in the classroom because they are "fueled by the occupationally generated anti-intellectualism of working-class parents" and their "lack of meaningful connection to their studies."[16] Joseph Heathcott calls working-class parents' emphasis on higher education "one of the great but ambivalent accomplishments for a working-class family."[17] Despite potential motivational roadblocks, some working-class students attend college for social and/or financial mobility. Michael Zweig notes that the working-class students he has taught "have gone to college because they want to get away from the life they've seen their parents endure."[18] Therefore, writing instructors may want to develop curriculum that teaches working-class students how to concertedly cultivate an understanding about how students' working-class identities can successfully intersect with academia. In my own efforts to support working-class students' transition to academia, I have developed a curriculum that focuses on discourse-community membership and identity to bridge working-class students' predisposed notions about education with the benefits of higher education.

The working-class students at my university, the University of Wisconsin–Stout, Wisconsin's only polytechnic, experience a similar challenge: finding a meaningful connection with their studies. Students' unofficial slogan for the university, "When in doubt, come to Stout," captures the ways in which our students struggle to find a place in higher education or struggle with understanding the purpose of a university degree. Because Stout is a regional university, many of its students are from rural, staunchly working-class regions of Wisconsin. And they are often more comfortable in a deer blind than in the classroom. According to an article in the *Chronicle of Higher Education*, rural students "are not always advised why they should go to college" and many rural students come from families that "have a deep reluctance to encourage, or even tolerate, 'learning beyond your station.'"[19] Conversely, many of Stout's students select the campus because of its close proximity to home, the small(er) campus size (ten thousand students), and the small-town community. Close to home but not too far away, Stout is located in the small manufacturing and farming town of Menomonie (sixteen thousand population) sixty miles east of Saint Paul and Minneapolis, Minnesota. Sixty-three percent of freshmen students are white locals from the counties surrounding Menomonie, where manufacturing, farming, technology, and factories are the dominant industries.[20]

While there are many different definitions of working class, I use particular markers to identify my working-class students: access to technology (and regular upgrades), parents' education, parents' occupation, location of family home (rural, urban, suburban), and history of family college attendance. Based on these markers, in my fall 2014 English 101 course, half my students come from working class families. My working-class students' parents have high-school degrees; some of them either received a technical/two-year college education or started a four-year college degree but did not finish. They are from small (seven hundred-plus population) rural townships to midsized (seventy thousand population) cities in Wisconsin or Minnesota where their parents own small businesses, work in feed mills, own farms, drive trucks, or work as secretaries and teachers' assistants, for example.

YOU WANT ME TO WRITE WHAT?: USING PROFILES IN ENGLISH 101

Very little has been written about the profile genre, especially its use in college writing curriculum. Profiles predominantly grace the pages of periodical magazines, such as the *New Yorker*, and textbooks, like *Writing Today*, in the form of profiling either a person or a place. According to Richard Johnson-Sheehan and Charles Paine, the authors of the textbook *Writing Today*, which I use in my first-year composition courses,

> Profiles are used to describe interesting people, their significance, and their contributions. They are not full-blown life stories. Instead, profiles try to create a snapshot of a person by taking a specific, focused angle that allows the write to capture something essential—an insight, idea, theme, or social cause. Some of the best profiles focus on people who seem ordinary but are representative of a larger issue.[21]

In my classroom, I use the profile to teach students how to observe and closely examine a subject or place; these are skills I believe are critical for first-year students' transitioning to a new discourse community. Before students can successfully interact with a new discourse community, they must learn how to observe and describe that community and its members. Writing is, as Peckham explains, "a fundamental act of literacy, of naming the world and writing one's way into it."[22] Requiring students to profile themselves is, in itself, a way they learn to write their way into their own world. The profile, however, it is not an easy genre to learn. Students struggle with providing observations or description while capturing an insight about their discourse community or themselves.

While the textbook provides clear genre guidelines for writing a profile, the assignment prompt provides students with a problem-solving task to explore how their discourse communities shapes their identities. Boiarsky notes that working-class students need problem-solving tasks to learn how "they can transfer the knowledge that they acquire from . . . one writing assignment to another" and "they need to perceive their courses as more than just the acquisition of pieces of information and sets of rules."[23] Writing the profile as a problem-solving task—teaching students how to observe and explore their own communities while assessing how their communities impact their identities—are tasks to be solved "rather than templates in which information can simply be inserted."[24] Problem-solving skills are important for working-class students because all students need guidance "learning to learn." According to Boiarsky, "Learning to learn means that students can enter a classroom and, regardless of the teacher's teaching style or the subject matter being taught, know how to select and use appropriate strategies to understand the course content sufficiently to discuss, read, and write about it."[25]

The Assignment

Introduced in the seventh week of the semester, the Discourse Community Identity Profile is a two-page, single-spaced text in which students profile themselves in a familiar discourse community with the purpose of exploring how their identities are shaped by their communities. To create a real-life writing situation, I selected *Stoutonia*, the campus newspaper, as the students' audience. I wanted students to write their profile with their university peers, staff, and faculty in mind. And to learn about technology and visual design, they were required to include two pictures of themselves in their discourse communities. While the addition of visual aids certainly helps readers connect with the writers, the pictures were meant to show students in their communities. However, the selection of the pictures became a problem-solving task as students decided how they wanted to represent their communities and their identities.

The purpose of the Discourse Community Identity Profile is to teach first-year students to explore how their identity is shaped by a discourse community they are members of, as well as, more implicitly, that discourse communities shape identities. I believe these points are important because as first-year students learn to acclimate to the new and familiar discourse communities on and around campus, learning to identify how discourse communities shape their members is critical to membership success. Whether their communities are social or academic, first-year students need to learn about the impact of discourse-community membership upon themselves and others around them. On the prompt, I list several ways in which students might explore how their identities have been shaped through clothing, media, written genres, places, hobbies, events, language, skills, and so forth.

In the first week of the profile, students read profiles of people from our *Writing Today* textbook, including a profile of Dave Grohl from the Foo Fighters, as well as a profile of Will Ferrell (*Vanity Fair* magazine) and Drake (*Rolling Stone* magazine). We explored the rhetorical situation (genre, audience, purpose) of each profile, analyzed accompanying images, and talked about what the profiles taught us about the identities of the profiled. In the second week I focused on cultural literacy. We read the *New York Times*'s "Faking Cultural Literacy," *Psychology Today*'s "Are You Culturally Literate?," and the *Simple Dollar*'s "The Value of Cultural Literacy." These readings introduced students to cultural literacy and how discourse communities shape our own literacies. In the third week, students outlined and workshopped their profiles, making sure their profiles incorporated the genre conventions.

Students submitted their profiles electronically before our next class period. On the day the profile was due, I assigned a reflection exercise at the beginning of class. Students were given ten minutes to answer these three questions:

1. What did you learn about discourse-community membership from this assignment?

2. Do you think discourse-community membership knowledge (i.e., knowing about how discourse communities work) will be useful to you this first year (and in the future)? Why or why not?

3. Have you noticed if your discourse-community knowledge has been useful so far this semester?"

These questions were meant to discover students' understanding of discourse-community membership, as well as determine whether or not they were beginning to apply course material to other areas of their lives. By the time students submitted their profiles, we had spent over ten weeks discussing discourse communities and their impact on our lives.

The communities students profiled ranged from sports (wakeboarding, skiing, and football) to friends (high-school friends, new dorm friends) to family. The following student examples were selected to demonstrate the different reflections written in response to the Discourse Communities Identity Profile assignment. Despite the differences, several common threads emerged from students' reflections. While I always hope students will see the relevance of the course content to their own academic and personal lives, students' responses indicate that, not surprisingly, they privilege their personal lives first. In particular, students remarked that the profile assignment taught them more about themselves, but only one student, a senior international student from China, was able to articulate that his math class could be a discourse community. Therefore, the reflections show instructors to what extent first-year students' looking inward trumps looking outward, such as connecting course content to academia.

"Made Me Research My Life More": Writing about
Identity as a Cathartic Process

Brett's profile, titled "Where 29 Meets 13," is a profile of his Colby, Wisconsin, high-school football team.[26] A small town of 1,616 residents, Colby is a tight-knit, everyone-knows-everyone type of town. Although Brett's profile explores how his small town created a tight bond on the football field, the crux of his profile explores how unexpected loss—the accidental deaths of many of his Colby friends—tightened the bond. In seventh grade, a friend died in a four-wheeling accident. While Brett was in high school, three more deaths occurred: the homecoming king, who was also the football team's star player, drowned, and two more friends died within months of each other. Brett's profile explores how the tragedy of untimely death spurred the football team toward an undefeated, fourth-straight conference title. The team played to honor their friends, regardless of the senselessness of the deaths. But, perhaps more important, these tragedies strengthened the bond between Brett and his teammates. In his conclusion, he writes,

> After high school, we kind of all scattered. Some of us moved away, mostly to Eau Claire and Menomonie for school, and some of stayed in the Colby

area and joined the workforce. But all the things we've been through will always keep us connected. Even though we moved away from home, were still always together to make it seem like we never moved away. I don't live in Colby anymore but it will always be my home. My friends are what keep my reminded of that. I love them and thank them for that.

While tragedy and football figure prominently in Brett's identity, his Colby friends have impacted him in another way—to pursue a life outside Colby and to complete his bachelor's degree. He explains,

Without football, and without the friends I have, I probably wouldn't even be writing this paper right now. I would still be working in a meat factory or doing concrete. Don't get me wrong I love working. I think it's important to work hard for what you want, but I didn't want to be doing that stuff for the rest of my life. In my group of friends we pushed each other to pursue our dreams and I will always love them for that.

Although Brett's point is salient in that it explains why he has chosen to attend college, he does not expand upon his decisions in his profile or reflection. The paragraph offers much insight to me about why he is in college, but Brett told me that exploring the tragedy of his friends' deaths was the most meaningful angle for him.

Even in his postprofile reflection shows that he knows the profile assignment was important for him. He says, "[It was] helpful to learn about discourse communities because I learned more about myself." But, despite the significance of how his community—Colby, his friends, and football—has affected and influenced his life, he is unable to see how discourse-community knowledge will be "usefull in school besides this class," despite my in-class application of the content to the campus community. Even though, at this point in the semester, he cannot anticipate transferring his knowledge to other campus communities, he does find value in the framework.

It will be usefull for me because of the knowledge I gained. . . . This class made me research my life a little bit more than I have. Even though I couldnt really get down everything in my two page paper, it was nice to try and get some of those feeling about my community on "paper." Its usually very difficult to talk about the things in my paper with people outside my community.

For Brett, the profile served as a cathartic process and safe space to explore a very difficult topic. And I am glad he trusted me enough to write about his loss. Students need to know their voices will be heard. Whether students' voices are heard, and whether the classroom is a safe space, impacts their perceptions of their place on campus, and, ultimately, their academic success. While I am not advocating that writing instructors treat first-year students or working-class students with kid gloves, I do believe the classroom must be a safe space in which the vulnerable feel supported.

Peter, who wrote about his family and their bond over skiing and snowboarding in "Snowboarding," writes about learning to ski on the big hill behind the family home in Michigan. His profile explores his transition from skiing to snowboarding, much to his dad's chagrin, "a big downhill skier." Peter, unlike Brett, blends two communities into his profile, his family and the snowboarding community. Although his profile is a bit disjointed, Peter is able to reflect more generally about how these communities have shaped his identity. In his conclusion he says,

> Being an insider in the snowboarding community has changed the way I have lived my life over the last twelve years. I have met so many people throughout my snowboarding career and made some of my best friends through snowboarding. The snowboarding team was a great experience overall and taught me how to push myself and progress without anyone motivating me. Not only has it allowed me to meet some of my best friends and to date and taught me some self-discipline, but it is something my family and I can all do together.

Like Brett's profile, Peter selected a sports-related community and explores how he has grown through his community involvement. Peter's conclusion shows his understanding of how identity can be influenced by both the character skills he learned (i.e., self-discipline) and the relationships that are maintained. Furthermore, he seems to recognize that relationships within a discourse community are reciprocal: both the community and individual benefit from the relationship.

Unlike Brett in his reflection, Peter is able to anticipate using his discourse-community knowledge in other areas of his life. He writes in his reflection, "I beleive that it will hel me now and in the futur because it recognized what it takes to be and insider and an outsider in various communiities. This would be useful in many diffferent situations." Like several of my students, Peter was able to specifically reflect upon the usefulness of discourse-community membership, particularly the work that goes into becoming an insider. His statement that he has learned "what it takes to be an insider" suggests he may be able to successfully apply our course content to learning how to become an insider in other communities. At least that is my hope.

Despite Peter's understanding of the work required to transition from outsider to insider, he does not explain how he will use his knowledge, nor does he say he has used it yet: "I havnt directly used my knowledge of discourse communities so far but I can see it helpng me in the future." Discourse-community frameworks can be complicated for first-year students to understand. Therefore, I understand why it would be difficult for Peter to articulate how he might use knowledge of discourse communities or to recognize he already is using his knowledge (which he probably is).

"Like a Large Family": The Benefits of Community Membership

Henry wrote his profile about the Green Bay Packers discourse community. This community is a large part of Wisconsin life, as it is not uncommon for Wisconsin Walmarts or other stores to allow their employees to dress in Packers gear on game day, as well as broadcast the Packers games over the store's loudspeakers. The importance of the Packers discourse community, to Henry, is that it is a statewide community. In his profile's opening line he writes,

> For me, being a member of the Packer community means that wherever I go in the state, there is always people on game day there with me to cheer on my favorite team.

Although Henry largely recounts his love for the Packers within his profile, it is apparent he values this community for more than just the team or their championships. Henry writes in his conclusion,

> The Packers are a great way to see family and friends. From Packer parties to the Thanksgiving Day game. There is always a way for people to bond over the game by either cheering or booing. From working at a sports bar I have had loads of experience with fans and Packer lovers. Even when you're not in Green Bay everyone makes you feel like you are. Win or Lose I will always be a true Packer fan my entire life.

Family and friends are very important communities to my students, not surprisingly. New to campus, they hold more tightly to their relationships back home. Henry's love for the team expands beyond friends and families, however. He seems to appreciate that the Packers community extends statewide. Henry can easily create or find a new community of Packers fans at Stout or somewhere else. In a way, the ease finding and fitting into a Packers community makes it easier for Henry to transition to college.

Despite Henry's profile's lacking content about how his identity has been impacted by the Packers discourse community, his reflection is quite thoughtful. Henry writes, "I think after this assignment it really gave me a purpose to join more clubs to meet more people. You never know if you could potentially be in larger communities by meeting more people. You don't know what that could lead to down the road." Henry was a very quiet and shy student who rarely spoke in class. Yet, his reflection illustrates the impact discourse community-related assignments can have on introverted students, even to helping them move outside their comfort zones. Also, his statement highlights the importance of reflection: reflection may highlight for instructors ways in which students are absorbing or applying the course material that may not be apparent in high-stakes writing assignments.

Henry is one of the few working-class students in my course who was able to articulate how he was going to apply his new-found discourse-community knowledge to the communities around him. He explains,

> I noticed things I think I would not have after learning about discourse communities. For example, when I joined my flag football team, I saw that it was comprised of a few smaller groups of people. The jocks, the nerds, and the average joe's. It made me think what these people are like outside of flag football. Now after the season is ended I continue to meet up with multiple people on my team that I never would have met if I had not joined.

Working-class students may be easily intimidated by academia and adjusting to a new campus community, but teaching them how to identify and evaluate discourse communities may help ease the transition. In addition, discourse-community assignments, such as the profile, encourage students to observe and respond to the world around them, which is a large part of learning how to become insiders in new communities.

In her profile, Erika wrote about the untimely death of her mother due to cancer and the challenges her family faced afterwards. Not surprisingly, Erika's identity, like most of my students, is rooted in her family. However, she cherishes her family community because of the support and stability it provides. She writes in her conclusion,

> Some people say that because I have acted like someone I shouldn't have had to be that I am weak because now "I don't know myself" or "don't know how to act my age and act like an adult." I think that is good. Yes, I had to grow up too fast. Yes I had to sacrifice things I should not have had to sacrifice. Yes I have fallen and been hurt. But that does not mean I can give up. I continue to fight my grief for my mother everyday but I try to leave a wake to happiness and example where ever I go. That is what I have learned in this irritating and trivial lesson. No matter how hurt you are, no matter how hard it is to get out of bed in the morning I will always have my family to help me. And that is all I need.

Because of her mother's death, Erika has needed to quickly grow up to help her siblings and father adjust to a new life together. As painful as her mother's death has been, and will continue to be, it brought the family closer together. Instead of focusing on her life as an individual, with individual wants and needs, Erika has focused her energy and effort on her family, knowing her community will support her in whatever ways necessary.

The idea of community, and how communities can support and value diverse members, is a critical component of Ericka's reflection. She writes,

> When a person is a part of a discourse communitiy they are a part of not only a group of people but a mini culture where they are seen as not only a person but a member. . . . I think the knowledge will help me better understand the different types of people and for others it can help them understand that people are not always the same. People value different things and it shows in how they act, speak and live.

Erika's understanding of family has influenced her conceptualizations of discourse-community memberships. A discourse community, for Erika, is a group in which people are not individuals but diverse members working toward a collective goal. A discourse community is a safe space where people can support and encourage each other. In many ways, Erika's understanding of discourse community is informed by her experiences with her family.

Cultivating "A Sense of Purpose": Recommendations and Conclusion

Working-class students need to know who they are before they can learn to transition into the campus community. Without a sense of self, or a sense of how their identities are shaped by the communities they are members of, working-class students may not be able to figure out how to concertedly cultivate identities that support their academic trajectory. Furthermore, working-class students need to decide to what extent they want academia to cultivate their identities—because it will. This does not mean academia will replace their old identities with new ones. But, as Brett wrote in his profile, choosing to go to college as opposed to continuing in a construction job meant he had to move away from Colby and cultivate a different life.

In the classroom, writing instructors may want to adopt writing assignments that allow working-class students to explore their own identities, how those identities are shaped, and how students might want to shape their own identities. Low- and high-stakes writing assignments about identity may help working-class students begin to cultivate their own identities, either in relation to their home discourse communities or new campus communities. Teaching working-class students to reflect upon their identities may provide a bridge between their home communities and academia so students recognize they have agency to direct and shape the identities they want to have. Furthermore, conversations about identity can lead to conversations about their collegiate identity and their purposes for attending college.

Instructors may want to offer a pre- and post-test at the beginning and at the end of the semester for which all students answer questions about their identities, what they want to achieve in college, or how they are struggling to adapt to college life. Pre- and post-tests allow instructors to gather data at the beginning and end of the semester to gauge the knowledge and skills their students have acquired. Pre- and post-test questions should be open ended and specific, such as, "what does it mean for you to be a member of a community?" or "in what ways has it been difficult for you to transition to college?" The answers to these questions can be used to facilitate conversation, to build community within the classroom, and to inform low- and high-stakes writing assignments.

In addition, writing instructors might emphasize how discourse-community concepts can help students find communities on campus that provide a family-like environment. Writing instructors can talk to their students about how to develop a microcommunity of support within larger, more intimidating communities, such as academia, to help students balance the familiar with the unfamiliar. Even though working-class students may not know how to apply discourse-community concepts in ways that might ease their transition to the college campus—a large reason for my emphasis on the framework within English 101—their new knowledge impacts them in other, critical ways.

Moreover, for instructors who intend to explicitly help their working-class students transition to the academic discourse community, assignments and in-class activities that tease out ways in which academia functions as a family-like discourse community may be useful. Another student, Joe, wrote in his reflection, "I learned that discourse community membership is important, Being a part of something gives me a sense of purpose." While Joe was not reflecting on academia in his reflection, his feelings of engagement can guide instructors in how to teach working-class students to think about academia as providing them with a sense of purpose, which is critical to retaining working-class students and helping them succeed while in college. Without a sense of purpose, working-class students may lack the internal drive or exigency to become insiders in the academic community. While academia and the campus community cannot mirror a family-like environment exactly, nor should it, there are traits, such as sense of place and support, that instructors can highlight to help working-class students develop their sense of academic purpose while in college.

As seen in my students' reflections, working-class students have more difficulty applying concepts of discourse-community membership to other areas of their lives. Although we had spent half the semester talking about how discourse-community membership could inform their lives and help them transition to new communities, most of my students wrote in their reflections that they had not begun applying it outside the classroom or did not see how the framework might be useful to them outside class. This difficulty in applying new knowledge is not unusual, however. Peckham explains, "Working-class students may also be less likely than middle-class students to see events from multiple perspectives . . . working-class students tend to resist the notion of shifting identities—for them, changing who you are to respond to the social context is what middle class people do."[27] Although my emphasis on discourse-community membership did not specifically focus on the word *change*, I did frequently use verbs such as *adapt*, *transition*, and *adjust* to describe how my students might want to negotiate with the new communities around them. But students were not particularly interested in discussing their transition to college or the ways in which the transition could be made more easily.

The sampling of student work I have included here offers a telling story: my students are most impacted by the communities in which they believe they enjoy a reciprocal relationship—they give to the community, and the community gives back. Many of my students liken their home community to a metaphorical family. This concept of family is a worth noting. According to Gerard Delanty, "Identity presupposes a capacity to distinguish between inside and outside; the self knows itself in terms of a relation to the other."[28] Therefore, for many of my students, being part of a community in which they were contributing, productive members significantly impacted their identities. And the course sequence gave students the language and terminology to articulate what they already knew: that being part of a community had impacted their lives in a variety of ways. It is obvious from my working-class students' writing that what they value most is *the constant*—the Packers fans who can be found anywhere and everywhere; the family and friends who ski together; the football team that has provided support through good times and tragic times; the family that has become closer due to a mother's death. In essence, my students valued communities that provided support, familiarity, and stability. My hope, in the end, is that my students left my English 101 class with a greater understanding of how their discourse communities shaped their identities and how they *can* concertedly cultivate their identities, should they wish to do so. It is also my hope that in learning to know themselves they will make conscious decisions to apply that knowledge as they transition to new discourse communities, like academia.

Notes

1. All students' names have been changed, and their writing style is unedited.
2. See Thomas, Porfilio, Gorlewski, and Carr, *Social Context Reform*; Hurst, *College and the Working-Class*; and Espinoza, *Working-Class Minority Students'*.
3. Boiarsky, Hagemann, and Burdan, "Working Class Students in the Academy," 17.
4. Ibid., 17. Emphasis mine.
5. Lareau, *Unequal Childhoods*, 5.
6. Linkon, Introduction to *Teaching Working Class*.
7. Boiarsky, Hagemann, and Burdan, "Working Class Students in the Academy," 17. Emphasis mine.
8. Henry, "Bodies at Home," 5.
9. Lareau, *Unequal Childhoods*, 3.
10. Brooman and Darwent, "'Yes, as the Articles Suggest,'" 19.
11. O'Keefe, "A Sense of Belonging."
12. Martin, "Pedagogy of the Alienated," 35.
13. Greenwald and Grant, "Border Crossing," 28.
14. Peckham, *Going North Thinking West*, 31.
15. Greenwald and Grant, "Border Crossing," 32–33.
16. Martin, "Pedagogy of the Alienated," 34, 35.
17. Heathcott, "What Kinds of Tools?," 106.
18. Zweig, *Working Class Majority*, 43.
19. "Rural Students: Common Obstacles."
20. Ibid.
21. Johnson-Sheehan and Paine, *Writing Today*, 57.
22. Peckham, *Going North Thinking South*, 1.
23. Boiarsky, "Learning to Learn," 27.
24. Ibid.
25. Ibid., 25.
26. In Brett's profile, he explains that Colby is located where Highway 29 meets Highway 13.
27. Peckham, *Going North Thinking South*, 72, 73.
28. Delanty, "Academic Identities," 131.

16

LITERACY DEVELOPMENT AS SOCIAL PRACTICE IN THE LIVES OF FOUR WORKING-CLASS WOMEN

Gail G. Verdi and Miriam Eisenstein Ebsworth

Literacy, in a traditional sense, is the ability to decode written texts and to encode oral language into writing. Yet many researchers and theorists argue that learning to read and write involves social activities influenced by interactions[1] and mediated by class affiliations.[2] In addition, gender, race, and ethnicity impact how individuals compose internal narratives driving motivation and academic performance.[3] Therefore, the narratives we construct through our exchanges with families, teachers, and peers frame our literate identities. The recent focus on the achievement of academic literacy by all learners has underscored the challenges that must be addressed by individuals from different backgrounds with alternative literacy traditions. Despite the concern that students from working-class and immigrant backgrounds do not reflect the standard literacy norms required by academic institutions, there are few studies investigating successful learners who are able to overcome these challenges.

Literate identities evolve over time, through relationships, and according to Jean Anyon and Ray Rist, are complicated when teachers view the literacy practices of students from working-class and poor families as deficient.[4] In addition, it has often been found that school curricula in working-class and poor communities are designed to focus on the control and reproduction of fragmented, isolated forms of knowledge. Such activities impede student engagement and contribute over time to students' resistance to acquiring the forms of literacy required for academic success, making them ripe for failure.[5] Other studies have also contributed to our understanding of how working-class children acquire relationships with words. Shirley Brice Heath, and later Denny Taylor and Catherine Dorsey-Gaines, studied the literate traditions of parents from different racial and social class communities, while Patrick Finn, building on the work of Anyon, focused on the different types

DOI: 10.7330/9781607326182.c016

of literacy taught in working-class, middle-class, professional, and elite schools.[6] Thus, our analyses in this study of working-class women's narratives reveal the forms of literacy their families used and how their families' relationships with the literate practices they experienced in schools impacted their identities as learners.

Our retrospective study identifies four successful women academics from working-class backgrounds and explores the evolution of their literacy, considering both the forms of resistance they exhibited as well as the strategies they used to succeed. Based on open-ended interviews, we consider how working-class girls/women are socialized through the dynamic nature of their affiliations in terms of language acquisition, literacy development, and cultural identity formation. In addition, much like Donna Dunbar-Odam's work, the purpose of this paper is not only to consider how the stories participants tell represent their desires for and acquisition of higher literacy but also to explore what strategies teachers might use in their own classrooms to help students from working-class backgrounds succeed in developing academic literacy.[7]

Choosing Participants

In selecting participants, we needed to operationally define what it means to be working class. As William Thelin and Genesea Carter indicate in the introduction of this volume, we concluded through a review of literature and conversations in various fora that there is more than one approach to this construct. However, it is also important to note that at the core of our participants' stories was their families' relationships with power. Consequently, for the purposes of this study, identifying oneself as coming from a working-class family meant being able to articulate the extent to which one had access to economic, cultural, educational, and work-related forms of power. After preliminary interviews, four women were chosen to participate in the study; each had grown up and lived in the New York metropolitan area. By focusing on the experiences of women who were born and raised around New York City, the scope of our study was narrowed, and opportunities to investigate in-depth variables that impacted participants' literacy development were expanded.

Four Working-Class Women

Ruth was born in Brooklyn in 1947. She describes herself as a multilingual and multicultural person who appears Caucasian but identifies racially as "human." She speaks several languages and has lived and worked in different countries. She went to a yeshiva but transferred to public high school in the eleventh grade. Ruth received a BA and a PhD from the City University of New York and an MA from a private university. She is currently an associate professor at a private college in New York. She grew up in a working-class, socialist, Jewish household. Her father left school to support his family. He worked at a range of jobs, including one at the Fulton Fish Market, while her mother worked at low-level accounting jobs, never having obtained her CPA.

Grace is an Italian American who was born in 1957 in Newark, New Jersey. She grew up in a multilingual, multicultural environment. She attended public schools K–12 and got her BA, MA, and PhD from private universities. She is an assistant professor at a public university in New Jersey. She has taught in preschools, high schools, and public and private universities. Her father was a milkman and her mother was a beautician; neither of her parents graduated from high school.

Terese is an African American woman, born in 1947 in New York City. She describes herself as bidialectal and multicultural. She characterizes her family as having a long history of working for powerful people in government. She attended public schools in Harlem and got her BA at the City University of New York. Before entering graduate school at a private university, Terese worked as a seamstress, dress designer, and administrative assistant. She has a PhD in English education and is an assistant professor at a public college in New Jersey. Terese did not live with her father as she was growing up. Her mother completed high school and worked as an administrative assistant.

Veronica is a bilingual, multicultural woman of color with some white ancestry, born in 1952 in Cuba. Veronica attended public schools in Cuba and the United States. She got her BA and MA at the City University of New York and her PhD from a private university. She is an assistant professor of education at a private college. Veronica's mother left Cuba without her father in 1962 and moved to the South Bronx with her seven children. Veronica's mother never finished school and was employed as a service worker.

THEORETICAL FRAMEWORK AND DATA COLLECTION

In order to maintain the women's individual voices and allow for a deeper understanding of the complex nature of working-class subcultures and the forms of literacy acquired within working-class homes and schools, the data were collected using unstructured phenomenological interviews resulting in first-person narratives.[8] This qualitative approach has been characterized by Irving Seidman as "interviewing as conversation."[9] Each conversation was based on responses to open-ended questions and follow-up discussions. Consequently, the four participants were looked upon as collaborators in the research, resulting in an interview process that provided opportunities to develop closer relationships with the women while exploring lived experiences.[10] The interview process consisted of three two-hour sessions. The preliminary interview focused on background information, at which time each participant was asked to describe her family, their linguistic and cultural backgrounds, and the forms of literacy used at home. The second stage of interviews required that the participants examine the manner in which literacy was presented and constructed within their working-class elementary and high-school classrooms. The third interview provided the opportunity to revisit relevant issues and events discussed previously and to explore these more deeply. In addition, at the end of each interview, the participants and the interviewer reflected on the process.

ANALYZING DATA

An interpretive analysis of data allowed the researchers to investigate participants' experiences through text-to-text renderings, reading the stories the women told, and looking for links and/or contradictions in theories discussed in previous research.[11] The stories told by the participants offered significant insights into how their families' literate practices influenced their attitudes toward reading and writing. Learning to read and write, therefore, came to represent the forms of literacy participants used at home, at work, and in their local communities

LITERACY, HOME, AND FAMILY

The portraits the participants shared of their families' literate traditions can be best understood as connected to the earlier work of Heath and Taylor and Dorsey-Gaines.[12] We integrated the reading and writing categories designed by Heath, and expanded on by Taylor and Dorsey-Gaines, in such a way that they serve as interpretive tools within the context of our study.

For reading, these categories include (1) instrumental: reading to gain information; (2) social-interactional: reading to maintain and gain information pertinent to social linkage; (3) news-related: reading to gain information and learn about third parties and distant events; (4)

recreational: reading for leisure, planning events, and to maintain social relationships; (5) confirmational: reading to check or confirm facts or to make announcements; and (6) critical/educational: reading to educate oneself, to fulfill educational requirements or school or college-course reading assignments to increase one's ability to consider and/or discuss political, social, aesthetic, or religious knowledge.

For writing, these categories are (1) reinforcement or substitution for oral messages: writing used when oral communication is not possible; (2) social-interactional: writing to establish, build, and maintain social relationships as well as writing to negotiate family responsibilities; (3) memory aids: writing to serve as a memory aid; (4) financial: writing to record numerals and amounts and purposes of expenditures and for signatures; and (5) expository: writing for work, school, for personal purposes.

Literate Practices in Working-Class Families

Grace's parents had acquired some literacy skills, even though her father left school in the third grade and her mother never graduated high school. As Grace noted, they were not literate in the same way she is today, reading for critical/educational purposes and writing expository and creative texts. What is significant in terms of social class is that the literate acts Grace described were linked to their usefulness in everyday life.

> We watched a lot of television. We would talk about the shows, and my parents would shout at the news. My mother and father did read, but mostly magazines and newspapers. My father read the *Daily News*. He would sit at the kitchen table watching television, smoking cigarettes and reading, mostly checking the results of the horse races. My mom read *Woman's Day* for recipes and household tips. Although my mother didn't read literature, she wanted me to be a reader.

In order to find out what was on television, Grace's parents read the television guide that was in the newspaper. Heath and Taylor and Dorsey-Gaines, noted above, refer to these activities as examples of instrumental literacy. Instrumental and financial literacies were also linked to the ability to read and write bills and keep track of business logs. In subsequent interviews, Grace noted that her mother, who was more literate than her father, had a better grasp of instrumental literacy. Grace's mother read things like applications for benefits, specials at the grocery store, recipes, and household tips in magazines. Both Grace's parents, however, read to gain information about third parties and about local, state, and national events. This is indicated in Grace's reference to reading the

Daily News and the *Star-Ledger* (news-related reading). They also read for recreation. Grace's father checked the results of the horse races, and her mother read *Woman's Day* for pleasure. Grace indicated that her parents used social-interactional literacy such as reading greeting cards, cartoons, and notices of local events—births, deaths, and marriages—as well as reading to confirm facts by checking income-tax forms and bills.

Ruth's comments were superficially consistent with those of Grace. Ruth said, "My parents were not that literate. My mother had a hard time writing, and I don't think my father read many books. They were more likely to watch television." Much like Grace's parents, Ruth's mother and father were literate. What Ruth means when she says they "were not that literate" is that the types of literate traditions they incorporated into their daily lives were based more on getting things done. Like Grace's parents, they read for instrumental information, for news, for recreation, to confirm information, and to some extent for social interaction. They did not read great works of literature. This type of reading would be considered reading to increase one's ability to discuss political, social, or aesthetic knowledge. Ruth also noted that her mother was not a fluent writer. Here, Ruth was referring to what Heath and Taylor and Dorsey-Gaines called *expository*, *creative*, or even *autobiographical* forms of writing. These are genres of writing that would indicate the ability to produce college or school papers, writing as a means of self-expression, or writing to understand oneself.

However, both Ruth's mother and Grace's mother could write in many different forms for practical purposes. For example, they could use words to substitute for oral messages (notes to teachers), for memory (lists), and for financial purposes (checks, forms). Similarly, both Grace and Ruth told stories of how their mothers influenced their attitudes about their abilities to become literate by taking them to the library for reading and to museums for culture: "My mother [Ruth's mother] took me to the library for my library card when I was in kindergarten. My mother always took me to the library and to museums . . . so even though her formal education was just about numbers not about reading and culture, she encouraged me to grow in these areas." Grace described the experience similarly: "Going to the library was an adventure. . . . She [my mother] encouraged me to take out a lot of books and return them to get more. So the library and museum that we could walk to were significant parts of my world outside of school as well as a place for my mother find a quiet space." In both portraits, the women indicated how their mothers gravitated toward libraries and museums located in their local communities. Within the rooms of children's libraries and the halls of museums, their mothers shared with them their dreams for their futures. The library card signified, for both mothers, a ticket to critical/educational literacy, the type of literacy they recognized they had not been able to acquire. Ruth did have a somewhat different experience than Grace due to her mother's and father's connection to unions and their interest in social justice. Ruth had the opportunity to engage in a type of oral discourse that pushed her to think about and talk about issues other than the everyday, but not because her family was particularly literate. She had this opportunity because she grew up in a household that immersed her in antiracist and anticlassist rhetoric and that did provide her opportunities to use description, explicit detail, and more abstract forms of thinking about how to solve problems.

Terese's family portrait contrasted with those of the communities in Heath's study in terms of African American working-class families and their literate traditions. Terese's family read and collected books. Therefore, growing up in Terese's home was very different from growing up working-class in a place like the Piedmont. Below, Heath describes the lack of books and reading material available in Trackton, the African American working-class community:

> Trackton residents have no such accumulation of reading materials; whatever comes into the community is usually either read, then burned or used for other purposes, or immediately discarded. There is no space or time assigned for reading. . . . Foremost among the types of reading and writing are those which are instrumental.[13]

The working-class subculture in which Terese grew up participated in literate traditions that were instrumental, social-interactional, news related, and conformational. However, in Terese's family, reading books was also tied to both recreation and critical/educational practices. Terese's mother was an administrative assistant and had to negotiate forms of literacy associated with job duties. In contrast to Ruth and Grace, who viewed reading as more of a solitary act, for Terese reading was social: "We got books for Christmas, and books for birthdays. Everybody in my family read, except for one aunt. We were read to at bedtime. It was a way of controlling us because there were five of us who were pretty close in age. We would read to each other, and my older sister would read to us." The social aspects of the literate traditions Teresa described were closely aligned to those attributed to the African American working-class community in Trackton. For Trackton adults, reading is a social activity; when something is read in Trackton, it almost always provokes narratives, jokes, sidetracking talk, and active negotiation of the meaning of written texts among the listeners; meanings are negotiated through the experiences of the group.[14]

For Terese and her siblings, reading was a collaborative activity, much as it is for the adults in Trackton. However, in Trackton this active engagement is limited to adults. Children in Trackton may hear the adults as they negotiate the meanings of instrumental texts, but they are not included in the group narratives. In contrast, the children in Terese's family read and were read to by adults, engaging the children in activities that required them to use their imaginations to read, perform, and create stories. Terese and her sisters learned both form and function of text this way. Although the types of reading described in Terese's portrait were more varied than those of the African American families in Trackton, her family didn't utilize the more formalized notions middle-class children are taught when learning to read and write. Terese's family motivated her to read, write, and perform texts, but they weren't doing this as a conscious preparation for school-based literacy performance. This view of literacy contrasts with Heath's observation regarding the working-class white people of Roadville's emphasis on individual achievement and the parents' need to draw school activities and values back into the home, constructing links through direct and extended talk to school knowledge.[15]

Veronica, in contrast, noticed that there were no books in her home and that her mother did not keep magazines around the house. She noted that this was true for her family in Cuba as well as her family in the United States. Her mother and other family members were able to read to gain information, for social-interactional purposes, and to confirm facts. However, there was very little news-related reading in her home, and there was no critical/educational reading except for what was brought home from school. Veronica's movement toward critical/ educational forms of literacy was acquired at school. The connection between her developmental narrative and school life appears twice, once in her portrait and once during our last interview. As she observed several times in her portrait, she linked her family's cultural beliefs about education with their lack of involvement in facilitating reading and writing at home. "In the Spanish culture that I come from, parents believe that the teacher knows what to do, not the parents. It is the teacher's responsibility to provide for your child's intellectual needs." During our last interview, Veronica described how she came to value reading and writing through school experiences. "My teacher was the one who took me to get my first library card. We did our homework in the library. We went there every day after school. We spent time at the library gossiping about boys as well as our schoolwork." What stands out in this excerpt, though, are the contradictions in Veronica's portrait. For example, her allusions to the lack of literate traditions within her home mirror those of the Trackton community in Heath's study. There were no adults in her home to monitor her reading comprehension because her parents didn't read to her or with her. But unlike the Trackton children, Veronica was fortunate to find teachers who filled in the gaps for her in elementary school. Whereas the Trackton children are presented with reading and writing as "decontextualized skills," Veronica, through her caring teachers, became a "contextualist who could predict and maneuver the scenes and situations by understanding the relatedness of parts to the outcome of identity of the whole."

While Veronica's teachers taught her to love reading, being a good student was a reaction to her mothers' limited literacy and life choices: "I wanted to go to college because my mother was on welfare, and I wanted to make sure that I wouldn't end up in that situation. It was a way out of poverty." This statement indicates that through what she knew of her mother's life, Veronica came to view literacy as her ticket out of the welfare system, building *a conceptual world* through integrating family and environment.[16]

Schools and Schooling in Working-Class Communities

Two major studies by Anyon and Finn based on the school lives of working-class students identified correlations among class, literacy development, and student engagement.[17] These studies reported the impact political, economic, and cultural factors had on institutional policies that determine the types of schools students attend, the academic track in which they are placed, and ultimately the jobs they perform after graduation. Faculty and administration at each type of school identified in figure 16.1 (working class, middle class, affluent professional, and executive elite) present knowledge, design tasks, control behavior, and influence student attitudes about learning through what has often been termed a *hidden curriculum.* This hidden curriculum is based on sociopolitical beliefs, whether conscious or unconscious, about what students can or cannot accomplish.

In order to determine the types of schools the women in this study attended, we designed a matrix (see figure 16.1) that outlined the framework and allowed us to add more depth to our interpretations. We also created a flow chart (figure 16.2) based on Anyon's and Finn's categories representing the forms of literacy participants learn to negotiate at

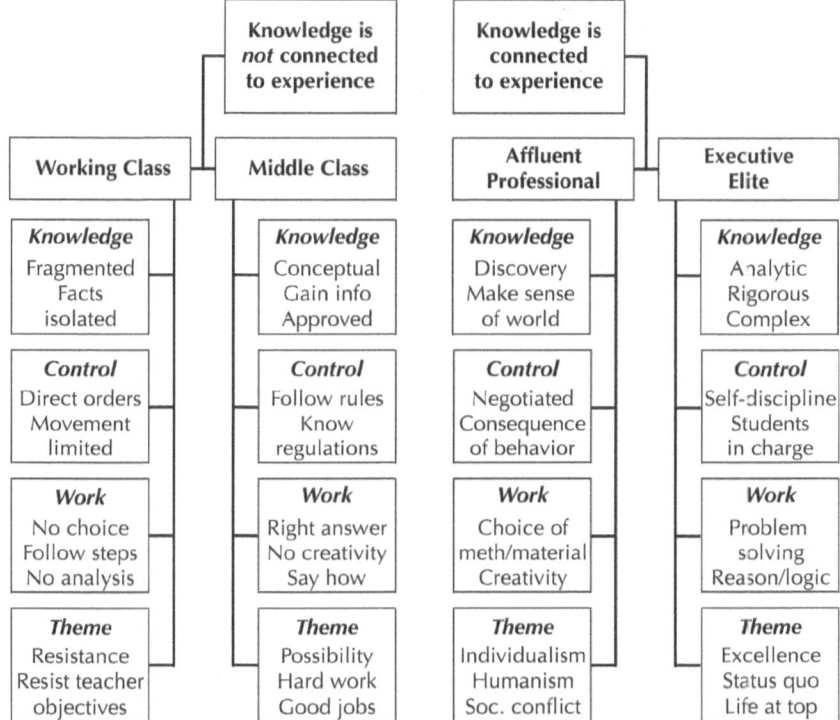

Figure 16.1. Class, control, language and literacy in schools (adapted from Anyon, "Social Class and the Hidden Curriculum of Work" and "Social Class and the Hidden Curriculum," and Finn, Literacy with an Attitude)

home (with family) and at school, ranging from the ability to move from oral language to writing (performative literacy) to forms of literacy that demand critical thinking and creative reasoning (powerful literacy).

As discussed in previous research, the higher on the socioeconomic spectrum a school lies, the more connected knowledge is to students' daily experience. Therefore, knowledge at executive elite schools and affluent professional schools provides students with forms of knowledge that engage students in discovery learning and complex forms of analysis. Similarly, these schools offer classroom contexts in which teacher control is negotiated with students, who are given choices of tasks and creative projects (affluent professional), and/or in which students are expected to exhibit forms of self-discipline that allow them to solve problems by using reason and logic (executive elite). Themes that arise from portraits of affluent professional schools highlight individualism or achieving personal success through one's own efforts while in executive elite schools students are socialized to perpetuate the status quo to maintain life at the top. Both the affluent professional and the executive elite provide students with experiences that contrast with working-class and middle-class schools.

Our Schools

The levels of literacy Grace developed in elementary and high school resembled the descriptions of children's literacy in Finn's working-class schools (see figure 16.2).

In the third grade, Grace was tested and tracked into lower-level classes. Tracking is the grouping of students homogeneously according to some measure of achievement. The rationale for tracking is that given students learn at different rates and children benefit from being placed into classes with students of similar capability. In high school, students are typically tracked into one of three groups: honors, college preparatory, or standard or basic skills. In elementary school, the tracking is subtle, with students being assigned by ability to reading groups with names like Bluebirds and Robins.

Consequently, Grace found herself in classes where students were extremely resistant to teachers' control and authority. As she talked about reading and writing in elementary school, she made connections between the types of knowledge presented in her classes, the work she did, teacher control, and resistance. "I remember reading from folded cards in a box, called SRA. We took cards, read the stories, and answered questions. There was no discussion . . . I learned to cheat, I stopped reading, and I just found the answer sheet and filled in the card. . . . The teacher sat at the front of the class reading the newspaper." From this experience, Grace learned knowledge was disconnected from experience. She was not reading authentic literature, and there was no opportunity for meaningful discussions. She was learning work was mechanical. The image above mirrors the experiences of assembly-line workers, in which no creative work goes on. The classroom reading activity was also a form of control. Rote activities (and cheating) replaced interaction and the acquisition of knowledge and skills. Furthermore, being in a lower track almost ensured Grace would only learn to read on a functional level. This level of literacy would enable her to follow directions but would not provide her with the skills needed to attend college. The same was true of the types of writing Grace was exposed to. "We learned to print and make circles and lines to write cursive. We copied down information

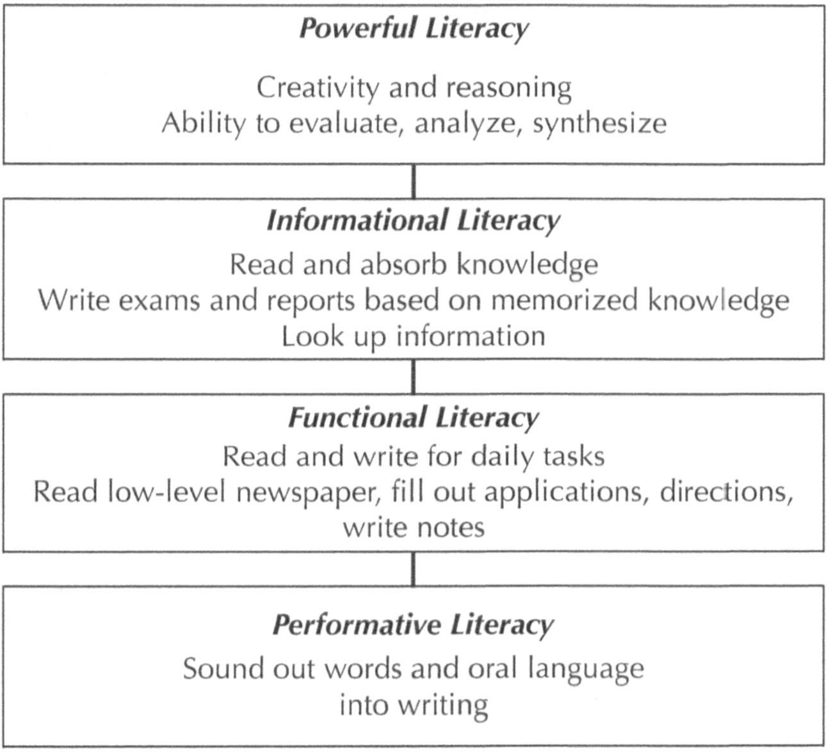

Powerful Literacy

Creativity and reasoning
Ability to evaluate, analyze, synthesize

Informational Literacy

Read and absorb knowledge
Write exams and reports based on memorized knowledge
Look up information

Functional Literacy

Read and write for daily tasks
Read low-level newspaper, fill out applications, directions,
write notes

Performative Literacy

Sound out words and oral language
into writing

Figure 16.2. Acts of literacy related to schools and schooling (adapted from Anyon, "Social Class and the Hidden Curriculum of Work" and "Social Class and the Hidden Curriculum," and Finn, Literacy with an Attitude)

and wrote short answers. I wrote a book report, which meant copying down information. . . . There was no connection between higher-order thinking and writing." Once again, the nature of the instruction here would prepare Grace to follow procedures (functional literacy) rather than to reason.

Resistance, in the form of playing dumb, was something Grace learned to use in high school, and it meant a major shift in her relationship to reading, writing, and studying that remained with her for many years. "I stopped studying. I learned to play dumb. I know it may sound strange, but I can pinpoint the moment. I was in Spanish class, looking at the poster of a matador. I looked at the teacher, and looked at the poster, and I just decided not to work." Resistance is a common theme in discussions of working-class students' school lives.[18] Grace changed from being young and eager to learn and read to being disengaged from learning. The unfortunate part of this scenario is that as a consequence of resisting and playing dumb and challenging the authority of the classroom, Grace was not equipped to analyze and transform her world. Such resistance ultimately disadvantages the students who engage in this behavior. School life in Newark may have been very different for students who were tracked into classes more academic and more challenging. They were more likely to be more engaged in learning and less likely to resist authority.

Ruth attended a small private yeshiva K–8. It was located in a working-class area, and most students came from working-class or lower-middle-class backgrounds. However, the centrality of literacy in the Jewish subculture created a unique environment. Here, she experienced learning that in some respects was more similar to that of students in a middle-class school, but with a subcultural twist. At first, in lower elementary school, learning took the form of play, and it was repetitive in nature. "I remember playing games in kindergarten like Hebrew bingo. We would have bingo cards, but instead of numbers there would be pictures, and a person would hold up a picture and say the word in Hebrew, and then if you had the picture on your card you would raise your hand and say, 'yesh li.' Which means 'I have it.'" Here, the knowledge presented to Ruth was based on performative literacy acts. She was being taught to recognize words and pictures as well as the sounds of the words. According to Ruth, expectations at her yeshiva were high for all students. As Ruth goes on to describe her later years at yeshiva, there is much more of a sense of how knowledge, work, teacher control, and student attitudes were constructed. "And I actually had about two hours, maybe, to do everything in English. We would get there at nine and pray until nine fifteen. Then we would work for an hour, have a fifteen-minute recess, and work until noon. . . . And then after lunch we had Hebrew language and literature, and we studied the Bible and prophets, and ethics and philosophy in Hebrew."

Much like the descriptions of the middle-class schools, Ruth's acquired knowledge within the context of her yeshiva was conceptual, and facts were not seen as isolated from each other. But the key here is that she was expected to gain information from socially approved sources such as the Bible and other specified texts. As in Anyon's and Finn's analyses of middle-class public schools, the yeshiva valued the knowledge in books as more important than the knowledge students might gain through experience. By studying ethics and philosophy, Ruth was able to make some connections to her life but only in the sense that what she learned would teach her how to be a better person through the sources sanctioned by yeshiva. Therefore, she learned how to find the "right answers." She also learned how to follow directions and how to read texts, listen to the teacher, answer questions, and do reports, typical activities in middle-class schools. In ninth grade, Ruth entered a yeshiva high school that catered to a more middle-class clientele. While Ruth never truly fit in there, she never experienced the kind of resistance Grace described in her working-class schools. Ruth admitted, however, that when she left yeshiva to go to a public high school, she saw students tracked into different classes, in part because of problems with authority but also due to inadequate academic development. Through the following portion of her interview, she shows us how resistant students and motivated students may be in the same building, but it's as though they attend different schools. "In my high school there were a lot of kids just like me, who were bright and from working-class families. In a school in which there were kids in gangs, kids on drugs, and kids with all kinds of terrible problems, someone who did her homework, and was bright and did well, was treated very well." Ruth distinguished herself from the students who were not so academically advanced, who showed resistance by avoiding their schoolwork, taking drugs, and joining gangs. She also noted that during her first semester, she was initially placed in a mid-level class, and was attacked in the hall for participating in class. She fought back and was eventually placed in the honors program

Veronica described in detail the complicated tracking system that existed in New York in the 1960s. Like Ruth, Veronica ascended into what she termed the talented and gifted track. But prior to winning access to the more privileged ranks, she spent time in lower-level classes. It was at this juncture that she learned a great deal about how race, class, immigrant status, and language acquisition determine the level of literacy one is exposed to. "I couldn't speak the language all that well when I started school. I was placed in what was then a three-nine class. This type of stratification is linked to the tracking system. A three-nine student was supposed to be slower. Students who were linguistically handicapped or disabled were pooled together." When Veronica arrived, she was not tested before she was placed in the class designated "developmentally disadvantaged." Her status as an Afro-Cuban second-language learner suggested to the administration of the school that she was not capable of performing any form of independent work. The basic premise behind classes for the "handicapped" is that the students in these placements need basic life skills. The teaching, therefore, is steeped in behaviorist paradigms. Veronica's description of the stratification she experienced indicates she was placed in a class that mirrored Anyon's and Finn's working-class schools, where knowledge was presented in fragments, movement was highly restricted, control was central, and the level of literacy taught in her three-nine class remained at the performative level. Veronica, as an immigrant with limited English, was placed in one of the classes reserved for the "least talented." The school was unaware of the content knowledge and literacy skills Veronica had obtained in her first language and made no effort to determine her first-language academic proficiency.

Fortunately, Veronica had teachers who were perceptive enough to move her out of this class and into a mid-level class; she transitioned from a performative curriculum to a functional one, mirroring the kind of working-class literacy Grace described. Veronica read out of textbooks, as Grace did, and she probably was even doing some work based on informative (middle-class) literacy skills, such as finding information. By fifth grade, she was tracked into the gifted-and-talented classes. For high school, her family, because they did not understand the system, did not see why entry into a specialized high school would benefit Veronica. "I also chose not to go to a specialized high school. . . . In New York students can take a placement test that enables them to attend a school that has a specific purpose like science or the arts. I didn't want to do that, but what I did want to do was to go to a school in a 'good neighborhood' in the North Bronx." In her new high school, most of the students came from middle-class white families. Veronica explained she had been socialized to believe schools were based on meritocracy. "I was taught that we live in an equitable society. If I studied hard, and got good grades, that I would succeed." As Anyon and Finn argue, Veronica was being assimilated into the ideals of the middle class in which her respect for authority would point her toward a college education and a better life than her immigrant parents experienced. She was rewarded for knowing the answers, techniques, and procedures she had been taught. Like Ruth, she learned how to follow the rules and regulations of the school and consequently those of mainstream society. Most of what she acquired was based on instrumental forms of literacy because she was competing to meet the expectations and standards of the school. Veronica said that even though she wrote and read extensively in high school, she never saw these activities as relating to her own life experiences. Moreover, she was never required to analyze or evaluate what she read. She was never asked to use writing to think critically about a topic that impacted her everyday life. Veronica had risen from a working-class school to a middle-class school, where knowledge is acquired so students can gain access to jobs and some higher education.

Terese prefaced her discussion of school structures and literacy by emphasizing the distinctions she made between reading at home and at school. "Reading at home was different than reading at school. We read big books because my aunt collected them, and they had books that were shaped differently. Those books were fun. But *Dick and Jane* was something we read in school. It was just something to do while you were there. Reading in school was work." In her narrative, Terese associated school reading with the forms of knowledge and work reflected in Anyon's and Finn's working-class schools and classrooms; school life mirrored that of the assembly line. Knowledge and work in Terese's class were monotonous, repetitive, and void of any connection to experience. But what stands out here is Terese's grasp of how reading at home was an activity that referenced concepts like play, real life, and social relationships. Reading at home was tactile and visceral. She was an active participant in the process. In contrast, reading at school was a passive experience for her. Terese's working-class school replicated stratified social structures through their presentation of knowledge and the mindless work they asked students to do. And when Terese's mother tried to help empower her daughter by cowriting a poem with her that was critical of our government, Terese learned how controversy could lead to bad grades. "I do remember that I wrote a poem in the seventh grade with my mother, and that tension developed over the contents of the text. My teacher wanted us to write a poem about the flag. But the poem was critical of the flag. And when I gave the poem to the teacher, she said, 'No you can't write these things.'"

As noted earlier, controversial topics are typically avoided in both working-class and middle-class classrooms. This story shows how this teacher linked Terese's apparent lack of patriotism with a lack of respect for the rules of the school. As a result, the teacher decided to teach Terese the lesson that powerful and critical forms of literacy that challenged local values were dangerous and should be avoided.[19] Terese also talked of balancing two disparate points of view. She became aware that she had been taught a form of functional literacy that would have inhibited her acquisition of knowledge based on real inquiry and critical thinking. At the same time, she felt that because she did not challenge the norms of the dominant culture, she was able to get through school without feeling submissive. From the perspective of critical literacy, Paulo Freire would contend that Terese was grappling with her own "conscientization" or "consciousness raising" as she struggled to make sense of progressive educational theories and her belief that she was shielded by not contesting the denial of her critical voice in school.[20]

Freire might also agree that what Terese needed was someone to help her make literacy dangerous.[21] She needed to recognize the social and economic interests that bound her together with other working-class students. Instead, Terese rationalized her experiences by separating them. She felt that the place for real acts of literacy was at home, while at school she learned how to disassociate herself from work, a strategy also observed in factory workers. Though Terese currently presents herself as having been relatively receptive, in fact she enacted resistance by separating herself through withdrawal and silence.

DISCUSSION

The results of this study demonstrate that working-class women's literate identities are complex and are impacted by the forms of reading and writing their families used in everyday life, key relationships that fostered participants' literacy development, and the forms of literacy teachers and administrators exposed them to in schools. The literacy narratives in our study revealed unique experiences based on race and ethnicity as well as shared features related to social class. These insights suggest implications for classroom practice we can infer from the narrative analyses. According to Jane Greer, literacy has come to be viewed as a "cultural practice," a way of constructing identities, creating social networks, enabling economic activities, and distributing power.[22] The stories told by the working-class women academics described in this chapter provide educators with a perspective on literacy development that reveals not only how literacy affects their students but also how their students can "seize" literacy that has meaning and utility in local contexts. When considering how the forms of family literacy used in their homes impacted their perceptions of themselves as readers and writers, three of the four women interviewed (Grace, Ruth, and Terese) described how viewing parents' and siblings' daily participation in reading and writing activities influenced their attitudes about themselves as educated, well-read learners. Although our participants' families did not utilize forms of literacy associated with critical/educational reading or expository writing, they did use most of the literate acts Heath and Taylor and Dorsey-Gaines outline in their research.[23] Therefore, three of the four working-class families in our study can be described as literate, even though the forms of literacy they experienced were different from many of those associated with middle-class, college-educated families. Extrapolating from these lived experiences, as teachers of working-class students, we must take into account the literate acts our students and their families are already engaged in and are capable of when they arrive in our class-rooms. It is imperative that we view our work through an additive lens. According to Norma González, Luis Moll, and Cathy Amanti, we should value the knowledge our students bring to reading and writing while encouraging them to develop more critical forms of literacy.[24]

Similarly, each participant (including Veronica) identified either parents or educators who introduced them to the library. This act of discovery can be seen as a rite of passage, a metaphor for a doorway to worlds beyond working-class streets. The library and the skills associated with using the resources within became significant spaces for all four of the working-class females in this study. For Grace and Ruth, the time they spent with their mothers in the library allowed them to interact and observe their mothers in an environment other than the home. Their mothers took them to the library and museums to immerse them in an educated culture. For Terese, who grew up surrounded by books, and who described reading as more of a social activity since she read with her siblings, it was her teachers who taught her how to use the library. Veronica, much like many second-language learners whose parents are struggling culturally and educationally, had to count on her relationships with teachers to introduce her to the world of books associated with the library and reading. Therefore, our findings resonate with those of Stephen Krashen and Ann Beck, who argue that schools and teachers in poor and working-class communities must become literacy advocates for their students and their families. Teachers should be educated to support parents and guardians in becoming reading and writing coaches. Through a critical-literacy approach, parents and teachers must be partners in encouraging working-class students in the acquisition of forms of critical literacies. Finally, communities must provide better access to libraries and books in poor and working-class neighborhoods. This action, along with the provision of parent literacy workshops, will result in higher reading scores, more pleasure reading, better writing, knowledge of grammar, and the acquisition of the forms of literacy required for college and career readiness.[25]

The women's literacy narratives collected in this study are representative success stories that transcend class, race, and/or ethnicity. All the women went on to acquire higher forms of literacy, succeed academically, and enter university culture. At the same time, the narratives show that even though the women came from families that shared, valued, and transmitted language through everyday literacy activities, the obstacles each experienced made the acquisition of academic (powerful) literacy a challenge. Our data confirm that teachers and schools often view the literate practices of working-class students as deficient. The process of evaluating and placing students into leveled cohorts often determines and limits the forms of literacy they are exposed to at school. Sharing stories that resonate with the experiences of the students described by Donna Marie San Antonio, the women in this study described how grouping influenced their social interactions and the way they perceived their own and their peers' intellectual competence.[26] Therefore, teachers and faculty instructing working-class students who are in the process of acquiring more powerful forms of literacy must also be mindful of how their attitudes toward those in their charge impact those learners' academic success. It is evident that ability grouping, while benefitting some, often results in or replicates school and societal divisions.[27] Ruth indicated that there were students in her public high school who were in classes focusing on lower forms of literacy but that she was ultimately treated well and introduced to higher forms of literacy because she was bright, did her homework, and didn't make trouble. Veronica described her ascendance to a middle-class school as a result of a system of meritocracy. What complicates Veronica's story, and what makes it resonate here, are the obstacles she faced and overcame.

Research shows that being a Latina from an immigrant family made up of nonreaders who did not speak Standard English fluently made it less likely that Veronica would achieve higher academic literacy.[28] Also, both Terese and Grace were placed in ability groups that projected on them gendered roles in working-class subcultures. They were placed in programs that trained them to become secretaries or administrative assistants. Terese's story is one that shows how her race, class, and gender initially placed her in an ability group that taught her how to accommodate to the roles prescribed for her as a young African American woman in school in the 60s. Yet Terese, unlike other women of her day, pushed the limits of a system set up to keep her in her place. But as Terese noted, "This may have had to do with my mother's rebellious attitude and the belief that she could be anything." Grace spoke of how different her story was from her sister's. "My sister never saw beyond marriage, a home, and a good job. It is not that she did not want to go to college, or have a career; she just didn't feel she had access to these things." In contrast to her sister's acceptance, and subtle resentment, Grace's resistance to being tracked into lower-level classes bubbled up in ways that were not always in her best interest.

John Ogbu and Herbert Simons and Finn would say Grace reacted by acting out or disassociating because she had internalized the feelings of an involuntary minority.[29] Grace, like other involuntary minority members, experienced cultural dissonance as oppositional rather than simply different and described accommodation as difficult. At first it may appear that the other women in this study were more like what Ogbu and Simons and Finn define as immigrant minorities.[30] During their interviews, they indicated that assimilation into mainstream culture was a necessary part of gaining social and academic success in school. And they seemed to believe, unlike Grace, that they could adopt the language and culture of the mainstream without compromising who they were.[31] Yet all four women pointed to a moment when their working-class sensibility turned into a form of critical consciousness and described how this consciousness led to a resistance of the mainstream, or what Henry Giroux terms "the ruling class."[32]

We participated in this resistance by becoming teachers of first-generation, working-class students. This act, although it may not be viewed as radical, allowed them to "flip the script" by developing a sense of agency through their work. They became advocates for their working-class students and provided opportunities for them to learn to read, write, and talk about the histories, traditions, daily rituals, and social relations of their communities, addressing the dissonance that often exists between the mainstream and their working-class subcultures. By giving students from working classes an opportunity to examine what is often left unexamined in classrooms, we offered them an opportunity to challenge the mainstream while acquiring strong critical literacy skills.[33] Therefore, we suggest that teachers of all socioeconomic backgrounds provide space (through assignments) for students to examine the impact race, class, gender, and sexual orientation have on our identities as learners.

CONCLUSION

The results of this study support much of what has been written in the literature on how working-class students experience public-school education. According to Mike Rose, things haven't changed all that much in the twenty-first century when we consider schools and schooling. "There can be 'no excuses' for the low performance of poor, immigrant, and racial and ethnic minority kids, as measured by the tests—I appreciate this 'no excuses' stance. Our schools have an unacceptable record with these populations; what we expect of them intellectually is a key element in their achievement."[34] If we look at the literature written on the impact social class has on educational opportunity, it is clear we continue to wrestle with the issue of providing quality teaching and learning in communities that service working-class students.[35] The stories told by the participants confirm that what is expected of working-class females in schools does impact their academic success. Yet, these working-class women found ways to navigate around test measures (ability grouping), as well as the ways teachers presented knowledge, work, and control. Three of the four participants resisted negative expectations of teachers. They also learned to straddle mainstream literacy while maintaining working-class identities. As academic writers they acquired powerful critical lenses that allowed them to make use of mainstream literate forms while challenging the restrictions a class-based society tried to impose. Teachers and curriculum developers should foster this development rather than try to restrict it.

The emphasis on familial relationships also appeared to be significant for the women, and their access to books and libraries provided opportunities to grow through literate experiences. Therefore, future research in writing pedagogy should explore the impact relationships at home and at school have on both male and female working-class students' academic success and focus on the importance of access to literature that may not be present in the home. A longitudinal study of curricula developed for working-class students, and particularly female working-class students, that is inclusive of rigorous problem solving, analysis, and complex tasks that support powerful forms of literacy should be developed and maintained over time, with special emphasis on the impact of gender.

While the data collected for this study were based on current views of subjective memories and perceptions, they can help us to consider what might be done to help poor and working-class students succeed better at developing academic literacy. Those of us who teach and advise working-class students at all levels are constantly asking ourselves, "What makes one student succeed and another fail?" By exploring the challenges faced by the women in this study, the strategies they used to navigate and negotiate both linguistic and cultural roadblocks, educators will recognize the importance of fostering a standards-conscious that utilizes standards as goals and tools rather than a starting point. Literacy curricula for all learners, irrespective of social class, must be both creative and critical and must foster connections between reading and writing across student differences in a learning community built on collaboration and cooperation.

Notes

1.   Gee, *Social Linguistics and Literacies.*
2.   Nieto, *Language, Culture, and Teaching.*

3. Bruner, *Acts of Meaning* Jones, *Girls, Social Class & Literacy* Jones, "Making Sense of Injustices" Verdi and Ebsworth, "Working-Class Women Academics."
4. Anyon, "Social Class" Rist, *Urban School.*
5. Finn, *Literacy with an Attitude.*
6. Heath, *Ways with Words* Taylor and Dorsey-Gaines, *Growing Up Literate* Firn, *Literacy with an Attitude* Anyon, "Social Class."
7. Dunbar-Odam, *Defying the Odds.*
8. Clandinin, *Handbook of Narrative Inquiry.*
9. Seidman, *Interviewing as Qualitative Research.*
10. Warren and Karner, *Discovering Qualitative Methods* Verdi and Ebsworth, "Working-Class Women Academics."
11. Warren and Karner, *Discovering Qualitative Methods.*
12. Heath, *Ways with Words* Taylor and Dorsey-Gaines, *Growing Up Literate.*
13. Heath, *Ways with Words*, 232.
14. Heath, *Ways with Words.*
15. Ibid.
16. Taylor and Dorsey-Gaines, *Growing Up Literate.*
17. Anyon, "Social Class"; Finn, *Literacy with an Attitude.*
18. Verdi and Ebsworth, "Working-Class Women Academics" Finn, *Literacy with an Attitude.*
19. Finn, *Literacy with an Attitude.*
20. Freire, *Pedagogy of the Oppressed.*
21. Finn, *Literacy with an Attitude.*
22. Greer, *Girls and Literacy in America.*
23. Heath, *Ways with Words* Taylor and Dorsey-Gaines, *Growing Up Literate.*
24. González, Moll, and Amanti, *Funds of Knowledge.*
25. Krashen, "Protecting Students"; Beck, "A Place for Critical Literacy."
26. San Antonio, *Adolescent Lives in Transition.*
27. Ibid.
28. Dunbar-Odam, *Defying the Odds.*
29. Ogbu and Simons, "Voluntary and Involuntary Minorities" Finn, *Literacy with an Attitude.*
30. Ibid.
31. Finn, *Literacy with an Attitude.*
32. Giroux, "Flipping the Script."
33. Ibid.
34. Rose, *Why School*, 49.
35. Nieto, *Language, Culture, and Teaching* Dunbar-Odam, *Defying the Odds.*

17

AN AFTERWORD TO *CLASS IN THE COMPOSITION CLASSROOM*
First-Year Writing as a Social Class Enterprise

James T. Zebroski

Freshman English is our sore subject.
Richard Ohmann

Who kids whom, and for how long?
Jay Robinson

We must force the frozen circumstances to dance by singing to them their own melody.
Karl Marx

My story starts in the last week of June in 1970. I took a Greyhound bus from my hometown of Warren, Ohio, to Columbus to go to orientation at Ohio State University. Somewhat unusual in my high school, if the bulletin board in the hall of Warren G. Harding High School was accurate, I was neither going away to an elite East Coast ivy league school or even Case Western Reserve in Cleveland, nor was I staying in town and attending either Kent State or Youngstown State, which were a short drive away. Why go away to a state university when we had very good ones practically in town? Why pay more for a college education when you could, as my dad insisted, stay at home, not pay for dorms and meals, work while going to school, and get the "same" education for less of a price?

But I was determined to not stay in town. I had to get out of Warren.

I did not even consider applying to more than one university—and certainly to no elite ones. Even at eighteen I was that practical. One of my best friends got into Harvard; another into Miami of Ohio, a "good" state school that was not even on the radar for me. Until my junior year in high school, I had thought, well, maybe Case Western Reserve in Cleveland, which was both away and close; then I received their catalog, discovering what their tuition and room and board cost; that was the end of Case Western Reserve. So I had applied only to Ohio

DOI: 10.7330/9781607326182.c017

*State despite the fact that among my friends, horror stories abounded—you are
just a number there; you don't have real teachers but TAs; they have TV lectures
rather than human lecturers; they rioted last year.*

*Ohio State became my goal for one reason, never having been to Columbus, let
alone the campus, and not knowing anyone who went there: the Warren Tribune
Chronicle had printed what was a wire service story that had noted that after Harvard, Ohio State was the university next highest in the financial aid it provided
students in the country. I also noted that the brochures and catalogs they sent
me in the mail—there was obviously no Internet at our house—had photos of a
campus that looked appealing. All my efforts from then on went into applying and
getting accepted as early as I could in order to get as much financial aid as I could.*

*I was on my own, very much at sea so to speak. I had no idea what I was
doing or how to make the college decision. No one could help me. I was the first
in my family to go to university, and my parents, while supportive, offered and
could offer little in terms of information or advice about the academic world.
Looking back more the forty-six years I am impressed both by how little I knew
and by how good my instincts were. That eighteen-year-old was already recognizing and theorizing social class.*

* * *

You have in your hands or on your screens an extraordinary volume,
Class in the Composition Classroom. This is one of the most important
books in the discipline that I have read in years. This book is extraordinary in several ways. At a time when some scholars in rhetoric and composition still argue we must cut our ties to teaching and particularly to
the so-called universal requirement, freshman composition, this book
focuses primarily on freshman composition.[1] At a time when people in
rhetoric and composition still see an untenable dualism, a rigid binary
between teaching and research, this book deconstructs that binary by
showing a range of research methods that focus on teaching but much
more on freshman composition. At a time when few scholars focus
on social class inside or outside rhetoric and composition, *Class in the
Composition Classroom: Pedagogy and the Working Class* returns to social
class, tracking its changes, updating and complicating concepts of social
class and working-class identity, and specifically attending to working-
class contributions to freshman composition but also to English departments, where we find most composition courses, and to the university
that encompasses both. This book shows social class is a helpful way of
viewing the dynamics of what I see (I am sure I am in the tiniest minority
in my own department on this) as the most important course we offer—
freshman composition.

This essay—and this book—complicate the crucial claim Lynn Z. Bloom made in 1996 that freshman composition is a middle-class enterprise.[2] I hope to expand that claim by arguing that freshman composition is a social class enterprise, that of all the sites in college or university, freshman composition is the exemplary location for studying and acting on social class. Not to say Bloom's essay is not critical as far as it goes, but what this book shows is that our students from a variety of backgrounds and social class identities also make a contribution to this course and what it is. *Class in the Composition Classroom: Pedagogy and the Working Class* is, in fact, one of the best descriptions of the deeper, invisible, unspoken values of middle-class culture as it encounters and tangles with other classes, other values, and especially the values of the working classes. While Bloom makes visible some of the unspoken middle-class values of academic discourse as envisioned by David Bartholomae and Patricia Bizzell[3] and others, this book adds the ignored reality that many of our students also have a say and have effects on first-year composition, bringing new voices, values, and assumptions, not to mention the multiple languages of their working-class cultural roots, to the so-called universal requirement. To be sure, they will need to take up Bloom's middle-class discourse, but—and it is a big but—that does not mean they must eliminate, eviscerate, or otherwise cast off their working-class culture or identities. It is precisely because freshman composition is a social class enterprise where ruling class meets working class, where discourse contests discourse, that it is perhaps the most interesting course I teach.[4] What you have no doubt discovered in reading these essays is that this book not only says that, it enacts it.

* * *

The temperature was in the mid-90s which, given the humidity, is very hot for Ohio. For me, who had been out of the Warren area maybe three times in my entire life, the trip alone that last week in June on the air-conditioned Greyhound to what for me was the distant metropolis, the distant, big city of Columbus, was a first great adventure. When I got into Columbus, I hired a taxi to take me to campus, and the driver asked if I had a student ID because campus had been closed since the riots after the Cambodian incursion in the Vietnam War in April. Hundreds of campuses had been shut down, and at Kent State, just down the road from my town (but also at Jackson State in Mississippi), students had been shot and killed by national guard soldiers. I had no ID—that was one of the things I was going to get at orientation. When we got to High Street and 15th, the main entrance of the university, the person in the booth checked, and we were waved through. They let me in. This time.

* * *

I wish I could leave it at that. A story. But I am expected in an essay like this to make an argument—as if my story is not an argument. My academic argument, then, begins with this book *Class in the Composition Classroom*. My claim is that it is a valuable heuristic to see that much that is important is shaped by power—which is what I mean when I say writing is political—that is, writing is situated in and comes out of power relations—and prime among those discourses is social class. First-year composition is especially a social class enterprise both because it is literally the gateway to university and because it is shaped by the culture of college departments of English, and this culture is, as Terry Eagleton shows, at the least ideological.[5] I would go further and claim that that culture of English departments tends to privilege ruling-class values and to denigrate or make invisible working-class culture and values. This is a problem for freshman composition, which is caught in between.

One of the joys of reading this book (several times actually) is to see the bigger picture that emerges from these grounded studies of class and composition. The patterns and omissions that arise from this book are themselves of great import as contributions to the most current study of social class. So what are some of these patterns?

- I know of no other book in the discipline of rhetoric and composition that focuses primarily on freshman composition and social class. To be sure, many books include essays that do such work, but they also include other topics, like the stories of the teachers who come out as working class or sometimes composition or literature course syllabi for teaching class. All of which is worthwhile. Yet this is the only book-length treatment on this topic.

- The book, in addressing this topic, makes a political statement and takes a courageous stand in the debate referred to above among those in the discipline who argue that rhetoric and composition needs to cut the ties with teaching and /or freshman composition. The debate is not mentioned—which is one of the most important techniques of strong argument, after all. But the focus in each essay on legitimate, rigorous, and significant research shows rather than tells. This book complicates the binary of research versus teaching (or service).

- This book contributes in its research to some critical questions in rhetoric and composition but also beyond. I have encountered no better description of the complications of traditional notions of social class and working class. Such work contributes in important ways to the research of Simon Head and others describing the brave new world of the twenty-first-century workplace.[6]

- This book traces out the diversity and complexity of freshman composition as it exists now, not one monolithic thing at all. It shows how the old freshman composition, if it ever existed as we remember it, does not exist now. Rather, freshman composition is populated by the widest variety of students that has existed since I went to Ohio State. Many of them are older. Most of them are either working or will be working as they take courses and try to complete degrees. Freshman composition is now shaped by an increasing number of schemes to get other non-working-class students out of it—dual enrollments, credit for exams, the abolition of remedial courses at the college level, and the dumping of non-English speakers into the course without preliminary coursework in English language or US culture. It is a political football at the state level in part because of the increasing need to standardize in order to transfer credit since more and more students do coursework at more than one college. Not your grandfather's freshman composition then.

- Finally, most important, this book does two related things—it includes many student voices from documents they wrote and inter-views with researchers. Student voices here are plentiful and loud. And this book allows students, teachers, administrators, and research-ers to tell their stories.

* * *

I was shocked by how lush and beautiful the campus and the Oval were. It was nicer than anything in Warren.

Among the other orientation activities, we were asked to take placement es-says for freshman English. I cannot remember the questions—there were some choices—but I do recall my essay was on comparing the music of Simon and Garfunkel with Gregorian chant, so I assume the questions tried to be "relevant" and allow for writing on a relevant topic. Evidently I did well enough because while I was not exempted out of freshman English (the required three courses of three hours each in a quarter system), I did exempt out of one quarter. Instead of taking English 101, 102, and 103 that first year, I was placed into 104 and 105, which gave a more condensed version of freshman English.

The English 104 course was an argument-writing course mostly on hot issues of the time. We used one textbook on critical thinking, which included traditional philosophical readings like Plato but also more current ones like Thoreau. There was a second book on the big issues of the time—it had a bright orange cover. We must have used James McCrimmon's Writing with a Purpose since Ohio State still was using that book when I came back to TA in 1978. All argument—never any so-called expressive writing.

The English 105 course was a course on literature and writing literary criti-cism. We had Ray Kytle's textbook, Clear Thinking for Composition. We also had a drama book and an anthology on poetry, which I still have—Poetry: A Themat-ic Approach by Sam Henderson and James Lee. The latter was unusual in that it collected poetry thematically but also included student-authored writing about poems with by-lines. The editors' note in their preface says, "In addition, there are representative explications in most of the thematic groupings. Some are from critical

journals; some are published here for the first time; some are written by students"[7]
This was radical for the time; a professor in English I took in my junior year told
that class not to go to the library or read the criticism, let alone read or peer review
each other's papers, which would have probably been seen as cheating. This ap-
proach was far more typical of the culture of the English Department in the 1970s.
All writing was individual and argument—no freshman English courses asked for
narrative, let alone story. Much writing was about literature.

* * *

Class in the Composition Classroom: Pedagogy and the Working Class raises
several questions for me. If I had to summarize the argument of the
collection as a whole, it would go something like this—freshman composition and working-class identity are radically changing; the old ways
of thinking about both neither describe nor help us teach or study writing. My bias is for this proposition because I could summarize my entire
academic project of the last several decades as something like this—to
understand writing, you must include *unauthorized writing*, that is, writing not approved or valued, often ephemeral writing that nonetheless
provides critical clues about composition.

A corollary follows from that focus on unauthorized writing—the
role of power in established conventions and institutions but also in
the resistance to and transformation of those. Another way to say that is
change. We are facing a world that has changed and is changing. What
"worked" when I was a student in freshman composition at Ohio State
in 1970–1971 will not work now. What worked in the 1980s and 1990s
when I first taught freshman composition will not work now. We need to
accept change, work with it.

So, first, freshman composition has changed. Our students in freshman composition have changed. What we teach and what our goals are,
what our curricula are, all are changing. Second, what counts as working
class has changed (and too what counts as ruling class). And finally, our
departments of English, if composition is located in them, are changing—or at least are facing the need to change or decline. My view: we
must commit to change, seeing it as a way to the future rather than looking for what remains the same, the path to the past. I take up each of
these points in the remainder of this essay.

* * *

Time passed. I graduated at the height of the recession in 1974 but got a job
teaching high school, working in the Columbus, Ohio, area for five years. I made
a conscious decision (I thought at the time and for decades after) that I would

go back for the PhD at Ohio State but work in English education on composi-
tion. My MA included a large number of literature courses, some of which I very
much enjoyed. As Joan Didion jokes, I could find the house-and -garden imagery
with the best of them—I was a ravenous reader—but I never quite knew why one
would want to do that for a living.

I never felt quite at home in the culture of the college English department. I ra-
tionalized my choice to study composition in 1978 as one of pragmatism—there
was an increasing number of jobs in the market for experts in composition—but
also a decision of realism—there were no faculty in English who focused on
writing per se.[8] Aside from not seeing how specializing in literature and taking
almost all my courses in British and American canonical authorized literature
would contribute to my study of composition, I admit now that I never really
felt comfortable in English, but I did feel comfortable in English education,
where faculty treated me as an equal. I was not apart from English—I TA-ed
in English, teaching freshman composition through this entire time, joined a
short-lived English TA strike, had conversations with English graduate students,
took a couple of literature courses, mostly in folklore, even went to a few English
Department functions. But my heart was mostly in English education and with
my writing students.

* * *

THE STORY OF ARGUMENT—1970 TO 2015

First-year composition has always depended on the local conditions—
what department it is located in, the students its college or university
serves, if it is located in the English Department, the makeup of the
English faculty and their areas of specialization, their view of literature,
and what might be called the *culture of the department.* As noted, until
about the mid-1980s, the freshman composition course, while influenced by increasing research on writing process, and with many exceptions to be sure, tended to be based on one of the many varieties of
current-traditional rhetoric that focused on what Sharon Crowley called
"EDNA"—exposition, description, narrative, argument.[9] The thinking
behind this focus was that these were kind of the basic building blocks of
language, and if we asked students to read examples of each mode and
then mimic the traits of each, they would advance to more complex writing that mixed these sorts of writing. This approach I call the *modes of dis-*
course version of current traditionalism. One of the early tasks of rhetoric and
composition was to complicate and ultimately dismantle this apparatus. [10]

While I never was allowed to write personal narrative when I took
freshman composition, we did do a variety of writing. I wrote about a

book I was keen on then called *African Genesis*, for example, a best seller on no reading list for any course I took. In my advanced composition course junior year, I was indeed allowed to use personal examples in an assignment on the ideal education. When I later taught freshman composition, nearly everyone assigned the modes. The textbooks were all about the modes, with a few exceptions. [11]

What is important for *Class in the Composition Classroom: Pedagogy and the Working Class* is that there is a tension in this volume between, on the one hand, an approach that privileges what I shall call *story* versus the ruling view now that everything, including the freshman composition curriculum, is *argument*. This is not simply a tension in this book. It is a contradiction in our field.

As the critical research of Andrea Lunsford and Karen Lunsford discovered, there has been a wholesale shift from a variety of forms in freshman composition to only papers that are argument. Lunsford and Lunsford point out an unexpected finding of their extensive study of error.

> The second trend we noted is a sea change in the types of papers teachers are asking students to write in first-year writing classes. . . . When we analyzed the kinds of papers represented in this study, we found a range of paper types. . . . These results strongly suggest that emphasis on personal narrative has been replaced by an emphasis on argument and research.

Lunsford and Lunsford also note that a national study by Kathleen Blake Yancey also found that an overwhelming majority of teachers indicated they focused on argument and research-based writing.[12] Todd De Stigter supports these findings by noting that the Core Standards also privilege argument in one of the most radical shifts in high-school and college writing over the past twenty years.[13] *Class in Composition Classroom* provides more space for its authors and students to story than is allowed in most freshman composition courses today.

In brief, my argument against argument is:

- Argument today entirely dominates both freshman composition and secondary-school writing. It is not unusual to find first-year courses that teach only argument.
- Story and argument is not a binary and instructors can and should value both at the same time. Effective texts do.
- Most of the texts students write in the university do not look like argument. Far more frequent is analysis.[14]
- This hegemony of argument is based on eliminating other forms. Even if one accepts the modes, there are three other forms beside argument. Could we argue that composition has been reduced by 75 percent?

- Argument displaces student voices and the voices important to students, especially in freshman composition.
- The research, such as we have, either questions the use of argument alone or supports inquiry that is more than argument.[15]
- Argument alone functions to remove student voices and the voices of their communities from academe.
- Argument alone works to sort working-class students out from more elite students. It is curious that professors (like me) and creative writers are allowed to tell stories but first-year writing students are now not.

Story *with* argument

- taps deeper sources for writing;
- gives voice to the otherwise silenced;
- witnesses and celebrates our communities;
- connects us to other stories and storytellers;
- makes social class visible in ways argument alone does not.

My point, then, is that we must change this "argument-only" curriculum that dominates. *Class in the Composition Classroom: Pedagogy and the Working Class* gives us a wonderful example of how to begin this transformation by demonstrating how argument and rigorous research can be combined with story in productive ways.

* * *

More time passed. I came to the University of Houston in 2007 to put into place a PhD program in rhetoric, composition, and pedagogy in the English Department, which was accomplished in two years. Yet as successful as the PhD program has been, resources after the initial three years have not been forthcoming, nor for the most part do doctoral students in literature and creative writing take our advanced course, despite the fact that this was the plan and despite the fact that if these students graduate and get jobs, they are likely to teach composition, including freshman composition. For five years, the RCP faculty made the argument again and again, in public forums and in committees, that we need added resources, particularly more full-time tenure-track faculty in rhetoric and composition. We were all told when we came here that we were research faculty and that no administration would be required. Nonetheless, when the nontenured faculty person who was doing this work was terminated, all this administration was added to our loads. There was no less expectation of rigorous research, but there was now much more work added on to our schedules and our load without any compensation. I work with amazing and wonderful rhetoric and composition colleagues, and we have shared the burden and managed things well. Still, we were and are desperate for more resources of some kind given this increase in load without increase in pay or compensation of any sort. We were refused every year and were always put on a priority list in such a way that the department never got to us. Conveniently.

* * *

THE NEW WORKING CLASSES

Class in the Composition Classroom is especially exemplary in its descriptions of how old concepts of social class and working class have changed. As the editors in their introduction note, Michael Parenti's view, that class is the division between those who have sufficient wealth that they could live on it and those who must work to provide for themselves and for the wealthy, is important. The Occupy movement made good use of this definition of social class. For creating broad social alliances, this is clearly the definition of social class that works best because it includes most people. It has the additional advantage that it goes beyond wealth to labor as the source of wealth and hence is compatible with Marx's analysis of capitalism.

Yet this book shows that the old Marxist idea of the industrial working class emerging from and organizing the manufacturing sector is less applicable. *Class in the Composition Classroom* shows people in a variety of places doing a variety of jobs and often not identifying with the working class or at least the older view of the working class.

I do not find this to be a problem but rather see it as proof of how capitalism has changed since Marx (something he predicted). Social classes have changed with capitalism. It is comparable to the variety of Marxisms that have sprouted up since Marx. As Frederic Jameson pointed out about this diversity in the 1970s,

> For it is perfectly consistent with the spirit of Marxism—with the principle that thought reflects the concrete social situation—that there should exist several different Marxisms in the world today, each answering the specific needs and problems of its own socio-economic system: thus, one corresponds to the postrevolutionary industrial countries of the socialist bloc, another—a kind of peasant Marxism—to China and Cuba and countries of the Third World, while yet another tries to deal theoretically with the unique questions raised by monopoly capitalism in the West.

I think much the same is true of social class. Capitalism must grow or die. So it should come as no surprise that the social classes have also developed. This book makes a stunning contribution to the discussion of working-class identity by tracing the changes in real, actually existing communities. We must embrace these changes.

What breaks, but also continuities, do we find?
Social class is now

- even more global—the market but also manufacturing and the divisions of labor are worldwide;
- even more local—where we are shapes how and who we are;
- rhetorical—social class is constituted in the material process of production but also in how we discourse about social class and what class identities fit;
- dynamic—Marx always insisted on historical analysis in part because capital is always morphing;

Given the increasing complexity of defining social class, what tendencies continue?

- Fragmentation in identities as well as in production is increasing. The new working classes are plural.
- Expansion is increasing. The working classes are even bigger than they were.
- Virtuality is increasing. Technology is where social class is increasingly made—in what amounts to online sweatshops. Simon Head's work tracks these changes and the ways technology has been Taylorized, so the more we work online, the more that work is monitored and controlled.[16]
- Intensification is increasing. Extreme inequality has exploded—less pay, more work for all but a few.[17]

All of these changes affect our students and our classrooms. This is the new reality. When this reality comes into contact with an outdated culture of college English departments, conflict ensues.

* * *

In this same five-year period, the English Department has approved and brought in sixteen new faculty, most of whom are specialists in literature, many of whom are from elite eastern universities. If numbers are an indication, the department's culture and values do not seem to be with composition. But it goes deeper than this. The departmental politics point to underlying differences of culture and value. And the divide seems to be increasing between the specialization required of English majors who study literature and the needs and values and culture of our undergraduate students. The divide is also between aspirations of high culture and a devaluing of popular culture and the cultures our students speak for in their stories, if they are allowed to tell stories. There is a hard-to-pin-down but nonetheless deep culture at work here, and it is classed. The political economy of the English Department, the ways labor is produced, circulated, rewarded, and punished, is at work.[18] But also there is what Eagleton calls an "ideology embedded in the study of elite and canonical texts." One might think the English Department is a machine for producing inequality. At a search-committee meeting, one of the new faculty from an elite East-Coast school called into question my claim that one of the candidates was effective with graduate students and another from an Ivy League school was not. It was implied that my claim could be dismissed as unimportant, that what seemingly really counted was the specialization and the predicted ability to publish—curiously, since the Ivy League candidate had hardly any conferences and no publications to their name. The candidate came and is a wonderful colleague; that is not the point. The point is that the culture of the English Department seems to be increasingly elitist.

* * *

THE CULTURE OF COLLEGE ENGLISH DEPARTMENTS

Change. We live in an ocean of change, but like fish in the ocean are not aware of water, we are hardly aware of it. The elite culture of college English departments has been analyzed for many decades now. Eagleton in his book *Literary Theory* shows that the definitions of literature in the traditional canon are ideological.[19] Traditional literary culture is about value. Values come out of communities but also out of social classes. The traditional English department culture validates upper-class values and denigrates or ignores working-class values.

Since Jay Robinson's "Literacy and the English Department," our discipline has been aware that the culture of the college English department is at odds with literacy and is marked by upper-class values. Robinson notes:

> English departments mean by the term literacy one particular and quite specialized thing: an easy familiarity with a certain body of texts, a particular attitude toward them, and special practices for reading texts so they will yield the appropriate attitude—attitudes which might lead a professor to call one student "cultured," another "urbane," and still another a "candidate for graduate school. . . . It is with the help of this system of discourse that we in English departments find means to ignore the needs of our students, especially those of our most needy students, and yet feel good about it.

I would add that the values behind this discourse are classed. There are many exceptions to be sure, but two words in my department embody the conflict between the upper class and working class discourse.

Passion. Whenever I ask undergraduates or graduates students why study English? why major in English?—questions I also asked when I served for many years on the Graduate Committee and read statements of intent—the reason they give most often is passion. "I am passionate about literature." "I am passionate about literature teaching." Are engineers—or doctors, lawyers, ministers, not to mention lowly composition faculty—less passionate about their area than literature and creative-writing folks seem to be? How does this word distinguish? And why? How does it construct the rest of us mere mortals—as lacking passion? Who benefits (and loses) if we see reality this way? *Cui bono*—who benefits?

Writer. The culture of English assigns *writer* to the creative writers (or of course to those great authors of the canon) despite the fact that everyone in our departments writes. How does one small group get to "own" the term *writer*? My creative-writing graduate students tell me that even within creative writing, there is a further division between "serious" writing (what our creative writers do and teach) versus "genre writing"—popular-culture writing that includes sci-fi, mysteries, horror, dystopian novels, and the like. Again, *cui bono*? And more important, does this culture of English welcome working-class students? Perhaps, but only at a price. Robinson compares composition with literature and the literati (a term for English professors who profess these values and popularized by Maxine Hairston).

> And because, as composition teachers, we somehow inherit the responsibility to bring our students into the academy *without* insisting that they leave their own lives and worlds behind . . . our task is more difficult (emphasis mine).

But I argue that valuing the traditional canon and requiring English students or even students in composition to pass muster means two things. Either students will believe *their* interests are less legitimate or they will hide them, not perhaps connecting such values to social class and the ruling class, and in that process they will be told implicitly again and again they do have to give up their lives and worlds. Or they will simply decide it is not worth the fight and they need to go elsewhere.

* * *

Current enrollments at all levels in my department have significantly gone down since I came here in 2007. I was brought in because the doctoral program in literature was already in a decade-long decline. RCP numbers, which have increased every year, are aggregated into the literature PhD numbers and so provide ballast for that program. The MA almost disappeared when TA support was cut by the higher administration. Most important, majors in English, which numbered over eight hundred when I came here, are now around six hundred, with no indication that the trend will change. I expect we will hit three hundred majors in five or six years. Even the creative-writing programs at all levels are having enrollment issues. I was told that five courses this term offered by five

*separate tenured faculty in literature did not make, that is, did not get high
enough enrollments to be offered. Two literature faculty whose courses did not
make are teaching freshman composition. In the meantime, the undergraduate
numbers in freshman composition, while declining very slowly, are still relatively
stable, and the enrollments in advanced composition have been rising each
term. I talk with students privately in freshman composition, advanced composition, and in the gay and lesbian literature course I offer as a popular-culture
course rather than an elite literature course. They tell me we have way too many
traditional British courses. They tell me most courses in literature are canonical,
rarely connecting to current popular culture. They tell me they are interested in
reading and writing but not the specialized decoding most English courses offer.
They tell me they might major in creative writing but their parents, who are paying for their education, would not support that major because what can one do
with a creative-writing degree except go on to get another creative-writing degree
at the master's level? A few of them tell me they would major in rhetoric and
composition rather than creative writing if we offered that major. Some of them
tell me they do not feel comfortable with the culture of the department and what
they see as its embrace of elite values.*

* * *

The culture of English needs changing, and Robinson was making
that argument prophetically three decades ago. The culture of English
must change to serve changing students but also to survive. Yet my students in private tell me they do not feel welcomed in most English
classes. So the ultimate call of *Class in the Composition Classroom* seems to
me to be a call for a change in this culture of English. But Jay Robinson's
final words[20] are also now, sixteen years later, mine. "'Literacy in the
English Department?' Maybe. But I doubt it."

* * *

Notes

1. Sharon Crowley argued for student choice about whether to take freshman composition in *Composition in the University*. Abolition of freshman composition was proposed in several essays in Petraglia, ed., *Reconceiving Writing, Rethinking Writing*. Gary
   Olson and Lynn Worsham argue for moving beyond the pedagogical imperative in
   Rhetoric and Composition as Intellectual Work. The most recent argument for moving
   beyond both freshman composition and teaching generally has been put forward
   by Sidney Dobrin, *Postcomposition*.
2. See Bloom, "Freshman Composition as a Middle-Class Enterprise."
3. Bartholomae, *Writing on the Margins: Essays on Composition and Teaching*; Bizzell,
   Academic Discourse and Critical Consciousness.
4. I have always insisted on teaching freshman composition regularly and do so to

this day. Chairs of English tend to see that as an inefficient use of faculty labor—the assumption and reality is "anyone" can and does teach freshman composition; not anyone can teach advanced graduate seminars or even advanced undergraduate courses.

5. Eagleton, *Literary Theory*, 13–14.
6. Head, *The New Ruthless Economy*; and Head, *Mindless.*
7. Henderson and Lee, *Poetry*, xii.
8. Obviously, Edward Corbett was there at the time and while I worked on the PhD. He was also then editor of *CCC*. Frank O'Hare came in the year I came. Still, the degree requirements were lit courses. It did not make sense to take the traditional canon coursework, which was then still mostly male, when my interest was in unauthorized writing, theory, and writing pedagogy.
9. Crowley, *The Methodical Memory*; but also Connors, *Selected Essays of Robert J. Connors*; and especially Connors, "The Rise and Fall of the Modes of Discourse."
10. Frank D'Angelo synthesized writing-process research with modes of discourse and patterns of development by arguing such products represented processes of mind, which is what he was aiming at in *Process and Thought in Composition*; James Kinneavy, William McCleary, and Neil Nakadate, in their textbook *Writing in the Liberal Arts Tradition*, do a similar mopping-up operation by distinguishing the aims of discourse from the forms or strategies of discourse.
11. The exceptions are notable. James McCrimmon, *Writing with a Purpose*, did not deal with the modes, nor did Sheridan Baker's *The Practical Stylist.* But nearly every reader did.
12. Lunsford and Lunsford, "'Mistakes Are a Fact of Life.'"
13. DeStigter, "On the Ascendance of Argument." De Stigter's empirical ethnographic research and theoretical analysis complements the argument I more briefly put forward here. His research shows "how the overemphasis on argumentation imposes unwarranted limits on what counts as valid thought, legitimate political subjectivity, and a feasible strategy for addressing economic inequality," 13. By showing that the public rationales for argument are neoliberal in their assumptions and concepts, DeStigter provides a tour de force argument of why it is necessary to have students write in a variety of forms including, but not limited to, argument.
14. See Miley, "Thirdspace Explorations in Online Writing Studios." But also the WPA 27-Question Survey (2A, 2B, 2C, 2D, 2E, 2F), which I have my undergraduates do in every one of my composition courses, supports this claim as well.
15. Hillocks, *Research on Written Composition*, but also see the recent study by Anderson, Anson, Gonyea, and Paine, "The Contributions of Writing to Learning and Development."
16. Simon Head, *The New Ruthless Economy*, but also Head's *Mindless.* Even academics are increasingly controlled through online labor. Staff must clock in on their computers and faculty must submit annual reports that have standardized assessment procedures for publications that count. My institution now has all course evaluations online as well. This is not even considering online courses usually taught—so far—in composition and largely by TAs and nontenured faculty.
17. See the impressive research of Thomas Piketty, *Capital in the Twenty-First Century*, who, by using extensive, reliable data collected over nearly two centuries of capitalism, shows unregulated capitalism tends to grow faster than wages and incomes of individuals, thus creating a systemic and increasing inequality. Unregulated capitalism creates extremes, including extremes of wealth and poverty, basically following Marx's analysis. But anyone who has had a job in the corporate, governmental, or academic sectors over the last few years already knows that work abetted by technology and a terrible labor market has increased and compensation has decreased.

We all work more and more for less and less—unless you are wealthy. Thirty-five years initiated by Ronald Reagan, through tax cuts for the wealthy, cuts in social programs, and antilabor laws and regulations, has created the most massive transfer of wealth in US history.

18. Zebroski, "The Political Economy of English."
19. Eagleton, *Literary Theory*, 13–14.
20. Robinson, "Literacy in the Department of English," 484.

BIBLIOGRAPHY

Adler-Kassner, Linda. "The Shape of the Form: Working-Class Students and the Academic Essay." In *Teaching Working Class*, edited by Sherry Lee Linkon, 85–105. Boston: University of Massachusetts Press, 1999.

Alcoff, Linda. "Cultural Feminism versus Post-Structuralism: The Identity Crisis in Feminist Theory." *Signs* 13, no. 3 (1988): 405–36. http://dx.doi.org/10.1086/494426.

Alexander, Kara Poe. "Implicit Response: Instructor Values and Social Class in the Literacy Narrative Assignment." PhD diss., University of Louisville, 2006.

Alexander, Kara Poe. "Successes, Victims, and Prodigies: 'Master' and 'Little' Cultural Narratives in the Literacy Narrative Genre." *College Composition and Communication* 62, no. 4 (2011): 608–33.

Alford, Barry, and Keith Kroll. *The Politics of Writing in the Two-Year College*. Portsmouth, NH: Boynton/Cook, 2001.

Allen, Paul. "Action, Reflection and Practice as an Electrician." In *Labor Writes 2013*, edited by Rebecca Fraser, Sophia Mavrogiannis, Sharon Szymanski, Masha Tupitsyn, and Christina Vallario, 35–57. Saratoga Springs: SUNY Empire State College, 2013.

Althusser, Louis. "Ideology and Ideological State Apparatuses." In *Lenin and Philosophy and Other Essays*. Translated by Ben Brewster. New York: Monthly Review, 1970.

Ambrose, Susan A., Michael W. Bridges, Michele DiPietro, Marsha C. Lovett, and Marie K. Norman. *How Learning Works: Seven Research-Based Principles for Smart Teaching*. New York: John Wiley and Sons, 2010.

Anderson, Paul, Chris M. Anson, Robert M. Gonyea, and Charles Paine. "The Contributions of Writing to Learning and Development: Results from a Large-Scale Multi-institutional Study." *Research in the Teaching of English* 50, no. 2 (2015): 201–35.

Anderson, Robin J. *Dynamics of Economic Well-Being: Poverty, 2004–2006*. Current Population Reports. US Census Bureau. March 2011. https://www.census.gov/prod/2011pubs/p 70-123.pdf.

Anyon, Jean. "Social Class and the Hidden Curriculum of Work." *Journal of Education* 162, no. 1 (1980): 67–92.

Anyon, Jean. "Social Class and the Hidden Curriculum." In *Critical Issues in Education: Anthology of Readings*, edited by Eugene F. Provenzo. Thousand Oaks, CA: SAGE, 2006.

Arizona Rural Policy Institute. *Demographic Analysis of the Navajo Nation Using 2010 Census and 2010 American Community Survey Estimates*. Window Rock: Northern Arizona University, n.d. http://azcia.gov/Documents/Links/DemoProfiles/Navajo%20Nation.pdf.

Aronowitz, Stanley. *How Class Works: Power and Social Movement*. New Haven, CT: Yale Press, 2003.

Aronson, J., and C. M. Steele. "Stereotypes and the Fragility of Academic Competence, Motivation, and Self-Concept." In *Handbook of Competence and Motivation*, edited by Andrew. J. Elliot and Carol. S. Dweck, 436–56. New York: Guilford, 2005.

Arum, Richard, and Josipa Roksa. *Academically Adrift: Limited Learning on College Campuses*. Chicago: University of Chicago Press, 2011. Kindle edition.

Attao, Kristine, and Washington State University Office of Student Support Services. "Request for Demographic Data." February 11, 2015.

Austin, J. L. *How to Do Things with Words: The William James Lectures Delivered at Harvard University in 1955*. Cambridge, MA: Harvard University Press, 1962.

DOI: 10.7330/9781607326182.c018

Bahr, Peter Riley. "Educational Attainment as Process: Using Hierarchical Discrete-Time Event History Analysis to Model Rate of Progress." *Research in Higher Education* 50, no. 7 (2009): 691–714. http://dx.doi.org/10.1007/s11162-009-9135-x.

Baker, Sheridan. *The Practical Stylist.* New York: Thomas Crowell, 1962.

Bandura, Albert. *Self-efficacy: The Exercise of Control.* New York: W. H. Freeman, 1997.

Barnett, Timothy. "'Love Letters': Narrating Critical Theory in the First-Year Writing Class." *Open Words* 7, no. 1 (2013): 21–40.

Barthes, Roland. *Mythologies.* London: Vintage, 1993.

Bartholomae, David. *Writing on the Margins: Essays on Composition and Teaching.* Pittsburgh: University of Pittsburgh Press, 2005.

Barton, David. *Literacy: An Introduction to the Ecology of Written Language.* 2nd ed. Malden, MA: Blackwell, 2007.

Bay, Libby. "Twists, Turns, and Returns: Returning Adult Students." *Teaching English in the Two-Year College* 26, no. 3 (1999): 305–12.

Bazerman, Charles. "Students Being Disciplined: Getting Confused, Getting By, Getting Rewarded, Getting Smart, Getting Real." Keynote speech presented at the Center for Interdisciplinary Studies of Writing 1994 Conference, "Looking Ahead: Writing In(tensively) in the Disciplines." Speaker Series No. 4. Minneapolis: University of Minnesota, 1996.

Bean, Janet. "Manufacturing Emotions: Tactical Resistance in the Narratives of Working Class Students." In *A Way to Move: Rhetorics of Emotion and Composition Studies,* edited by Dale Jacobs and Laura R. Micciche, 101–12. Portsmouth, NH: Boynton/Cook, 2003.

Beck, Ann. "A Place for Critical Literacy." *Journal of Adolescent & Adult Literacy* 48, no. 5 (2005): 392–400.

Beech, Jennifer. "Redneck and Hillbilly Discourse in the Writing Classroom: Classifying Critical Pedagogies of Whiteness." *College English* 67, no. 2 (2004): 172–86. http://dx.doi.org/10.2307/4140716.

Benmayor, Rina. "Digital 'Testimonio' as a Signature Pedagogy for Latina Studies." *Equity & Excellence in Education* 45, no. 3 (2012): 507–24. http://dx.doi.org/10.1080/10665 684.2012.698180.

Berger, Bennet. *Working Class Suburb.* Berkeley: University of California Press, 1960.

Bergmann, Linda S., and Janet Zepernick. "Disciplinarity and Transfer: Students' Perceptions of Learning to Write." *WPA: Writing Program Administration* 31, no. 1–2 (2007): 124–49.

Berkhofer, Robert F. *The White Man's Indian: Images of the American Indian from Columbus to the Present.* New York: Vintage, 1979.

Bernstein, Basil. *Class, Codes and Control.* Vol. 1, Theoretical Studies towards a Sociology of Language. London: Routledge & Kegan Paul, 1971. http://dx.doi.org/10.4324/9780203014035.

Bernstein, Basil. *Class, Codes, and Control.* Vol. 1, Theoretical Studies towards a Sociology of Language. New York: Routledge, 2003.

Berry, Patrick. "Critical Remediation: Locating Eliza." *Kairos* 11, no. 3 (2007): n.p.

Bizzell, Patricia. *Academic Discourse and Critical Consciousness.* Pittsburgh, PA: University of Pittsburgh Press, 1992.

Black, Laurel Johnson. "Stupid Rich Bastards." In *This Fine Place So Far from Home: Voices of Academics from the Working Class,* edited. by C. L. Barney Dews and Carolyn Leste Law, 13–25. Philadelphia, PA: Temple University Press, 1995.

Bloom, Leslie Rebecca. "'When One Person Makes It, We All Make It': A Study of Beyond Welfare, a Women-Centered Community-Based Organization That Helps Low-Income Mothers Achieve Personal and Academic Success." *International Journal of Qualitative Studies in Education: QSE* 22, no. 4 (2009): 485–503. http://dx.doi.org/10.1080/0951 8390902740597.

Bloom, Lynn Z. "Freshman Composition as a Middle-Class Enterprise." *College English* 58, no. 6 (1996): 654–65. http://dx.doi.org/10.2307/378392.

Boltanski, Luc. *Mysteries and Conspiracies: Detective Stories, Spy Novels and the Making of Modern Society*. Malden, MA: Polity, 2014.

Boiarsky, Carolyn R., ed. *Academic Literacy in the English Classroom: Helping Underprepared and Working Class Students Succeed in College* Portsmouth, NH: Boynton/Cook, 2003.

Boiarsky, Carolyn R. "Learning to Learn: Helping Students Become Independent Thinkers." In *Academic Literacy in the English Classroom: Helping Underprepared and Working Class Students Succeed in College*, edited by Carolyn R. Boiarsky, 22–62. Portsmouth, NH: Boynton/Cook, 2003.

Boiarsky, Carolyn R., Julie Hagemann, and Judith Burdan. "Working Class Students in the Academy: Who Are They?" In *Academic Literacy in the English Classroom: Helping Underprepared and Working Class Students Succeed in College*, edited by Carolyn R. Boiarsky, 1–21. Portsmouth, NH: Boynton/Cook, 2003.

Bourdieu, Pierre. *Distinction: A Social Critique of the Judgment of Taste*. Translator Richard Nice. Cambridge, MA: Harvard University Press, 1984.

Bourdieu, Pierre. *Language and Symbolic Power*. Cambridge, MA: Harvard University Press, 1993.

Bowles, Samuel, and Herbert Gintis. *Schooling in Capitalist America: Educational Reform and the Contradictions of Economic Life*. New York: Basic Books, 1976.

Brady, Laura. "Fault Lines in the Terrain of Distance Education." *Computers and Composition* 18, no. 4 (2001): 347–58. http://dx.doi.org/10.1016/S8755-4615(01)00067-6.

Brandt, Deborah. *Literacy and Learning: Reflection on Writing, Reading, and Society*. San Francisco, CA: John Wiley and Sons, 2009.

Brandt, Deborah. *Literacy in American Lives*. Cambridge: Cambridge University Press, 2001. http://dx.doi.org/10.1017/CBO9780511810237.

Brandt, Deborah. "Sponsors of Literacy." In *Literacy: A Critical Sourcebook*, edited by Ellen Cushman, Eugene R. Kintgen, Barry. M. Kroll, and Mike Rose, 555–71. New York: Bedford St. Martin's, 2001.

Brereton, John. *The Origins of Composition Studies in the American College, 1875–1925*. Pittsburgh, PA: University of Pittsburgh Press, 1996.

Bridwell-Bowles, Lillian. "Freedom, Form, Function: Varieties of Academic Discourse." *College Composition and Communication* 46, no. 1 (1995): 46–61. http://dx.doi.org/10.2307/358869.

Brint, Steven, and Jerome Karabel. *The Diverted Dream: Community Colleges and the Promise of Educational Opportunity in America, 1900–1985*. New York: Oxford University Press, 1989. ERIC Document No. 309827.

Brint, Steven. "The Educational Lottery." *Los Angeles Review of Books*, November 15, 2011.

Britton, James. *Language and Learning: The Importance of Speech in Children's Development*. Portsmouth, NH: Boynton/Cook, 1970.

Brodkey, Linda. "Writing on the Bias." *College English* 56, no. 5 (1994): 527–47. http://dx.doi.org/10.2307/378605.

Brooks, Joanna, and Fern Cayetano. "The (Dis)location of Culture: On the Way to Literacy." In *Teaching Working Class*, edited by Sherry Lee Linkon, 56–68. Boston: University of Massachusetts Press, 1999.

Brooman, Simon, and Sue Darwent. "'Yes, as the Articles Suggest, I Have Considered Dropping Out': Self-Awareness Literature and the First-Year Student." *Studies in Higher Education* 37, no. 1 (2012): 19–31. http://dx.doi.org/10.1080/03075079.2010.490580.

Bruner, Jerome. *Acts of Meaning: Four Lectures on Mind and Culture*. Cambridge, MA: Harvard University Press, 2007.

Buck, Jo Ann, Sallyann H. Fitzgerald, Yulanda McKinney, Jude Okpala, Leslie Roberts, Marilyn Valentino, and Xiao Wang. "Guidelines for the Academic Preparation of English Faculty at Two-Year Colleges." 2004. http://www.ncte.org/library/NCTEFiles/Groups/TYCA/TYCAGuidelines.pdf.

Burgess, Jean. "Hearing Ordinary Voices: Cultural Studies, Vernacular Creativity and Digital Storytelling." *Continuum: Journal of Media and Cultural Studies* 20, no. 2 (2006): 201–14. http://dx.doi.org/10.1080/10304310600641737.

Burke, Kenneth. *Attitudes Toward History*. 3rd ed. Berkeley: University of California Press, 1984.

Burke, Kenneth. *A Grammar of Motives*. New York: George Braziller, 1955.

Burke, Kenneth. *Permanence and Change: An Anatomy of Purpose*. 3rd ed. Berkeley: University of California Press, 1984.

Burke, Kenneth. *A Rhetoric of Motives*. Berkeley: University of California Press, 1969.

Burnham, Christopher. "Expressive Pedagogy: Practice/Theory, Theory/Practice." In *A Guide to Composition Pedagogies*, edited by Gary Tate, Amy Rupiper, and Kurt Schick. New York: Oxford University Press, 2001.

Butler, Judith. *Gender Trouble*. New York: Routledge, 1990.

Carmona, Ariel. "Cal State's Early Start Program Sparks Opposition." CalWatchdog.com. July 30, 2012. http://calwatchdog.com/2012/07/30/cal-states-early-start-program -sparks-opposition/.

The Carnegie Classification of Institutions of Higher Education. Carnegie Classifications. 2015. http://carnegieclassifications.iu.edu/.

Carney-Crompton, Shawn, and Josephine Tan. "Support Systems, Psychological Functioning, and Academic Performance of Nontraditional Female Students." *Adult Education Quarterly* 52, no. 2 (2002): 140–54. http://dx.doi.org/10.1177/074171360205200 2005.

Cheryan, Sapna, Victoria C. Plaut, Paul G. Davies, and Claude M. Steele. "Ambient Belonging: How Stereotypical Cues Impact Gender Participation in Computer Science." *Journal of Personality and Social Psychology* 97, no. 6 (2009): 1045–60. http://dx.doi.org /10.1037/a0016239.

Cho, Sung-Woo, James Jacobs, and Christine Zhang. "Demographic and Academic Characteristics of Pell Grant Recipients at Community Colleges." Community College Research Center. CCRC Working Paper No. 65. New York: Community College Research Center, Teachers College, Columbia University: Columbia University, 2013. https://academiccommons.columbia.edu/catalog/ac:170463.

Chua, Amy, and Jed Rubenfeld. *The Triple Package: How Three Unlikely Traits Explain the Rise and Fall of Cultural Groups in America*. New York: Penguin, 2014.

Clandinin, D. Jean. *Handbook of Narrative Inquiry*. Thousand Oaks, CA: SAGE, 2006.

Clark, Burton R. *The Academic Life. Small Worlds, Different Worlds. A Carnegie Foundation Special Report*. Princeton, NJ: Carnegie Foundation for the Advancement of Teaching, 1987.

Clark, Burton R. "The 'Cooling-Out' Function in Higher Education." *American Journal of Sociology* 65, no. 6 (1960): 569–76. http://dx.doi.org/10.1086/222787.

Clason, Dennis L., and Thomas J. Dormody. "Analyzing Data Measured by Individual Likert-Type Items." *Journal of Agricultural Education* 35, no. 4 (1994): 31–35. http://dx .doi.org/10.5032/jae.1994.04031.

Coffey, Marjorie D. "Literacy Narratives across the Curriculum. "MA thesis, Oregon State University, 2011.

Cohen, Arthur, and Florence Brawer. *The American Community College*. San Francisco, CA: Jossey-Bass, 2008.

Cohen, Geoffrey, Julio Garcia, Nancy Apfel, and Allison Master. "Reducing the Racial Achievement Gap: A Social-Psychological Intervention." *Science* 313, no. 5791 (2006): 1307–10 http://dx.doi.org/10.1126/science.1128317.

Collins, Chuck, Jennifer Ladd, Maynard Seider, and Felice Yeskel. *Class Lives. Stories from across Our Economic Divide*. Ithaca, NY: ILR Press, 2014.

Complete College America. The Bill and Melinda Gates Foundation. http://postsecond ary.gatesfoundation.org/report/complete-college-america-the-game-changers/.

Guerra, Jennifer. "Coming Out as Poor at an Elite University." *All Things Considered*. WUOM Radio. Ann Arbor, MI: January 29, 2015. http://stateofopportunity.michigan-radio.org/post/coming-out-poor-elite-university.

Connell, R. W. *Masculinities*. Cambridge: Polity, 1995.

Connors, Robert. "The Rise and Fall of the Modes of Discourse." *College Composition and Communication* 32, nos. 1–12 (1981): 444–55.

Connors, Robert J. *Selected Essays of Robert J. Connors*. Boston, MA: Bedford/St. Martins, 2003.

Coovadia, Imraan. *Transformations: Essays*. 1st ed. Cape Town: Umuzi, 2012.

Corbin, Juliet, and Anselm Strauss. *Basics of Qualitative Research: Techniques and Procedures for Developing Grounded Theory*. Thousand Oaks, CA: SAGE, 2014.

Corkery, Caleb A. "Narrative and Personal Literacy Developing a Pedagogy of Confidence-Building for the Writing Classroom." PhD diss., University of Maryland, 2004.

Coston, Bethany M., and Michael Kimmel. "Seeing Privilege Where It Isn't: Marginalized Masculinities and the Intersectionality of Privilege." *Journal of Social Issues* 68, no. 1 (2012): 97–111. http://dx.doi.org/10.1111/j.1540-4560.2011.01738.x.

Cox, Rebecca D. *The College Fear Factor: How Students and Professors Misunderstand One Another*. Cambridge, MA: Harvard University Press, 2009. http://dx.doi.org/10.4159/9780674053663.

Crowley, Sharon. *Composition in the University*. Pittsburgh: University of Pittsburgh Press, 1998.

Crowley, Sharon. *The Methodical Memory*. Carbondale: Southern Illinois University Press, 2010.

Cruz, Cindy. "Making Curriculum from Scratch: 'Testimonio' in an Urban Classroom." *Equity & Excellence in Education* 45, no. 3 (2012): 460–71. http://dx.doi.org/10.1080/10665684.2012.698185.

D'Angelo, Frank. *Process and Thought in Composition*. Boston: Little, Brown, 1985.

de Certeau, Michel. *The Practice of Everyday Life*. Berkeley: University of California Press, 1984.

DeJoy, Nancy C. *Process This: Undergraduate Writing in Composition Studies*. Logan: Utah State University Press, 2004.

Delanty, Gerard. "Academic Identities and Institutional Change." In *Changing Identities in Higher Education: Voicing Perspectives*, edited by Ronald Barnett and Roberto Di Napoli, 124–33. Oxford: Routledge, 2007.

de Leon, Josephine. *2009–2010 Diversity Report Card: A Report on the Demographics of the Students, Faculty and Staff of the University of New Mexico*. Albuquerque: University of New Mexico Office for Equity and Inclusion, 2010. http://diverse.unm.edu/wp-content/uploads/2010/03/DRC2-2008-2009-labeled.pdf.

Deleuze, Gilles, and Félix Guattari. *A Thousand Plateaus: Capitalism and Schizophrenia*. Minneapolis: University of Minnesota Press, 1987.

Delgado Bernal, Dolores, Rebeca Burciaga, and Judith Flores Carmona. "Chicana/Latina 'Testimonios': Mapping the Methodological, Pedagogical, and Political." *Equity & Excellence in Education* 45, no. 3 (2012): 363–72. http://dx.doi.org/10.1080/10665684.2012.698149.

Del Sole, C. "The Things I Carry." In *Labor Writes 2014*, edited by Rebecca Fraser, Thomas Kerr, MaryHelen Kolisnyk, Sophia Mavrogiannis, Keisha Spradley, Desmond Palmer, and Chris Vallario, 34–35. Saratoga Springs: SUNY Empire State College, 2014.

Deil-Amen, Regina. "'Warming Up' the Aspirations of Community College Students." In *After Admission: From College Access to College Success*, edited by James E. Rosenbaum, Regina Deil-Amen, and Ann E. Person, 40–65. New York: Russell Sage Foundation, 2006.

Desrochers, Donna M., and Rita J. Kirshstein. *College Spending in a Turbulent Decade: Findings from the Delta Cost Project. A Delta Data Update, 2000–2010*. Washington, DC: American Institutes of Research, 2012.

DeStigter, Todd. "On the Ascendance of Argument: A Critique of the Assumptions of Academe's Dominant Form." *Research in the Teaching of English* 50, no. 1 (2015): 11–34.

Dewey, John. *Experience and Education.* New York: Simon & Schuster, 1997.

Dews, C. L. Barney, and Carolyn Leste Law. *This Fine Place So Far from Home: Voices of Academics from the Working Class.* Philadelphia, PA: Temple University Press, 1995.

Difino, Joseph. "My Life as an Electrician." In *Lights On: A View of the Electrical Industry Through the Eyes of Local 3 Apprentices,* edited by Rebecca Fraser, 80–87. Saratoga Springs: SUNY Empire State College, 2009.

DiMaria, Frank. "Working-Class Students: Lost in a College's Middle-Class Culture." *Education Digest* 72, no. 1 (2006): 60–65.

Dobrin, Sidney. *Postcomposition.* Carbondale: Southern Illinois University Press, 2011.

Dobrin, Sidney I., J. A. Rice, and Michael Vastola, eds. *Beyond Postprocess.* Logan: Utah State University Press, 2011.

Donehower, Kim, Charlotte Hogg, and Eileen Schell. *Rural Literacies.* Carbondale: Southern Illinois University Press, 2007.

Downs, Douglas, and Elizabeth Wardle. "Teaching about Writing, Righting Misconceptions: (Re)envisioning 'First-Year Composition' as 'Introduction to Writing Studies.'" *College Composition and Communication* 58, no. 4 (2007): 552–84.

Driscoll, Dana Lynn, and Jennifer Wells. "Beyond Knowledge and Skills: Writing Transfer and the Role of Student Dispositions." *Composition Forum* 26 (2012). http://composi tionforum.com/issue/26/beyond-knowledge-skills.php.

Dugan, Andrew. "Americans Most Likely to Say They Belong to the Middle Class." Gallup. November 30, 2012. http://www.gallup.com/poll/159029/americans-likely -say-belong-middle-class.aspx

Dunbar-Odom, Donna. *Defying the Odds: Class and the Pursuit of Higher Literacy.* Albany: SUNY Press, 2007.

Eagleton, Terry. *Literary Theory: An Introduction.* Minneapolis: University of Minnesota Press, 1996.

Edwards, Mike. "Economies of Writing, Without the Economics: A Rhetorical Analysis of Composition's Economic Discourse in *JAC* 32.3–4." *Rhetoric Review* 33, no. 3 (2014): 244–61. http://dx.doi.org/10.1080/07350198.2014.917514.

Eller, Dani. "Literacy Narrative." 2011. www.dani-eller.com.

Espinoza, Roberta. *Working-Class Minority Students' Routes to Higher Education.* New York: Routledge, 2012.

Farr, Marcia. "Essayist Literacy and Other Verbal Performances." *Written Communication* 10, no. 1 (1993): 4–38. http://dx.doi.org/10.1177/0741088393010001001.

Ferguson, Stephen. "Reflections of Work." In *Labor Writes 2015,* edited by Rebecca Fraser, Thomas Kerr, Alison Dundy, Chris Vallario, and Desmond Palmer, 34–35. Saratoga Springs: SUNY Empire State College, 2015.

Ferretti, Eileen. "Between Dirty Dishes and Polished Discourse: How Working-Class Moms Construct Student Identities." In *Teaching Working Class,* edited by Sherry Lee Linkon, 69–84. Boston: University of Massachusetts Press, 1999.

Ferster, Bill. *Teaching Machines: Learning from the Intersection of Education and Technology.* Baltimore, MD: Johns Hopkins, 2015.

Finn, Patrick J. *Literacy with an Attitude: Educating Working-Class Children in Their Own Self Interest.* 2nd ed. Albany: SUNY Press, 2009.

Flower, Linda. "Talking across Difference: Intercultural Rhetoric and the Search for Situated Knowledge." *College Composition and Communication* 55, no. 1 (2003): 38–68. http://dx.doi.org/10.2307/3594199.

Foster, Victoria, Michael Kimmel, and Christine Skelton. "What About the Boys?': An Overview of the Debates." In *What About the Boys?: Issues of Masculinity in Schools,* edited by Wayne Martino and Bob Meyenn, 1–23. Philadelphia, PA: Open University Press, 2001.

Foucault, Michel. *The History of Sexuality, Volume 1: An Introduction.* New York: Vintage Books, 1978.

France, Alan W. "Assigning Places: The Function of Introductory Composition as a Cultural Discourse." *College English* 55, no. 6 (1993): 593–609. http://dx.doi.org/10.2307/378696.

Freire, Paolo. *Pedagogy of the Oppressed.* New York: Seabury, 1970.

Freire, Paulo. *Pedagogy of the Oppressed.* New York: Continuum, 1990.

Fromm, Erich. *The Sane Society.* New York: Rinehart & Company, 1955.

Fulkerson, Richard. "Composition at the Turn of the Twenty-First Century." *College Composition and Communication* 56, no. 4 (2005): 654–87.

Fussell, Paul. *Class.* New York: Ballantine, 1984.

Ganderton, Philip T., and Richard Santos. "Hispanic College Attendance and Completion: Evidence from the High School and Beyond Surveys." *Economics of Education Review* 14, no. 1 (1995): 35–46. http://dx.doi.org/10.1016/0272-7757(94)00034-4.

Garcia, Romeo. 2013. "The Tyranny of Argument: Rethinking the Work of Composition." Reviews of the 2013 Conference on College Composition and Communication. *Kairos* 18, no. 1: 122–24.

Gee, James Paul. *An Introduction to Discourse Analysis: Theory and Method.* London: Routledge, 1999.

Gee, James Paul. *Social Linguistics and Literacies: Ideology in Discourses.* 3rd ed. New York: Routledge, 2008.

"Genesee Community College Students Experience Homelessness for One Night." United States Federal News Service. *HighBeam Research*, May 17, 2007.

Gibson-Graham, J. K. "Economy." In *New Keywords*, edited by Tony Bennett, Lawrence Grossberg, and Meaghan Morris, 94–97. Malden, MA: Blackwell, 2005.

Gibson-Graham, J. K. *A Postcapitalist Politics.* Minneapolis: University of Minnesota Press, 2006.

Gilyard, Keith. *Voices of the Self: A Study of Language Competence.* Detroit, MI: Wayne State University Press, 1991.

Giroux, Henry. "Flipping the Script: Rethinking Working-Class Resistance." Truthout. June 8, 2015. http://www.truth-out.org/news/item/31238-flipping-the-script-rethinking-working-class-resistance.

Gold, Lawrence N. "Improving College Access for Needy Adults Under Existing Federal Programs." In *Financing Nontraditional Students: A Seminar Report*, 33–46. Washington, DC: ACE, 1992.

González, Norma, Luis C. Moll, and Cathy Amanti. *Funds of Knowledge: Theorizing Practices in Households, Communities, and Classrooms.* New York: Taylor and Francis, 2005.

Google. Google Ngram Viewer. 2013.

Grall, Timothy S. *Custodial Mothers and Fathers and their Child Support: 2007.* Current Population Reports. US Census Bureau. November 2009. http://www.icbl.hw.ac.uk/ltdi/cookbook/info_likert_scale/index.html.

Greenberg, Milton. "The New GI Bill is No Match for the Original." *Chronicle of Higher Education* 54, no. 46 (2008): A 56. ERIC document no. EJ806467.

Greenwald, Richard, and Elizabeth A. Grant. "Border Crossings: Working-Class Encounters in Higher Education." In *Teaching Working Class*, edited by Sherry Lee Linkon, 29–38. Boston: University of Massachusetts Press, 1999.

Greer, Jane. *Girls and Literacy in America.* Santa Barbara, CA: ABC-CLIO, 2003.

Gouldner, Alvin. *The Future of Intellectuals and the Rise of the New Class.* Oxford: Oxford University Press, 1982.

Gutiérrez, Kris D. "Developing a Sociocritical Literacy in the Third Space." *Reading Research Quarterly* 43, no. 2 (2008): 148–64. http://dx.doi.org/10.1598/RRQ.43.2.3.

Hagedorn, Linda Serra. "The Pursuit of Student Success: Community College Interventions, and Programs: Directions and Challenges Facing Community Colleges." In *Higher*

Education: Handbook of Theory and Research. Vol. 25, edited by John C. Smart, 181–218. London: Springer Dordrecht Heidelberg, 2010. http://dx.doi.org/10.1007/978-90 -481-8598-6_5.

Hall, Anne-Marie, and Christopher Minnix. "Beyond the Bridge Metaphor: Rethinking the Place of the Literacy Narrative in the Basic Writing Curriculum." *Journal of Basic Writing* 31, no. 2 (2012): 57–82.

Hansen, Karen. "My Blue Collar Skills." In *Labor Writes 2013*, edited by Rebecca Fraser, Sophia Mavrogiannis, Mary Roma, Sharon Szymanski, Masha Tupitsyn, and Christina Vallario, 29–30. Saratoga Springs: SUNY Empire State College, 2013.

Hardt, Michael, and Antonio Negri. *Empire.* Cambridge, MA: Harvard University Press, 2000.

Harrington, Michael. *The Other America.* New York: Simon and Schuster, 1997.

Harris, Joseph Harris. *A Teaching Subject: Composition Since 1966.* New York: Prentice Hall, 1997.

"The Harry Van Arsdale Jr. Memorial Association Biography." The Harry Van Arsdale Jr. Memorial Association. Accessed February 4, 2015. http://www.harryvanarsdalejr.org/bio graphy.htm.

Hartsock, Nancy C. M. "The Feminist Standpoint: Developing the Ground for a Specifically Feminist Historical Materialism." In *Discovering Reality: Feminist Perspectives on Epistemology, Metaphysics, Methodology, and Philosophy of Science*, edited by Sandra Harding and Merrill B. Hintikka, 283–310. Dordrecht: D. Reidel, 1983.

Haushofer, Johannes, and Ernst Fehr. "On the Psychology of Poverty." *Science* 344, no. 6186 (2014): 862–67. http://dx.doi.org/10.1126/science.1232491.

Hawk, Byron. *A Counter-History of Composition: Toward Methodologies of Complexity.* Pittsburgh, PA: University of Pittsburgh Press, 2007.

Hawk, Byron. "Reassembling Post-Process." In *Beyond Postprocess*, edited by Sidney I. Dobrin, J. A. Rice, and Michael Vastola, 75–93. Logan: Utah State University Press, 2011.

Head, Simon. *The New Ruthless Economy: Work and Power in the Digital Age.* New York: Oxford University Press, 2003.

Head, Simon. *Mindless: Why Smarter Machines Are Making Dumber Humans.* New York: Basic Books, 2014.

Heath, Shirley Brice. *Ways with Words: Language, Life, and Work in Communities and Classrooms.* Cambridge: Cambridge University Press, 1983.

Heath, Shirley Brice. *Words at Work and Play: Three Decades in Family and Community Life.* Cambridge: Cambridge University Press, 2012.

Heathcott, Joseph. "What Kinds of Tools? Teaching Critical Analysis and Writing to Working-Class Students." In *Teaching Working Class*, edited by Sherry Lee Linkon, 106–22. Amherst: University of Massachusetts Press, 1999.

Henderson, Sam, and James Lee, eds. *Poetry: A Thematic Approach.* Belmont, CA: Wadsworth, 1969.

Henry, Sue Ellen. "Bodies at Home and at School: Toward a Theory of Embodied Social Class Status." *Educational Theory* 63, no. 1 (2013): 1–16. http://dx.doi.org/10.1111/edth .12006.

Hewett, Beth L. "Fully Online and Hybrid Writing Instruction." In *A Guide to Composition Pedagogies.* 2nd ed., edited by Gary Tate, Amy Rupiper Taggart, Kurt Schick, and H. Brooke Hessler, 194–211. New York: Oxford University Press, 2014.

Hill, Jean. *New Mexico Highlands University Self-Study Report.* Las Vegas: New Mexico Highlands University, 2009. Accessed January 12, 2015, http://its.nmhu.edu/IntranetUp loads/001808-self_study_i-93200943002.pdf.

Hillocks, George. *Research on Written Composition.* Urbana, IL: NCTE, 1986.

Hochschild, Arlie R. *The Managed Heart Commercialization of Human Feeling.* Berkeley: University of California Press, 1983.

Horner, Bruce, and Min-Zhan Lu. "Working Rhetoric and Composition." *College English* 72, no. 5 (2010): 470–94.

hooks, bell. *Teaching Community: A Pedagogy of Hope*. New York: Routledge, 2003.

hooks, bell. *Teaching to Transgress*. New York: Routledge, 1994.

Hull, Glynda. "Hearing Other Voices: A Critical Assessment of Popular Views on Literacy and Work." In *Literacy: A Critical Sourcebook*, edited by Ellen Cushman, Eugene R. Kintgen, Barry Kroll, and Mike Rose, 660–83. Boston, MA: Bedford St. Martin's, 2001.

"Hungry and Homeless in College." *The Kresge Foundation*, March 14, 2017. http://kr esge.org/library/hungry-and-homeless-college.

Hurst, Allison L. *The Burden of Academic Success: Loyalists, Renegades, and Double Agents*. Lanham, MA: Lexington Books, 2010.

Hurst, Allison L. *College and the Working Class: What It Takes to Make It*. Rotterdam: Sense, 2012. http://dx.doi.org/10.1007/978-94-6091-752-3.

Huws, Ursula. *The Making of a Cybertariat: Virtual Work in a Real World*. New York: Monthly Review Press, 2003.

ICF International. *Working for California: The Impact of the California State University System*. California State University. May 2010. https://www.calstate.edu/impact/docs/CSU ImpactsReport.pdf

Ivani , Roz. *Writing and Identity: The Discoursal Construction of Identity in Academic Writing*. Amsterdam: John Benjamins, 1998. http://dx.doi.org/10.1075/swll.5.

Jacobs, Bruce A. *Race Manners: Navigating the Minefield between Black and White Americans*. New York: Arcade, 1999.

Jaffe, Barbara. "Changing Perceptions, and Ultimately Practices, of Basic Writing Instructors through the *Familia* Approach." In *Teaching Writing with Latino/a Students: Lessons Learned at Hispanic-Serving Institutions*, edited by Cristina Kirklighter, Diana Cardenas, and Susan Wolff Murphy, 169–90. Albany: SUNY Press, 2007.

Jarratt, Susan C., Katherine Mack, Alexandra Sartor, and Shevaun E. Watson. "Pedagogical Memory: Writing, Mapping, Translating." *WPA: Writing Program Administration* 33, no. 1–2 (2009): 46–73.

Johnson, Daniel M., and David A. Bell. *Metropolitan Universities: An Emerging Model in American Higher Education*. Denton: University of North Texas Press, 1995.

Johnson, Hans. "Higher Education in California: New Goals for the Master Plan." Public Policy Institute of California. April 2010. http://www.ppic.org/main/publication.asp ?i=916.

Johnson-Sheehan, Richard, and Charles Paine. *Writing Today*. Boston, MA: Longman, 2013.

Johnstone, Barbara. "Locating Language in Identity." In *Language and Identities*, edited by Carmen Llamas and Dominic Watt, 29–36. Edinburgh: Edinburgh University Press, 2010.

Jones, Stephanie. *Girls, Social Class & Literacy: What Teachers Can Do to Make a Difference*. Portsmouth, NH: Heinemann, 2006.

Jones, Stephanie. "Making Sense of Injustices in a Classed World: Working-Poor Girls' Discursive Practices and Critical Literacies." *Pedagogies* 7, no. 1 (2012): 16–31. http://dx.doi .org/10.1080/1554480X.2012.630493.

Joshi, Prathibha V., Kris A. Beck, and Christian Nsiah. "Student Characteristics Affecting the Decision to Enroll in a Community College: Economic Rationale and Empirical Evidence." *Community College Journal of Research and Practice* 33, no. 10 (2009): 805–22. http://dx.doi.org/10.1080/10668920802708843.

Kasworm, Carol. "Adult Student Identity in an Intergenerational Community College Classroom." *Adult Education Quarterly* 56, no. 1 (2005): 3–20. http://dx.doi.org/10.1177 /0741713605280148.

Kasworm, Carol, and Gary R. Pike. "Adult Undergraduate Students: Evaluating the Appropriateness of a Traditional Model of Academic Performance." *Research in Higher Education* 35, no. 6 (1994): 689–710. http://dx.doi.org/10.1007/BF02497082.

Kelly, Lou. *From Dialogue to Discourse: An Open Approach to Competence and Creativity.* Glenview, IL: Scott Foresman, 1972.

Ketai, Rachel Lewis. "Race, Remediation, and Readiness: Reassessing the 'Self' in Directed Self-Placement." In *Race and Writing Assessment,* edited by Asao B. Inoue and Mya Poe, 155–68. New York: Peter Lang, 2012.

Kevern, J., Chris. Ricketts, and Christian Webb. "Pre-Registration Diploma Students: A Quantitative Study of Entry Characteristics and Course Outcomes." *Journal of Advanced Nursing* 30, no. 4 (1999): 785–95. http://dx.doi.org/10.1046/j.1365-2648.1999 .01175.x.

Kimmel, Michael. *Guyland: The Perilous World Where Boys Become Men.* New York: Harper Perennial, 2008.

Kinneavy, James, William McCleary, and Neil Nakadate. *Writing in the Liberal Arts Tradition.* New York: Harper and Row, 1990.

Kirby, Lisa A. "Cowboys of the High Seas: Representations of Working-Class Masculinity on Deadliest Catch." *Journal of Popular Culture* 46, no. 1 (2013): 109–18. http://dx.doi.org /10.1111/jpcu.12018.

Klausman, Jeffrey. "Mapping the Terrain: The Two-Year College Writing Program Administrator." *Teaching English in the Two-Year College* 35, no. 3 (2008): 238–51.

Krashen, Stephen. "Protecting Students Against the Effects of Poverty: Libraries." *New England Reading Association Journal* 46, no. 2 (2011): 17–21.

Lareau, Annette. *Unequal Childhoods: Class, Race, and Family Life.* Berkeley: University of California Press, 2003.

Leacock, Eleanor Burke. *The Culture of Poverty; a Critique.* New York: Simon and Schuster, 1971.

Leary, Mark R., Katharine M. Patton, Amy E. Orlando, and Wendy Wagoner Funk. "The Impostor Phenomenon: Self-Perceptions, Reflected Appraisals, and Interpersonal Strategies." *Journal of Personality* 68, no. 4 (2000): 725–56. http://dx.doi.org/10.1111/1467 -6494.00114.

LeCourt, Donna. *Identity Matters: Schooling the Student Body in Academic Discourse.* Albany: SUNY Press, 2004.

LeCourt, Donna. "Performing Working-Class Identity in Composition: Toward a Pedagogy of Textual Practice." *College English* 69, no. 1 (2006): 30–51. http://dx.doi.org/10.2307 /25472187.

Lewis, Oscar. *Five Families: Mexican Case Studies in the Culture of Poverty. A Mentor Book.* New York: New American Library, 1965.

Lindquist, Julie. "Class Affects, Classroom Affectations: Working through the Paradoxes of Strategic Empathy." *College English* 67, no. 2 (2004): 187–209. http://dx.doi.org/10 .2307/4140717.

Lindquist, Julie. *A Place to Stand: Politics and Persuasion in a Working-class Bar.* Oxford: Oxford University Press, 2002.

Lindquist, Julie, and David Seitz. *The Elements of Literacy.* New York: Longman, 2009.

Linkon, Sherry Lee, ed. Introduction to *Teaching Working Class,* edited by Sherry Lee Linkon, 5–6. Amherst: University of Massachusetts Press, 1999.

Lubrano, Alfred. *Limbo: Blue-Collar Roots, White-Collar Dreams.* Hoboken, NJ: John Wiley & Sons, 2004.

Lunsford, Andrea, and Karen Lunsford. "'Mistakes Are a Fact of Life': A National Comparative Study." *College Composition and Communication* 59, no. 4 (2008): 781–91.

Lytle, Susan L. "Living Literacy: Rethinking Development in Adulthood." In *Literacy: A Critical Sourcebook,* edited by Ellen Cushman, Eugene R. Kintgen, Barry Kroll, and Mike Rose, 376–401. Boston, MA: Bedford St. Martin's, 2001.

Mack, Nancy. "Being the Namer or the Named: Working-Class Discourse Conflicts." *JAC* 27, no. 1–2 (2007): 329–50.

Mack, Nancy. "Critical Memoir and Identity Formation: Being, Belonging, Becoming." In *Critical Expressivist Practices in the College Writing Classroom*, edited by Roseanne Gatto and Tara Roeder, 55–68. Anderson, SC: Parlor, 2014.

Mack, Nancy. "Ethical Representation of Working-Class Lives: Multiple Genres, Voices, and Identities." *Pedagogy* 6, no. 1 (2006): 53–78. http://dx.doi.org/10.1215/15314200-6-1-53.

MacRorie, Ken. *Uptaught: A Professor Discovers His Students on the Way to a New University.* Rochelle Park, NJ: Hayden, 1970.

Mahala, Daniel, and Jody Swilky. "Telling Stories, Speaking Personally: Reconsidering the Place of Lived Experience in Composition." *JAC* 16, no. 3 (1996): 363–88.

Mahle-Grisez, Lisa. "Reframing the Seductive Narrative of 'Success' in Open Admissions." *Open Words* 4, no. 2 (2010): 48–65.

Martin, Jonathan. "Pedagogy of the Alienated: Can Freirian Teaching Reach Working Class Students?" *Equity & Excellence in Education* 41, no. 1 (2008): 31–44. http://dx.doi.org/10.1080/10665680701773776.

Martin, Justin. *Rebel Souls: Walt Whitman and America's First Bohemians.* Philadelphia, PA: Da Capo, 2014.

Mavrogiannis, Sophia. Introduction to *Pipe Dreams: A Manifesto for Local 1 Apprentices*, edited by Sophia Mavrogiannis, Rebecca Fraser, and Thomas Kerr, 1–3. Saratoga Springs: SUNY Empire State College, 2011.

Mayers, Tim, Leann Bertoncini, and Sharon O'Dair. "Two Comments on Sharon O'Dair's 'Class Work: Site of Egalitarian Activism of Site of Embourgeoisement?'" *College English* 66, no. 5 (2004): 558–65. http://dx.doi.org/10.2307/4140736.

McCarty, Teresa. *Language, Literacy, and Power in Schooling.* Mahwah, NJ: Erlbaum, 2005.

McComiskey, Bruce. *Teaching Composition as a Social Process.* Logan: Utah State University Press, 2000.

McCrimmon, James. *Writing with a Purpose.* 3rd ed. Boston: Houghton Mifflin, 1963.

McIntosh, Peggy. "White Privilege and Male Privilege: A Personal Account of Coming to See Correspondences Through Work in Women's Studies." College Art Association. Wellesley: Center for Research on Women, 1988.

Makinen, Judy A., and Timothy A. Pychyl. "The Differential Effects of Project Stress on Life-Satisfaction." *Social Indicators Research* 53, no. 1 (2001): 1–16. http://dx.doi.org/10.1023/A:1007140527056.

Merriam, Sharon B., Rosemary S. Caffarella, and Lisa M. Baumgartner. *Learning in Adulthood: A Comprehensive Guide.* 3rd ed. San Francisco, CA: Jossey-Bass, 2007.

Merrill, Michael. "About the Van Arsdale Center." The Harry Van Arsdale Jr. Center for Labor Studies. Saratoga Springs: SUNY Empire State College, 2016. https://www.esc.edu/labor-studies-center/labor-studies-program/.

Merrill, Michael. "Why Trade Unionists Need to Go to College." Accessed February 5, 2015. https://www.esc.edu/labor-studies-center/labor-studies-program.

Messner, Michael. *Politics of Masculinity: Men in Movements.* Lanham, MD: AltaMira, 2000.

Metzgar, Jack. "Are 'the Poor' Part of the Working Class or in a Class by Themselves?" *Labor Studies Journal* 35, no. 3 (2010): 398–416. http://dx.doi.org/10.1177/0160449X09335472.

Micciche, Laura. "When Class Equals Crass: A Working-Class Student's Ways with Anger." In *Blundering for a Change: Errors and Expectations in Critical Pedagogy*, edited by John Paul Tassoni and William H. Thelin, 24–36. Portsmouth, NH: Boynton/Cook, 2000.

Michigan Almanac." Office of Budget and Planning at the University of Michigan. 5th ed. Ann Arbor: University of Michigan, 2015.

Miley, Michelle. "Thirdspace Explorations in Online Writing Studios: Writing Centers, Writing in the Disciplines, and First Year Composition in the Corporate University." PhD diss., University of Houston, 2013.

Moffett, James. *Teaching the Universe of Discourse.* Boston, MA: Houghton Mifflin, 1968.

Mogey, Nora. "Evaluation Cookbook: So You Want to Use a Likert Scale?" Learning Technology Dissemination Initiative. Last modified March 25, 1999. http://www.icbl.hw .ac.uk/ltdi/cookbook/info_likert_scale/index.html.

Moran, Charles. "Technology and the Teaching of Writing." In *A Guide to Composition Pedagogies*, edited by Gary Tate, Amy Rupiper, and Kurt Schick, 203–23. New York: Oxford University Press, 2001.

Morrison, Mary K. "The Old Lady in the Student Lounge: Integrating the Adult Female Student into the College Classroom." In *Two-Year College English: Essays for a New Century*, edited by Mark Reynolds, 26–36. Urbana, IL: NCTE, 1994.

Mutnick, Deborah. "Rethinking the Personal Narrative: Life-Writing and Composition Pedagogy." In *Under Construction: Working at the Intersections of Composition Theory, Research, and Practice*, edited by Christine Farris and Chris M. Anson, 79–92. Logan: Utah State University Press, 1998.

Muzzatti, Stephen L., and C. Vincent Samarco. *Reflections from the Wrong Side of the Tracks: Class, Identity, and the Working Class Experience in Academe*. Lanham, MD: Rowman and Littlefield, 2006.

Navajo Nation Regional Partnership Council. *2010 Needs and Assets Report: Navajo Nation.* August 31, 2010. http://www.azftf.gov/WhoWeAre/Board/Documents/Sept27,10%20 Board%20Materials/Attachment_11l_Navajo%20Nation%20_NA_2010%20RPT.pdf.

New York College of Technology. "About City Tech." CUNY. Accessed June 10, 2015. http://www.citytech.cuny.edu/aboutus/collegefacts.shtml.

New York City College of Technology. City University of New York, System Retention and Graduation Rates of Full-Time First-Time Freshman in Associate Programs by Year of Entry: NYCCT. CUNY. Accessed June 10, 2015. http://www.cuny.edu/irdatabook /rpts2_AY_current/RTGS_0001_FT_FTFR_ASSOC_COMP-NY.pdf.

New York College of Technology. "New York City College of Technology: Facts 2014–15." CUNY. Accessed June 10, 2015. http://www.citytech.cuny.edu/files/aboutus/facts .pdf.

Nieto, Sonia. *Language, Culture, and Teaching: Critical Perspectives.* 2nd ed. New York: Rout-ledge, 2010.

"Non-traditional Students Benefit from CSU Plan." *SFGate*, March 17, 2000. http://www.sf gate.com/opinion/editorials/article/Non-Traditional-Students-Benefit-from-CSU -Plan-2795199.php.

Nowacek, Rebecca. *Agents of Integration: Understanding Transfer as a Rhetorical Act.* Carbondale: Southern Illinois University Press, 2011.

O'Brien, Tim. *The Things They Carried.* New York: Houghton Mifflin, 1991.

O'Connor, Alice. "Poverty and Paradox." *Hedgehog Review* 6, no. 3 (November 2014): 20–29.

O'Neill, Peggy, Cindy Moore, and Brian Huot. *A Guide to College Writing Assessment.* Logan: Utah State University Press, 2009.

Ogbu, John, and Herbert Simons. "Voluntary and Involuntary Minorities: A Cultural-ecological Theory of School Performance with Some Implications for Education." *Anthropology & Education Quarterly* 29, no. 2 (1998): 155–88. http://dx.doi.org/10.1525/aeq.1998.29 .2.155.

O'Keefe, Patrick. "A Sense of Belonging: Improving Student Retention." *College Student Journal* 47, no. 4 (2013): 605–13.

Oldfield, Kenneth, and Richard Greggory Johnson. *Resilience: Queer Professors from the Working Class.* Albany: SUNY Press, 2009.

Oliver, Kelly. *Witnessing: Beyond Recognition.* Minneapolis: University of Minnesota Press, 2001.

Olson, Gary, and Lynn Worsham. *Rhetoric and Composition as Intellectual Work.* Carbondale: Southern Illinois University Press, 2002.

Orellana, Marjorie Faulstich. "Moving Words and Worlds: Reflections from 'the Middle.'" In *Reframing Sociocultural Research on Literacy: Identity, Agency, and Power*, edited by Cynthia Lewis, Patricia Enciso, and Elizabeth Birr Moje, 123–36. New York: Routledge, 2009.

Pajares, Frank. "Self-Efficacy Beliefs, Motivation, and Achievement in Writing: A Review of the Literature." *Reading & Writing Quarterly* 19, no. 2 (2003): 139–58. http://dx.doi.org /10.1080/10573560308222.

Parenti, Michael. *Land of Idols: Political Mythology in America*. New York: Bedford St. Martin's, 1994.

Park, Gloria. "'Writing IS a Way of Knowing': Writing and Identity." *ELT Journal* 67, no. 3 (2013): 336–45. http://dx.doi.org/10.1093/elt/cct012.

Parks, Steve, and Nick Pollard. "Emergent Strategies for an Established Field: The Role of Worker-Writer Collectives in Composition and Rhetoric." *College Composition and Communication* 61, no. 3 (2010): 476–509.

Pascarella, Ernest T., Christopher T. Pierson, Gregory C. Wolniak, and Patrick T. Terenzini. "First-Generation College Students: Additional Evidence on College Experiences and Outcomes." *The Journal of Higher Education* 75, no. 3 (May–June 2004): 249–84.

Pascoe, C. J. *Dude, You're a Fag: Masculinity and Sexuality in High School*. Berkeley: University of California Press, 2007.

Peary, Alexandria. "The Hidden Ethos Inside Process Pedagogy." *Pedagogy* 14, no. 2 (2014): 289–315. http://dx.doi.org/10.1215/15314200-2400512.

Peckham, Irvin. "Complicity in Class Codes: The Exclusionary Function of Education." In *This Fine Place So Far from Home: Voices of Academics From the Working Class*, edited by C. L. Barney Dewes, and Carolyn Leste Law, 263–76. Philadelphia, PA: Temple University Press, 1995.

Peckham, Irvin. *Going North Thinking West: The Intersections of Social Class, Critical Thinking, and Politicized Writing Instruction*. Logan: Utah State University Press, 2010.

"Pell Grants: The Cornerstone of African-American Higher Education." *Journal of Blacks in Higher Education*, 2010. Accessed February 2015. http://www.jbhe.com/features/65_pell grants.html.

Penrose, Ann M. "Academic Literacy Perceptions and Performance: Comparing First-Generation and Continuing-Generation College Students." *Research in the Teaching of English* 36, no. 4 (2002): 437–61.

Petraglia, Joseph, ed. *Reconceiving Writing, Rethinking Writing*. Mahwah, NJ: Erlbaum, 1995.

Pew Research Center. "Most See Inequality Growing, but Partisans Differ over Solutions." Pew Research Center. January 23, 2014. http://www.people-press.org/2014/01/23/most -see-inequality-growing-but-partisans-differ-over-solutions/.

Piff, Paul K., Daniel M. Stancato, Stéphane Côté, Rodolfo Mendoza-Denton, and Dacher Keltner. "Higher Social Class Predicts Increased Unethical Behavior." *Proceedings of the National Academy of Sciences of the United States of America* 109, no. 11 (2012): 4086–91. http://dx.doi.org/10.1073/pnas.1118373109.

Piketty, Thomas. *Capital in the Twenty-First Century*. Cambridge, MA: Belknap, 2014. http://dx .doi.org/10.4159/9780674369542.

Pincus, Fred L. "The False Promises of Community Colleges: Class Conflict and Vocational Education." *Harvard Educational Review* 50, no. 3 (1980): 332–61. http://dx.doi.org /10.17763/haer.50.3.y733663386302231.

Pollack, William. *Real Boys: Rescuing Our Sons from the Myths of Boyhood*. New York: Henry Holt, 1998.

Postman, Neil, and Charles Weingartner. *Teaching as a Subversive Activity: A No-Holds-Barred Assault on Outdated Teaching Methods-with Dramatic and Practical Proposals on How Education Can Be Made Relevant to Today's World*. New York: Dell Publishing, 1969.

Powell, Pegeen Reichert. *Retention and Resistance: Writing Instruction and Students Who Leave*. Logan: Utah State University Press, 2013.

Pratt, Mary Louise. "Arts of the Contact Zone." *Profession* 91 (1991): 33–40.

Prelli, Lawrence J., Floyd D. Anderson, and Matthew T. Althouse. "Kenneth Burke on Recalcitrance." *Rhetoric Society Quarterly* 41, no. 2 (2011): 97–124. http://dx.doi.org/10.1080/02773945.2011.553768.

Preston, Jacqueline. "The Fertile Commonplace: Collective Persuasions, Interpretive Acts, and Dialectical Spaces." PhD diss., University of Wisconsin–Madison, 2011.

Preston, Jacqueline. "(Project)ing Literacy: Writing to Assemble in Postcomposition FYW Classroom." *College Composition and Communication* 67, no. 1 (2015): 35–63.

Probyn, Elspeth. *Blush: Faces of Shame.* Minneapolis: University of Minnesota Press, 2005.

Provasnik, Stephen, and Michael Planty. *Community Colleges: Special Supplement to The Condition of Education 2008: Statistical Analysis Report. NCES 2008–033.* Washington, DC: National Center for Education Statistics, 2008.

Pryor, John, Kevin Eagan, Laura Palucki Blake, Sylvia Hurtado, Jennifer Berdan, and Matthew H. Case. *The American Freshman: National Norms Fall 2012.* Los Angeles: Higher Education Research Institute, 2012.

Quinnan, Timothy William. *Adult Students "At-Risk": Culture Bias in Higher Education.* Westport, CT: Bergin & Garvey, 1997.

Ranciere, Jacques. *Preface to Proletarian Night (1981).* Abahlali baseMjondolo. Umhlaba Izindlu neSithunzi Land Housing Dignity, n.d. http://abahlali.org/files/proletarian_nights_excerpt.pdf.

Ratcliffe, Krista. *Rhetorical Listening: Identification, Whiteness, Gender.* Carbondale: University of Southern Illinois Press, 2005.

Ray, Emma Bah, David H. Holben, and John P. Holcomb. "Food Security Status and Produce Intake Behaviors, Health Status, and Diabetes Risk among Women with Children Living on a Navajo Reservation." *Journal of Hunger & Environmental Nutrition* 7, no. 1 (2012): 91–100. http://dx.doi.org/10.1080/19320248.2012.649670.

Redd, Teresa M. "'Tryin to Make a Dolla Outa Fifteen Cent': Teaching Composition with the Internet at an HBCU." *Computers and Composition* 20, no. 4 (2003): 359–73. http://dx.doi.org/10.1016/j.compcom.2003.08.012.

Reiff, Mary Jo, and Anis Bawarshi. "Tracing Discursive Resources: How Students Use Prior Genre Knowledge to Negotiate New Writing Contexts in First-Year Composition." *Written Communication* 28, no. 3 (2011): 312–37. http://dx.doi.org/10.1177/0741088311410183.

Renny, Christopher. "New Working-Class Studies in Higher Education." In *New Working Class Studies,* edited by John Russo and Sherry Lee Linkon, 209–20. Ithaca, NY: Cornell University Press, 2005.

Reyes, Kathryn Blackmer, and Julia E. Curry Rodriguez. "'Testimonio': Origins, Terms, and Resources." *Equity & Excellence in Education* 45, no. 3 (2012): 525–38. http://dx.doi.org/10.1080/10665684.2012.698571.

Reynolds, Thomas J., and Charles R. Lewis. "The Changing Topography of Computer Access for Composition Students." *Computers and Composition* 14, no. 2 (1997): 269–78. http://dx.doi.org/10.1016/S8755-4615(97)90027-X.

Ribero, Ana. "Global Voices: DePaul Voices on Linguistic Diversity." University Center for Writing-Based Learning. Chicago, IL: DePaul University, 2011–12.

Ricoeur, Paul. *Freud and Philosophy: An Essay on Interpretation.* New Haven, CT: Yale University Press, 1977.

Rist, Ray. *The Urban School: A Factory for Failure.* Piscataway, NJ: Transaction, 2002.

Robinson, Bill, William S. Robinson, and Pam Altman. *Integrations: Reading, Thinking, and Writing for College Success.* London: Engage, 2003.

Robinson, Jay L. "Literacy in the Department of English." *College English* 47, no. 5 (September 1985): 482–98.

Rochkind, Jon, and Jean Johnson. "How Higher Education Can Support Working Students." *Diversity & Democracy* 13, no. 3 (2010): 8–9.

Rose, Mike. *Back to School: Why Everyone Deserves a Second Chance at Education.* New York: New Press, 2012.

Rose, Mike. "The Language of Exclusion: Writing Instruction at the University." *College English* 47, no. 4 (1985): 341–59. http://dx.doi.org/10.2307/376957.

Rose, Mike. *Lives on the Boundary: A Moving Account of the Struggles and Achievements of America's Educationally Underprepared.* New York: Penguin Books, 2005.

Rose, Mike. *The Mind at Work: Valuing the Intelligence of the American Worker.* New York: Penguin, 2004.

Rose, Mike, Why School: Reclaiming Education for All of Us . New York: New Press, 2014.

Rounsaville, Angela, Rachel Goldberg, and Anis Bawarshi. "From Incomes to Outcomes: FYW Students' Prior Genre Knowledge, Meta-Cognition, and the Question of Transfer." *WPA: Writing Program Administration* 32, no. 1 (2008): 97–112.

"Rural Students: Common Obstacles, Different Settings." *Chronicle of Higher Education,* November 3, 2006. http://www.chronicle.com/article/Rural-Students-Common/3 1372.

Saavedra, Cinthya M. "Language and Literacy in the Borderlands: Acting upon the World through 'Testimonios.'" *Language Arts* 88, no. 4 (2011): 261–69.

Salisbury University. "Salisbury University Mission Statement 2014." Accessed February 2015. http://www.salisbury.edu/Info/mission.html.

Samuel-Nakamura, Christine. "Uranium and Other Heavy Metals in the Plant-Animal-Human Food Chain near Abandoned Mining Sites and Structures in an American Indian Community in Northwestern New Mexico." PhD diss., University of California, Los Angeles, 2013. http://escholarship.org/uc/item/9w29f7d6.pdf.

San Antonio, Donna Marie. *Adolescent Lives in Transition: How Social Class Influences the Adjustment to Middle School.* New York: SUNY Press, 2004.

Sánchez, Raúl. *The Function of Theory in Composition Studies.* New York: SUNY Press, 2012.

Sarup, Madan. *Identity Culture and the Postmodern World.* Athens: University of Georgia Press, 1996.

Sayer, Andrew. *The Moral Significance of Class.* Cambridge: Cambridge University Press, 2005. http://dx.doi.org/10.1017/CBO9780511488863.

Scharf, Adria. "Scripted Talk." In *The Changing World of Work,* edited by Marjorie Ford, 105–12. New York: Pearson, 2006.

Schendel, Ellen, and Peggy O'Neill. "Exploring the Theories and Consequences of Self-Assessment through Ethical Inquiry." *Assessing Writing* 6, no. 2 (1999): 199–227. http://dx .doi.org/10.1016/S1075-2935(00)00008-8.

Schon, Donald A. *Beyond the Stable State.* San Francisco, CA: Jossey-Bass, 1971.

Schwartz, Pepper. "The Social Construction of Heterosexuality." In *Composing Gender,* edited by Rachel Groner and John F. O'Hara, 186–203. New York: Bedford St. Martin's, 2014.

Scott, J. Blake. "The Literacy Narrative as Production Pedagogy in the Composition Classroom." *Teaching English in the Two-Year College* 24, no. 2 (1997): 108–17.

Scott, Tony. "Creating the Subject of Portfolios: Reflective Writing and the Conveyance of Institutional Prerogatives." *Written Communication* 22, no. 1 (2005): 3–35. http://dx .doi.org/10.1177/0741088304271831.

Scott, Tony. "Writing Work, Technology, and Pedagogy in the Era of Late Capitalism." *Computers and Composition* 23, no. 2 (2006): 228–43. http://dx.doi.org/10.1016/j.comp com.2005.08.008.

Sedgwick, Eve Kosofsky. *Epistemology of the Closet.* Berkley: University of California Press, 1990.

Seider, Scott C., Samantha A. Rabinowicz, and Susan C. Gillmor. "Changing American College Students' Conceptions of Poverty through Community Service Learning." *ASAP: Analyses of Social Issues and Public Policy* 11, no. 1 (2011): 105–26. http://dx.doi.org /10.1111/j.1530-2415.2010.01224.x.

Seidman, Irving. *Interviewing as Qualitative Research.* 4th ed. New York: Teachers College Press, 2012.

Seitz, David. "Making Work Visible." *College English* 67, no. 2 (2004): 210–21. http://dx.doi.org /10.2307/4140718.

Seitz, David. *Who Can Afford Critical Consciousness?: Practicing a Pedagogy of Humility.* New York: Hampton, 2004.

Selfe, Cynthia L., and Gail E. Hawisher. *Literate Lives in the Information Age: Narratives of Literacy from the United States.* Mahwah, NJ: Erlbaum, 2004.

Sennett, Richard, and Jonathan Cobb. *The Hidden Injuries of Class.* New York: Alfred A. Knopf, 1972.

Shinji, Ikari. "The Value of the Things I Carry Daily." In *Labor Writes 2014,* edited by Rebecca Fraser, Thomas Kerr, MaryHelen Kolisnyk, Sophia Mavrogiannis, Keisha Spradley, Desmond Palmer, and Chris Vallario, 36–37. Saratoga Springs: SUNY Empire State College, 2014.

Shor, Ira. *Critical Teaching and Everyday Life.* Boston, MA: South End, 1989.

Shor, Ira. *Empowering Education: Critical Teaching for Social Change.* Chicago: University of Chicago Press, 1992.

Shor, Ira. *When Students Have Power: Negotiating Authority in a Critical Pedagogy.* Chicago, IL: University of Chicago Press, 1997.

Shor, Ira. "Why Teach about Social Class?" *Teaching English in the Two-Year College* 33, no. 2 (2005): 161–70.

Siefer, Angela. *The Internet Is Important to Everyone.* OCLC WebJunction. September 18, 2013. http://www.webjunction.org/news/webjunction/the-internet-is-important-to-everyone.html.

Silva, Jennifer. *Coming Up Short: Working-Class Adulthood in an Age of Uncertainty.* Oxford: Oxford University Press, 2013. http://dx.doi.org/10.1093/acprof:oso/9780199931460.001.0001.

Skeggs, Beverley. "Imagining Personhood Differently: Person Value and Autonomist Working-Class Value Practices." *Sociological Review* 59, no. 3 (2011): 496–513. http://dx .doi.org/10.1111/j.1467-954X.2011.02018.x.

Skeggs, Beverley. "New Formations of Spectacular Selves." Economic and Social Research Council ESRC Identities and Social Action Programme Launch. UK Economic and Social Research Council, 2005. https://www.gold.ac.uk/media/documents-by-section /departments/research-centres-and-units/research-centres/centre-for-urban-and -comm/IdentitiesProjectNewFormationsOfSpectatularSelves.pdf.

Soliday, Mary. "Translating Self and Difference through Literacy Narratives." *College English* 56, no. 5 (1994): 511–26. http://dx.doi.org/10.2307/378604.

Steck, Laura West, Jennifer N. Engler, Mary Ligon, and Erin Cosgrove. "Doing Poverty Learning Outcomes among Students Participating in the Community Action Poverty Simulation Program." *Teaching Sociology* 39, no. 3 (2011): 259–73. http://dx.doi.org/10 .1177/0092055X11407347.

Stein, Wayne J. *Tribally Controlled Colleges: Making Good Medicine.* Vol. 3, American Indian Studies. New York: Peter Lang, 1992.

Stenberg, Shari, and Amy Lee. "Developing Pedagogies: Learning the Teaching of English." *College English* 64, no. 3 (2002): 326–47. http://dx.doi.org/10.2307/3250737.

Stephens, Nicole. "A Cultural Mismatch: The Experience of First-Generation College Students in Elite Universities." PhD diss., Stanford University, 2009.

Stephens, Nicole M., Hazel Rose Markus, and Sarah M. Townsend. "Choice as an Act of Meaning: The Case of Social Class." *Journal of Personality and Social Psychology* 93 (2007): 814–30. http://dx.doi.org/10.1037/0022-3514.93.5.814

Stephens, Nicole, Stephanie A. Fryberg, and Hazel Rose Markus. "When Choice Does Not Equal Freedom: A Sociocultural Analysis of Agency in Working-Class American Contexts." *Social Psychology and Personality Science* 2 (2011): 33–41. http://dx.doi.org/10 .1177/1948550610378757.

Stephens, Nicole, Stephanie A. Fryberg, Hazel Rose Markus, Camille S. Johnson, and Rebecca Covarrubias. "Unseen Disadvantage: How American Universities' Focus on Independence Undermines the Academic Performance of First-Generation College Students." *Journal of Personality and Social Psychology* 102, no. 6 (2012): 1178–97. http://dx .doi.org/10.1037/a0027143.

Sternglass, Marilyn S. *Time to Know Them: A Longitudinal Study of Writing and Learning at the College Level.* Mahweh, NJ: Erlbaum, 1997.

Street, Brian V. *Literacy in Theory and Practice.* Cambridge: Cambridge University Press, 1984.

Stuber, Jenny Marie. "Integrated, Marginal, and Resilient: Race, Class, and the Diverse Experiences of White First-Generation College Students." *QSE: International Journal of Qualitative Studies in Education* 24, no. 1 (2011): 117–36. http://dx.doi.org/10.1080 /09518391003641916.

Stuckey, Elspeth. *The Violence of Literacy.* Portsmouth, NH: Heinemann, 1991.

Sullivan, Patrick. "An Essential Question: What Is 'College-Level' Writing?" In *What Is "College-Level" Writing?*, edited by Patrick Sullivan and Howard Tinberg, 1–28. Urbana, IL: NCTE, 2006.

Taylor, Denny, and Catherine Dorsey-Gaines. *Growing Up Literate.* Portsmouth, NH: Heinemann, 1988.

Taylor, Mac. "Initial Review of CSU's Early Start Program." A Legislative Analyst's Office (LAO) Brief. January 2014. http://www.lao.ca.gov/reports/2014/education/early -start/CSU-Early-Start-011414.pdf.

Terenzini, Patrick T., Leonard Springer, Patricia M. Yaeger, Ernest T. Pascarella, and Amaury Nora. "First-Generation College Students: Characteristics, Experiences, and Cognitive Development." *Research in Higher Education* 37, no. 1 (1996): 1–22. http://dx .doi.org/10.1007/BF01680039.

Thomas, Paul, Brad J. Porfilio, Julie Gorlewski, and Paul R. Carr, eds. *Social Context Reform: A Pedagogy of Equity and Opportunity.* New York: Routledge, 2014.

Thompson, Stephanie. "Bridging ESL and Academic English: Opening Literacy Narratives to Code-Meshing." Paper presented at the Conference on College Composition and Communication Convention, Indianapolis, IN, March 22, 2014.

Thurston, Kay. "Mitigating Barriers to Navajo Students' Success in English Courses." *Teaching English in the Two-Year College* 26, no. 1 (1998): 29–38.

Tinberg, Howard B. *Border Talk: Writing and Knowing in the Two-Year College.* Urbana, IL: NCTE 1997.

Tinberg, Howard. "Theory as Healing." *Teaching English in the Two-Year College* 24, no. 4 (1997): 282–90.

Tingle, Nick. "Opinion: The Vexation of Class." *College English* 67, no. 2 (2004): 222–30. http://dx.doi.org/10.2307/4140719.

Tokarczyk, Michelle M., and Elizabeth A. Fay. *Working-Class Women in the Academy: Laborers in the Knowledge Factory.* Amherst: University of Massachusetts Press, 1993.

Trudgill, Peter. *Sociolinguistics: An Introduction to Language and Society.* New York: Penguin, 2000.

Tuck, Eve. "Suspending Damage: A Letter to Communities." *Harvard Educational Review* 79, no. 3 (2009): 409–27. http://dx.doi.org/10.17763/haer.79.3.n0016675661t3n15.

Uehling, Karen. "Older and Younger Adults Writing Together: A Rich Learning Community." *Writing Instructor* 15, no. 2 (1996): 61–69.

United States Census Bureau. "Poverty." United States Census. Last revised September 16, 2016. https://www.census.gov/hhes/www/poverty/data/.

United States Census Bureau. "Glossary." *Poverty.* Accessed February 16, 2017. https://www .census.gov/topics/income-poverty/poverty/about/glossary.html.

US Department of Education. National Center for Education Statistics. *Digest of Education Statistics,* table 329. NCES, 2008. https://nces.ed.gov/programs/digest/d08/tables/dt 08_329.asp.

US Department of Education. Office of Postsecondary Education. "Federal TRIO Programs: Current-Year Low-Income Levels." US Department of Education. Last modified March 8, 2016. https://www2.ed.gov/about/offices/list/ope/trio/incomelevels.html

US Department of Education Office of Postsecondary Education. "Federal TRIO Programs—Home Page." Last modified December 12, 2016. https://www2.ed.gov/about /offices/list/ope/trio/index.html?exp=4.

US Department of Education. "No Child Left Behind: Elementary and Secondary Education Act." https://www2.ed.gov/nclb/landing,jhtml.

US Department of Education. "Technology Literacy Challenge Fund." Archived Information. Last modified March 4, 2003. https://www2.ed.gov/offices/OESE/SST/tlcf.html.

US Department of Health and Human Services. "2014 Poverty Guidelines." ASPE: Office of the Assistant Secretary for Planning and Evaluation. December 1, 2014. https://aspe .hhs.gov/poverty/14poverty.cfm.

US Department of Labor. Bureau of Labor Statistics. "Occupational Outlook Handbook." 2015. https://www.bls.gov/ooh/.

University of Michigan Office of Budget and Planning. "The Michigan Almanac." Accessed February 14, 2015. http://obp.umich.edu/wp-content/uploads/almanac/Almanac _Ch3_Dec2013.pdf.

University of Michigan Mission and Integrity. "Mission Statement." 2009. http://www.acc reditation.umich.edu/mission/.

University of Michigan Office of the Registrar. "University of Michigan Total Enrollment Overview." 2014. http://www.ro.umich.edu/report/14enrollmentsummary.pdf.

University of Michigan Student Life Research. "What Proportion of UM Students Are First-Generation?" 2016. https://studentlife.umich.edu/research/article/what-proportion -um-students-are-first-generation-4.

University of Michigan Student Profile Comparison with Other Highly Selective Public and Very Highly Selective Private Institutions. University of Michigan. 2013. http://www.crlt.umich.edu /sites/default/files/resource_files/StudentProfileDatafor2013.pdf.

University of New Mexico. "UNM's Mission." http://www.unm.edu/welcome/mission .html.

Valadez, James R. "Searching for a Path out of Poverty: Exploring the Achievement Ideology of a Rural Community College." *Adult Education Quarterly* 50, no. 3 (2000): 212–30. http://dx.doi.org/10.1177/07417130022087017.

Veracini, Lorenzo. *Settler Colonialism: A Theoretical Overview.* New York: Palgrave, 2010. http://dx.doi.org/10.1057/9780230299191.

Verdi, Gail, and Miriam Eisenstein Ebsworth. "Working-Class Women Academics: Four Sociolinguistic Journeys." *Journal of Multicultural Discourses* 4, no. 2 (2009): 183–204. http://dx.doi.org/10.1080/17447140802372788.

Villanueva, Victor. "The Political Economy of Basic Writers." Paper presented at the Annual Convention of the Conference on College Composition and Communication, Indianapolis, IN, March 19–22, 2013.

Virtanen, Beth L. "Working-Class Students in Higher Education: Playing on an Uneven Field." *Michigan Academician* 34 (2003): 445–75.

Wardle, Elizabeth A., and Doug Downs. *Writing about Writing: A College Reader.* Boston, MA: Bedford St. Martin's, 2014.

Warren, Carol A. B., and Tracy Xavia Karner. *Discovering Qualitative Methods: Field Research, Interviews and Analysis.* New York: Oxford University Press, 2010.

Warren, Stephen. "Grandmothers in the Classroom: How College English Teachers Can Help Those Non-Traditional Students." Paper presented at the 23rd annual meeting of the College English Association, Pittsburgh, PA, March 27–29, 1992.

Watson, Anne, Michael Kehler, and Wayne Martino. "The Problem with Boys' Literacy Underachievement: Raising Some Questions." *Journal of Adolescent & Adult Literacy* 53, no. 5 (2010): 356–61. http://dx.doi.org/10.1598/JAAL.53.5.1.

Watters, Audrey. "Is It Time to Give Up on Computers in Schools?" *Hybrid Pedagogy*, June 30, 2015. http://www.hybridpedagogy.com/journal/is-it-time-to-give-up-on-computers-in-schools/.

Weber, Max. *Economy and Society*. Berkeley: University of California Press, 1978.

Welsch, Kathleen A. *Those Winter Sundays: Female Academics and Their Working-Class Parents*. Lanham, MA: University Press of America, 2005.

Weisberger, Ronald. "Community Colleges and Class: A Short History." *Teaching English in the Two-Year College* 33, no. 2 (2005): 127–41.

Wenger, Etienne. *Communities of Practice: Learning, Meaning, and Identity*. Cambridge: Cambridge University Press, 1998. http://dx.doi.org/10.1017/CBO9780511803932.

West, Candace, and Don H. Zimmerman. "Doing Gender." *Gender & Society* 1, no. 2 (1987): 125–51. http://dx.doi.org/10.1177/0891243287001002002.

Williams, Bronwyn T. "Heroes, Rebels, and Victims: Student Identities in Literacy Narratives." *Journal of Adolescent & Adult Literacy* 47, no. 4 (2003): 342–45.

Williams, David Cratis. "Kenneth Burke as Dialectician: Seminar Report." *Kenneth Burke Society Newsletter* 9, no. 1 (December 1993): 17–18, 20.

Wordsworth, William. *Preface to Lyrical Ballads*. Famous Prefaces. The Harvard Classics, 1909–14. Bartleyby.com. http://www.bartleby.com/39/36.html.

Yancey, Kathleen Blake. *Reflection in the Writing Classroom*. Logan: Utah State University Press, 1998.

Young, Vershawn Ashanti. "'Nah, We Straight': An Argument Against Code Switching." *Journal of Advanced Composition* 29, no. 1–2 (2009): 49–76.

Zebroski, James Thomas. *Thinking Through Theory: Vygotskian Perspectives on the Teaching of Writing*. Portsmouth, NH: Boynton/Cook, 1994.

Zebroski, James T. "The Political Economy of English: The 'Capital' of Literature, Creative Writing, and Composition." In *Economies of Writing: Revaluations in Rhetoric and Composition*, ed. Bruce Horner, Brice Nordquist, and Susan Ryan, 68–84. Logan: Utah State University Press, 2017.

Zembylas, Michalinos. *Teaching with Emotion: A Postmodern Enactment*. Greenwich: Information Age, 2005.

Zorn, Diana M. "Enactive Education: Dynamic Co-Emergence, Complexity, Experience, and the Embodied Mind." PhD thesis, University of Toronto, 2011.

Zweig, Michael. "Six Points on Class." *Monthly Review* 58, no. 3 (July-August 2006). http://dx.doi.org/10.14452/MR-058-03-2006-07_11.

Zweig, Michael. *The Working Class Majority: America's Best Kept Secret*. Ithaca: Cornell University Press, 2012.

ABOUT THE AUTHORS

AARON BARLOW teaches at New York City College of Technology (CUNY). His recent work includes editing *Doughboys on the Western Front: Memories of American Soldiers in the Great War* and writing *The Depression Era: A Historical Exploration of Literature*. He is faculty editor of *Academe*, the magazine of the American Association of University Professors.

CORI BREWSTER is professor of writing and rhetoric at Eastern Oregon University and board chair of Oregon Rural Action, a grassroots organization working for social and environmental justice in northeast Oregon. Her work on rural rhetorics and literacies has appeared in several collections, including *Reclaiming the Rural* (Donehower, Hogg, and Schell 2012), *The Ecopolitics of Consumption* (Davis, Pilgrim, and Sinha 2015), and *Crossing Borders, Drawing Boundaries* (Wojhan and Couture 2016). Her article "Basic Writing through the Back Door: Community-Engaged Courses in the Rush-to-Credit Age" was selected for inclusion in *Best of the Independent Rhetoric and Composition Journals, 2015*. Her current work focuses on public agricultural rhetorics and the rhetorics of race, access, and rurality in public higher education.

GENESEA M. CARTER is an assistant professor of English and the associate director of Composition at Colorado State University. Her work, which has appeared in *Composition Studies, Journal of Teaching Writing*, and elsewhere, focuses on digital literacy, multimodal pedagogy, access, and posthuman rhetorics. She blogs about life, happiness, and motivation at geneseacarter.com.

PATRICK CORBETT is an assistant professor of English at New York City College of Technology (CUNY), where he teaches courses in professional and technical writing, first-year writing, and linguistics. He had worked previously in diverse fields including textile manufacturing, information technology, healthcare policy research, and motion picture development before becoming a teacher and scholar of writing. Patrick's research focuses on the unseen activities and cultural dimensions found in the everyday use of communications tools.

HARRY DENNY, associate professor of English, directs the Writing Lab at Purdue University. His scholarship focuses on composition studies, writing center theory and practice, cultural studies, and research methods. Harry's first monograph, *Facing the Center: Toward an Identity Politics of One-to-One Mentoring* (Utah State University Press), explores how sociocultural dynamics impact the everyday interaction of writing conferences. His other scholarship has explored those issues in relation to writing centers, particularly as sites for community-building and for cross-cultural/disciplinary dialog. He is currently finishing the anthology *Out in the Center: Public Controversies, Private Struggles* (coedited with Anna Sicari, Rob Mundy, Lila Naydan, and Richard Severe), which deepens conversations about identity politics by foregrounding the authentic voices and experiences of tutors and administrators navigating everyday sessions and the disclosure and embodiment of difference. Away from the Writing Lab at Purdue, Harry spends time cycling and refereeing wrestling matches between his twin hounds, as well as tormenting people in life with ear-worm songs.

CASSANDRA DULIN received her PhD from the University of Texas at El Paso and has presented her work at the Conference on College Composition and Communication and elsewhere.

MIRIAM EISENSTEIN EBSWORTH is director of Doctoral Programs in Multilingual Multicultural Studies at New York University, Steinhardt. She is research editor of the *Journal of Writing and Pedagogy* and is incoming chair of the Research and Evaluation SIG for the National Association for Bilingual Education. A consultant on the development of Action through Words: Learning English—Learning about the United Nations, her research includes second language writing, heritage language education, intercultural pragmatics, and technology-enhanced language learning. She is coeditor of the forthcoming text *Maintenance in the Sociology of Language and Religion Framework*, to be published by Multilingual Matters, and is an advocate for emergent bilingual learners and immigrant families.

MIKE EDWARDS is an assistant professor of rhetoric and composition at Washington State University and author of *Postcapitalist Economics and Technologies of Composition*, forthcoming from the University of Pittsburgh Press. His work, which has appeared in *Pedagogy*, *Rhetoric Review*, and elsewhere, focuses on the intersections of economics, technologies, and rhetorics. He likes cats.

REBECCA FRASER is an associate professor of writing and literature at the Harry Van Arsdale Jr. Center for Labor Studies at Empire State College at the State University of New York. She is the coauthor, with Sophia Mavrogiannis, of "'I Don't Write, I Work': Writing and Reading with Trade Union Apprentices" in *Principles, Practices, and Creative Tensions in Progressive Higher Education: One Institution's Struggle to Sustain a Vision* (Sense Publishers, 2017). She is also the coauthor, with Barrie Cline, of an Empire Pillar Grant under development titled *Breaking Divides: An Exhibition and Examination of Trade Unionists' Art and Writing*. Finally, she is the originator and managing editor of the Van Arsdale's annual anthology of student art and writing, titled *Labor Writes* and produced in the class or in response to an assignment. In her free time, Fraser likes to spend her time taking photographs and water coloring. Recently, she had a foursome mixed media painting in a show titled "Super Woman" in Jersey City.

BRETT GRIFFITHS is a teacher-writer-scholar-activist and the director of the Reading and Writing Studios at Macomb Community College. She writes academic articles, poetry, and nonfiction. Her scholarly interests focus on student support, genre theory, and the development and support of faculty identities and recognition of their rights and responsibilities in open-access institutions. Her work has appeared or is forthcoming in *CCC*, *Teaching English in the Two-Year College*, and other journals.

ANNA V. KNUTSON is a doctoral candidate in the Joint Program in English and Education at the University of Michigan. Anna is interested in learning transfer, digital literacies, and writing program administration. Her dissertation research explores how feminist-identified students negotiate the relationship between their literacy and rhetorical learning in social media and academic contexts. She has coauthored articles published in *Computers and Composition*, *Kairos*, and *College English*. When she's not researching or teaching writing, Anna is probably watching horror films or playing with her Chihuahua.

LIBERTY KOHN is associate professor of rhetoric and composition at Winona State University. His scholarship focused on public writing, technical writing, and genre has been featured in various journals, including the *Journal of Technical Writing and Communication*, *The Journal of Interdisciplinary Humanities*, *Technoculture*, and *The Journal of Literacy and Technology*. His scholarship based in teacher training and student development has appeared in *Composition Forum* and *Technology in the Literature Classroom* (Bedford/St. Martin's). Kohn serves as writing center director and has served as WAC coordinator and chair of faculty development. He is currently finishing a book titled *Mapping Publics*, which identifies methods for teaching sustainable and free-market rhetorics in the writing classroom. Liberty is a first-generation college student who planned on becoming a guitar legend but accidentally became an academic. He begrudges neither his guitar nor academia for this accident.

NANCY MACK is a professor of English at Wright State University and the author of *Engaging Writers with Multigenre Research Projects* and two volumes about teaching grammar with poetry. She edited a special issue of the *English Journal* about bullying and has published several articles and chapters on memoir, emotional labor, working-class, and composition theories.

HOLLY MIDDLETON is associate professor of English and director of the First-year Writing Program at High Point University. She is a founding coeditor of the journal *Literacy in Composition Studies* and has published on the history of composition, the teaching of reading in composition, and information literacy. She is currently collaborating on a longitudinal study on undergraduate research practices and source engagement.

ROBERT MUNDY is an assistant professor of English and Writing Program Director at Pace University. His research focuses on composition studies, writing center theory and practice, and gender/masculinity studies. He has published on the intersection of gender and class, multicultural competence, masculinities in the media, and rhetoric of leadership communication.

MISSY NIEVEEN PHEGLEY is the director of Composition and Assessment at Southeast Missouri State University. Her research focuses on assessment and teacher training. She is currently working on a project examining concurrent enrollment and modes of instructional delivery. She is also a yoga instructor, a coffee snob, a lover of bikes and shoes, and a fan of super-hoppy beer.

JACQUELINE PRESTON is a professor at Utah Valley University in the Literacies and Composition Department. She is coauthor of the text *The Write Project: A Concise Rhetoric for the Writing Classroom*. Her work is published in a number of journals including *Community Literacies Journal* and *College, Composition, and Communication*. Her most recent publication is a chapter featured in *Writing Program Architecture: Thirty Cases for Reference and Research*. She is currently working on a book-length project that explores how advances in new materialist thought inform first-year composition.

JAMES E. ROMESBURG is an assistant professor of English and director of College Writing at the University of Wisconsin–Platteville. James has been teaching first-year composition, professional writing, and literature at the university level for over a decade, receiving his PhD from the University of Louisville's Rhetoric and Composition Program in August 2011. He completed his master's and bachelor's degrees in English at Clemson University in Clemson, South Carolina. His research interests focus mainly on writing program administration and the role formal literacy education plays in working-class lives—particularly the literacy practices first-generation and nontraditional students bring to their college writing classrooms and how literacies that deviate from the academic/rational rhetorical paradigm are received in higher education.

EDIE-MARIE ROPER is a PhD student in rhetoric and composition at Washington State University. Roper is a first-generation college graduate and participates in student support programs for low-income and first-generation students. Her current research focuses on the use of personal narratives in nonfiction writing and the persuasive power of structures in nonfiction writing. But she's really just here for the stories.

AUBREY SCHIAVONE is a teaching assistant professor in the University Writing Program at University of Denver. She recently earned her doctorate in English and education at University of Michigan. Her doctoral work culminated in her dissertation project—a qualitative interview study designed to examine potential connections between the speaking and writing literacies working-class first-generation college students practice in first-year writing courses and the literacies they practice outside of first-year writing in home, work, and extracurricular contexts. In addition to her research with working-class first-generation college students, she also studies the role of multimodal composition in writing instruction. Outside her academic interests, she loves bluegrass music, knitting, and her dog Bella.

WILLIAM H. THELIN is a professor at the University of Akron. He has published in journals such as *College English* and *College Composition and Communication* and authored the textbook *Writing without Formulas*, as well as coedited the collection *Blundering for a Change: Errors and Expectations in Critical Pedagogy*. He has been associated with the standing group of the 4C's, Working-Class Culture and Pedagogy, since its inception and is currently co-chairing the group. In his life away from academia, he enjoys bowling, karaoke, and poker, and he is a fanatical Cleveland sports fan. Go Browns!

CHRISTIE TOTH is an assistant professor in the University of Utah's Department of Writing and Rhetoric Studies. Her research has appeared in *Assessing Writing, College Composition and Communication, College English, Composition Studies, Journal of Basic Writing, Mentoring Across Cultures and Disciplines, Teaching English in the Two-Year College*, and *Writing Program Administration*, as well as the collections *Higher Education: Handbook of Theory and Research Writing Assessment, Social Justice, and Advancement of Opportunity*. She also coedited, with Patrick Sullivan, the critical sourcebook *Teaching Composition in the Two-Year College*. She collaborates with Salt Lake Community College colleagues and students on a variety of inter-institutional initiatives. She is currently working on a book about transfer students and community college-university relations in composition studies.

GAIL G. VERDI is an assistant professor in the Department of Elementary Education and Bilingual Education at Kean University. Her research and publications include articles and chapters on literacy development, working-class studies, and the influence second languages and dialects have on student success. She has taught elementary English learners and composition at CUNY and NYU's Expository Writing Program as well as general education courses, language arts, and second language acquisition courses at both the graduate and undergraduate level. She was an executive board member of NJTESOL/NJBE and chair of NJTESOL/NJBE's Graduate Student Forum from 2009 to 2012. She has served as an executive board member of the NJDOE Bilingual Advisory Board, the National Association of Bilingual Education's Research SIG chair, and the Kean Future Teacher Academy director. She received a PhD in English ed/applied linguistics and an MA in TESOL from NYU. She also has a BA in elementary education/early childhood from Seton Hall.

JAMES T. ZEBROSKI is author of the book *Thinking through Theory: Vygotskian Perspectives on the Teaching of Writing*. He has written numerous articles and chapters on critical theory and composition. He has especially focused on unauthorized writing. He teaches at University of Houston, where he founded the Rhetoric, Composition, and Pedagogy PhD Program in 2010.

INDEX

www.ingramcontent.com/pod-product-compliance
Lightning Source LLC
Chambersburg PA
CBHW030512120726
47904CB00005B/1429